LANGUAGE
FOR
DAILY
USE

Voyager Edition

BROWN

Curriculum and Instruction

Dr. Dorothy S. Strickland

Professor of Education
Department of Curriculum and Teaching
Teachers College, Columbia University

Consulting Educators

Dr. Richard F. Abrahamson, Consultant for Literature
Professor of Education
Department of Curriculum and Instruction
College of Education, University of Houston

Dorothy M. Doyle
Instructional Coordinator, Language Arts, K-12
Parkway School District
Chesterfield, Missouri

Donna Babb Frinks
Teacher of Gifted Education
Academic Resource Center
Leon County School District
Tallahassee, Florida

Hildagarde Gray
Librarian
St. John the Baptist School
Pittsburgh, Pennsylvania

Elizabeth Handford
Curriculum Consultant
Southside Christian School
Greenville, South Carolina

Sheryl Jones
Consultant for Computer Applications in Language Arts
Arvada Senior High
Jefferson County R-1
Arvada, Colorado

Helen Levy
Librarian
Springdale Elementary School
Princeton City School District
Cincinnati, Ohio

Ruth Ann Plate, Ed. D.
Director of Secondary Education
Willoughby-Eastlake Schools
Willoughby, Ohio

James W. Reith
Coordinator of Language Arts and Fine Arts
Scottsdale Unified School District #48
Scottsdale, Arizona

Sister Marie Rosarine, S.S.J.
Language Arts Chairperson
Archdiocese of Philadelphia
Philadelphia, Pennsylvania

Edmund A. Sullivan
Supervisor of English
Evansville-Vanderburgh School Corporation
Evansville, Indiana

David Zaslow
Writer-in-Residence
Southern Oregon Public Schools
Ashland, Oregon

LANGUAGE
FOR
DAILY
USE

Voyager Edition

HBJ HARCOURT BRACE JOVANOVICH, PUBLISHERS

Orlando   San Diego   Chicago   Dallas

ACKNOWLEDGMENTS

For permission to reprint copyrighted material, grateful acknowledgment is made to the following sources:

The Associated Press: From "Tinkerer returns 'old soldier' to duty" and from "Nine handicapped adventurers achieve Mount Rainier's summit" in *The New Haven Register,* July 3, 1981.

Atheneum Publishers, Inc.: "Flashlight" from *Flashlight and Other Poems* by Judith Thurman. Copyright © 1976 by Judith Thurman. Published by Atheneum, New York, 1976. "Red" from *I Feel the Same Way* by Lilian Moore. Copyright ©1967 by Lilian Moore. Published by Atheneum, New York, 1967.

Doubleday & Company, Inc.: "Dogs That Have Known Me" from *Please Don't Eat the Daisies* by Jean Kerr. Copyright ©1957 by The Condé Nast Publications, Inc. Adapted from *D'Aulaire's Book of Greek Myths* by Ingri and Edgar Parin D'Aulaire. Copyright ©1962 by Ingri and Edgar Parin D'Aulaire.

E. P. Dutton, Inc.: From "The Boy Who Could Not Swim" in *Thor Heyerdahl: Viking Scientist* by Wyatt Blassingame. Copyright ©1979 by Wyatt Blassingame.

Farrar, Straus & Giroux, Inc.: "Springtime" from *Spin a Soft Black Song* by Nikki Giovanni. Copyright ©1971 by Nikki Giovanni. From *The Treasure* by Uri Shulevitz. Copyright ©1978 by Uri Shulevitz.

Hammond Incorporated, Maplewood, NJ: Map of Japan from *Hammond Contemporary World Atlas.*

Harcourt Brace Jovanovich, Inc.: "Fog" from *Chicago Poems* by Carl Sandburg. Copyright 1916 by Holt, Rinehart and Winston, Inc.; renewed 1944 by Carl Sandburg. From "Prairie" in *Cornhuskers* by Carl Sandburg. Copyright 1918 by Holt, Rinehart and Winston, Inc.; copyright 1946 by Carl Sandburg. From "Haze" in *Smoke and Steel* by Carl Sandburg. Copyright 1920 by Harcourt Brace Jovanovich, Inc.; copyright 1948 by Carl Sandburg. From *Serve Me a Slice of the Moon* by Marcie Hans. ©1965 by Marcie Hans. Pronunciation Key and entries reprinted and reproduced from *The HBJ School Dictionary.* Copyright ©1985 by Harcourt Brace Jovanovich, Inc. Glossary entries from *Cascade.* Copyright ©1982 by Harcourt Brace Jovanovich, Inc.

Harper & Row, Publishers, Inc.: "To Some Sixth-Graders in Los Angeles" and "To Jill L_____" from *Letters of E. B. White,* collected and edited by Dorothy Lobrano Guth. Copyright ©1976 by E. B. White.

Houghton Mifflin Company: "Pacific 'Ring of Fire'" from *Information Please Almanac 1980.* Copyright ©1979 by Houghton Mifflin Company.

Alfred A. Knopf, Inc.: "January" from *A Child's Calendar* by John Updike, illustrated by Nancy Ekholm Burkert. Copyright ©1965 by John Updike and Nancy Burkert. Adapted from "Father Wakes Up the Village" in *The Best of Clarence Day.* Copyright 1934, 1935 by Clarence Day; renewed 1962 by Katherine B. Day. "Velvet Shoes" from *Collected Poems of Elinor Wylie.* Copyright 1921 by Alfred A. Knopf, Inc.; renewed 1949 by William Rose Benét.

Macmillan Publishing Co., Inc.: From "Swift Things Are Beautiful" in *Away Goes Sally* by Elizabeth Coatsworth. Copyright 1934 by Macmillan Publishing Co., Inc.; renewed 1962 by Elizabeth Coatsworth Beston. "What is Once Loved" from *Alice-All-by-Herself* by Elizabeth Coatsworth. Copyright 1937 by Macmillan Publishing Co., Inc.; renewed 1965 by Elizabeth Coatsworth Beston.

Julian Messner, a division of Simon & Schuster, Inc.: Adapted from "The Land We Love" in *Celebrate America* by Nancy Henderson. Copyright ©1978 by Nancy Henderson.

The New Haven Register: Editorial " 'Quiet Dust' and vibrant company" from *The New Haven (CT) Register,* July 4, 1981.

New York Daily News: From "Rides in with memories" in the *Daily News,* June 23, 1981. Copyright 1981 by New York News, Inc.

The New York Times: "Hold Fast Your Dreams" by Louise Driscoll. Copyright ©1918 by The New York Times Company.

The Aaron Priest Literary Agency, Inc.: From "Go-to-Pot Month" in *At Wit's End* by Erma Bombeck. ©1981 by Erma Bombeck.

Reader's Digest: From "All in a Day's Work," contributed by Carol Wirges and from "Life in These United States," contributed by Juanita J. Van Wagenen in *Reader's Digest,* August 1981.

Sayre Publishing, Inc.: From *The Honorable Shirley Chisholm* by Nancy Hicks. Published by Lion Books, 1971.

Mrs. James Thurber: From "The Night the Ghost Got In" in *My Life and Hard Times* by James Thurber. Copyright ©1933, 1961 by James Thurber. Published by Harper & Row, Publishers, Inc.

Viking Penguin Inc.: Adapted from *My Lord, What A Morning* by Marian Anderson. Copyright ©1956; renewed ©1984 by Marian Anderson.

World Book-Childcraft International, Inc.: From the index entry on "Japan" in *The World Book Encyclopedia.* ©1982 by World Book—Childcraft International, Inc.

CONTENTS

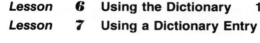

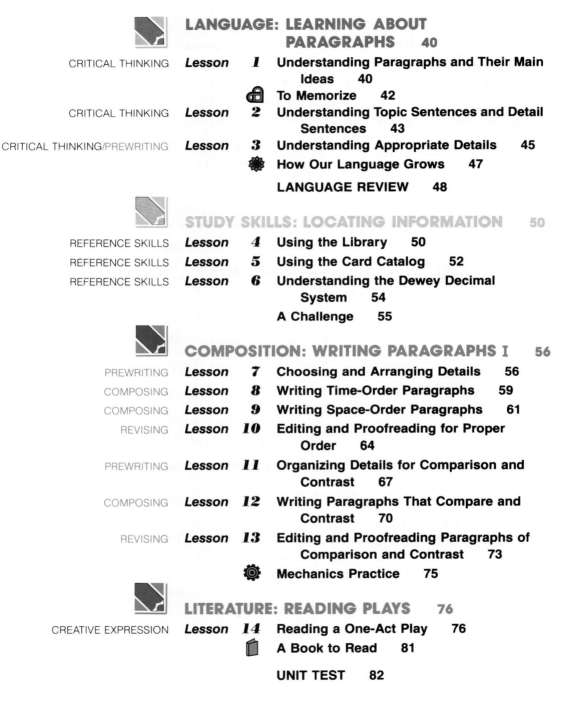

UNIT 6   225

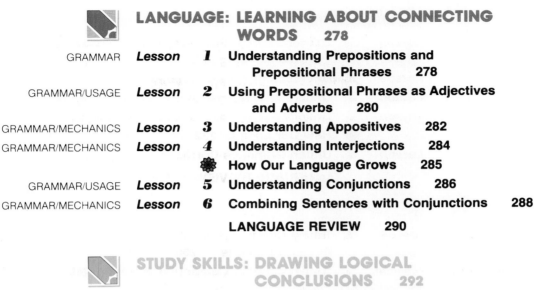

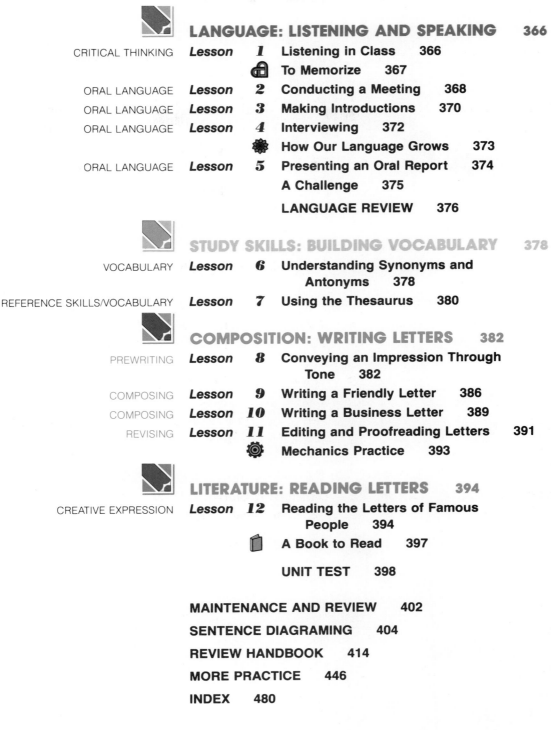

LANGUAGE
Learning About
Sentences

STUDY SKILLS
Locating and
Studying Words

COMPOSITION
**Writing
Sentences**

LITERATURE
**Reading Biography
and Autobiography**

The dark clouds roll over the horizon, and the wind gusts furiously. A storm rages. Look at the photograph. What can you add to this story beginning?

In order to tell a story you need to express thoughts. Think about the ideas you added to the story. Were all of them statements? What other kinds of sentences might you use to tell about the storm?

Before a storm the clouds look *ominous.* Perhaps you do not know the definition of the word *ominous.* Where can you go for help? Of course, you know that a dictionary defines words. A dictionary can be useful in other ways too. In this unit you will learn what other information you can find in a dictionary.

Take another look at the photograph. How can you tell that the storm is nearing an end? When you answered that question, how did you begin your sentence? In this unit you will learn how to vary sentences to make your writing vivid and interesting. In addition, you will read selections from a biography and an autobiography, and you will use these as models to write a brief biography of your own.

Now sharpen your thoughts, turn the page, and you are ready to begin!

◀ *Clearing after the storm, Monhegan Island, Maine*

LANGUAGE

Lesson 1: Understanding Kinds of Sentences

Read these word groups about ancient Egypt.

1. The history of Egypt goes back 5,000 years.
2. What a long history Egypt has!
3. In the Nile Valley the pharaohs.
4. How old are the pyramids?
5. Read this book about Egypt.

Which of these groups is missing some information? Add some words of your own to make it complete.

Think and Discuss

A sentence does not leave you hanging, wondering what will come next. Instead, it expresses a complete thought and ends with a punctuation mark.

- A **sentence** is a group of words that expresses a complete thought. It begins with a capital letter and ends with a punctuation mark.
- A **declarative sentence** makes a statement. It ends with a period.
- An **interrogative sentence** asks a question. It ends with a question mark.
- An **imperative sentence** makes a request or gives an order. It ends with a period.
- An **exclamatory sentence** shows surprise or strong feeling. It ends with an exclamation point.

What kind of sentence is number 2?

Practice

A. Copy these sentences. Add capital letters and punctuation marks. Then write which kind of sentence each one is.

1. let me see that sample of writing
2. what kind of writing is this
3. what strange writing it is
4. egyptian writing is called hieroglyphics
5. hieroglyphics began as picture writing
6. look at this book on hieroglyphics
7. what does that picture show
8. it is a picture of a pyramid
9. how huge it seems
10. egyptian artists used hieroglyphics on pyramid walls

B. Complete these sentences by adding words of your own. Then write which kind of sentence each one is.

11. How did the Egyptians build _____?
12. Mummies have been found _____.
13. Look at _____.
14. What a beautiful _____!
15. Was all of this treasure _____?
16. Who discovered _____?
17. Please give me _____.
18. What a tall _____!
19. This mummy case is _____.
20. Only a historian can tell _____.

Apply

C. **21.–30.** Write ten sentences about another country you have studied or a wonderful place you have seen. Write at least two declarative, two interrogative, two imperative, and two exclamatory sentences. Be sure to punctuate your sentences correctly. Then write which kind each one is.

Lesson 2: Understanding Complete Subjects and Predicates

Maria Rodriguez made some sentence flash cards for school. Here are three of them.

1. The boys climbed Mr. Lara's fence.
2. Charles fell into the tomato patch.
3. His friend Arthur saw Charles fall.

Maria knew that sentences have two main parts. What does each part tell?

Think and Discuss

The two main parts of every sentence are the **subject** and the **predicate**. All the words in the subject are called the **complete subject**. All the words in the predicate are called the **complete predicate**. Either one may be a single word or a group of words.

Name the complete subject and the complete predicate in sentences 2 and 3. What do the underlined parts mean?

> - The **complete subject** is all the words that make up the subject of a sentence. The subject is the part about which something is said.
> - The **complete predicate** is all the words that make up the predicate of the sentence. The predicate is the part that tells something about the subject.

Practice

A. Copy these sentences. Draw one line under each complete subject and two lines under each complete predicate.

1. Arthur lost his balance.
2. He fell off the fence too.

3. Barbara and Linda saw the boys in the garden.
4. The vegetables had not been squashed.
5. Barbara and Linda helped the boys clean up.

B. Add either a complete subject or a complete predicate to these word groups. Write your new sentences, drawing one line under each complete subject and two lines under each complete predicate.

6. fences
7. climbed a fence one day
8. fell onto the street
9. a neighbor
10. was not seriously hurt
11. a good friend
12. had been lucky
13. could have been hit
14. stone walls and ledges
15. no children

Apply

C. 16.–25. Write ten sentences about someone you know who did something amusing. Then draw one line under each complete subject and two lines under each complete predicate.

A Challenge

These mixed-up sentences do not make sense. Copy the sentences and draw one line under each complete subject and two lines under each complete predicate. Then unscramble the sentences so that each subject is followed by a predicate that makes sense.

1. Our school was too big to fit through the doors.
2. Fred were there with Creepy, their pet python.
3. Allison and Andy was not in the gym.
4. The winner of the contest had a "Biggest Pet" contest in the gym.
5. Bulky, Penny's pet elephant, brought his huge turtle.

Lesson 3: Understanding Simple Subjects and Predicates

Read these sentences.

1. Many people enjoy puzzles.
2. Enzo gave Giovanna a puzzle book.
3. Giovanna solves puzzles every day.

Name the complete subject and the complete predicate in each sentence. Which complete subject has two words?

Think and Discuss

In every subject there is a key word called the **simple subject.** Like the complete subject, the simple subject may be a single word or a group of words. Like the complete subject, the simple subject is the part about which something is said. The simple subject of sentence 1, for example, is *people.*

In the same way, the key word in the complete predicate is called the **simple predicate.** It, too, may be one word or several. Like the complete predicate, the simple predicate tells something about the subject. The simple predicate of sentence 1 is *enjoy.* The key word is always the *most important* word or words in each sentence part. Name the simple subject and the simple predicate in sentences 2 and 3. In which sentences are the complete subject and the simple subject the same?

> • The **simple subject** is the key word or words in the complete subject of a sentence.
> • The **simple predicate** is the key word or words in the complete predicate of a sentence.

Practice

A. Copy these sentences. Draw one line under each simple subject and two lines under each simple predicate.

1. A cryptogram is a word puzzle.
2. The words are written in code.
3. The solver must break the code.
4. Solvers should be clever people.
5. Some puzzles include hidden words.
6. The solver must search for each one.
7. Enzo likes crossword puzzles best.
8. These puzzles use definitions as clues.
9. Enzo keeps a dictionary nearby.
10. Sometimes he must check his answers in the dictionary.

B. Complete these sentences by adding a simple subject or a simple predicate. Draw one line under each simple subject and two lines under each simple predicate.

11. Scrabble _____ an interesting word game.
12. _____ must make words from the letters they receive.
13. Some players _____ a double or triple word score.
14. One _____ might add letters to the other's word.
15. The person _____ credit for both words.
16. Giovanna _____ in a scrabble contest once.
17. The best _____ were adults.
18. Of all the students, _____ earned the highest score.

Apply

C. 19.–30. Write twelve sentences about a puzzle or a game that you enjoy. Tell how it can be solved or won. Then draw one line under each simple subject and two lines under each simple predicate.

Lesson 4: Identifying the Subjects of Sentences

Luisa and Jorge were talking about autumn. This is what they were saying.

1. When does autumn begin?
2. Look it up on the calendar.
3. Does Ramon have a calendar?
4. Ask him.

Try to find the simple subject of each sentence. Interrogative and imperative sentences often make subject hunting more difficult than usual.

Think and Discuss

The subject of an interrogative sentence is not always found at or near the beginning of the sentence. Yet you can still locate it easily. As with other sentences, ask yourself whom or what the sentence is about. Sentence 1, for example, is about autumn, so *autumn* is the subject.

In imperative sentences, however, the subject is not usually stated. The speaker or writer means that the subject is *you,* the person to whom the command or request is given. This kind of subject is called an **understood subject** because the subject's name is understood in the speaker's mind. Most imperative sentences have *you* (understood) as their subject.

> • *You* **(understood)** is the subject of an imperative sentence.

Name the subjects of sentences 2, 3, and 4. How many times is *you* (understood) the subject?

Practice

A. Copy these sentences. Underline each subject. Write (*you*) after each sentence in which the subject is *you* (understood).

1. Did Nara borrow a calendar?
2. Give the calendar to me.
3. Why does autumn begin so late in September?
4. Why do the leaves change color?
5. Read this book about the changing leaves.
6. Look at this picture.
7. Read the paragraph underneath.
8. What does the paragraph say?
9. How often does the writer mention chlorophyll?
10. Count them yourself.

B. Copy these sentences, adding the proper punctuation. Underline each subject. Write (*you*) after each sentence in which the subject is *you* (understood).

11. Ask Mr. Chung about the leaves
12. Why don't you ask him
13. Please give me that leaf
14. Where is the chlorophyll
15. Don't tell me about Jack Frost
16. Be quiet
17. Why is the room so quiet
18. Listen to the leaves falling
19. Is their chlorophyll gone
20. Aren't you tired of chlorophyll yet

Apply

C. **21.–30.** Write five interrogative and five imperative sentences about autumn. Underline the subject of each sentence. Write (*you*) after each sentence that has an understood subject.

Lesson 5: Understanding Word Order in Sentences

Miriam wrote about an adventure she had during the summer. Here are four of her sentences.

1. The old house was completely dark.
2. I was all alone.
3. Suddenly, across the hall shone a light.
4. A candle was floating in the air!

Which of Miriam's sentences is written in a different word order from the rest? What is unusual about the subject of this sentence?

Think and Discuss

In most sentences the subject comes before the predicate. This is called **natural** word order. Sometimes, however, the natural order is reversed. The writer may want to call attention to a certain sentence or build suspense in a story. In such a case, the predicate would come before the subject. This is called **inverted** word order.

Find the subjects of sentences 1 through 4 above. Tell which sentences are in natural order and which are in inverted order. Now read the next two sentences in Miriam's adventure.

5. Nearer and nearer came the light.
6. My heart beat wildly!

Which one is in natural order? Which is in inverted order?

Practice

A. Copy these sentences. Underline each subject. Then write *natural* after each sentence in natural order and *inverted* after each sentence in inverted order.

1. The elevator began its trip to the tenth floor.
2. It stopped suddenly.
3. From under the door poured thick black smoke.

4. Alarms clanged all over the building.
5. From below came the shouts of the fire fighters.
6. Now I was really nervous.
7. Bravely I kept silent.
8. Underneath our car worked the fire fighters.

B. Complete these sentences about the elevator rescue. Tell whether each is in natural or inverted order.

9. Others in the car ____.
10. Louder clanged ____.
11. From above came ____.
12. Suddenly the air ____!
13. Slowly the elevator ____.
14. Into the car came ____.
15. With a smile she ____.
16. In great relief I ____.

Apply

C. 17.–21. Write five sentences completing Miriam's adventure. Write two in inverted order.

HOW OUR LANGUAGE GROWS

One way languages change and keep up to date is by adopting new words for inventions. Just how new are these words?

Though today we usually think of the word *rocket* along with space travel, the word's original meaning described the shape of a stick used in spinning wool or flax. With inventions and discoveries, old words like *rocket* may be used in new ways.

Sometimes prefixes, root words, and suffixes from Greek and Latin are combined in words to name inventions. *Airplane, locomotive, submarine,* and *astronaut* are all combinations of such word parts. Knowing the meanings of a few word parts can help you discover the meanings of many new words.

What do the names of these inventions mean: *astrodome, helicopter, subway, television, hydrofoil?*

LANGUAGE REVIEW

Understanding Kinds of Sentences   pages 2–3

Copy these sentences. Write *declarative, interrogative, imperative,* or *exclamatory* after each sentence.

1. Did you really bake this bread?
2. It tastes delicious!
3. The recipe was my grandmother's.
4. Please cut me another slice.
5. It is a whole-grain bread.
6. I love it!

Understanding Complete Subjects and Predicates   pages 4–5

Copy these sentences. Draw one line under the complete subject and two lines under the complete predicate.

7. John Locke was an English thinker and writer.
8. Locke lived in the late 1600's.
9. A revolution took place in England in 1688.
10. Locke wrote a book about overthrowing the king.
11. No ruler could take away all of the people's rights.
12. Locke's ideas became part of the American Declaration of Independence.

Understanding Simple Subjects and Predicates   pages 6–7

Copy these sentences. Draw one line under the simple subject and two lines under the simple predicate.

13. Thomas Jefferson wrote the Declaration of Independence.
14. Some ideas in this document came from French thinkers.
15. Jefferson knew the writings of John Locke too.
16. The Declaration of Independence stated many important ideas.
17. No one could rule without the consent of the American people.
18. Few documents have ever had such importance in history.

Identifying the Subjects of Sentences   pages 8–9

Copy these sentences. Underline the simple subject in each
one. If the subject of a sentence is *you* (understood), write *you*
in parentheses ( ) after the sentence.

19. Who knows the capital city of Burma?
20. What did Diane ask about Burma?
21. Please hand me the atlas.
22. Look at the map.
23. Is Rangoon the capital?
24. Don't give me any more trouble.
25. Who is giving you trouble?
26. Am I giving you trouble?
27. Give me a chance.
28. Look at the chart.
29. Doesn't it prove something?
30. Please forget the whole thing.

Understanding Word Order in Sentences   pages 10–11

Copy these sentences. Write *natural* after each sentence in
natural order. Write *inverted* after each sentence in inverted order.

31. Ancient Athens was a busy city.
32. Homes and shops lined the streets.
33. On a high hill stood the Parthenon.
34. Over the city gazed the goddess Athena.
35. She was the special protector of Athens.
36. Inside the Parthenon stood her huge statue.
37. She watched over the citizens at work and at play.
38. Athena often helped the soldiers in battle.
39. Into the midst of battle rushed the fierce goddess.
40. After battles, the Athenians heaped gifts before her statue.

Applying Sentences

41.–50. Write ten sentences about your city or town. Remember
to write only complete thoughts. Use capital letters and
punctuation marks.

STUDY SKILLS

Lesson 6: Using the Dictionary

Notice the way in which the words are arranged on this model dictionary page.

---

rad·i·cand [rad′ə·kand′] *n.* The number written under a radical sign: 8 is the *radicand* of $\sqrt[3]{8}$.

rad·i·ces [rad′i·sēz′] A plural of RADIX.

ra·di·i [rā′dē·ī] Plural of RADIUS.

ra·di·o [rā′dē·ō] *n., pl.* **ra·di·os,** *v.* **ra·di·oed, ra·di·o·ing** **1** *n.* The devices and methods by which sounds or other signals are changed into variations of an electromagnetic wave that travels through space to a receiver where the signals are recovered. **2** *adj. use:* a *radio* beam; a *radio* broadcast. **3** *n.* A receiver, transmitter, or other radio apparatus. **4** *v.* To send (a message) or communicate with (someone) by radio. **5** *n.* The radio business or industry.

ra·di·o·ac·tive [rā′dē·ō·ak′tiv] *adj.* Containing a nucleus which is inherently unstable in some way and which decays toward a more stable configuration by emitting matter or energy.

ra·di·um [rā′dē·əm] *n.* A strongly radioactive metallic element found in ores of uranium. Its salts are sometimes used in medicine.

ra·di·us [rā′dē·əs] *n., pl.* **ra·di·i** or **ra·di·us·es** **1** A straight line from the center of a circle or sphere to the circumference or surface. **2** A circular area or boundary measured by the length of its radius: only two stores within a *radius* of 15 miles. **3** The thicker and shorter bone of the forearm.

ra·dix [rā′diks] *n., pl.* **rad·i·ces** or **ra·dix·es** The base of a number system: The *radix* of the decimal system is 10.

Think and Discuss

The words on the model page are in **alphabetical order.** You must know alphabetical order to use most reference books.

In this lesson you will use alphabetical order to find words in the dictionary. You will gain practice in alphabetizing not only by the first letter of words, but also by the second, third, fourth, and fifth letters. Which word, for example, would come first, *steam* or *stage; group* or *grovel?*

If you divided the alphabet into three equal parts, the first part would include the letters *A* to *F;* the second, *G* to *P;* the third, *Q* to *Z.* In which third would you find the word *opera?* Where would you find *benefit?* In which third is *valiant?*

The words in boldface at the top of the model dictionary page are **guide words.** They tell you the first and last words on that page. Other words on the page are listed alphabetically between these two. Tell why you would *not* find these words on this page: *rain, rescue, rabbit, rise, ragweed.*

Practice

A. Write these words in alphabetical order. After each word write 1, 2, or 3 to indicate in which third of the dictionary the word can be found.

1. whistle	2. year	3. tackle
4. native	5. barter	6. danger
7. statue	8. greed	9. errand
10. cart	11. arrange	12. frighten
13. vertical	14. weight	15. lag

B. Write each row of words in alphabetical order.

16. inquiry	ivory	icicle	iron	imagine
17. team	tender	teacher	there	theme
18. poetic	podium	point	poacher	pocket
19. strain	stream	strange	straighten	stress

C. Write the words that would fall between the guide words *pressure* and *previously.*

20. pretend	21. present	22. pride
23. presume	24. pretzel	25. prime
26. prey	27. preview	28. presto
29. prince	30. president	31. prelude
32. press	33. pretty	34. prepay

Apply

D. **35.–49.** In your dictionary locate each word in Practice A. On your paper write the word, the page number of the dictionary, and the guide words for the page on which you found the word.

Lesson 7: Using a Dictionary Entry

A dictionary gives more than just the definitions of a word. Read the sample entry.

> **rul·er** [ro͞o′lər] *n.*   **1** A person who rules or governs, as a king or queen.   **2** A straight-edged instrument for use in measuring or in drawing lines.

What information other than the meanings of the word *ruler* does the entry give?

Think and Discuss

You can learn the **pronunciation** of words by looking at the *phonetic respelling* in parentheses ( ) or brackets [ ] after the entry word. A short pronunciation key like this one is often found on dictionary pages.

a	add	i	it	oͦo	took	oi	oil
ā	ace	ī	ice	oͦo	pool	ou	pout
â	care	o	odd	u	up	ng	ring
ä	palm	ō	open	û	burn	th	thin
e	end	ô	order	yoͦo	fuse	th	this
ē	equal					zh	vision

ə = { a in *above*   e in *sicken*   i in *possible*
      { o in *melon*   u in *circus*

Each **symbol** in the phonetic respelling stands for a sound in the word. If a word has more than one syllable, the accented syllable or syllables is shown. Accented syllables are shown with accent marks. In words with more than one accent, the heavy accent is a dark mark. The light accent is smaller. For example, in the word *preliminary,* the second syllable has a heavy stress and the fourth a lighter stress.

pri lim′ ə ner′ ē

The entry word shows both the correct spelling of the word and how to divide it at the end of a writing line. Look at the entry word for *ruler.* How many syllables does it have? If you were dividing the word at the end of a line, how would you separate the word *ruler?*

Many words in the dictionary have more than one meaning. How many meanings does the entry for *ruler* have? In the sentence "I measured it with a ruler," which meaning of *ruler* is used?

Practice

A. Examine the list of words below. Look up each word in your dictionary to check the spelling. If a word is spelled incorrectly, write the correct spelling on your paper. Next to each word copy the pronunciation given in the dictionary.

1. island
2. tiranny
3. appear
4. shiney
5. skowl
6. flounder
7. knowledge
8. exaggerate
9. breth
10. colum

B. Read the sentences below. The underlined word in each sentence has more than one meaning. Find the underlined words in your dictionary, and copy the meaning as it is used in the sentence.

11. The key doesn't fit the <u>lock</u>.
12. The <u>bank</u> is closed today.
13. A link from this chain is <u>missing</u>.
14. Please open the <u>blind</u>.
15. I <u>store</u> food in the refrigerator.

C. 16.–20. Use the dictionary to find another meaning for each of the words in Practice B. Write a sentence for each word using the other meaning.

Apply

D. 21.–30. Pick ten new words from any literature lesson in your book. Look up each in the dictionary and learn its pronunciation. Write a sentence to show that you understand each meaning that is given. Show how you would divide each word into syllables.

COMPOSITION

Lesson 8: Prewriting
Brainstorming for Specific Words

Your sentences will be effective if the words are specific. Which is the most specific of these three word groups?

big   very tall   three miles high

Think and Discuss

When a writer makes words more **specific,** he or she takes a general word and narrows it down. You can do the same. Start with a word like *green.* Then think of a more particular kind of green, like *light green* or *dark green.* Finally, think of the most specific kind of green that suits your sentence. A very specific kind of light green, for example, might be *lime green* or *apple green.* A very specific kind of dark green might be *forest green* or *olive green.*

You might find it helpful to set up a chart that shows your progress from general to specific. Here is a sentence that could be made more specific.

Betty wore a *blue* dress to the party.

		turquoise
		robin's egg blue
		aquamarine
blue	blue-green	peacock blue
General Word →	**More Specific** →	**Most Specific**

Notice that there are many specific words for *blue-green.* If this had been your sentence, you would have thought of as many kinds of *blue-green* as you could. Then you would have chosen the word that came closest to the color of Betty's dress. What are some other very specific words for *blue-green*? Suppose you wrote this sentence.

Betty *spoke* to me.

What would be a more specific word or phrase for *spoke*? What words would be most specific of all?

How to Brainstorm for Specific Words

1. **Start with a general word.**
2. **Think of another word that means the same but that is more particular than the general word.**
3. **Think of as many words as you can that are even more particular than your second word. List each of those words.**
4. **Choose the word from your list that fits most exactly in your sentence.**

Practice

A. These groups of words progress from general to specific. Fill in the blanks with words that are general, more specific, or most specific.

1. warm, humid, _____
2. _____, delighted, triumphant
3. hard, _____, impossible
4. _____, downpour, _____
5. pastry, _____, _____

B. Read sentences 6 through 10. Rewrite them, substituting a specific word for each underlined word. Follow the guidelines in the box.

6. The Tuileries is a <u>nice</u> garden in Paris.

7. Gothic cathedrals in France boast <u>big</u> windows and <u>colorful</u> stained glass.
8. Versailles, King Louis XIV's <u>house</u>, offers guided tours of the <u>many</u> buildings.
9. The Louvre, the <u>biggest</u> museum in France, displays many artistic treasures.
10. The Musée de Cluny is an old monastery that has been converted into a <u>small</u> museum.

Apply

C. Soon you will be writing some sentences about a scene. These guidelines will help you choose specific words.

Choose Your Topic
● Choose a scene that you know very well and could describe easily. Make a list of objects in the scene. If you wish, you may use a photograph as a guide.

Choose Your Audience
● Decide who, besides your teacher, will read your sentences. You will want to choose specific words that your audience will understand.

Make a Chart
● List the objects that are in your scene in a column down the left side of your paper. Leave plenty of room between them.
● Work with one object at a time. Write a general word, a more specific word, and then a list of most specific words that might describe each object. Work across your paper.
● Use the model on page 18 and the guidelines in the blue box on page 19 to help you.

Review Your Work
● Look over your objects and word lists. Add any specific words that may occur to you. Circle the ones that describe each object best.
● Save your work for the Apply exercise in Lesson 9.

Lesson 9: Composing
Writing Effective Sentences

Which of Gabrielle's sentences is the better one?

1. The Rhine is an important French river.
2. The Rhine River is the main inland waterway of Europe.

Think and Discuss

As Gabrielle wrote her report on the land and climate of France, she tried to make her sentences **effective.** That is, she made her words as specific as possible. She tried to use all four kinds of sentences, and she varied them whenever she could.

Gabrielle tried to choose only words that said exactly what she meant. That is why she rewrote sentence 1 to take out the "lazy" word *important*. What specific words did Gabrielle add in sentence 2?

Gabrielle's second sentence is also better in terms of content. Sentence 1 is very general. It does not tell *why* the Rhine is important. Sentence 2 does this, however, and even suggests its use both in pleasure and commerce.

To understand how Gabrielle varied her sentences, read this section of her report.

> The plains of northern France contain some of the richest land in the country. Along the Seine River stretch miles of dairy farms, apple orchards, and vineyards. Although this region is largely devoted to farming, it is still heavily populated. One-sixth of the country's people live in the area around Paris alone!
>
> From which area come the raw materials used in French industry? Vast deposits of iron ore lie to the east of the northern plains. Here the iron is mined. Then it is sent by rail to steel plants in the central cities.

Of the eight sentences in this part of Gabrielle's report, six are declarative, one is interrogative, and one is exclamatory. It is not unusual for declarative sentences to occur most often in this kind of writing. Yet variety is still possible. Two of the eight sentences, for example, are in inverted order. Moreover, when compared to the other sentences, one of them is quite short. Not only does this sentence contain valuable information, but it provides a change of pace from the longer sentences. All of these devices of variety help make writing effective.

Keep these guidelines in mind when writing sentences of your own.

How to Write Effective Sentences
1. **Choose only specific words.**
2. **Use as many of the four kinds of sentences as possible.**
3. **For variety, include sentences in inverted order.**
4. **Vary the length of your sentences.**

Practice

A. Rewrite these sentences using specific words and devices of variety wherever possible. Use an encyclopedia for additional information.

1. The Garonne River is in the lowlands of France.
2. Other rivers are also in the area.
3. Beaches are along the coast.
4. There are pine forests and plains in the area too.
5. Grapes grow in this area.
6. Wine is made from these grapes.
7. Natural gas comes from the area near Landes.
8. An important seaport is Bordeaux.
9. The temperature is about 40 degrees in winter.
10. The temperature is over 70 degrees in summer.

B. Study the section of Gabrielle's report that is printed in your book. Then close the book and write the passage as your teacher dictates it.

Apply

C. Take out the word lists you prepared for Lesson 8. You now have a head start in writing your sentences.

Write Your Sentences

● Write a sentence or two about each object in the scene you have chosen. From your list of *most specific* words, select the word or words that best fit each sentence.

● Vary your sentences according to the guidelines in the blue box on page 22.

Review Your Work

● Look over your sentences. Be sure you have examples of declarative, interrogative, and exclamatory sentences. At least one sentence should be in inverted order.

● Save your sentences for revising in Lesson 10.

To Memorize

Step by step one ascends the staircase.

Turkish proverb

Word by word great books are written.

Italian proverb

Put these two proverbs into your own words. Do they have the same meaning?

Lesson 10: Revising
Editing and Proofreading Sentences

Editing and Proofreading Marks

≡ capitalize

⊙ make a period

∧ add something

⩟ add a comma

ⱽ ⱽ add quotation marks

⤙ take something away

○ spell correctly

¶ indent the paragraph

/ make a lowercase letter

∿ transpose
tr

Read these sentences from Gabrielle's report.

> 1. Paris is the capital of france
> 2. Paris is the capital and largest city of France.

What changes did she make to sentence 1?

Think and Discuss

After writing sentences, you usually read them over to make corrections. This process is called **revising,** and the marks you can use to help you are called **editing and proofreading marks.** The most useful ones are shown on this page.

Look at these model sentences from Gabrielle's report. She has already revised them to make them more varied and thus more effective.

> 3. The French Alps *and the Jura Mountains* form the border of Italy and Switzerland.
> 4. The famous ski area of Chamonix lies deep in the mountains.

Notice that in addition to corrections in capitalization and punctuation, the marks have helped Gabrielle change the *structure* of her sentences. In sentence 4 she used the *tr* marks and arrows to change the places of her sentence parts. The new sentence is in inverted order, a change from the sentence in natural order above it. How do the extra words make sentence 3 more effective?

How to Revise Sentences

Editing

1. **Be sure that your sentences give all the information about your topic that you planned.**
2. **Be sure your sentences make sense.**
3. **Check for very specific words. Be sure that your audience will understand them.**
4. **Be sure that you have varied your sentences in length and in type.**

Proofreading

5. **Be sure that your sentences are correctly capitalized and punctuated. Check for correct spelling.**

Practice

A. 1.–2. The two sentences in Think and Discuss have already been revised. Rewrite them as they should appear in Gabrielle's finished report.

B. Copy sentences 3 through 20. Then revise them for variety to make them more effective. Use the editing and proofreading marks to help you. Finally, rewrite the sentences as you would want them to appear in your finished work.

3. The climate of France is different in different areas.
4. This area has mild winters and cool summers.
5. Inland areas have hot summers and cold winters.

6. Mountain areas receive much rain in the summer.
7. The Alps and Jura Mountains are very snowy.
8. There are glaciers in the Alps.
9. Cold north winds blow over southern France.
10. These winds are called mistrals.
11. Mistrals cause damage to crops.
12. The Riviera is in the south of France.
13. The Riviera is near the Mediterranean Sea.
14. The Riviera is an important tourist place.
15. The Alps keep the north winds from the Riviera.
16. The Riviera is warmed by breezes from the Mediterranean Sea.
17. The climate of France is varied.
18. Tourists enjoy the beaches.
19. Tourists enjoy the mild weather.
20. Tourists go to the mountains for winter sports.

Apply

C. Find the sentences you wrote for Lesson 9. Read them to be sure they make sense.

Edit Your Sentences
- Check your **content.** Did you include the first two items in the box on page 25?
- Check your **style.** Style refers to your vocabulary and the variety in your sentence structure. Did you include items 3 and 4 in the box on page 25?

Proofread Your Sentences
- Use item 5 in the blue box on page 25 as a guide.
- Copy your revised sentences onto a clean sheet of paper.

MECHANICS PRACTICE

Capitalizing and Punctuating Sentences

- Capitalize the first word of a sentence.

  We are doing our homework.

- Capitalize the word *I*.

  Jeremy and I like social studies.

- Use a period at the end of declarative and imperative sentences.

  This book is interesting. Read it.

- Use a question mark at the end of an interrogative sentence.

  Have you finished yet?

- Use an exclamation point at the end of an exclamatory sentence.

  What a terrific story this is!

Copy these sentences. Use capital letters and punctuation marks wherever they are needed. (There may be more than one sentence in each numbered line.)

1. an ocean is a large body of salty water
2. what do we call a large body of fresh water
3. a large body of fresh water is a pond
4. you are wrong a large body of fresh water is a lake
5. bring me a dictionary and i will check the definition
6. i will if you ask me nicely
7. please bring me the dictionary
8. well at least i was right about lakes
9. listen to this
10. along the rocky coast are many fine harbors
11. they were carved out of the land by the invading sea
12. many islands dot these harbor channels
13. an island is a tract of land surrounded by water
14. stop reading at once jeremy has found something good
15. hurray jeremy has made the discovery of the year

LITERATURE

Lesson 11: Understanding Biography and Autobiography

The word *biography* comes from two Greek roots, *bio* (life) and *graphy* (writing). The word *autobiography* comes from the Greek root *auto* (self) plus *bio* and *graphy*.

Now that you know the roots that make up these words, can you tell the meaning of *biography* and *autobiography?*

Think and Discuss

Read this passage from the life story of a famous singer, Marian Anderson, to learn if it is a biography or an autobiography.

My parents did not consider themselves singers, but when they sang it pleased me. I remember Father's singing while he dressed, bits of "Asleep in the Deep," never finishing it. I don't recall feeling that there was anything special about his voice, but maybe there was and I was too young to know. Mother liked to sing at home, and as a youngster she had sung in church choirs. On rainy evenings, when we could not go out to sit on the steps and visit with our neighbors, Mother, my sisters, and I might sing for our own amusement—old American songs, hymns, and spirituals.

When I was about eight years old Father got us a piano. He bought it from his brother who had had it in his home, where no one used it. When it arrived at our house, what excitement and joy! We ran our fingers over it, listening delightedly to the notes of the scale. Father, I remember, permitted me to sit on his knee. I tried playing a scale with five fingers, slipping the thumb under the hand to get all eight notes without a break, the way I had seen people play in school and church. When Father put his hand on the piano, I tried to guide his fingers to play a scale. Because he was understanding, he hit two notes with one finger, and his scale did not come out as well as mine.

I did not have music lessons; there was not enough money for a teacher. However, we did acquire from somewhere a card, marked with the notes, that one could set up directly back of the keys. With the help of this, we learned some simple melodies. But it did not occur to me that I might be able to learn to play the piano properly. I was walking along the street one day, carrying a basket of laundry that I was delivering for my mother, when I heard the sound of a piano. I set down my basket, went up the steps and looked into the window. I knew it was wrong to peep, but I could not resist the temptation. I saw a woman at a piano, playing ever so beautifully. Her skin was dark like mine. I realized that if she could, I could.

As Mother had said so often, "Remember, wherever you are and whatever you do, someone always sees you." I remembered that woman, who never knew the effect she had on me, when I tried years later to study the piano. I loved music, but I had taken it for granted that it must be for others.

Who tells Marian Anderson's story? What does she discover in this short passage?

Here is a story about the life of Norwegian explorer Thor Heyerdahl. He once sailed in a raft from South America to the Pacific Islands to prove that people long ago might also have crossed the Pacific. Read this passage to discover if it is a biography or an autobiography.

Thor liked to stand in front of a window watching the ships come and go through Oslo Fjord. He wondered where they went and what strange lands lay beyond the horizon.

One winter day Thor went to watch blocks of ice being cut from a nearby lake. The ice was to be used in the brewery owned by Thor's father. Thor, happy to be out of doors, began to run excitedly about on the lake. He jumped onto a block of ice that had been cut free from the rest. Under the boy's weight it tilted slightly. Arms waving, Thor plunged into the icy water.

Fear and the shock of the cold water paralyzed him. He did not know how to swim. Fortunately, the air trapped inside his clothing kept him floating for a few moments. To the child, his mind black with terror, these moments seemed to last forever.

A workman reached him, caught the collar of his coat, and pulled him to safety.

The next summer Thor's father tried to teach him to swim. But even the thought of putting his face beneath the surface terrified Thor. "He'll learn as he gets older," his father said.

But Thor's fear of the water did not fade. Later his father hired a professional swimmer to teach the boy. Thor wanted to swim. He watched the teacher carefully. He learned exactly what he was supposed to do. But as soon as he stepped into the water, he would feel terror cold inside himself. And the instant his face went beneath the surface, blind panic took over.

This happened time and again. From his teacher Thor learned everything there was to know about swimming—in theory. But in actual practice he simply could not swim. Finally his teacher told Mr. Heyerdahl, "This boy is never going to learn," and quit.

Though he was afraid of the water itself, Thor was fascinated by the beach, the shells, the life of the sea. He was still very young when he started a collection of seashells. As he grew older, his father introduced him to some of the commercial fishermen in Larvik. The boy spent hours around the fish houses, watching the boats being unloaded, asking questions. Fishermen brought him strange creatures that had been caught in the nets.

Thor's mother took him to the zoological museum in Oslo, the capital of Norway. He had never seen a museum before. He wandered wide-eyed from one exhibit to the next. When at last he was pulled away, he told his mother, "There's no museum in Larvik. So I'm going to start one."

Even at that age, if Thor set a goal for himself, he stuck to it. He talked his father into allowing him to use an old building near the brewery. The boy already had his collection of shells and the creatures of the sea, as well as butterflies and other insects. Now he began to collect all sorts of wildlife. Some of the other schoolchildren brought their collections. Before he finished high school, Thor had a real museum.

Does Thor Heyerdahl tell his own story? What happens in the passage?

You have read parts of two forms of a life story. A **biography** is the story of a person's life written by another person. An **autobiography** is the story of one's life written by oneself. Both forms usually follow time order.

Practice

A. Read these short passages. Then copy each underlined name and occupation onto your paper. Write *B* next to each one that comes from a biography. Write *A* next to each one that comes from an autobiography.

1. <u>Dylan Thomas, writer:</u> It was the first time I had stayed in grandpa's house. The floorboards had squeaked like mice as I climbed into bed, and the mice between the walls had creaked like wood as though another visitor was walking on them.

2. <u>James Thurber, writer:</u> The ghost that got into our house on the night of November 17, 1915, raised such a hullabaloo of misunderstandings that I am sorry I didn't just let it keep on walking, and go to bed. It caused my mother to throw a shoe through a window of the house next door.

3. <u>Shirley Chisholm, congresswoman:</u> She developed a close relationship with her grandmother, who was not a big woman but seemed that way to the children. Emmeline Seale was very stern but also very kind. Her gentleness made her seem like a godmother to the children, and they listened closely when she would gather them around her to talk about life.

Apply

B. Get ready to write an imaginary autobiography.

Prewriting
- Imagine that you are a famous space explorer, scientist, or artist. Choose an event in your life that you would like to recount.
- Make a list of specific words to use in your work.

Composing
- Write about the event as if it were part of a real autobiography. It may be humorous or serious.
- Use specific words and varied sentences.

Revising
- Read your imaginary autobiography. Check that your wording is specific and that you have varied your sentences.

A BOOK TO READ

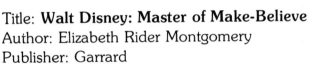

Title: **Walt Disney: Master of Make-Believe**
Author: Elizabeth Rider Montgomery
Publisher: Garrard

The birth of Mickey Mouse, the magical creation of Walt Disney's pen, is shrouded in mystery and legend. One story is that the artist had befriended a tiny mouse and had even taught him to stay within a penciled circle on the drawing board. Years later while searching for a fresh idea, he sketched the lovable big-eared mouse that is known by millions today.

From a childhood filled with cruelty and hunger, Disney rose to international fame and founded an entertainment empire. He produced the first color cartoon, the first full-length cartoon movie, *Snow White and the Seven Dwarfs,* and the most famous amusement parks in the world. *Walt Disney: Master of Make-Believe* is a brief biography of a man whose genius has entertained the whole world.

1 UNIT TEST

● **Kinds of Sentences**   pages 2–3

Number your paper from 1 to 7. Next to each number write the letter that tells you which kind of sentence each one is. Use this code.

A. declarative   B. interrogative   C. imperative   D. exclamatory

1. Anna Elizabeth Dickinson was active during the Civil War.
2. What did she do?
3. She spoke of the need to end slavery.
4. Tell me more about her.
5. She also spoke for women's rights.
6. Did you know that she was called the Joan of Arc of the North?
7. What courage she must have had!

● **Complete Subjects and Predicates**   pages 4–5

Copy these sentences. In each sentence draw one line under the complete subject and two lines under the complete predicate.

8. Chief Joseph ruled the Nez Percé tribe.
9. He would not let the government take his people's land.
10. A war began soon after that.
11. Chief Joseph's warriors won several battles.
12. The government's forces were stronger, however.
13. Chief Joseph ordered a retreat to Canada.
14. Government troops could not stop him.

● **Simple Subjects and Predicates**   pages 6–7

Copy each sentence. Circle the simple subject and the simple predicate.

15. This brave chief led his people more than 1,000 miles.
16. General Nelson A. Miles stopped the retreat only 40 miles from the Canadian border.

17. The Nez Percé people surrendered sadly.
18. Chief Joseph loved his people — and peace.
19. He has been called the Indian Napoleon.

● The Subjects of Sentences   pages 8–9

Copy these sentences. Underline each simple subject. Write *(you)* after sentences in which the subject is *you* (understood).

20. When may I go to bat?
21. Wait your turn.
22. Please hit a home run.
23. What is that pitcher doing?
24. Do not swing yet.
25. Where did the ball go?
26. Run for home!
27. The catcher has dropped the baseball.
28. What will the runner do?
29. Taka is running toward second base.
30. Look at her!
31. What speed she has!
32. Will Taka go on to third base?
33. Maybe Linda will hit a home run.
34. Ask the coach for the players' records.
35. Bring them to me right away.

● Word Order in Sentences   pages 10–11

Copy these sentences. Write *natural* or *inverted word order* after each.

36. On the starting blocks stood the swimmers.
37. The starting gun went off.
38. Into the water dove the six swimmers.
39. Suddenly two swimmers pulled ahead.
40. Up came a hand at the end of the pool.
41. A new champion grinned at the cheering fans.
42. On the stage stood Conchita.
43. The judge handed her a blue ribbon.
44. The audience clapped wildly.
45. Conchita's family was happy and proud.

● The Dictionary   pages 14–15

If the guide words on a dictionary page are *dust* and *ecology,* which of these words would be found on that page? Write the answers on your paper.

1. eagle	**2.** dryer	**3.** duster	**4.** echo
5. domino	**6.** edge	**7.** ebony	**8.** economical
9. duty	**10.** dynamite	**11.** electric	**12.** dwelling
13. draft	**14.** easel	**15.** earthquake	

● The Dictionary Entry   pages 16–17

The slanted word in each of these sentences has more than one meaning. Look up each slanted word. Copy the definition that tells what the word means in the sentence.

16. That is a very *clear* photograph, Lauren.

17. Mr. Gotrocks kept his money in a *safe.*

18. I love the *lemon* color of these towels.

19. Will Mom *patch* the hole in your jeans?

20. Stay away from that *bold* cliff.

21. Our teacher, Ms. Quong, made the meaning quite *clear.*

22. Rwanda is wearing her new *down* jacket.

23. The actor spoke his lines in a *hollow* voice.

24. The mayor has taken *measures* to cut down on noise.

25. Pedro called the meeting to *order.*

26. Janice helped her parents *pick* the crops.

27. At that *point,* the visitors left.

28. Our carnival *ran* for a whole week.

● Prewriting, Composing, and Revising—Sentences   pages 18–26

1. Copy these words on your paper. Next to each word, write a more specific word.

hot	nice	pretty	wet
happy	storms	cold	rains

Use your specific words to write sentences about the seasons. Write four declarative sentences, one about each season. Then write two interrogative, one imperative, and one exclamatory sentences. Edit and proofread your sentences.

● Mechanics Practice   page 27

Capitalize and punctuate these sentences correctly.

2. what season of the year do you enjoy most
3. autumn is a lovely season
4. leaves turn various colors
5. the mountains are covered with their brilliant hues
6. how cool the air feels in autumn
7. this lake is clear but cold
8. let's walk across this meadow
9. what a beautiful day this is
10. i have seen more beautiful days than this
11. stop trying to spoil our good time
12. i just meant that the leaves have not changed color yet
13. come here and i will show you a beautiful tree
14. are these oak or maple leaves
15. the red ones are sugar maple leaves
16. what color do oak leaves become
17. oak leaves turn yellow in the fall
18. look at this leaf
19. what a beautiful color it is
20. don't go near that bush
21. that is a sumac bush
22. it is beautiful but poisonous
23. what a terrible rash i got last year
24. i will never forget how miserable i was
25. you are making me feel itchy

● Biography and Autobiography   pages 28–33

Imagine that two books are being written about someone you know.
Write two sentences for each type of information listed below. One
sentence should look as though it would appear in a biography.
The other sentence should look as though it would appear in an
autobiography.

- the date and place of that person's birth
- that person's favorite food as a child
- that person's best subject in school
- that person's favorite activity as a child

LANGUAGE
Learning About Paragraphs

STUDY SKILLS
Locating Information

Do you know how to snap clear photographs? If you do, you know that you have to decide what you want others to see. You usually focus on a particular person or thing. What did the photographer focus on in the picture on the left? Why might the photographer have chosen that particular rock formation? Describe the other things you see in the picture.

Pretend you are going to write a paragraph about the scene in the photograph. What should your focus, or main idea, be? Think of an exciting sentence about the rock formation. Now that you have the rock formation as a focus, or main idea, what details might you choose for your paragraph? After you have decided on your details, you will need to put them in order. In this unit you will learn about order in paragraphs. You will study the topic sentence and three different ways to organize details in your writing.

Suppose you want to find out more information about rock formations. If you go to the library, you will have to know where to locate the facts you want. In this unit you will learn how to use the card catalog to gather information on subjects, books, and authors. You will also read a play, *The Land We Love,* and use it as a model for writing a short scene of your own.

Now focus your thoughts and start the unit!

◀ *Delicate Arch, Arches National Park in Utah*

LANGUAGE

Lesson 1: Understanding Paragraphs and Their Main Ideas

Stephanos loves chocolate. Read this passage he found in a library book.

Chocolate is a food made from the seeds of a tree called the cacao. The cacao tree grows best in a warm, wet climate near the equator. Most of the world's cacao beans, or seeds, come from such an area in West Africa. Brazil also produces much of this raw material from which chocolate treats of all kinds are made.

What kind of information does this passage give? How is the first line of a paragraph set apart from all the others?

Think and Discuss

The book Stephanos read gave him a great deal of information about chocolate. Each set of facts was organized into a separate paragraph in which only a single idea was discussed. This kind of organization helped Stephanos move easily from one main idea to the next.

> • A **paragraph** is a series of sentences that develops a single topic. The topic upon which the paragraph is based is its **main idea.**

Look back at the paragraph Stephanos read. Its main idea is to show where the raw material of processed chocolate comes from.

Now read these paragraphs, which are also taken from Stephanos's book.

The first steps in processing cacao seeds are roasting and grinding. The roasted nibs, which are cacao seeds without their shells, are ground to release the *cocoa butter* inside. During grinding, the nibs and cocoa butter form a liquid called *chocolate liquor.*

Chocolate products are all manufactured from the chocolate liquor. *Baking chocolate,* the bitter product used in cakes and cookies, is simply chocolate liquor solidified and formed into squares. *Cocoa powder* is chocolate liquor from which some of the cocoa butter has been removed. The hard substance that remains is then reground into a fine, reddish-brown powder.

When you look for the main idea of a paragraph, you ask yourself, "What *single topic* does this paragraph develop? What *one thought* can I take from it?" The main idea of the second paragraph is that roasting and grinding are the first steps in processing cacao into chocolate. What is the main idea of the third paragraph?

Practice

A. Read these paragraphs. Then write in your own words the main idea of each one.

1. Milk chocolate is the most popular of all chocolate products. It is made from chocolate liquor, milk solids, and granulated sugar. Extra cocoa butter is also added for richness. These materials are put through a series of rollers, and the process takes over three days to complete. After this time the chocolate is hardened and is made into bars.

2. Sweet chocolate and semisweet chocolate go through the same manufacturing process as milk chocolate. The only difference is that milk solids are not added to the mixture. Most sweet and semisweet chocolate is sold to candy makers who use it to cover the creamy, nutty, and chewy centers of boxed candy.

3.   Cacao beans were first used by the Maya Indians of Central America and the Aztec Indians of Mexico. The cacao bean played an especially important role in the religion of the Aztecs, who believed that one of their prophets had given them the first cacao seeds. According to the Aztec legend, the prophet had taken the seeds from heaven and had sown them in his garden. When he ate the fruit, he gained great wisdom and knowledge.

Apply

B. 4.–8. Write in your own words and in sentence form five main ideas that might be used to compose five paragraphs. The main ideas need not be on the same subject, but each must be suitable for a paragraph.

To Memorize

Hold fast your dreams!
Within your heart
Keep one still, secret spot
Where dreams may go,
And sheltered so,
May thrive and grow—
Where doubt and fear are not
Oh, keep a place apart
Within your heart,
For little dreams to go.

Louise Driscoll

What might happen to dreams if doubt and fear were allowed to enter their secret place? Do you think it is important for people to have dreams? Why or why not?

Lesson 2: Understanding Topic Sentences and Detail Sentences

Imac had come from Peru to the United States as an infant. Read this paragraph from a book about Peru that she found.

There are three main land regions in Peru. The coast, on the western side of the country, is a long, narrow area along the Pacific Ocean. The highlands consist of mountains and valleys in the center of Peru. The selva, the eastern region of the country, is made up mainly of rain forests and jungles.

What is the main idea of this paragraph? Does any one sentence express this idea?

Think and Discuss

Sometimes a paragraph will contain one sentence that expresses its main idea. Such a sentence is called a **topic sentence.** It is most often found at the beginning or the end of the paragraph. The other sentences, called **detail sentences,** support the topic sentence by adding details that complete the paragraph. A topic sentence that *begins* the paragraph lets the reader know what is coming. It also helps the writer to keep to the topic. At the *end* of a paragraph, the topic sentence often sums up what has been said.

> - A **topic sentence** is one that expresses the main idea of a paragraph.
> - A **detail sentence** supports the topic sentence by adding details.

What is the topic sentence of Imac's paragraph on Peru? Which ones are the detail sentences?

Read this paragraph from another part of Imac's book.

Since the sixteenth century when Peru was conquered by the armies of Spain, Spanish has been the only language used in government and business. In 1975, however, the Inca language *Quechua* was accepted on the same basis as Spanish. Although Quechua is spoken mainly by the highland people, many Spanish-speaking Peruvians are also learning it. Today both Spanish and Quechua are the official languages of Peru.

What is the topic sentence of this paragraph?

Practice

A. Copy these sentences. Next to each write *topic sentence* if it expresses a main idea or *detail sentence* if it states a detail.

1. They tamed llamas and began to grow potatoes, which grew wild in the highlands.
2. Gradually the Indians learned to farm.
3. Scholars believe that the first people to live in Peru were Indians from North America.
4. Later, potatoes became an important food in Peru.
5. They were known and used by the Indians long before they were discovered by the rest of the world.

B. Write a topic sentence for each of these subjects.

6. your favorite European country
7. the climate of your home town or city
8. your city's place in American history
9. a product for which your city or state is known
10. a language you would like to learn

Apply

C. 11.–14. Choose one of the topic sentences you wrote in Practice B. Write four detail sentences that support it. Arrange your sentences in paragraph form.

Lesson 3: Understanding Appropriate Details

Read this paragraph.

Field Day at school was a grand success! There was a huge crowd and the races were very exciting. Everyone in my class entered the mini-marathon. My cousin Tina spent the weekend at our house. The mini-marathon was the most fun because we ran with our families. Each family in the race received a trophy.

Which sentence does not belong in the paragraph?

Think and Discuss

As you know, the main idea of a paragraph is often stated in a topic sentence. When all the detail sentences support the main idea, the paragraph has **unity.** Any sentence that departs from the main idea must be taken out.

A paragraph is **coherent** when each detail sentence follows the one before it in logical order. Except for the sentence that must be deleted, the paragraph about Field Day is coherent. The detail sentences begin by mentioning races, then move to the mini-marathon, a kind of race, and end with the trophies, the results of the race.

Practice

A. Copy these topic sentences and the detail sentences that follow. Underline any sentence that does not keep to the topic.

1. Our school had a Field Day.
   a. It was held in the park.
   b. Our school has a football team.
   c. Students and their families were invited.

2. Besides races, there were many other events.
   a. Our class competed against the seventh grade in a tug-of-war.
   b. The younger classes had a jump-rope contest.
   c. Everyone received a new T-shirt.

3. Field Day ended with a family picnic.
   a. Some of the teachers cooked the hot dogs.
   b. The kite-flying contest was the last event.
   c. Each family brought a special dish.
   d. These foods were placed on a long table for everyone to share.

4. Even the losers were winners on Field Day.
   a. Each winning class treated each losing class to some apples.
   b. Most classes that were losers in one event were winners in another event.
   c. The archery event was canceled because no one could find the arrows.
   d. The members of most classes ate at least three apples.

5. Everyone in school talked about Field Day for weeks.
   a. Next year Field Day will be held in September.
   b. No one will forget the fifth-grade runner who fell into a mud puddle.
   c. Grade three will always remember that they won the sack race.
   d. Grade seven will probably be reminding us for weeks that they won the tug-of-war.

B. On the next page there is a topic sentence that is followed by several detail sentences. Copy the topic sentence. Then write the detail sentences in logical order.

Topic Sentence: Running has become a popular activity and sport.

6. Joggers can be seen on almost any road or city street.
7. Dedicated joggers also run after school or work.
8. At noon many spend their lunch hours running.
9. Even late at night a few lone joggers make their way through the quiet streets.
10. In the morning some people jog to work.

Apply

C. 11. Choose one of the topic sentences in Practice A. Add other details in sentences that support the main idea in the topic sentence. Then write the sentences in correct paragraph form.

HOW OUR LANGUAGE GROWS

If you were in England, you might hear someone say that she has to "ring up her solicitor on a trunk call." The person is saying that she must make a long distance call to her lawyer. What we call *quotation marks,* the British call *inverted commas.* Our *TV* is their *telly.*

At a *petrol station* in London you might hear a driver ask the attendant to "check the accumulator and the hooter." Would you know that a *petrol station* is a gas station, an *accumulator* is a battery, and a *hooter* is a horn? These differences are like the regional dialects we have in the United States.

British and American spellings for some words are also different. On a separate sheet of paper, write the American spelling for each of these words.

1. tyre   2. centre   3. axe   4. recognise   5. programme
6. honour 7. grey   8. colour 9. colonise   10. pyjamas

LANGUAGE REVIEW

Paragraphs and Their Main Ideas   pages 40–42

Read these paragraphs. Write the main idea of each paragraph in your own words.

1.   The first English settlers to come to America faced great dangers on the way. They crossed the ocean, crowded together in small boats. The voyage took many months. People often became sick because there were no fresh fruits or vegetables in their diets. Some died for lack of proper medical care. The small wooden crafts often arrived in America with fewer passengers than had left England. It took courage and strength for anyone to come to the New World.

2.   When people from other countries arrived, they saw a world that seemed very strange to them. Europe had been heavily settled, and the cities were crowded. In America, forests covered the land as far as they could see. There were no cities. America was very different from the world they had known.

3.   As people travel and settle in new places, their languages travel too. English changes and grows as foreign words are added to it. For example, imagine a girl who is dressed in a khaki shirt, denim pants, and moccasins, and who pours ketchup on her macaroni. To describe her, you would use words from all over the world. *Khaki* is a Hindustani word meaning "dust colored." *Denim* was first manufactured in France, where it was called *serge de Nimes. Moccasin* is an Algonquin word, and *ketchup* is a Malay word for a sauce. *Macaroni,* of course, is Italian.

Topic Sentences   pages 43–44

4.–6. Copy the topic sentence from each of the three paragraphs in the previous exercise.

7.–11. Read these sentences. Then write the sentences as a paragraph in the order that makes the most sense. Underline the topic sentence of the paragraph.

7. They grew tired of the same daily work.
8. More and more people began to leave the farms.
9. In the nineteenth century many Americans were not happy living on farms.
10. The cities in the East offered them a chance to earn money and live more exciting lives.
11. As a result, cities grew and expanded.

Details in Paragraphs   pages 45–47

Copy this topic sentence and the numbered detail sentences that follow it. Underline the sentences that support the topic sentence.

Machines are used in every step of cloth-making.

12. In the fields machines pick cotton.
13. Boll weevils can damage cotton crops.
14. Cotton is a good fabric.
15. Machines spin cotton into thread and weave it into cloth.
16. The dyeing, decorating, and sewing are also done with machines.
17. Dyed cotton is expensive.

Read this topic sentence and the numbered detail sentences that follow it. Choose the detail sentences that support the topic sentence. Then write those sentences and the topic sentence in correct paragraph form.

Early cities in America were trading and shipping centers.

18. These young cities were built near bodies of water.
19. Sailing ships and boats were the chief means of transportation.
20. Goods were taken from the docks to the trading posts in carts.
21. The cities are better than farms.

Applying Paragraphs

22. Choose one of these subjects. Then write a paragraph to develop it. Include a topic sentence.

    an imaginary kingdom, schools of the future, the strangest machine in the world, the ideal vacation, the most exciting career of all

STUDY SKILLS

Lesson 4: Using the Library

Hana made this list of things she wanted to find.

a picture book for her three-year-old brother
the March 1985 issue of *Consumer Reports*
a map of Illinois
a cookbook with casserole recipes in it
a novel by Virginia Hamilton

Name at least three places in which Hana might find some of this information. Where could she find *all* of it?

Think and Discuss

A library is a rich source of information. In it you can find just about any kind of information you might need. Most libraries have rooms or sections with various types of reading material in each one.

The **reference** section contains dictionaries, indexes, encyclopedias, atlases, and almanacs. Many people need to use these books often, so you must use them while you are in the library.

You may borrow most other books in a library. These other books are divided into two main groups. Works of **fiction** include novels and short stories. Fiction books are arranged alphabetically according to the last name of the author. **Nonfiction** books contain factual material, and they are arranged according to subject. Some libraries keep books for readers under 14 years of age in an area called the **juvenile** section. The **young adult** section (if the library has one) is for somewhat older or more experienced readers.

A library is also a storehouse of newspapers and magazines. The **periodicals** section contains local and national newspapers and often newspapers from other countries. It may display a number of recent magazines. Older issues of magazines and newspapers, often going back several years, are also kept there.

Practice

A. Write these authors' names in the order in which they would appear on a library shelf.

1. Robert C. O'Brien
2. Beverly Cleary
3. Emily Neville
4. Theodore Taylor
5. Joan Aiken
6. C. S. Lewis
7. Robert Silverberg
8. Louisa May Alcott
9. Richard Peck
10. Scott O'Dell

B. Copy these sources of information. Next to each one write whether it would be found in the *reference, fiction, nonfiction,* or *periodicals* section of a library.

11. a map of Puerto Rico
12. the novel *A Wrinkle in Time*
13. a book about coal mining
14. a biography of Theodore Roosevelt
15. the *World Almanac*
16. a copy of your local newspaper
17. a collection of stories by Edgar Allan Poe
18. the current issue of *Time* magazine
19. a history of professional baseball
20. a book about raising vegetables

C. Write the paragraph that your teacher will now dictate to you.

Apply

D. 21.–28. Visit your school or public library. Write the titles of two books or other sources of information that you find in *each* of its four sections.

Lesson 5: Using the Card Catalog

Kent had been given a puppy for his birthday. His mother suggested that he read about dogs in a book called *Dogs: Records, Stars, Feats, and Facts*. Where might Kent find this book?

Think and Discuss

The easiest way for Kent to find *Dogs: Records, Stars, Feats, and Facts* is to go straight to the **card catalog** of his nearest library. The card catalog is a cabinet of small drawers. Each card in the catalog contains information on a book in the library. These cards are arranged in alphabetical order.

The card catalog contains three kinds of cards. If you know the title of the book you want, look up the **title card.** If you know the author, look up the **author card.** Author cards are alphabetized according to the author's last name. If you have no particular book in mind, look for the **subject card.** Study these examples of the three types of cards.

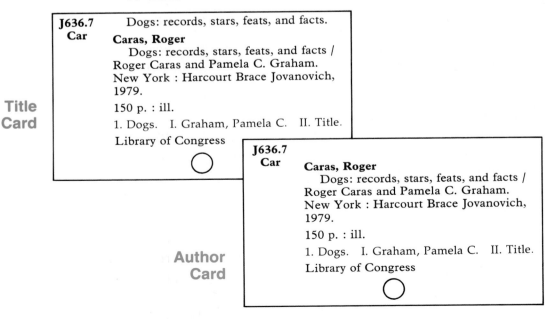

Title Card

J636.7
Car

Dogs: records, stars, feats, and facts.

Caras, Roger
 Dogs: records, stars, feats, and facts /
Roger Caras and Pamela C. Graham.
New York : Harcourt Brace Jovanovich,
1979.

150 p. : ill.

1. Dogs. I. Graham, Pamela C. II. Title.

Library of Congress

Author Card

J636.7
Car

Caras, Roger
 Dogs: records, stars, feats, and facts /
Roger Caras and Pamela C. Graham.
New York : Harcourt Brace Jovanovich,
1979.

150 p. : ill.

1. Dogs. I. Graham, Pamela C. II. Title.

Library of Congress

DOGS

J636.7
Car

Subject
Card

Caras, Roger
    Dogs: records, stars, feats, and facts /
Roger Caras and Pamela C. Graham.
New York : Harcourt Brace Jovanovich,
1979.

    150 p. : ill.

    1. Dogs. I. Graham, Pamela C.   II. Title.
Library of Congress

Which card will Kent look at to find the book he wants?

The number in the upper left-hand corner of each card is the **call number.** It tells you where to find the book on the library shelves. If the call number begins with a *J,* you will find the book in the **juvenile** section.

Practice

A. Study the cards shown in this lesson. Answer these questions on your paper.

1. Who wrote this book?
2. Is it illustrated?
3. When was it published?
4. Where was it published?
5. Who published it?
6. What is its call number?

B. Copy this book information. Next to each item write whether you would use the *title card,* the *author card,* or the *subject card* to find it.

7. books about unusual inventions
8. the novel *Danny Dunn and the Homework Machine*
9. a book about Chinese watercolor painting
10. a book by Virginia Olsen Baron

Apply

C. 11.–14. Use the card catalog in your school or public library to look up a novel, a biography, an American history book, and a book of poems. Write the author, title, and call number for each.

Lesson 6: Understanding the Dewey Decimal System

By using the card catalog, Kent found that his library had a copy of the book he wanted. Now all he had to do was find it. If you were Kent, what would you do?

Think and Discuss

Each card in the card catalog has in the upper left corner a code made of numbers and letters. This code is known as a **call number.** Each call number fits into the **Dewey Decimal System,** in which nonfiction books are arranged according to subject areas. Here are the ten main subject areas of the Dewey Decimal System. Next to each main subject are topics that might be found under that heading. The numbers to the left show the call numbers under which books on that subject will be found.

000–099   General works (encyclopedias, atlases, newspapers)

100–199   Philosophy (ideas about the meaning of life, psychology)

200–299   Religion (world religions, mythology)

300–399   Social science (government, law, business, education)

400–499   Language (dictionaries, grammar books)

500–599   Pure science (mathematics, chemistry, plants, animals)

600–699   Applied science (how-to books, engineering, radio)

700–799   Arts and recreation (music, art, sports, hobbies)

800–899   Literature (poems, plays, essays)

900–999   History (travel, geography, biography)

Practice

A. Copy these book titles. Next to each title write the Dewey Decimal System number under which each book would appear.

Example: *American History 900–999*

1. *The Government of Peru*
2. *World Atlas*
3. *Basic American English*
4. *Soccer Made Easy*
5. *Gods of Ancient Greece*
6. *Navajo Indian Poems*
7. *All About Snakes*
8. *Home Repair Manual*

B. A certain library shelf holds books with the call numbers 807.1–809.3. Write the books that would be on that shelf in the order in which they would appear.

9. *Nature Poems*   808.3
10. *Hero Poems*   803.6
11. *Poetry About Animals*   807.6
12. *All About Poetry*   809.1
13. *Poems by Sixth-Graders*   806.1
14. *Poems for Children*   807.4
15. *Story Poems*   808.4
16. *Classroom Poetry*   809.4

Apply

C. Go to the library and look up a book on each of these subjects. Write its title, author, and call number, as well as the main subject area under which it appears.

17. a book on origami
18. a biography about Mozart
19. a Spanish dictionary
20. a book about the planets

A Challenge

Make up a Dewey Decimal System of your own. Instead of books, however, classify other objects such as tools or careers. You must have ten separate categories in your new system.

COMPOSITION

Lesson 7:   Prewriting
Choosing and Arranging Details

Tanya was planning a report about a snow-sculpture exhibit she had seen. She had been so impressed with the many sculptures that she wrote about them in her journal. How might Tanya choose and arrange details from her journal for her report?

Think and Discuss

Tanya decided to start with a diagram that included the highlights of the exhibit. Here is her diagram.

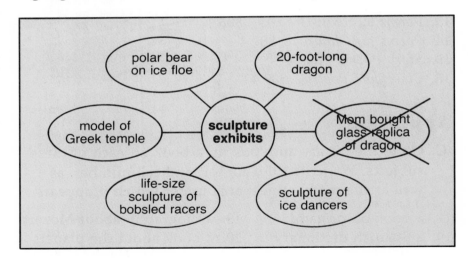

As Tanya looked over her diagram, she realized that one entry did not belong, and she crossed it out. Why would the crossed-out item be unsuitable for her report?

Then Tanya had to decide how to order the details she had chosen. After rereading her journal entry, she made two lists, each arranged in a different order.

A. Exhibits in the order in which *I visited them* (Time Order)	B. Exhibits as they were arranged *on show grounds* (Space Order)
1. bobsled racers 2. dragon 3. polar bear 4. ice dancers 5. Greek temple	1. Greek temple 2. ice dancers 3. bobsled racers 4. polar bear 5. dragon

Were both types of order suitable for Tanya's report? Why or why not? Could a trip to a museum or gallery be arranged in both types of order? For what other kinds of reports might such an arrangement be used?

How to Choose and Arrange Details

1. **Choose only details that support your topic. Cross out any that do not belong.**
2. **Plan your details in some sort of logical order.**
3. **Decide whether your details could be arranged in time order or space order.**
4. **Make a short list showing the order in which you will mention your details.**

Practice

A. Make a diagram like the one on page 56. Write the items on this page and the next page in the circles in the diagram. Leave out any items that do not belong.

- grilled hamburgers over open fire
- played softball
- Mary Ellen home with cold
- rowed out on lake
- things we did on our picnic

- sang songs around fire
- it rained for one-half hour
- hiked around lake

B. Make a list showing these items in logical order.
- The picnic area is south of the softball field.
- A small wooded area lies west of the lake and north of the tennis courts.
- The lake is in the center of the park.
- To the east of the lake lies the softball field.
- Due north of the lake is the ranger station.
- The tennis courts lie to the west of the picnic area and to the south of the woods.

Apply

C. Plan a time-order and a space-order paragraph.

Choose Your Topic
- If you have a journal, use it for ideas. If you do not have a journal, you might begin one now.
- For the time-order paragraph choose a familiar routine. For the space-order paragraph choose an arrangement of objects.

Choose Your Audience
- You will probably find it enjoyable to write for someone who will appreciate your topic. Choose words that are suitable for this audience.

Make Diagrams and Lists
- For each paragraph make a diagram like the one on page 56. The diagram should show possible details to support your topic.
- When you have chosen your details, list them in logical order.

Review Your Work
- Look over your diagrams and lists. Take out any items that would not support your topic. Add any that might occur to you.
- Be sure each list is in the proper order.
- Save your work for Lessons 8 and 9.

Lesson 8: Composing
Writing Time-Order Paragraphs

Read this paragraph about the beginning of a storm.

The baseball game had just begun. Soon storm clouds gathered overhead. Thunder and lightning followed. Next it began to rain heavily. Some fans left when the downpour started, but the players continued. Then the field became soggy. Finally the umpire called off the game.

Which words in the paragraph indicate time?

Think and Discuss

When you tell a story or describe an event, it is important to state facts clearly and in the proper order. When facts and events are presented in the proper order, a paragraph has coherence. The model paragraph, for example, would not make sense if sentence 6 were placed first. How would you describe the order of the sentences in the paragraph? What time words tie the sentences together? Time order is one of the ways to tell a story, describe an event, or give directions.

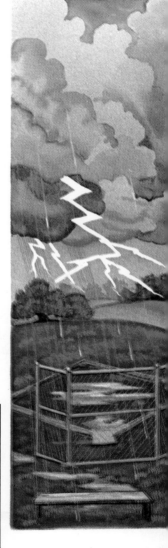

How to Write a Time-Order Paragraph

1. Before you begin to write the paragraph, make notes on the order of events that you will describe.
2. Put the events in the order in which they happen.
3. Try to use words like *first, next, then,* and *finally* to tie sentences together.
4. Refer to your notes as you write the paragraph.
5. Check your work to see that one sentence leads to the next in a sensible way.

Practice

A. Read these sentences. Number the sentences so that they make sense in time order. Then write the sentences in paragraph form.

1. By the next morning streets, sidewalks, and houses were covered with ten inches of snow.
2. Soon the sidewalks were covered, and snow began to pile up in doorways and on rooftops.
3. The snowstorm began with a few tiny flakes that melted as soon as they touched the ground.
4. Throughout the following night the snow continued.
5. After a while the flakes stopped melting.

B. 6. Read this paragraph. Rewrite it correctly.

Suddenly traces of green seem to sprout everywhere. The trees have tiny buds, and the grass is fresh and new. It is easy to tell when spring is here. The crocuses pop out of the ground first, even when snow still covers the grass. Before long, more flowers are blooming, and a sweet fragrance fills the air.

C. 7. Study the time-order paragraph you wrote for Practice A. Then close your books and write the paragraph as your teacher dictates it.

Apply

D. Reread the material you wrote for Lesson 7.

Write a Topic Sentence
● Tell what you are going to write about.

Write Detail Sentences
● Write a sentence or two for each of your details.
● The last detail sentence will be a conclusion.

Review Your Work
● Reread your time-order paragraph. Be sure you have joined your detail sentences with time words.
● Save your paragraph for revising in Lesson 10.

Lesson 9:   Composing
Writing Space-Order Paragraphs

Maska and Imala were an American Indian boy and girl who had been transported to a strange place by an old Indian chant. This paragraph tells what they saw.

Directly before them lay a vast plain covered with reddish grass and shrubs. About a mile straight ahead, sheer golden cliffs seemed to rise out of the earth, reaching an incredible height. From what Maska thought might be breaks in the cliff walls glittered thousands of tiny ruby lights. Nothing stirred. Toward the horizon stretched the deep, silent violet sky.

In what order is this strange landscape described?

Think and Discuss

In describing a scene of any kind, it is a good idea to do so in a certain order. You might, for example, begin with the things that are near and gradually move farther away. You could begin at a distance and move closer. You might even begin at your left or right and describe the scene in a circular movement that ends where you began. Whichever kind of space order you choose, it is important to let your paragraph flow smoothly from one detail to the next. The reader should be able to follow your description mentally as easily as he or she would take in a real scene. Good planning helps you to build up the effect you want your paragraph to have.

Look back at the description that introduces this lesson. What effect do you think the writer wanted to produce?

Practice

A. Copy the underlined topic sentence. The remaining four sentences should be arranged in the same order as the paragraph on page 61. Write them in paragraph form.

1. <u>Maska remembered a scene very much like this one from a long-ago dream.</u>

2. The distant cliffs had been a soft blue.
3. In his dream, only the sky was exactly the same, a dense violet canopy with amethyst clouds shifted about by the restless wind.
4. Instead of ruby lights, a thousand eyes had stared out at him from the cliff walls.
5. In the dream, however, the plain in front of him had been divided into sections of rust and golden grasses.

B. 6. This mixed-up paragraph should begin at a distance and end close by. Rewrite it correctly.

Although the creatures were still nearly a mile away, they were advancing rapidly, parting the sea of red grass as they rode. It had not come from the distant creatures but was quite near, perhaps arising from a cavern at their very feet! Suddenly a howl rose in the still air. Just then, Imala thought of the howl. At this, Maska and Imala turned and saw, from a distant valley, a dark line of creatures moving in their direction.

Apply

C. Reread the space-order diagram and list that you wrote for Lesson 7.

Write a Topic Sentence
- Some paragraphs taken from longer works do not have a clear-cut topic sentence. Since you are writing a single paragraph, however, you should first tell what your topic is.

Write Detail Sentences
- Write a sentence or two for each detail you listed. Follow the order you set up in your list.
- Use the guidelines in the blue box on page 62 to help you.

Review Your Work
- Reread your space-order paragraph. Be sure your description proceeds in logical order. It may be left to right, near to far, or in a circular pattern.
- Save your paragraph for revising in Lesson 10.

Editing and Proofreading for Proper Order

Claire had written a space-order paragraph describing a scene in Scotland. When she read it over, however, she realized that two of the sentences were not in correct space order. In addition, she noticed four misspellings and several other small errors. What could she do to make the changes before she wrote her final copy?

Think and Discuss

Here is the first draft of Claire's paragraph and the changes she finally made. Her space order was meant to begin at ground level and move up.

Editing and Proofreading Marks

Mark	Meaning
≡	capitalize
⊙	make a period
∧	add something
∧ (comma)	add a comma
ỷ ỷ	add quotation marks
⌙	take something away
○	spell correctly
¶	indent the paragraph
/	make a lowercase letter
∼ tr	transpose

The moor country of scotland is a trecherous *treacherous* but beautiful area ⊙ much of the ground is swampy ∧ and those who do not know the right paths often do not get thru *through*. Nevertheless, the grassy vallys *valleys* are a bright and healthy green. The sky is sometimes a brilliant blue ∧ but often a misterious *mysterious* gray mist hangs over the moors like a soft velvet drape. Fields of lavender and violet heather *tr* mark every hilltop.

After which sentence should the circled sentence go?

Claire's paragraph began with a topic sentence. Notice that since she mentioned *first* that the area was dangerous, her *first* detail sentence explained that characteristic. Discussing points in the sequence in which they are introduced creates a good paragraph.

Making the last sentence of the rough draft the next-to-last sentence restores correct space order to Claire's work. What two *major changes* would have to be made if Claire wanted to move from *air* to *ground*?

How to Revise for Proper Order

Editing

1. Be sure you have written a topic sentence that tells what your paragraph is about.
2. Be sure your detail sentences support your topic sentence.
3. Be sure time-order paragraphs list details in the order in which they happened.
4. Be sure space-order paragraphs proceed smoothly in one general direction. Details should be arranged according to your prewriting plan.
5. Be sure that your vocabulary is neither too easy nor too difficult for your audience.
6. Be sure that you have tied your detail sentences together with words that were suggested in your composing lessons.

Proofreading

7. Check your paragraphs for correct spelling, punctuation, and mechanics.

Practice

A. 1. Rewrite Claire's paragraph in final form. Follow the marks that helped her make the changes.

B. 2. Copy this time-order paragraph as it is, and add marks to show how you would change it. Then write the paragraph in final form.

A thick gray mist encircled what seemed like the entire world. Finally, breaking out of the low clouds and nearing the top of the mountain, we passengers seemed to be the only people living in the clear light of day. Later, as the train climbed to a few hundred feet, the mist lessened, and I began to see waving grass, small shrubs, and heather. The first thing I saw that morning in Scotland was — absolutely nothing!

C. 3. Write a time-order paragraph describing the gradual arrival of spring or autumn in your part of the country. Revise it for proper order, capitalization, and punctuation. When all your changes have been made, copy the paragraph in final form. Give both copies to your teacher.

Apply

D. Now you will revise your time-order and space-order paragraphs.

Edit Your Paragraphs

- Check your **content.** Use items 1–4 in the blue box on page 65 as a guide. Be sure all your detail sentences follow each topic sentence in a logical order.
- Check your **style.** Items 5 and 6 in the same blue box should help you.

Proofread Your Paragraphs

- Correct all errors in spelling, punctuation, and mechanics.
- Be sure that you indented the first word of each paragraph.
- Copy your revised paragraphs onto clean sheets of paper.

Lesson 11:   Prewriting

Organizing Details
for Comparison and Contrast

Students often write paragraphs, especially as test answers, to compare or contrast. Once, on a social studies test, Masako was asked to tell in what ways the civilizations of Greece and Rome were different. If you had only a few minutes to plan your answer, how would you set it up?

Think and Discuss

Masako knew several ways in which he could contrast Greece and Rome. However, he also knew that his answer would be better understood if he could organize it logically. Here is a sample outline he jotted on a sheet of scrap paper.

Qualities	Greece	Rome
1. geography	1. small mountainous country	1. large country with rolling hills
2. government	2. independent city-states	2. empire governing vast area
3. main interests	3. philosophy, art, literature	3. law, business, expansion

The qualities, or characteristics, that Masako could most easily write about are listed in the first column. He decided to mention these qualities, in the order listed, in the topic sentence of his answer paragraph. Then, to write his detail sentences, he would take each quality in order, mentioning Greece first and Rome second each time.

Look at this partly written comparison outline.

Qualities	Oak Trees	Maple Trees
1. where found in U.S.	1. eastern half, Maine to Florida	1. _____ _____
2. type of tree	2. _____ _____	2. deciduous (lose leaves)
3. _____	3. _____	3. _____

How would you fill in the blanks for qualities 1 and 2? Where would you list the qualities in your paragraph? How would you arrange your detail sentences? Think of another quality that oaks and maples have in common and list it in your outline.

How to Organize Details for Comparison and Contrast

1. **In one column make a list of qualities that you can clearly compare or contrast.**
2. **Fill in the headings for columns 2 and 3 as in the model.**
3. **Write brief phrases under each heading.**

Practice

A. Make an outline form like the model on page 67. Arrange these parts for a paragraph of comparison.

- Qualities
- amphibian (lives on land and in water)
- how its life begins
- Frog
- kind of animal
- hatches from egg laid by female
- food eaten
- Turtle
- eats a great many insects

B. Complete this form for a paragraph of contrast.

Qualities	Warm Colors	Cool Colors
1. sample colors in category	1. _____ _____	1. greens, blues, and violets
2. sample objects in category	2. sun, firelight, flowers, sunsets	2. _____ _____
3. observer reactions	3. observers feel warm, cozy, contented, relaxed	3. _____ _____ _____ _____

Apply

C. Prepare to set up two outlines, one for a paragraph of comparison, and one for a paragraph of contrast.

Choose Your Topic
● Choose topics that have obvious likenesses and differences.

Choose an Audience
● If you want to practice answering test questions, you might decide to write for a teacher in a certain subject area. Your choice of words could then be more technical than for a general audience.

Make Your Outline
● Follow the form on page 67 for both types of outline.
● Add the qualities you will use to compare and contrast; then fill in the appropriate details.
● Numbering the items in your outline will help you follow the correct order later.

Review Your Work
● Reread your two outlines. Be sure that everything is listed in the proper order. If you should think of additional details, write them in.
● Save your outlines for the Apply exercise in Lesson 12.

Lesson 12:   Composing

Writing Paragraphs That Compare and Contrast

Franklin thought that eagles and robins have a great deal in common. Read this paragraph he wrote.

Eagles and robins are similar in their basic appearance, in their homes, and in the way they care for their young. First of all, both eagles and robins are birds, and both fly. Both build nests for their eggs. Both eagles and robins feed their young until they are ready to leave their nests and care for themselves.

In what three ways does Franklin think eagles and robins are similar?

Think and Discuss

Some paragraphs show ways in which things are alike. Others show ways in which they are different. The first is called a **paragraph of comparison.** In writing it, you think of several qualities that your two subjects have in *common.* In the second type, the **paragraph of contrast,** you decide which qualities are the most *unlike,* and you concentrate on those.

Most of your comparison or contrast paragraphs should have no more than two subjects, and no more than three qualities should be discussed. Can you think of a good reason for this?

Look back at Franklin's paragraph. Notice that he chose his three points of comparison and stated them in a *topic sentence.* He placed this sentence first in the paragraph. Then, in the same order in which he introduced each quality, he showed how both eagles and robins are alike. By organizing his paragraph in this way, he prepared his readers for *what* he would write and *in what order* he would write it. At the same time he kept himself on track with his subject.

Now read Odessa's paragraph of contrast. She, too, chose eagles and robins as her subjects and the same three qualities that Franklin had chosen to compare. Odessa, however, thought that there were greater differences than likenesses between the two.

Eagles and robins are quite different in appearance, in their homes, and in care of their young. Eagles, for example, are much larger than robins, with powerful muscles and stronger beaks and claws for food gathering. The huge nests of eagles are built high, on mountaintops or in very tall trees, far away from humans. Robins, on the other hand, build delicate nests in ordinary trees or even in birdhouses. Although they are not tame, they do not seem to mind living near people. Finally, although eagles feed their young mice, snakes, and rabbits, robins give their fledglings insects and worms to eat.

How does this paragraph compare with the first one?

How to Compose Paragraphs of Comparison or Contrast

1. **Choose no more than two subjects for each paragraph.**
2. **Choose no more than three qualities to compare or contrast.**
3. **State your subjects and the qualities you will discuss in a topic sentence.**
4. **Place the topic sentence first in the paragraph.**
5. **As you write, discuss each quality in the same order in which you introduced it.**

Practice

A. Copy these topic sentences. After each, write *comparison* or *contrast,* depending on the kind of paragraph it would best introduce.

1. Cats and dogs both make wonderful pets.
2. Trees and shrubs are alike in many ways.
3. Living near a beach is more enjoyable than living in a forest.
4. Celery and carrots are both popular vegetables.
5. It is easier to drive a car than a truck.
6. Going on a cruise is more fun than going camping.
7. Frogs and fish are both common water creatures.
8. Roller skating takes much more skill than ice skating.
9. Short stories and novels are very much alike.

B. For each pair of subjects list three qualities that could be discussed in a paragraph. Then write whether the qualities would be better as points of comparison or of contrast.

10. oceans and lakes
11. birds and insects
12. trees and shrubs
13. rivers and forests
14. airplanes and trains
15. singing and dancing

Apply

C. Reread your outlines from Lesson 11. Follow them closely to write your paragraphs.

Write a Topic Sentence
- State what you will compare or contrast. Mention the qualities in the order listed in your outline.

Write Detail Sentences
- Follow the order of your outline. The guidelines in the blue box on page 71 should help.

Review Your Work
- Reread both paragraphs. Be sure they match your outlines both in *content* and in order.
- Save your work for revising in Lesson 13.

Lesson 13:   Revising

Editing and Proofreading Paragraphs of Comparison and Contrast

Read Naomi's improved contrast paragraph.

> ⌐Crows and turkeys differ from one another in
> many ways, among which are their sizes, the
> *noises*
> ⟨nises⟩ they make, and especially their intelligence⊙
> First of all, the crow is a much smaller bird
> *Next*
> than a turkey. ∧ A crow's usual call is a ⟨haorse⟩
> *hoarse*
> "caw," while a turkey utters a throaty "gobble-
> gobble." Finally the crow is usually considered
> the smarter bird. ~~Parrots are also very smart.~~⌐
> Turkeys, on the other hand, are probably the
> least intelligent birds of all.

Think and Discuss

Why did Naomi delete a sentence that introduced a third subject? What other changes did she make?

Editing and Proofreading Marks

≡ capitalize

⊙ make a period

∧ add something

⅄ add a comma

⌄⌄ add quotation marks

⌐ take something away

◯ spell correctly

⌐ indent the paragraph

/ make a lowercase letter

∼ transpose
tr

How to Revise a Paragraph That Compares or Contrasts

Editing
1. **Be sure that your topic sentence tells whether you are comparing or contrasting.**
2. **Discuss the qualities in the same order in which they were introduced.**
3. **Delete any unnecessary sentences.**
4. **Be sure your vocabulary suits your audience.**

Proofreading
5. **Check spelling, punctuation, and mechanics.**

Practice

A. Write Naomi's paragraph as it should be. Use the changes she made.

B. Look at this paragraph of contrast. Notice the sentences that do not belong. Rewrite this paragraph, taking out the unsuitable sentences.

     The snowy owl and the burrowing owl are quite different in their sizes, their nesting habits, and the lands they inhabit. The snowy owl can be as tall as 60 centimeters, while the tiny burrowing owl is only 20 centimeters tall. The snowy owl nests on the ground in the tundra regions around the Arctic Sea. It eats mainly lemmings. The burrowing owl nests underground in burrows made by other animals. It lives in North and South America. An owl lives in a tree outside my window. I can hear it every night.

Apply

C. Find the paragraphs of comparison and contrast that you wrote for Lesson 12. Read over what you have written.

Edit Your Paragraphs
- Check your **content.** Did you include items 1-3 in the box on page 73?
- Check your **style.** Did you include item 4 in the box on page 73?

Proofread Your Paragraphs
- Check for errors in spelling, punctuation, and mechanics. Be sure the first word of each paragraph is indented.
- Copy both paragraphs onto clean sheets of paper.

MECHANICS PRACTICE

Punctuating Paragraphs and Times of Day

- Indent for each new paragraph.
- Divide words at the end of a line with hyphens.

The train was very late when it arrived at Bridgeport last night.

- Use a colon between the hour and the minutes when writing the time of day.

I took the 9:20 train from Stamford last night.

- Use periods after the letters A.M. and P.M.; capitalize A.M. and P.M.

I rise at 5 A.M. and go to bed at 9 P.M.

Write this paragraph and the following sentences correctly.

1. At 115 pm Jiro boarded a local train in New Haven, Connecticut. At 140 pm an elderly woman with a pair of knitting needles boarded the train in Stratford. For some strange reason she kept shaking the knitting needles as though they were castanets. As the train continued to Bridgeport, Fairfield, and Southport, Jiro watched her. It was not until 220 pm, however, that Jiro realized what the woman had been doing. Leaving the train at Stamford, the happy lady took off her headphones and turned her cassette player up so that everyone could hear the music.

2. You can take the 502 pm express train or the 520 pm local.
3. If you miss the 520 pm train, take the 542 pm.
4. The 607 pm express train is your last chance.
5. Does the 502 pm express go to New Haven?
6. Yes, but you will have to take the 520 pm or the 542 pm if you want to get off in Stamford.
7. A 500 am train stops in Riverside and Greenwich.
8. Does the 631 am train stop in Westport?

LITERATURE

Lesson 14: Reading a One-Act Play

Plays are meant to be acted out or at least read aloud. A good play, however, can be enjoyed even when it is read silently. On these occasions, reading a full-length play can be very much like reading a novel. Why is this?

Think and Discuss

Every play has three important characteristics. The first is a set of **characters** whose roles or parts are taken by the actors. Through their **dialog,** or spoken lines, the characters relate to one another and to the audience. As they speak, the **plot,** or action, of the play is advanced.

As you have already noticed, a full-length play is much like a novel. Both have characters, dialog, and plot. A one-act play, however, is more like a short story. How is this true?

The play that follows takes place on Ellis Island, New York, where for many years immigrants coming to the United States were identified and checked. As you read, notice how the characters relate to one another. Notice, too, how their dialog keeps the plot in motion.

The Land We Love

Nancy Henderson

Characters

George	**Father**	**Danny**
Reuben	**Amos**	**Rachel**
Grandmother	**Mother**	**Tourists**
Inspectors	**Translator**	

(Music of "America the Beautiful" is heard. The scene is a big bare hall at Ellis Island. The time is now. A group of people are being shown around by **George,** *a park attendant.)*

George: Step this way, ladies and gentlemen. This building is called the Registry Hall. It is the place where more than 12 million people passed through, from 1890 to 1954. As many as 12,000 were processed in this room in a single day. Now, please keep together; you must not wander away from the tour. When it ends, the boat will be waiting to take you back to Manhattan.

Woman: I was hoping to stay longer and walk around some on my own.

George: Sorry, ma'am. The buildings are old and decaying. It's dangerous to wander around. We'd like to restore the place — but the whole job will cost about a hundred million.

Reuben *(an older man):* Rules, rules! The place hasn't changed too much.

George: You were here before?

Reuben: Many years ago. I came through this hall as an immigrant from Poland. My mother and father sold everything and bought steerage passage for us to come to America.

George: A large family?

Reuben: Seven children — ten of us, counting my grandmother. When we finally arrived at Ellis Island, our troubles seemed to be just beginning. I'll never forget those inspectors looking us over, waiting with large tags to mark us.

George: They had to separate the sick from the well. Nobody was allowed in who wasn't able to work.

Reuben: We didn't know what was happening. We couldn't speak a word of English.

(The group becomes **Reuben's** *family. The girls take out kerchiefs and tie them around their heads.* **Reuben** *becomes a young boy.* **George** *puts on an official cap with a visor and becomes an* **Inspector.** *Several more* **Inspectors** *enter from left, carrying white cards with large*

letters on them. **Reuben** *and his group cross to stage right. The inspectors gather together at stage left. The two groups keep a space between them at center, crossing it when they communicate with each other.*)

Reuben: We knew the marks would work against us, and we were frightened. The worst was my brother, Amos. He had been given an *E* because his eyes were inflamed. We were waiting for him to come back from the medical examination.

(**Amos** *comes in, very upset, wearing a large E. He pantomimes to his family that he is going to be sent back.*) Amos had trachoma, the doctor said. If you had trachoma, you were deported. Children under ten had one parent sent back with them. But Amos was fourteen, which meant he would have to go alone.

(*The* **Mother** *and* **Father** *weep and make gestures protesting the decision.* **Amos** *is led away by two* **Inspectors.** *He is looking back sadly, waving to his family.*)

Inspector 2: Now—what is the family name?

Translator: Klebanovski.

Inspector 2: I don't believe it. What town do they come from?

Translator: The name of the town is Kleck. K-l-e-c-k.

Inspector 2 (*writing*): Let's give them that name. A lot easier.

Translator: What if they don't want to change it?

Inspector 2: Don't bother me with that. What better way to start a new life, in a new country, than with a new name? Here, it's on their paper now—the Kleck family.

Reuben: Maybe they were right sometimes, changing names. My father was very upset at first. But when we children went to school, we were so glad to have a name everyone could pronounce. And now we're all quite used to being Klecks instead of Klebanovskis. I still wonder how we got through that day. But after all the standing in line and going from room to room, we gathered our belongings (*They pick up pillow cases full of clothes.*) and went down a long corridor where a sign was pointing to the city we had dreamed about for so many years.

(**Inspector 2** *holds up a large red arrow with lettering inside that reads* "**To New York.**" *It points off left. They follow it;* **Reuben** *is last. Other* **Inspectors** *and* **Translator** *go off.* **George** *removes his official cap and returns as a present-day guide.*)

George: How did everything work out?

Reuben (*crossing down to* **George**): My mother and father got jobs in a shirt factory, earning about three dollars a week, each. My brother Daniel and I worked there after school. My sisters did what they call "home work." Maybe you know what home work is? It has nothing to do with school.

George: I believe it's piece work that children bring home from a factory.

Reuben: Right. We lived in two rooms and saved every penny we could. In two years we had enough money to send to Amos so he could come over first class on a ship. We had learned that first and second class passengers never had to go to Ellis Island. They are examined on the ship, and it was a very easy examination. So Amos returned in style and got in this time, and we had a reunion. What a reunion! (**Reuben** *meets* **Amos** *at right. They hug, and hurry over to the family; everybody hugs and cries. The rest of the family go off left, and* **Reuben** *comes back to* **George**). Of course he still had trachoma!

George: And you got your law degree?

Reuben (*beaming*): After many years. And one day it finally dawned on me that this America was *my country*. And I long to spend the rest of my life making it always a better place for other people, because it did so much for me.

George: But each of you brought something—added something of your own. That's what makes our nation great.

Reuben: All these people, striving to live together, refusing to give in to failure—at last succeeding together—this is what makes America the land we love. (*Music "America the Beautiful" comes in.*)

Practice

A. Copy these sentences, adding the correct answers.

1. The action of a play is known as its _____.
2. The lines the actors speak are called _____.
3. The people whose names appear next to their words in the written play are the _____.
4. The reader can tell which lines the actors speak and which lines are stage directions because _____.
5. The action of this play moves by starting in the_____ time, changing to the_____ time, and ending in the _____ time.

B. Answer these questions in complete sentences.

6. How does the plot change suddenly in the beginning?
7. The plot of a story, novel, or play usually revolves around some conflict or difficulty. What conflicts can be found near the beginning of the play?
8. How does Reuben use dialog to advance the action in the middle part of the play?
9. The main character of the story or a play is usually called the *protagonist*. Who is the protagonist of this play? The person who opposes the protagonist is the *antagonist*. Who is the antagonist in this play?
10. Mention two ways in which the plot at the end of the play is similar to the plot at the beginning.
11. Mention three details that show how conflicts continue until the play is nearly over.

Apply

C. Write a scene about Amos's return to Poland. Tell what he does there and how he gets back to America.

Prewriting

- Divide a sheet of paper into three parts. Label them "Amos's Return to Poland," "Amos in Poland," and "Amos's Return to America."
- Under each heading, list actions that might take place.
- Read over what you have written. Keep your plot simple. Cross out unimportant details.

Composing

- Write your scene using your three sets of notes. Include dialog and stage directions.

Revising

- Read your scene to yourself. Use the definitions in the green box on page 80 to help you revise.
- Copy your scene onto clean paper.

A BOOK TO READ

Title: **The Dark Is Rising**
Author: Susan Cooper
Publisher: Atheneum Press

"When the Dark comes rising, six shall turn it back,
Three from the circle, three from the track;
Wood, bronze, iron; water, fire, stone;
Five will return, and one go alone."

On the day of his eleventh birthday, Will Stanton discovers that he has been given a special gift—he is the last of the Old Ones, a group of immortals who have been dedicated to keeping the world from being destroyed by the forces of evil, the Dark.

The Dark Is Rising is a Newbery Honor Book. It is only one of a series of fantasies that Susan Cooper has written about the conflict between the Light and the Dark.

2 UNIT TEST

Understanding Paragraphs pages 40–47

Read these paragraphs. Then number your paper from 1 to 10. Write the *letter* that shows which sentence answers each question. Use this code:

a. sentence 1 **b.** sentence 2 **c.** sentence 3 **d.** sentence 4
e. sentence 5 **f.** sentence 6

Paragraph 1

Certain stars rise just before or after the sun. The time and position of each rising and setting star change with the seasons. If you watched carefully and kept records for many years, you would be able to predict the coming of each season. You could also measure times of the year by noting where on the horizon the sun rises and sets daily. As the planets change position in the skies, you could even note the changing cycles of life on earth. The skies are a wonderful calendar for anyone who watches and records.

Paragraph 2

This planet Earth is the only home we know. Venus is too hot and Mars is too cold. I saw some pictures of Venus and Mars. Earth, however, is just right for human beings. Its atmosphere permits plants and animals to live and grow. Since there is nowhere else for us to go, we must take care of the planet we have.

1. Which sentence in paragraph 1 is the topic sentence?
2. Which is the third detail sentence in paragraph 1?
3. Which is the first detail sentence in paragraph 1?
4. Which is the second detail sentence in paragraph 1?
5. Which sentence in paragraph 1 is a detail sentence that does not mention a planet or star?
6. Which sentence in paragraph 2 does not belong?
7. Which sentence in paragraph 2 states the main idea?

8. Which is the third detail sentence in paragraph 2?
9. Which is the fourth detail sentence in paragraph 2?
10. Which sentence in paragraph 2 is the topic sentence?

The Library   pages 50–51

In which room or section of the library would you find these items? Copy the name of each item. Then copy the *letter* indicating the correct place. Use this code:

a. periodical reading room   **b.** nonfiction section
c. fiction section   **d.** juvenile section   **e.** reference section

1. almanacs   2. biographies   3. short stories
4. magazines   5. novels   6. children's books
7. story poems   8. newspapers   9. encyclopedias

The Card Catalog   pages 52–53

Copy this list. After each item write whether you would look for a *title, author,* or *subject card* in the card catalog to find it.

10. a book of African folktales
11. a book called *Bel Ria*
12. a book about Ceylon
13. poems by David McCord
14. a book about animal communication
15. the autobiography of Helen Keller
16. a book called *The Phantom Tollbooth*
17. a book by E. B. White

The Dewey Decimal System   pages 54–55

Copy each book title. Write the numbers of the Dewey Decimal System under which each book would appear.

18. *Encyclopaedia Britannica*
19. *Bulfinch's Mythology*
20. *Anatomy for the Dancer*
21. *American Government: Readings and Documents*
22. *Logic*
23. *Wild Animals*
24. *History of England*
25. *Building Birdhouses*

Prewriting, Composing, and Revising — Time-Order and Space-Order Paragraphs   pages 56–66

1. Choose one of these topics. Write five details about your topic in a diagram or a list. Number the details using time or space order.

   - getting ready for bed
   - the view from your bedroom window
   - a neighborhood park
   - a visit to a museum
   - a football game
   - setting the table
   - taking a photograph
   - a classroom

   Use your diagram or list to write a time-order or a space-order paragraph. Be sure to include a topic sentence. Using editing and proofreading marks, revise your paragraph. If you write a time-order paragraph, be sure the details are in the proper order. Check that you have used time words to tie your sentences together. If you write a space-order paragraph, your description should proceed in one general direction. Check your paragraph for correct spelling, punctuation, and other mechanics. Then rewrite the paragraph in final form.

Prewriting, Composing, and Revising — Paragraph of Comparison and Contrast   pages 67–74

2. Choose one of these pairs of topics. Outline three qualities you might use to compare or contrast this topic. Then add three details about each part of the topic, based on the qualities you listed. Write the details you choose next to the qualities on your outline.

   - apples and oranges
   - Memorial Day and Independence Day
   - cotton and wool
   - spring and fall
   - the St. Louis Cardinals and the New York Yankees
   - soccer and hockey
   - dogs and cats
   - television and movies

Use the outline to develop a paragraph of comparison or contrast. Be sure to write a topic sentence and to follow the other guidelines you have learned. Using editing and proofreading marks, revise your paragraph. Check the order in which you discuss the qualities you are comparing or contrasting. Make any other changes or corrections that are necessary. Then rewrite your paragraph in final form.

● Mechanics Practice   page 75

Capitalize and punctuate these times correctly.

3. 8 00 a m   **4.** 10 01 p m   **5.** 5 02 p m   **6.** 6 55 a m

Imagine that these words occur at the end of a line. Divide them correctly using the proper punctuation.

7. station   **8.** meeting   **9.** barnyard   **10.** cattle

Rewrite these sentences correctly.

11. the train for seattle arrives at 1 52 pm
12. it leaves phoenix at 10 20 on friday
13. is it better to take the 2 00 plane instead
14. please hand me the schedule for flights be tween indianapolis and toledo
15. the 5 30 plane is very late
16. the plane that should have left at 12 00 mid night did not take off until 2 07 am

● Plays   pages 76–81

Copy these sentences. Write the correct answer in each space.

1. A story that is meant to be acted out is called a _____.
2. The words the actors say are called the _____.
3. Through their words the actors advance the _____, or action.
4. The people the actors "become" are known as the _____.
5. Reading a one-act play is very much like reading a _____.
6. A full-length play is more like a _____.
7. Full-length plays and one-act plays have _____, _____, and _____.
8. Plays are enjoyed most when _____ or read aloud.

MAINTENANCE and REVIEW

Kinds of Sentences   pages 2–3

Copy these sentences. After each write whether it is *declarative, interrogative, imperative,* or *exclamatory.* Add correct punctuation.

1. What do you know about French food
2. I know that an appetizer is an *hors d'oeuvre*
3. What a strange expression that is
4. Please hand me that menu
5. What is *homard*
6. Don't you know a lobster when you see one
7. Never mind; don't tell me any more

Complete and Simple Subjects and Predicates   pages 4–7

Copy these sentences. Underline complete subjects once and complete predicates twice. Then circle the simple subjects and simple predicates.

8. This dish is called *Coquilles St. Jacques.*
9. It is made of scallops in wine and cream.
10. *Coquilles St. Jacques* is listed under *Poisson.*
11. *Poisson* means fish.
12. That dish is also called an *entrée.*
13. I would like a simple roast beef dinner.
14. Roast beef is *rosbif au jus* in French.
15. *Rosbif au jus* is roast beef in its own gravy.

Word Order in Sentences   pages 10–11

Copy these sentences. After each write whether it is in *natural* or *inverted* order.

16. Where are potatoes on this menu?
17. Hand it to me.
18. From behind a tall plant came the waiter.
19. "Potatoes are called *pommes de terre.*"
20. *Pommes* are called *apples* in my dictionary.

21. Are you sure?
22. Next to our table sat a kindly looking man.
23. *"Pommes de terre* are potatoes."
24. Then I will have *pommes de terre frites.*
25. I hope those are french fries!

Paragraphs   pages 40–47

Read these paragraphs. Then answer the questions that follow.

Many modern English words come from Anglo-Saxon and Norman French. The Anglo-Saxons were a tribe of Germanic people who lived in England during the Middle Ages. They gave us such words as *hwaet (what)* and *daeg (day).* In 1066 the Normans came from France and conquered England. Their leader was named William the Conqueror. The Normans gave us the words *fleur* (flower) and *forêt* (forest).

The names of foods that have come to us from these two languages have an interesting history. The words for foods from Italy are also interesting. Our modern English words *sheep* and *cow* come from the Anglo-Saxon words *sceap* and *cū.* That is because the Anglo-Saxons were mostly servants who cared for the living animals. The names for the meat of these animals, however, come from the Norman words *moton* (mutton) and *buef* (beef). That is because the Normans were the masters who knew the animals mostly as dishes on the dinner table.

26. What is the main idea of paragraph 1?
27. Which sentence in paragraph 1 is a detail sentence that does not belong there?
28. If paragraph 1 has a topic sentence, copy it on your paper. If not, write *no topic sentence.*
29. If paragraph 2 has a topic sentence, copy it on your paper. If not, write *no topic sentence.*
30. How many detail sentences are there in paragraph 2?
31. Which sentence in paragraph 2 is a detail sentence that does not belong there?
32. What is the main idea of paragraph 2?
33. What is the job of the detail sentences in a paragraph?

An erupting volcano is an impressive sight! It is also important news. Where might you read about it first? Pretend you are a newspaper reporter. Describe what you see in the exciting photo.

How did you use words such as *Hawaii, lava, fire,* and *smoke* in your description? These words are nouns. Remember, nouns name persons, places, or things. A newspaper reporter would find it impossible to write a news story without using any nouns at all.

Suppose you want to tell the newspaper readers what causes a volcano to erupt. How can you find out? In this unit you will learn about three important reference books. You will find out what kind of information you can gather from an encyclopedia, an atlas, and an almanac.

Look at the volcano photograph again. What effects might the volcanic eruption have on the surrounding land or on the wildlife? In this unit you will learn how to write a clear paragraph that focuses on a cause, or a reason, for something happening and the effects, or results.

Finally you will learn about newspaper writing. You will read three types of news items and select one as a model for writing.

Sharpen your reporter's eye, and turn the page!

◀ *Eruption of Mount Kilauea in Hawaii*

LANGUAGE

Lesson 1: Understanding Common and Proper Nouns

Antoine and Jamal were reading about ancient Greece in their history book. Here is part of their lesson.

Athens was one of the greatest cities in ancient Greece. The Greeks were famous for their beautiful temples and gardens. Of all their buildings the Parthenon was probably the most beautiful.

Which eight words in this paragraph name persons, places, or things? Which are the simple subjects of sentences?

Think and Discuss

It would be impossible for Antoine and Jamal to read a book without finding names of persons, places, and things. These words are **nouns.** Some nouns such as *cities* are general words that name *any* person, place, or thing. These are called **common nouns. Proper nouns** such as *Athens* name particular persons, places, or things. Proper nouns are always capitalized.

> - A **noun** is a word that names a person, place, or thing.
> - A **common noun** names *any* person, place, or thing. It begins with a small letter.
> - A **proper noun** names a *particular* person, place, or thing. It begins with a capital letter.

Now look at this sentence.

> The Greeks built the Parthenon to honor Athena, the goddess of wisdom.

How many nouns are there? If you found four, you are *almost* right. There is a fifth noun, the word *wisdom*. Even though it is not the name of a thing you can see, feel, hear, smell, or taste, it is still a noun because it names an *idea*. Other nouns that name ideas are *courage, beauty,* and *love*.

Practice

A. Copy these sentences. Draw one line under the common nouns and two lines under the proper nouns.

1. Greece and Troy fought a long war.
2. The Greeks wanted to get into Troy.
3. They made a wooden horse and hid soldiers in it.
4. The Trojans brought the object inside the gates.
5. That night the men crept out of their hiding place.

B. Complete each sentence with the kind of noun in parentheses ( ).

6. _____ was one of the countries that fought the Trojan War. (proper noun)
7. The Greeks came to Troy in _____. (common noun)
8. The city was protected by _____. (common noun)
9. Today _____ lies in ruins. (proper noun)
10. Another _____ was built over it. (common noun)

Apply

C. 11.–20. Write ten sentences about your neighborhood, town, or city. Use at least six common nouns and six proper nouns. Circle the common nouns and underline the proper nouns you have chosen.

Lesson 2: Understanding Singular and Plural Nouns

Mr. Ramirez came to work one day with scratches on both arms.

"What happened to you?" asked his friends in surprise. "Did some mice think you were a cheese?"

"Nothing so exciting," laughed Mr. Ramirez. "I was playing tug-of-war with my St. Bernard dog, and *I* was the one he was tugging!"

Find four nouns that refer to more than one person, place, or thing.

Think and Discuss

The nouns *day, cheese,* and *dog* each name only one thing. They are **singular nouns.** *Days, cheeses,* and *dogs* each refer to more than one. They are **plural nouns.**

- A **singular noun** names *one* person, place, or thing.
- A **plural noun** names *more than one* person, place, or thing.

Study this chart.

How to Form the Plurals of Nouns

1. **Form the plurals of most nouns by adding** *s.*
   friend — friends, dog — dogs
2. **Add** *es* **to nouns that end in** *z, s, x, sh,* **or** *ch.*
   buzz — buzzes, bus — buses, fox — foxes,
   flash — flashes, bench — benches
3. **If a noun ends in** *y* **with a vowel before it, add**
   s. **If the noun ends in** *y* **with a consonant**
   before it, change the *y* **to** *i* **and add** *es.*
   monkey — monkeys, lady — ladies

How to Form the Plurals of Nouns *(continued)*

4. To form the plural of nouns that end in a vowel and *o*, add only an *s.* For some nouns that end in a consonant and *o*, add *es.*
   radio — radios, hero — heroes
5. To form the plural of most nouns ending in *f* or *fe*, change the *f* to *v* and add *es.* For others, simply add *s.* leaf — leaves, safe — safes
6. The plurals of some nouns are formed by a vowel change within the singular form.
   man — men, foot — feet, child — children
7. Some nouns are the same in the singular as they are in the plural. deer — deer, salmon — salmon

If you are not sure how to form the plurals of certain nouns, check your dictionary. You may wish to memorize the plurals you do not already know.

Practice

A. Write the plurals of the following words.

1. duck	**2.** ostrich	**3.** family	**4.** studio	**5.** veto
6. giraffe	**7.** sheep	**8.** wife	**9.** tomato	**10.** ox

B. Copy the following sentences. Write *singular* or *plural* above each underlined noun.

11. A zookeeper has many worries.
12. All the monkeys and their babies must be fed.
13. Each animal should be free from sickness.
14. Seven elephants must have baths.
15. The screeches of birds in a bush startled several turtles.

Apply

C. 16.–25. Write ten sentences about your favorite zoo animals. Use as many plurals as possible.

Lesson 3: Understanding Abbreviations

Joanna writes notes to herself in a daily reminder notebook. Here is an entry.

> Mon., Dec. 13
> Get stamps at P.O.
> Send note to:
>   Gov. Ruth Lorenson
>   Kansas City, KS 66103

Which words have been shortened?

Think and Discuss

We sometimes use shortened forms of nouns. These shortened forms, called **abbreviations,** are usually followed by periods. Many abbreviations are forms of proper nouns. These abbreviations are written with a capital letter.

Most standard dictionaries contain a complete list of abbreviations. Here are some of those commonly used.

Titles: Mr. = Mister, Dr. = Doctor
Days of the week: Sun. = Sunday, Tues. = Tuesday
Months: Jan. = January, Feb. = February
Streets: St. = Street, Dr. = Drive, Pl. = Place
States: CT = Connecticut, NM = New Mexico

From the examples given above, what are the two most common ways of forming abbreviations?

Practice

A. Using a dictionary or other reference book, write the abbreviations for the following words.

1. Texas	**2.** Avenue	**3.** Friday	**4.** Mountain
5. November	**6.** River	**7.** Boulevard	**8.** Colorado

B. For which words do the following abbreviations stand?

9. Wed.　**10.** CA　**11.** Apr.　**12.** U.S.A.　**13.** Oct.
14. Sq.　**15.** MN　**16.** UHF　**17.** N.Y.C.　**18.** Rev.

C. Write the abbreviations of the underlined words.

19. On <u>Thursday</u>, <u>January</u> 18, I went to my dentist, <u>Doctor</u> Painless, of 264 Pine <u>Lane</u>.

20. Doctor Painless's title is <u>Doctor of Dental Surgery</u>.

21. While my mouth was full of cotton, Doctor Painless told me she was from <u>Saint</u> Paul, <u>Minnesota</u>.

22. She also said that her old friend, <u>Representative</u> Govern Ment, lives in <u>Fort</u> Worth, <u>Texas</u>.

23. Doctor Painless and her friend will meet in <u>South</u> Apopka, <u>Florida</u>, on <u>Wednesday</u>, <u>February</u> 18.

24. My friends, <u>Senator</u> Voting Forme and <u>Attorney</u> Liveby Thelaw are coming to <u>North</u> <u>Fort</u> Polk, <u>Louisiana</u>, on <u>Monday</u>, <u>March</u> 25.

25. Maybe all five of us could meet in <u>New York</u> on <u>Sunday</u>, <u>April</u> 7.

Apply

D. Write the following addresses using the complete words for which the abbreviations stand.

26. Mr. George Harris, Jr.　　**27.** Dr. Sarah Jones
　　Harris Bros., Inc.　　　　　　400 Madison Ave.
　　35 W. 5th St.　　　　　　　　Pasadena, CA 91101
　　N. Ft. Myers, FL 33903

A Challenge

You are among the first group of people to set up a permanent colony on another planet. Write a short paragraph explaining the kinds of land, people, and creatures you might find there.

Lesson 4: Understanding Possessive Nouns

As you ride along the highway or walk along the streets of your town or city, have you ever paid much attention to billboards or store signs? Many tell who owns certain places: Fred's Diner, Marie's Restaurant, Anderson's Hardware. What punctuation mark do these names have in common?

Think and Discuss

Noun forms that show ownership are called **possessives**. Possessive nouns are easy to identify and write. They follow three basic rules.

How to Form Possessive Nouns
1. Form the possessive of a singular noun by adding an apostrophe and an *s*. Do this even if the singular noun already ends with an *s*.
   Ling's paper, *Charles's* book
2. Form the possessive of a plural noun that ends in *s* by adding an apostrophe only.
   girls' answers, *cats'* whiskers
3. Form the possessive of a plural noun that does not end in an *s* by adding an apostrophe and an *s*.   *children's* teams

---

Practice

A. Write the possessive form of each noun.

1. Mr. Adams	2. men	3. foxes
4. Lois	5. puppies	6. women
7. Fred	8. thieves	9. Alice
10. Cass	11. boss	12. Rex
13. Mrs. Rey	14. sister	15. Garth

B. Copy these singular nouns. Then write the singular possessive, the plural, and the plural possessive. You should have four columns.

16. pony   **17.** elf   **18.** bird   **19.** trio   **20.** ox

Apply

C. 21.–25. Write five sentences of your own using singular possessive nouns. Then rewrite the sentences, changing the nouns to plural possessives. Try to use at least two irregular plural nouns.

HOW OUR LANGUAGE GROWS

Late in the eighth century people from Denmark invaded England. The Anglo-Saxons living in England during this time spoke what we today call Old English. The Anglo-Saxons and the Danes lived and worked side by side, using the same kinds of everyday words. It is difficult, therefore, to tell exactly how much Danish influenced English.

We do know, however, that many words we use with the /sh/ sound, such as *ship* and *fish,* came from Old English. Many of those with an /sk/ sound, such as *skull* and *ski,* came from Danish. Also, if it had not been for this Scandinavian influence on our language, we might still be saying *yive* for *give.* The use of both the hard *g* and the *k,* as in *egg* and *kid,* can often be traced to Scandinavian origins. Perhaps the greatest Scandinavian contribution to Modern English are the pronouns *their, they,* and *them.*

Using a dictionary that shows word origins, find the original meaning of these words: *law, sky, window, skirt, want, meek, wrong.*

LANGUAGE REVIEW

Common and Proper Nouns   pages 90–91

Copy these sentences. Underline the nouns. Then write *common* over the common nouns and *proper* over the proper nouns.

1. The voters came out early on Election Day.
2. On Tuesday the Suarez family had a picnic.
3. Relatives had arrived from South America.
4. Dr. Lois Suarez will be on vacation during August.
5. The agency reserved a room for Dr. Suarez in England.

Singular and Plural Nouns   pages 92–93

Copy these sentences. Underline the nouns. Then write *singular* over the singular nouns and *plural* over the plural nouns.

6. At Logan Airport three planes were 30 minutes late.
7. The terminal was crowded with eager passengers.
8. Dr. Suarez finally boarded her plane.
9. The airline showed a first-run movie on the flight.

Copy these nouns. Then write the plural of each one.

10. match   11. dawn   12. toy   13. dance   14. gown
15. flash   16. fox   17. baby   18. beach   19. gash
20. trolley   21. waltz   22. cave   23. window   24. dress

Copy these sentences. Use the plural form of the nouns in parentheses ( ).

25. How many _____ have you seen? (salmon)
26. Three _____ are in that pond. (sunfish)
27. This animal park even has _____, _____, _____, and _____. (wolf, coyote, lynx, bear)
28. Can you feed the _____? (deer)
29. Were those _____ I saw? (kangaroo)
30. They certainly were not _____, _____, _____, and _____. (giraffe, ostrich, camel, buffalo)

Abbreviations pages 94–95

Copy these nouns. Write the abbreviations for each.

31. Street	**32.** River	**33.** Kentucky	**34.** Drive
35. Reverend	**36.** Maine	**37.** Sunday	**38.** Senator
39. Tuesday	**40.** March	**41.** Station	**42.** October
43. September	**44.** Road	**45.** January	**46.** Mister

Possessive Nouns pages 96–97

Copy these sentences. Use the possessive form of each word in parentheses ( ).

47. The _____ faces were clean. (boys)

48. The _____ toys were in the attic. (children)

49. Did you see that _____ tail? (wolf)

50. Where is the _____ den? (fox)

51. The _____ uniforms were white. (sailors)

52. The _____ bike is missing. (woman)

53. The _____ carriage is on the porch. (baby)

54. Where are the _____ instruments? (trio)

55. Who is that _____ teacher? (class)

Write the possessive forms of these nouns.

56. ox	**57.** grass	**58.** mice	**59.** days	**60.** fern
61. lives	**62.** dove	**63.** life	**64.** folly	**65.** salmon

Applying Nouns

Write a paragraph on one of these topics.

- the mountains, bodies of water, or other natural features of your state
- a description of a creature that you might find on another planet
- the natural features of a foreign country you might like to visit someday

Include as many special plurals and possessive nouns in your paragraph as possible.

STUDY SKILLS

Lesson 5: Using the Encyclopedia

Toshiro had been born in the United States, but he wanted to learn something about his family's native land, Japan. His friend Caren suggested that he start by reading the articles on Japan in an encyclopedia. Why was this good advice?

Think and Discuss

An **encyclopedia** is a great storehouse of information on almost every subject there is. Because so much knowledge has to fit between its covers, most encyclopedias come in sets of many volumes. For the same reason, encyclopedias do not offer a great deal of information on their subjects but instead provide an overview of each one.

The subjects in an encyclopedia are arranged in *alphabetical order.* The first letter or letters of the subjects found in each volume are printed on the spine, or narrow side, of every book in the set. If several different volumes all contain information on your subject, the *index* will tell you just which ones to use. The index is usually in the last volume of the set.

At the end of each encyclopedia article you will probably find *cross-references,* a list of other articles that might give you more information on your subject. These cross-references will also appear in alphabetical order in the index.

The index in the encyclopedia Toshiro used devoted over half a page to the subject of Japan. Here is part of the information the index contained. Each entry in italic, or slanted, type indicates a subtopic of the article on Japan in the *J* volume.

Index Entry

Japan J:30 *with pictures and maps*
See also the Reading and Study
  Guide on this topic
Asia (Way of Life in East Asia)
  A:750
Earthquake (table) **E:19**
Fan **F:30**
Flag *picture on* **F:179**
Food *pictures on* **F:291, F:294**
House of Representatives (Lower
  Houses in other countries)
  H:354
World (Arts and Recreation of
  the World) **W:350**

Religion
  Japan (Religion) **J:38** *with picture*
  Asia (Religions) **A:751**
  Feasts and Festivals (In Buddhism)
    F:62 *with picture*
  Religion (Shinto) **R:213–214** *with*
    picture
  Shinto **S:327**

Social and cultural life
  Japan (Way of Life) **J:37–39** *with*
    pictures

Technology and science
  Ship (Merchant Fleets of Other
    Countries) **S:346h**

Practice

A. Using the set of encyclopedias pictured on this page, write the *number* of the volume you would use for information on these subjects.

1. Egypt   2. icebergs   3. dolphins
4. rockets   5. meteors   6. X-rays
7. baseball   8. opera   9. Argentina

B. Using the index entry on Japan, answer these questions.

10. What volumes contain pictures of religious events in Japan?
11. On what page of what volume can you find a picture of the Japanese flag?
12. In what volume would you look to find out about the social life of the Japanese people?
13. What subtopic contains material on Japanese shipping?
14. What information on earthquakes in Japan does the encyclopedia contain?

Apply

C. 15.–20. Choose a foreign country in which you are interested. List *six* references from an encyclopedia index that will give you information about that country.

Lesson 6: Using Atlases and Almanacs

Toshiro was very interested in the way Japan had been formed from volcanoes deep in the sea. Once he had learned all he could about Japanese volcanoes from the encyclopedia, his teacher, Mrs. Stewart, urged him to check an atlas and an almanac.

Think and Discuss

An **atlas** consists mainly of maps. The maps and other charts in the atlas show the size, climate, population, and natural features of every region in the world. In addition, an atlas gives information on agriculture, industry, and natural resources. It also includes the capitals, languages, religions, and money used in every country listed.

Almanacs are printed every year. They give the latest information available on many current topics of interest. Among these are business, sports, and government. The people who have made news in these areas during the past year are also included. Information appears on the latest events from every state in the country and from every country in the world.

A certain map in Toshiro's atlas showed valleys, plains, and mountains. From it Toshiro learned that most of Japan is still a mountainous country. He was impressed by a line of mountains that looked like a spine down a person's back.

From the almanac Toshiro learned that Japan belonged to a volcanic region in the Pacific Ocean called the "Ring of Fire." Toshiro's almanac listed the six most important volcanoes in Japan. It also included the features of each one and the latest year in which each had erupted. On the next page are the entries Toshiro found in each book.

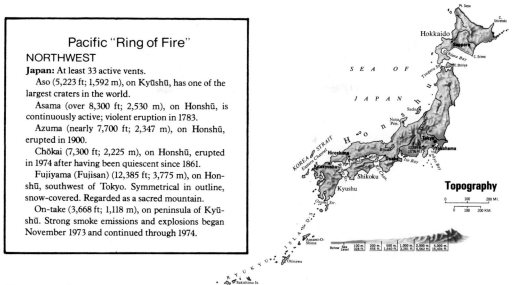

Pacific "Ring of Fire"

NORTHWEST

Japan: At least 33 active vents.

Aso (5,223 ft; 1,592 m), on Kyūshū, has one of the largest craters in the world.

Asama (over 8,300 ft; 2,530 m), on Honshū, is continuously active; violent eruption in 1783.

Azuma (nearly 7,700 ft; 2,347 m), on Honshū, erupted in 1900.

Chōkai (7,300 ft; 2,225 m), on Honshū, erupted in 1974 after having been quiescent since 1861.

Fujiyama (Fujisan) (12,385 ft; 3,775 m), on Honshū, southwest of Tokyo. Symmetrical in outline, snow-covered. Regarded as a sacred mountain.

On-take (3,668 ft; 1,118 m), on peninsula of Kyūshū. Strong smoke emissions and explosions began November 1973 and continued through 1974.

Practice

A. Which of these questions can best be answered by using an *atlas* and which by an *almanac*? Copy these questions and write the name of the reference you would use to answer each one.

1. Who was the governor of Iowa in 1982?
2. Where is Ethiopia?
3. What countries border Sweden?
4. What is the state flower of Idaho?
5. Where were the Olympic Games held during the winter of 1976?
6. What is the highest point in Wyoming?
7. How long is a solar day?

B. 8.–14. Use an atlas and an almanac to answer the seven questions in Practice A.

Apply

C. 15.–20. Make a list of three questions that can be answered by looking only in an atlas. List three more that can be answered by looking only in an almanac. Exchange lists with a classmate and find the answers to each other's questions.

COMPOSITION

Lesson 7: Prewriting
Planning a How-to Paragraph

The students in Mrs. Bluehouse's class were trying to write paragraphs that explained how to follow a process. However, they were having difficulty sorting out the details that were unnecessary. Sometimes the students had so many steps that the really important ones were lost in the clutter. How might they simplify a process paragraph?

Think and Discuss

One of the students finally came up with an idea that would help the others write *only* important steps. This is called a framed paragraph.

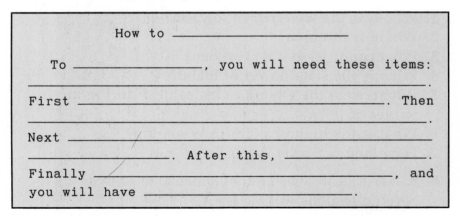

How to _____

To _____, you will need these items:
_____.
First _____. Then
_____.
Next _____
_____. After this, _____.
Finally _____, and
you will have _____.

By limiting themselves to a list of equipment and five steps, the students easily completed the "frame." What other signal words, or **transitional expressions,** might be substituted for the ones already used?

After practicing with the framed paragraph, Mrs. Bluehouse's students had no difficulty writing other paragraphs of their own. In what ways might they have changed the framed paragraph to suit their new topics? What other kinds of paragraphs might be written with this form as a guide?

How to Plan a How-to Paragraph

1. **Begin with a title that tells which process you will explain.**
2. **Start your outline paragraph by listing the equipment you will need for the process.**
3. **Jot down some transitional expressions that might be helpful.**
4. **Fill in each blank with a word or two that summarizes a particular step. At this point you do not have to write complete sentences.**

Practice

A. Complete this framed paragraph with transitional expressions.

How to Repot a Plant

   To repot a plant, you will need soil, gravel, a pot, and a plant. _____ line the pot with gravel. _____ fill the pot halfway with soil. _____ put the plant into the pot. _____ fill the pot with soil and pat it down.

B. Make a framed paragraph for one of these topics. Follow the guidelines in the blue box.

- How to Make a Milk Shake
- How to Make a Stuffed Toy
- How to Peel a Potato
- How to Bathe a Dog
- How to Make a Sandwich
- How to Make Lemonade

Apply

C. Now you will use a framed paragraph to plan the steps in a process of your own.

Choose a Topic

- Think of a process that you can explain easily and that might prove interesting to others.

Choose Your Audience

- Try to tailor your topic to a particular audience. If you explain how to build a model plane, for example, your audience might be an arts and crafts club.

Make a Framed Paragraph Outline

- Follow the guidelines in the blue box on page 105. Limit yourself to five steps as in the model on the first page of this lesson.

Review Your Work

- Look over your "frame" and the notes you made in the blanks. Would following these steps explain your process adequately?
- If five steps do not explain the process clearly enough, you have two choices. You may change your topic to a simpler one or rethink the topic so that you have only five *important* steps. Remember, this process should help you weed out items of lesser importance and concentrate on those that really matter.
- Save your final "frame" and its notes for the Apply exercise in Lesson 8.

Lesson 8: Composing

Writing a How-to Paragraph

Read the following paragraph.

A headband is simple to make. First you will need a strip of felt about 2 in. (5 cm) wide and 20 in. (50 cm) long, some felt scraps in various colors, scissors, a hole puncher, glue, and a piece of string. Try the long strip of felt for size around your head from the forehead to the back. Then with the scissors cut off whatever felt you do not need. Next punch one hole in the felt at each end, being careful not to place the hole too close to the edge of the material. Otherwise the material might tear. After the holes are punched, join the ends by tying or lacing the string through them. Finally cut the felt scraps into various patterns and glue them onto the headband as decoration.

What kind of order is used for writing these directions? Why do you think this order was chosen?

Think and Discuss

You have already studied how to write time-order paragraphs. When you are giving directions as in a how-to paragraph, the order is also important. For this reason, transitional expressions such as *first, then, next,* and *finally* are helpful. In the paragraph about the headband, transitional expressions introduce each step in the process. They allow the paragraph to flow smoothly. Transitional expressions also help make a paragraph coherent. In a coherent paragraph every fact is presented in a logical order.

What is the purpose of the first sentence? Why are the materials listed next? What might happen if you cut the piece of felt *before* you tried it around your head?

Practice

A. Here is a topic sentence for a how-to paragraph followed by six steps. Copy the topic sentence. Then finish the paragraph by putting the steps in the correct order. Add a transitional expression to the beginning of each detail sentence after the first one.

You might enjoy making a cardboard drum.

1. You will need an empty oatmeal box, tape, glue, construction paper, felt, scissors, and paint.
2. Tape the top of the oatmeal box so that it will remain closed.
3. Glue or tape construction paper to the sides of the box.
4. Cut the felt so that it fits on the top and bottom of the box.
5. Glue the felt to the top and bottom.
6. Paint designs on the top and sides of the box.

B. Listed below are a topic sentence and a set of directions in the wrong order. Rewrite the paragraph correctly.

Cornbread is delicious and easy to prepare.

7. Fill a well-greased loaf pan with the batter.
8. You will need 2 cups (.48 l) of cornbread mix, a loaf pan, 4 tablespoons (60 ml) of oil, 2 eggs, lightly beaten, and ¾ of a cup (180 ml) of milk.
9. Bake at 375° F (343° C) for 20 minutes.
10. Blend the oil, cornbread mix, eggs, and milk.
11. Stir until smooth.

Apply

C. Find your framed paragraph and the notes you made in it for Lesson 7. Look over the steps you listed.

Write Your Topic Sentence

- Write which process you will explain. You may include your list of equipment here or write it in a separate sentence.

Write Detail Sentences

- Follow the notes you made in your "frame." At this point, of course, you should be writing complete sentences.
- Feel free to change your transitional expressions as well as their placement. These expressions clarify your steps, but they do not always have to be the first words in a sentence.

Review Your Work

- Reread your how-to paragraph. Do your sentences all support the topic?
- Do the transitional expressions give the paragraph coherence?
- Does your choice of words suit your audience?
- Add your title to the top of the paragraph.
- Save your paragraph for revising in Lesson 9.

Lesson 9: Revising

Editing and Proofreading a How-to Paragraph

What changes did Carlos make in his revised paragraph?

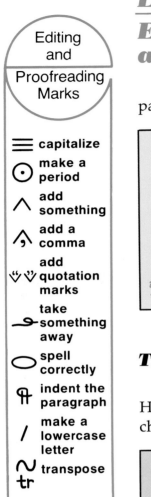

Editing and Proofreading Marks

≡ capitalize

⊙ make a period

∧ add something

∧ add a comma

ᵛᵛ add quotation marks

⟋ take something away

◯ spell correctly

¶ indent the paragraph

/ make a lowercase letter

∼ transpose
tr

How to Make a Clay *Pot* ~~out of Clay~~

It is simple to make a clay pot. You will need clay and a good kiln. First Roll pieces of clay into strips. Next form a ⟨cay⟩ clay bottom for to your pot. Second layer the round strips until they take on tr the pot shape. Let it dry for an hour, and it is finally ready for the kiln.

Think and Discuss

Carlos added transitional expressions to his paragraph. He also moved a sentence. Why did he make these changes? Why did he not have to explain what a *kiln* is?

How to Revise a How-to Paragraph

Editing
1. Be sure that your paragraph explains a process.
2. Be sure your opening sentences give your topic and list the equipment needed.
3. Check your detail sentences. Be sure they give clear directions in the proper order.
4. Be sure your words suit your audience.
5. Add transitional expressions.

Proofreading
6. Correct all errors in spelling, punctuation, or other mechanics.

Practice

A. Write Carlos's paragraph as it should be.

B. Read this paragraph. Add transitional expressions. Then rewrite it, putting the sentences in the correct order.

Making a dollhouse for a young child can be fun. Cut out windows and doors. Cut out cardboard furniture and furnish your house. Glue the boxes together so the rooms are where you want them. Decide which boxes you will use for which dollhouse rooms. Gather together several boxes, glue, and scissors.

Apply

C. Reread the how-to paragraph you wrote for Lesson 8.
Edit Your Paragraph
- Check your **content.** Did you include items 1–3 in the box on page 110?
- Check your **style.** Did you include items 4 and 5 in the blue box on page 110?
Proofread Your Paragraph
- Correct all errors in spelling, punctuation, and mechanics. Pay particular attention to the spelling of any technical words you used.
- Copy your paragraph onto a clean sheet of paper.

Lesson 10: Prewriting

Planning Paragraphs of Cause and Effect

Reuben was planning a paragraph for health class. He wanted to explain what happened when he stopped eating cookies and ate fruit instead. If eating fruit was a **cause,** what good **effects** might Reuben mention?

Think and Discuss

An easy way to show the relationship between causes and effects is to draw a simple diagram. Here is the one Reuben used to plan his health paragraph.

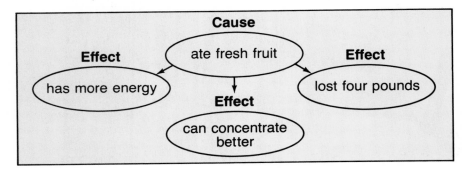

Which item tells what made the others happen? What happened as a result of the first action?

Lila's paragraph also involved causes and effects. She planned to show how her improved health resulted from a regimen she followed. Here is her diagram.

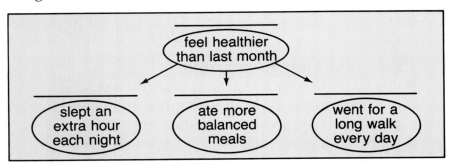

How would you label Lila's diagram? With which item do you think Lila will begin her paragraph? Why? Notice that the arrows indicate whether the paragraph will move from cause to effect or from effect to cause.

Practice

A. Complete these diagrams on a sheet of paper. Then label each one correctly.

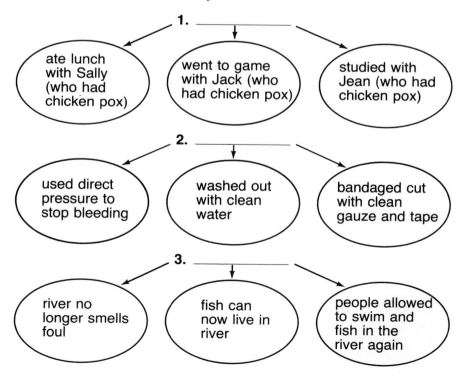

COMPOSITION/PREWRITING: A Cause/Effect Paragraph **113**

B. Diagram these two topics on a clean sheet of paper. Each topic given goes in the top circle. The first topic is a cause. The second is an effect.

4. Isabel and her family go hiking together often.
5. Robert has scored 100 on the last three health quizzes.

Apply

C. Now you will plan two paragraphs of your own. One will begin with a *cause* and the other will begin with an *effect*.

Choose Your Topics
● You might want to write about something that happened to you. Otherwise, you might choose topics from a subject you are studying.

Choose Your Audience
● Remember that your choice of words should suit the person or group for whom you are writing.

Make Your Diagrams
● Follow the models on page 112. The guidelines on page 113 should help you fill in each diagram.
● Remember to label both diagrams. This will make it easier for you to refer to them.

Review Your Work
● Look over each diagram separately. Are the causes *really* actions that make things happen? Are the effects *really* results?
● If a better cause or effect occurs to you, delete the weakest item and put the stronger one in its place. Be sure the new item fits logically in the diagram.
● Save both diagrams for the Apply exercise in Lesson 11.

Lesson 11: Composing

Writing Paragraphs of Cause and Effect

Jimmy Lee wrote this paragraph as an assignment for English class.

> Recently my father cut down the tree in our backyard. Since then I have noticed that our house is much warmer in summer without the cool shade of the leaves. I miss the chirping of the birds just before I get up in the morning. Worst of all, the yard looks so bare and empty without our tree that it makes me feel lonely.

Which of these sentences shows a cause, or a reason, for something happening? Which ones show effects, or results?

Think and Discuss

Paragraphs involving causes or effects are not usually difficult. A paragraph of **effects,** such as Jimmy Lee's, often begins with a topic sentence that states a *cause.* The rest of the paragraph consists of examples to support it, all involving *effects.* Each effect is a result of the action stated in the topic sentence.

In a similar way, a paragraph of **causes** might begin with a topic sentence stating an *effect.* This time the rest of the paragraph will consist of example sentences, all involving *causes.* Read this paragraph.

> My friend Angela won first prize in the state figure skating competition. This does not surprise me, because she gets up at six o'clock every morning to practice. She practices for two hours before school and for three or four hours after school. Moreover, she has great strength, excellent timing, and the will to achieve whatever goal she sets for herself.

Which effect introduces the paragraph? How many sentences that contain causes follow?

The topic sentence in both of these paragraphs was placed first to make the sentences that followed easier to understand. If you wish, however, you may write the body of your paragraph first and save the topic sentence for last. This gives your concluding sentence a dramatic touch. Read this paragraph.

```
    Yesterday we called the fire department rescue
team. As soon as they arrived, they set a tall
ladder against our maple tree. Then fire fighter
Hansen climbed the ladder as far as she could. Next
she inched out on a large branch to make her
rescue. My dad will never try to cut off high tree
branches again.
```

Is this a paragraph of causes or of effects? Where is the topic sentence and what kind of statement does it make?

Name the transitional expressions that were used in the paragraph. Why are transitional expressions necessary in paragraphs of cause and effect?

How to Write Paragraphs of Cause and Effect

1. **Begin paragraphs of effect with a *cause*. The detail sentences should all involve *effects*.**
2. **Begin paragraphs of cause with an *effect*. The detail sentences should all involve *causes*.**
3. **Use transitional expressions to help your sentences flow smoothly.**
4. **Try writing a paragraph of cause or effect in reverse order for a touch of drama. Your concluding sentence will be your topic sentence.**

Practice

A. Copy these topic sentences. After each write *cause* or *effect*. Then copy the detail sentences that you think support the topic sentence.

1. Marcy looks wonderful since she has lost 20 pounds.
   a. She ate only balanced meals.
   b. She exercised for an hour every day.
   c. She read many books of poetry.
   d. Her snacks were fresh fruit and vegetables.
2. Corita received all A's on her last report card.
   a. Math had been her most difficult subject.
   b. She asks questions about anything she does not understand.
   c. She does her homework right after school.
   d. She plans ahead for all her long-term assignments.
3. Mrs. Chin was taking her little boy out in his stroller when a bee stung her on the neck.
   a. Mrs. Chin let go of the stroller's handle.
   b. The stroller began to roll down the hill.
   c. My friend Regina ran after the stroller and saved Mrs. Chin's little boy.
   d. Mrs. Chin had stopped to talk to a neighbor.
4. Our town made over $30,000 on its last carnival.
   a. With the money two new parks will be built.
   b. The raffle alone brought in $11,000.
   c. One hundred teenagers will have summer work helping to build the parks.
   d. There will be two new playgrounds for the children.

B. Copy these topic sentences. Numbers 5 and 7 are *causes;* 6 and 8 are *effects*. Write four detail sentences to support each topic sentence.

5. Richard was careless walking down the street.
6. Laura has won a beautiful first-place ribbon.
7. Jan is very interested in science.
8. Bob has finally learned to roller-skate.

Apply

C. Look over the diagrams you made in Lesson 10. Check again to be sure that they make sense. Then use the diagrams to write two paragraphs.

Write Topic Sentences

● Write a topic sentence for each paragraph. Use the notes you made in the top circle of each diagram.

● Be sure one topic sentence introduces a paragraph of causes and the other introduces a paragraph of effects.

Write Detail Sentences

● Each set of detail sentences should support the topic sentence by giving either causes or effects. Again, follow the notes you made in your diagrams.

● Keep your audience in mind as you explain the causes or effects. Be sure to choose words and phrases that they will understand.

● Tie your detail sentences together with transitional expressions.

Review Your Work

● Reread your paragraphs over one at a time.

● Do they follow the diagrams you made?

● Do the detail sentences flow logically from your two topic sentences?

● Did you remember to give a title to each paragraph?

● Save your work for revising in Lesson 12.

To Memorize

Sometimes one must travel far to discover what is near.

The Treasure, Uri Shulevitz

What do you think the author means about traveling far to find something that is really quite near?

Lesson 12: Revising

Editing and Proofreading
Paragraphs of Cause and Effect

Leigh had just written a paragraph on health advances in the nineteenth century. As she reread it, however, she realized she had been much too wordy. As a result, her writing was not *clear*. What advice might you give to Leigh as she revises?

Think and Discuss

This is Leigh's revised paragraph.

> *The years after 1850 saw vast improvements in health care. As you may know, Joseph Lister* advocated *(avocated) the use of antiseptics in surgery. Pasteurization of foods was developed. Robert Koch, a name that often appears in history books, developed water filtration, which helped prevent cholera. The Civil War ended.*

Editing and Proofreading Marks	
☰	capitalize
⊙	make a period
∧	add something
⌄⸴	add a comma
⌄⌄	add quotation marks
⸜	take something away
◯	spell correctly
¶	indent the paragraph
/	make a lowercase letter
∼ tr	transpose

Why might Leigh have taken out *As you may know* and *a name that often appears in history books* in sentences 2 and 4?

Leigh also deleted the last sentence of her paragraph. Since the paragraph is one of cause and effect, the detail sentences should all be causes and should support the topic sentence, which states an effect. Does the last sentence support the topic sentence? Why or why not?

Leigh's changes have helped to make her paragraph clearer. She has also followed the rules for writing a paragraph of cause and effect.

> **How to Revise Paragraphs of Cause and Effect**
>
> *Editing*
> 1. **Check your topic sentence. Be sure it contains a clear example of a cause or an effect.**
> 2. **Check your detail sentences. A cause should be followed by *effects* and an effect by *causes.***
> 3. **Check your entire paragraph for unity. There should be no sentences that do not support the topic.**
> 4. **Check your paragraph for clarity. There should be no unnecessary words.**
>
> *Proofreading*
> 5. **Correct all errors in spelling, punctuation, and mechanics.**

Practice

A. Rewrite Leigh's paragraph, making all the corrections she indicated.

Apply

B. Find the cause and effect paragraphs you wrote for Lesson 11. Read over what you have written to be sure they make sense.

Edit Your Paragraphs

- Check your **content.** Did you include items 1 and 2 from the blue box?
- Check your **style.** Did you include items 3 and 4 from the blue box?

Proofread Your Paragraphs

- Correct errors in spelling, punctuation, and mechanics.
- Be sure you indented the first word in each paragraph.
- Copy your revised paragraphs onto clean sheets of paper.

MECHANICS PRACTICE

Capitalizing and Punctuating Noun Forms

- Capitalize all proper nouns.

     Who was Pliny?

- Use periods in abbreviations.

     It happened at 2:00 P.M.

- Use commas to separate days and years.

     It was a calm day on August 23, A.D. 79.

- Use apostrophes in possessive forms of nouns.

     Pliny's uncle's house was beautiful.

Rewrite these sentences correctly.

1. mt vesuvius erupted on august 24 AD 79.
2. What did you learn about the eruption in pompeii?
3. A writer named pliny the younger left us an account.
4. The eruption began about 2:00 pm with a burst of smoke.
5. Across the bay of naples tiles shook loose from plinys house.
6. Did an earthquake occur shortly after 2:00 pm?
7. Yes, and it caused a huge tidal wave in the bay of naples.
8. Fire, dust, and cinders rained down on plinys uncles house.
9. Lava poured from the volcanos mouth, and the strong smell of sulfur filled the air.
10. Who survived in plinys family?
11. Everyone survived except plinys uncle, who died as he tried to get away in the familys boat.
12. Although many peoples lives were lost, the eruption of mt. vesuvius is important to todays historians.
13. The ruins of pompeii and the nearby town of herculaneum have told us much about the ancient romans way of life.
14. Plinys letters tell us what the ruins do not.
15. Plinys time is known as the silver age of latin literature.

LITERATURE

Lesson 13: Reading News Stories, Feature Articles, and Editorials

Read this news story.

PARADISE, Wash. (AP)—Five blind climbers with Braille maps, one man with an artificial leg, an epileptic, and two deaf people completed a joyful climb on Friday, July 3. On that day they reached the top of 14,410-foot Mount Rainier.

The nine climbers could be heard over two-way radio, cheering and clapping as they waved flags and hugged each other at their success. They wanted to prove that handicapped people could do things that most people thought were impossible for them.

The climb nearly ruined the artificial leg of Chuck O'Brien, 35, of Philadelphia, who lost his limb in the Vietnam War. "But I'll make it," he said. "My spirit is really up."

First to reach the top were O'Brien; blind Kirk Adams, 19, of Snohomish, Wash.; and deaf Alec Naiman, 27, of New York City. With them was their guide, veteran climber Jim Whittaker, the first American atop Mount Everest.

Also reaching the top were Sheila Holzworth, 19, of Des Moines, Iowa, blinded at age 10; and Frederick Noesner, 34, of Glenside, Pa., who lost his sight in childhood. Douglas Wakefield, 39, of Arlington, Va., blind since birth; and Paul Stefurak, 25, of Federal Way, Wash., followed next. After them climbed Justin McDewitt, 29, of Rosemont, Pa., blind since birth.

They planned to hike back to the base camp to sleep and then to descend to Paradise Lodge at the 5,400-foot level by about noon Saturday.

What is this story about? Does it offer *facts* or *opinions*?

Think and Discuss

There are three main types of newspaper articles: **news stories, feature articles,** and **editorials.** News stories report events that have recently taken place; they present facts rather than opinions. The article about the climbers, for example, is a news story. Feature articles also present *facts.* They differ from news stories mainly in that they concentrate only on one or two angles, or parts of the story, but present them in greater depth. An editorial, on the other hand, is a written *opinion* on some newsworthy situation.

Most news stories and feature articles contain the answers to six basic news-gathering questions.

<u>Who</u> was involved?
<u>What</u> happened?
<u>When</u> did the event take place?
<u>Where</u> did it happen?
<u>Why</u> did it happen?
<u>How</u> did it happen?

The newspaper reporter always makes sure these questions are answered, preferably in the first paragraph of the story. Omitting any of them would make it incomplete. Look back at the news story about the handicapped climbers. Are all the basic questions answered?

Now read this feature article.

North Adams, Mass. (AP) — A little town that refused to let its oldest soldier die is throwing a party today. The party marks the return of a Civil War statue that became a pile of stones one night in the headlights' white glare.

It took three years and the careful labor of a Yankee artist to piece together the statue of the Union soldier. It was first dedicated here on the Fourth of July in 1878 when the town was less than a year old.

Back in his place at the head of the green where Union soldiers trained for battle, the old soldier is getting a parade and a brass band today. "The old fellow means a lot to us," said Charles Lamb, the mayor of this town of 17,000 people near the Vermont border. "He's a sign of our heritage."

When a car smashed the statue three years ago, police carefully picked up the pieces. Experts said it would take at least $30,000 to repair. So the citizens gave it the Humpty Dumpty try. They laid out the pieces of the statue at the town sewage plant and tried to put them back together again.

When things looked very bad, Carl Robare, a lifelong artist, appeared. Friends and neighbors in nearby Stamford, Vt., where Robare lives, said that he could repair anything. "I felt bad seeing him lying there in the sewer plant," Robare said. "After all, I grew up with him."

After Robare put in 240 hours of work with a homemade cement, the two legs, battered 700-pound body, half head, musket part, and box full of pieces had become a new soldier. Mayor Lamb said that the city wants to put a fence around the statue now that it is finally back in one piece.

Did you notice that the feature article *sounded* different from the news story? The difference is in the tone of the article, the writer's *attitude* toward the subject. The news story, for example, is very businesslike. It seems as though the reporter's only concern was to present the facts. In the feature article, however, the reporter has a much more relaxed attitude toward the subject. The article is factual, but the vocabulary is casual, and the result is a feature written more for enjoyment than for its value as news.

Finally, read this editorial.

Almost everything memorable in the history of New Haven — and of our whole country — is briefly touched in the 17 acres of Grove St. Cemetery. Almost every stone and grave marker reflects in some way the passage of our American ancestors over 150 years.

Starting at Roger Sherman's grave on this Independence Day, the deeds and the records run in all directions. Many are buried here.

Eli Whitney, the inventor of the cotton gin.

Charles Goodyear, who discovered the way to vulcanize rubber and thus put the world on soft-rolling wheels.

Noah Webster, the writer of the first dictionary of the American language.

Admiral Andrew Foote, who created a steam-run navy after the Civil War.

Out by the gate, Yehudi Ashmun, who created the colony of Liberia in Africa and who began today's search for black identity and pride.

Jedidiah Morse, Yale scholar and the father of American geography.

James Hillhouse, a U.S. senator, the tree-lover who made this the Elm City. There are so many others: Yale President Ezra Stiles who watched the British invasion of New Haven from his town's highest steeple; the widow of Samuel F.B. Morse who invented the telegraph; and Ann Gerry, the widow of Elbridge Gerry who signed the Declaration of Independence for Massachusetts.

The graveyard is filled with names that gave New Haven grace as a frontier town and that serve it still today.

The writer of an editorial presents facts, as those of stories and features do. *Unlike* the other two, however, the editorial writer uses the facts to state an *opinion.* The reader may or may not agree with the writer's opinion. The tone of the writing lies somewhere between that of the news story and the feature. In general, the three different kinds of newspaper writing offer three varied ways of getting out the news.

Remember This

1. <u>News stories</u> and <u>features</u> report facts.
2. <u>Editorials</u> report facts and offer opinions.
3. <u>Features</u> stress only one or two angles of a news item.
4. News stories and feature articles answer the six basic questions: *who, what, when, where, why, how.*

Practice

A. Answer these questions in complete sentences.

1. What is the purpose of a news story?
2. What is the purpose of an editorial?
3. What is meant by the *tone* of a piece of writing?
4. How does the tone of a piece of writing affect the vocabulary the writer chooses?

B. Use the three selections to answer these questions.

5. Copy one sentence from the news story that you would consider formal or businesslike in tone.
6. Copy one sentence from the feature article that you would consider informal in tone.
7. Copy one sentence from the editorial that is somewhere between the tone of the news story and the tone of the feature article.

Apply

C. Get ready to write a news story, feature article, or an editorial.

Prewriting
- Choose a topic that will appeal to many people.
- Do some research for background information. Take notes to use in your writing.

Composing
- Write an introduction that states your topic.
- List facts for news stories and features, opinions with supporting examples for editorials.
- Follow the form of the model you have chosen. Choose a tone that fits the category you have selected.
- Follow the guidelines in the green box.

Revising
- Be sure your facts support your topic.
- Check your work for errors in spelling, punctuation, and mechanics.
- Copy your revised work onto clean paper.

A BOOK TO READ

Title: **Mrs. Frisby and the Rats of NIMH**
Author: Robert C. O'Brien
Publisher: Atheneum

Mrs. Frisby, widow of the late Jonathan Frisby, was raising her family of field mice alone, and she had a terrible problem. In trying to solve this problem, Mrs. Frisby meets a colony of most extraordinary rats: rats that have electric lights, an elevator, and an extensive library in their burrow. Strange events take place as the rats try to help Mrs. Frisby and her family.

Mrs. Frisby and the Rats of NIMH won the Newbery Medal in the year it was published.

3 UNIT TEST

● **Common and Proper Nouns**   pages 90–91

Read these sentences. Then copy the questions that follow. Add the *letter* of each correct answer.

                a   b   c
A. The city held a parade on Columbus Day.

      a   b   c
B. Crowds watched from both sides of Fifth Avenue.

            a   b   c
C. The marchers turned onto Lexington Avenue.

            a   b   c
D. The doctors and nurses at Columbus Hospital watched the activity.

     a   b   c
E. Police controlled the crowds near the East River.

1. The proper noun in sentence A is ———.
2. The common noun in sentence B is ———.
3. The common noun in sentence C is ———.
4. The proper noun in sentence D is ———.
5. The common noun in sentence E is ———.

● **Singular and Plural Nouns**   pages 92–93

Copy these sentences. Underline the nouns. Then write *singular* or *plural* above each one.

  6. Worms love my garden.
  7. This garden has many plants.
  8. The tomatoes have worms in them.
  9. Gardening takes many hours of work.
10. This rake was a gift from my dad.

Forming Plurals of Nouns   pages 92–93

Copy these nouns. Write the plural form of each one.

11. watch   **12.** file   **13.** catch   **14.** box
15. pass   **16.** boy   **17.** ash   **18.** knave
19. ant   **20.** wrench **21.** folly   **22.** knight

Copy these sentences. Use the correct plural form of the nouns in parentheses ( ).

23. The cow had four _____. (calf)
24. The _____ were grazing on the hill. (sheep)
25. Who owns those _____? (canoe)
26. I asked the _____ about it. (man)
27. They were chasing the _____. (mouse)
28. Look at those _____. (hoof)
29. These animals all live long _____. (life)

Abbreviations   pages 94–95

Copy these words. Next to each write its correct abbreviation.

30. August   **31.** Railroad **32.** April   **33.** Friday
34. Mister   **35.** Sunday   **36.** Mount   **37.** Utah
38. River   **39.** Road   **40.** Ohio   **41.** Doctor
42. Avenue   **43.** October   **44.** Colonel **45.** Major

Possessives   pages 96–97

Copy these sentences. Add the correct possessive form of each word in parentheses ( ).

46. The _____ alignment should be corrected. (wheels)
47. The _____ seat is uncomfortable. (driver)
48. The _____ department is crowded. (men)
49. The _____ covers don't fit. (boxes)
50. My _____ sole is worn out. (shoe)
51. Mr. _____ office is near mine. (Moss)
52. The _____ bottle fell off the table. (baby)
53. My _____ coats are in the closet. (friends)
54. _____ bike is red and yellow. (Janice)
55. _____ bike is blue. (Mary Eagle Feather)

Encyclopedias   pages 100–101

A set of encyclopedias is arranged like this. Copy each subject. Write the volume *number* that would be used for each one.

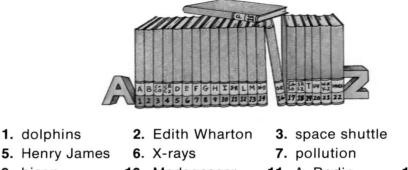

1. dolphins
2. Edith Wharton
3. space shuttle
4. tennis
5. Henry James
6. X-rays
7. pollution
8. chlorine
9. bison
10. Madagascar
11. A. Rodin
12. vitamins

Atlases and Almanacs   pages 102–103

Copy this list. Then write whether you would find the information in an *atlas* or an *almanac.*

13. the winner of the last senatorial election in your state
14. the current population of the United States
15. a map showing the natural resources of Nigeria
16. a chart showing the languages spoken in Europe
17. the names of the countries that border the Gulf of Mexico

Prewriting, Composing, and Revising—How-to Paragraph
pages 104–111

1. Set up a framed paragraph with directions for one of these topics.
   - How to Tie a Square Knot
   - How to Make Scrambled Eggs
   - How to Load Film into a Camera
   - How to Replace a Bicycle Chain
   - How to Load Software into a Computer

Then write a how-to paragraph on the topic you chose. Be sure to include transitional expressions. When you revise your paragraph, check that your directions are clear and in the correct order. Correct all mistakes in spelling, punctuation, and other mechanics. Then rewrite your paragraph in final form.

Prewriting, Composing, and Revising—Paragraph of Cause and Effect   pages 112–120

2. Choose one of these topic sentences. Make a diagram showing causes or effects for the sentence. Label the parts of your diagram *cause* or *effect.*

   - Bob did not take care of the garden he planted.
   - My sister is allergic to anything made from milk.
   - The Earth is warmer than it used to be.

Use the diagram to develop a paragraph of cause or effect. Revise your paragraph. Concentrate on its *clarity* of presentation, but mark all errors in spelling and punctuation as well. Then rewrite your paragraph in final form.

Mechanics Practice   page 121

Capitalize and punctuate these sentences correctly.

3. At 1 00 p m the fire alarm sounded at school.
4. It was thursday, november 10 1983.
5. Quickly mr coggins guided us out of mr bigelows room.
6. The fire fighters arrived at 1 03 pm
7. Capt dodge discovered a short circuit in the alarm in mr coggins office.

The Newspaper   pages 122–127

Read this article. Then list on your paper the six questions each feature article must answer, and write the answers the article gives.

   Tall, handsome Roy Rogers rode into town yesterday, and it's hard to believe that the "King of the Cowboys" is celebrating his 50th year in show business this week. . . . "It's a long time between New York premieres," he said during an interview in the Essex House. "My first picture, *Under Western Skies,* opened here at the Criterion Theater in 1938." . . . Since then it's been happy trails for Roy and his wife of 34 years, Dale Evans. . . .
   Today Roy will present one of his horses called "Broadway Trigger" to the New York City Police Department's Mounted Unit in Central Park. "What better way to celebrate 50 years of performing?" he asked.

LANGUAGE
Learning About Verbs

STUDY SKILLS
Organizing Information

Have you ever seen the launch of a space shuttle? How would you describe the scene as the space shuttle leaves the launch pad? The photograph on the left shows the *Challenger* in action. What words might you use to describe the action that you see in the picture? As you know, words that express action are *verbs*. What verbs describe the sounds the *Challenger* makes?

Verbs not only express action but also tell *when* things occur. Verbs express time. They tell whether something happened last week or yesterday, whether something is happening now, or whether something will happen tomorrow.

In addition to studying verbs in this unit, you will examine the parts of a book. Suppose you want to find out whether your science book has a chapter on space travel or whether your book mentions the *Challenger*. Perhaps you need to find a definition for the term *space shuttle*. In this unit you will learn which sections of your book contain the type of information you need.

Finally you will study a book report, and you will read a myth, "Demeter and Persephone," which was written long before people knew about space travel. Using this story as a model, you will then create a myth of your own.

Now turn the page and take off!

◄ *Space shuttle launch at Cape Canaveral, Florida*

LANGUAGE

Lesson 1: Understanding Action Verbs

Read this paragraph.

Dwayne dreamed about a robot one night. The robot obeyed his orders. It woke him every morning. It played baseball with him after school. Its computer helped him with his homework.

Find an example of a simple predicate in the paragraph.

Think and Discuss

Every complete sentence must have a predicate, which contains a **verb** to make it complete. If the verb tells what the subject *does,* it is an **action verb.**

> - A **verb** is a word that expresses action or being.
> - An **action verb** expresses physical or mental action.

Now read these sentences.

1. All day long the robot worked for Dwayne.
2. Everyone thought of chores for it.

The verb *worked* is an action verb that expresses physical action. The verb *thought* is an action verb that expresses mental action.

Look again at the paragraph about Dwayne. Which four verbs show action performed with the body, or a physical action? Which verb shows an action of the mind?

Practice

A. Copy these sentences. Underline each action verb that expresses physical action. Circle each action verb that expresses mental action.

1. Some factories use robots.
2. The robots do the boring or dangerous jobs.
3. They load and unload heavy machines.
4. Robots never think about long hours.
5. Once workers sent flowers to a broken robot.

B. 6. Listen carefully and write the paragraph that your teacher will dictate.

Apply

C. 7.–16. Imagine that someone just gave you a robot. Write ten sentences that tell what it can do. Underline the action verbs in each sentence.

HOW OUR LANGUAGE GROWS

Myths are stories of the supernatural. They deal with imaginary superhuman beings: gods, goddesses, and monsters. Our language has borrowed many words from these ancient stories, especially those handed down to us by the Greeks.

The Greek goddess of the earth was named *Gaea.* From her name we have the words *geography, geology,* and *geometry.* In a famous Greek story the *sirens* were creatures whose sweet music lured ships into dangerous waters. Today we use the word *siren* to represent a warning of danger. *Pan* was the god of shepherds. His music sometimes frightened people into a *panic.*

1. *Hypnos* was the god of sleep. What word comes from his name?
2. From which hero's name do we get the word for a strong person?

Lesson 2: Understanding Linking Verbs

What is the single action verb in this paragraph?

Kitty O'Neil is a famous sports personality. At one time she was a champion diver. When sickness kept her from the Olympics, Kitty became a car and motorcycle racer. Soon she was a well-known stunt person. Today she is among the best stunt people in the world.

Think and Discuss

Verbs that do not show action, but express *being* instead, are called **linking verbs.** They link, or join, the subject of a sentence with a word or words in the predicate. Linking verbs help tell what a subject *is* or *is like.* In the paragraph about Kitty O'Neil, for example, the linking verb *is* in the first sentence joins the subject, *Kitty O'Neil,* to the words *sports personality.* The verb identifies Kitty O'Neil.

- A **linking verb** links, or joins, the subject of a sentence with a word or words in the predicate.

Most linking verbs are forms of the verb *be* such as *am, is, are, was, were, will be, have been, has been,* or *had been.* Other verbs that are similar in meaning such as *seem, appear, become, taste,* or *smell* are also linking verbs.

Look at the second sentence of the paragraph. *She* is the subject and *was* is the linking verb. *Diver* is the word in the predicate that is linked to the subject by the verb. What is the subject of the fourth sentence? Name the linking verb and the words in the predicate that are linked to the subject.

Practice

A. Copy these sentences. Underline each linking verb.

1. Kitty O'Neil is a remarkable person.
2. She has been deaf since childhood.
3. Her mother was the person who taught Kitty to read.
4. Kitty's mother was a Cherokee from Texas.
5. Kitty has always been athletic.

B. Copy the sentences that have linking verbs. Underline each linking verb. Circle the subject and the word in the predicate to which the verb links it.

6. As a stunt person, Kitty is completely fearless.
7. Her deafness is an aid to concentration.
8. She is the women's record holder for land speed.
9. At 5 feet 3 inches and 100 pounds, Kitty appears frail.
10. She is strong, however, both in body and in spirit.

Apply

C. 11.–15. Choose another person in science, sports, art, or music. Write a paragraph describing what this person has achieved in his or her life. Use at least five linking verbs in the paragraph.

To Memorize

There are no gains without pains.

Benjamin Franklin

This proverb comes from *Poor Richard's Almanac*, a collection of witty sayings. What is the message of this proverb? Do you agree with it?

Lesson 3: Understanding Helping Verbs and Main Verbs

Read these sentences.

1. The Eagles are playing an important baseball game.
2. The other team, the Lions, have been hitting well.
3. The Eagles, however, can boast two secret weapons: great teamwork and their pitcher, Glennette.

Did you know that, like the Eagles, verbs often work in teams? In every sentence two or three words have teamed up to form the verb. Can you name them?

Think and Discuss

Sometimes a simple predicate is made up of two or more words. One of them is a **main verb** and one or more is a **helping verb.** The main verb expresses the action in the sentence. The helping verb helps the main verb do its job.

In sentence 1 *playing* expresses the action. The helping verb *are* helps the main verb by showing time and number. That is, it shows that the game is being played at the present time. It also indicates that several people are playing. The second sentence has a three-word verb. *Hitting* is the main verb and *have been* is the helping verb.

> - The **main verb** is the verb that expresses action or being.
> - The **helping verb** is the verb that helps the main verb express its action. Most helping verbs are forms of *be*, *have*, and *do*.

When studying sentences that use helping verbs, you should watch for three things. Sometimes the helping verb and main verb are separated by words such as *not* or *never*. In a question, the subject often comes between the two parts of the verb. Finally, a helping verb such as *have* can be a main verb in one sentence and a helping verb in another.

Read these sentences.

4. Sam has never hit a home run.
5. Have you seen Glennette pitch lately?
6. The Eagles have won eight games this season.
7. The Eagles have a great team.

Name the verbs in sentences 4–7. In which sentence is *have* a main verb?

Practice

A. Copy these sentences. Underline the verbs.

1. The players are walking onto the field.
2. The big day has come at last.
3. The Eagles have practiced all week.
4. They are prepared for this game.
5. The Eagles have never played the other team.
6. Glennette is practicing her pitch.

B. Copy these sentences. Underline the main verb in each sentence. Circle the helping verb.

7. The fans are watching Glennette.
8. She has never thrown such a fast ball!
9. The Lions' hitter has struck out!
10. Now the Eagles have taken the field.
11. On the first pitch Sam has hit a home run.
12. The Eagles have won the game!

Apply

C. **13.–22.** Imagine that you are reporting on an important sports event. Write ten sentences describing what you see. Use a main verb and a helping verb in each of your sentences.

Lesson 4: Understanding Principal Parts of Regular Verbs

Read these sentences.

1. Many animals <u>live</u> in Africa.
2. Some species <u>lived</u> there before people did.
3. Most species have <u>lived</u> there for centuries.

How do the three forms of the verb *live* differ from one another?

Think and Discuss

All verbs have three important forms called **principal parts.** From these come all other verb forms. Study this list of some common principal parts.

Present	Past	Past Participle
change (s)	changed	(has, have, had) changed
cry (ies)	cried	(has, have, had) cried
learn (s)	learned	(has, have, had) learned
rush (es)	rushed	(has, have, had) rushed

The first principal part, the **present,** is the simplest form of the verb. Notice that its endings vary. The second principal part, the **past,** is formed by adding *d* or *ed* to the present form. (If the verb ends in *y,* change *y* to *i* before adding the ending.) The **past participle,** which is the third principal part, is formed by using the helping verb *has, have,* or *had* with the past form of the verb.

Verbs in which the past and past participle are formed by adding *d* or *ed* to the present form are called **regular verbs.**

> • The three basic forms of a verb are its **principal parts.** The principal parts are the **present,** the **past,** and the **past participle.**

Practice

A. Copy these sentences. After each write which principal part of the underlined verb was used.

1. Gazelles <u>race</u> across the open plains of Africa.
2. Monkeys <u>have</u> always <u>climbed</u> trees in the jungle.
3. Vast herds of elephants once <u>roamed</u> the grasslands.
4. Hunters, however, <u>killed</u> many for their ivory tusks.
5. Today few <u>remain</u> in their natural habitat.
6. Ostriches <u>have wandered</u> over the southern plains.
7. Crocodiles <u>inhabit</u> many of Africa's rivers.
8. From his leafy home, one monkey <u>has called</u> to another.
9. Back and forth they <u>chattered</u>.
10. Even an interested bird <u>joins</u> the conversation.

B. 11.–20. Write the three principal parts of each of the verbs underlined in Practice A.

C. Copy these sentences. Complete each with the correct principal part of the verb in parentheses ( ). After each sentence write the name of the part you used.

21. Many kinds of plants _____ in Africa.   (thrive)
22. Olive trees have always _____ in northern areas.   (live)
23. The cork oak _____ the material for this table.   (furnish)
24. Date palms have always _____ delicious fruit.   (supply)
25. Furniture makers _____ mahogany here.   (obtain)
26. Growers _____ tons of coffee beans last year.   (raise)
27. Cedar trees _____ sweet-smelling wood.   (provide)
28. During storms, deserts have often been _____.   (change)
29. Plants that once _____ dead sometimes revive.   (seem)
30. Cactus roots can _____ water deep underground.   (reach)

Apply

D. 31. Write a paragraph about a plant or animal that comes from Africa. Use the principal parts of five regular verbs in your paragraph.

Lesson 5: Understanding Principal Parts of Irregular Verbs I

Read these sentences.

1. Today Bart <u>goes</u> to the country.
2. He <u>went</u> there once last week.
3. He has <u>gone</u> there only once before.

Each verb is a principal part of the verb *go*. What differences do you see between these verbs and the verbs you learned in Lesson 4?

Think and Discuss

The past and past participle of some verbs are not formed by adding *d* or *ed* to the present form. Such verbs are called **irregular verbs.** Look at these three groups of irregular verbs. The second and third principal parts of each group are formed in different ways.

	Present	**Past**	**Past Participle**
Group 1	come(s)	came	(has, have, had) come
	go(es)	went	(has, have, had) gone
	run(s)	ran	(has, have, had) run
Group 2	begin(s)	began	(has, have, had) begun
	drink(s)	drank	(has, have, had) drunk
	ring(s)	rang	(has, have, had) rung
	sing(s)	sang	(has, have, had) sung
	swim(s)	swam	(has, have, had) swum
Group 3	bring(s)	brought	(has, have, had) brought
	catch(es)	caught	(has, have, had) caught
	say(s)	said	(has, have, had) said
	sell(s)	sold	(has, have, had) sold
	think(s)	thought	(has, have, had) thought

In the first group, the vowel is changed in the past form. The past participle is either the same or nearly the same as the present form. The verbs in the second group have an *i* in the present form. The *i* is changed to an *a* in the past and to a *u* in the past participle.

In the third group, the past and past participle forms are similar. The only difference is that the past participle has a helping verb.

Practice

A. Copy these sentences. Underline the irregular verbs. After each sentence, write which principal part was used.

1. Bart thinks of easy ways to do everything.
2. Now he has thought of a way to avoid mowing the lawn.
3. This morning Bart went to a farmer's house.
4. The farmer no longer sells any of his sheep.
5. He has begun to rent his sheep as lawn mowers.

B. Copy these sentences. Use the correct form of the irregular verb in parentheses ( ). Write which principal part you used.

6. Bart waited while a man _____ the sheep.   (catch)
7. He _____ some lemonade on the porch.   (drink)
8. He _____ about sheep "mowing" lawns.   (think)
9. He could have _____ in the nearby pond.   (swim)
10. He _____ for a mile every day.   (run)

Apply

C. 11.–20. Write ten sentences about a dog who helps to do household chores. Use the principal parts of the irregular verbs in this lesson. Underline each of these irregular verbs, and after each sentence write which part you used.

Lesson 6: Understanding Principal Parts of Irregular Verbs II

Can you answer these questions?

1. When does the verb grow rhyme with knew?
2. When does the verb tear rhyme with worn?
3. When does the verb freeze rhyme with chose?

To answer the questions, you must know the principal parts of the first underlined verb in each question. Can you figure out the answers?

Think and Discuss

Study these groups of irregular verbs.

	Present	Past	Past Participle
	do(es)	did	(has, have, had) done
	eat(s)	ate	(has, have, had) eaten
	fly(ies)	flew	(has, have, had) flown
	give(s)	gave	(has, have, had) given
Group 4	grow(s)	grew	(has, have, had) grown
	know(s)	knew	(has, have, had) known
	ride(s)	rode	(has, have, had) ridden
	take(s)	took	(has, have, had) taken
	write(s)	wrote	(has, have, had) written
	break(s)	broke	(has, have, had) broken
	choose(s)	chose	(has, have, had) chosen
Group 5	freeze(s)	froze	(has, have, had) frozen
	speak(s)	spoke	(has, have, had) spoken
	tear(s)	tore	(has, have, had) torn
	wear(s)	wore	(has, have, had) worn

Notice that for some of these verbs the present and past participle are similar. For others the past and past participle are similar.

After you have studied the chart, name the principal parts of each verb mentioned in sentences 1–3.

Practice

A. Copy these sentences. Underline the irregular verbs from this lesson. After each sentence, write which principal part was used.

1. During the nineteenth century, many American cities grew quite large.
2. Single-family houses took up too much space.
3. In New Orleans the Baroness Pontalba spoke to architects.
4. In their plan they had done something new.
5. Soon workers broke ground for two apartment houses.
6. Today the Pontalba Apartments have grown famous.
7. The renters take pride in their historic homes.

B. Complete each sentence with the correct form of the verb in parentheses ( ). After each sentence, write which principal part was used.

8. Baroness Pontalba must certainly have _____ what she was doing. (know)
9. She had been _____ much good advice. (give)
10. She _____ beautiful iron balconies for her apartments. (choose)
11. The balconies _____ the apartments a special touch. (give)
12. Many have _____ miles to see this attraction. (ride)
13. Others have _____ to New Orleans from Europe. (fly)
14. Much has been _____ about the area in which the baroness's apartments stand. (write)
15. It has been _____ as the French Quarter for years. (know)

Apply

C. 16.–25. Write ten sentences about another historic American city. Use the verbs from this lesson, and identify the principal part of each one.

Lesson 7: Understanding Verb Tenses: Present, Past, and Future

Read this airport information board.

Flight 393 departs from gate 5. Now boarding.
Flight 881 will depart from gate 3.

Your flight is 881. Has it left yet? How do you know?

Think and Discuss

You already know that verbs express time. The word used to express a *particular* time is **tense**. The first three tenses are the **present**, the **past**, and the **future**.

> - The time expressed by a verb is its **tense**.
> - The **present tense** expresses action that is taking place *now*.
> - The **past tense** expresses action that took place at *some definite time in the past*.
> - The **future tense** expresses action that will take place at *some time in the future*.

Present Tense

I arrive	we arrive
you arrive	you arrive
he, she, it arrives	they arrive

Past Tense

I arrived	we arrived
you arrived	you arrived
he, she, it arrived	they arrived

Future Tense

I will arrive	we will arrive
you will arrive	you will arrive
he, she, it will arrive	they will arrive

Notice that the present tense has the same form as the first principal part and that the past tense has the same form as the second principal part. The future tense is made from the first principal part plus the word *will*.

Practice

A. Copy these sentences. Underline the verbs. After each sentence, write the tense of each verb.

1. Marie took a plane from St. Louis to Chicago.
2. The plane left Lambert Airport at 10:42 A.M.
3. The flight lasted about an hour.
4. Will the plane arrive in Chicago early?
5. Now Marie waits in the terminal for Michael.
6. He will meet her at the terminal.
7. Michael finally reaches the terminal at noon.
8. Michael tells Marie about his morning.
9. His car ran out of gas at 11:00 A.M.
10. Michael's trip to the airport took as much time as Marie's flight to Chicago.

B. Complete these sentences with the correct tense of each verb in parentheses ( ).

11. Tino _____ to Rome every year. (*fly,* present)
12. He always _____ first-class tickets. (*buy,* present)
13. He _____ a delicious dinner. (*eat,* present)
14. Last April he _____ on a new airline. (*fly,* past)
15. The steward _____ his dinner. (*forget,* past)
16. Later, the movie projector _____ down. (*break,* past)
17. He _____ awake all night. (*stay,* past)
18. Tino _____ in Rome two hours late. (*arrive,* future)
19. The airline _____ about his problems. (*hear,* future)
20. They _____ him a free flight next year. (*offer,* future)

Apply

C. 21.–30. In ten sentences, finish the story about Tino. Use the present, past, and future tenses of verbs.

Lesson 8: Understanding Verb Tenses: Present Perfect Tense

Read this paragraph.

Careers in communications <u>have</u> always <u>attracted</u> creative people. Most editors, publishers, and film directors <u>have reached</u> their present positions after years of hard work. Many <u>have studied</u> years to learn more about their jobs.

What do all the underlined verbs have in common?

Think and Discuss

When you tell others about events that have happened in the past, you often use the past tense. Sometimes, however, an event might have begun in the past but is still going on. It might have taken place in some *indefinite* past time. In such cases the **present perfect tense** is used.

This tense is easy to form. Simply use the past participle of the verb with the helping verb *have* or *has.* Study this chart.

Present Perfect Tense

I have arrived	we have arrived
you have arrived	you have arrived
he, she, it has arrived	they have arrived

How and where does the form of the helping verb change? This same helping verb is also used when a noun is the subject.

> ● The **present perfect tense** expresses action that took place at *some indefinite time in the past* or that began in the past and is *still going on.*

Practice

A. Copy these sentences. Underline all verbs that are in the present perfect tense.

1. Some people in communications have always written the news.
2. Angela has applied for a job in a printing plant.
3. The manager has accepted her for the job.
4. She has never worked in a printing plant, however.
5. Therefore the manager has assigned her to work with the inks on the four-color presses.
6. Other people like Angela have started working in communications in similar jobs.
7. One magazine editor has worked at every job in magazine publishing.

B. Complete each sentence with the present perfect tense of each verb in parentheses ( ).

8. Since movies were first made, the work of film directors _____ on-the-job training.   (require)
9. Film editors _____ some poor films into great successes.   (change)
10. Radio and television writers _____ many shows successful.   (make)
11. Yet wardrobe people and script clerks _____ their skills as well.   (contribute)
12. Skills of many kinds _____ people to communicate with others all over the world.   (help)

Apply

C. 13.–20. Imagine that you have a career in the communications field. Write eight sentences describing what you do. Use the present perfect tense at least five times.

Lesson 9: Understanding Verb Complements

Driving through a bad storm, Trenell and his father were listening to the car radio. Because of the static, this is all they heard.

〰️〰️〰️ Summer Olympics, 19 〰️〰️〰️
Today an American diver won 〰️〰️〰️
〰️〰️〰️ Japanese champion was〰️〰️ 〰️〰️
diver Greg Louganis broke〰️〰️ 〰️〰️ 〰️〰️

Trenell had no idea what might have happened at the diving event. From what he had heard, what do you think had taken place?

Think and Discuss

Trenell was annoyed because he had not heard the **complements,** the words that completed the meaning of the announcer's verbs. In the broadcast, the three verbs *won, was,* and *broke* all needed complements to make sense. Some verbs, however, do not need them.

> - A **direct object** follows an *action* verb and receives its action.
> - A **predicate nominative** follows a *linking* verb and tells what the subject is.
> - **Transitive verbs** are action verbs that are followed by direct objects.
> - **Intransitive verbs** include all linking verbs and any action verbs not followed by direct objects.

Suppose in the diving event the American won the gold medal. *Medal* received the action of the verb *won* and is a **direct object.** Suppose the Japanese champion was the *runner-up. Runner-up* follows the linking verb and tells what the Japanese champion was. It is a **predicate nominative.** Which verb is transitive? Which is intransitive?

Practice

A. Copy these sentences. Underline each verb, and after the sentence write *transitive* or *intransitive*. If the verbs have complements, circle them, and after the sentence write *direct object* or *predicate nominative*.

1. The Olympic official was a capable person.
2. She opened the ceremony.
3. Then she gave the torch to the first runner.
4. The runner was a sprinter from Brazil.
5. He passed the torch to the next runner.
6. The second runner was not really a racer.
7. She was a gymnast from Norway.
8. She carried the torch to the next runner.
9. One runner fell along the way.
10. The torch, however, did not go out.

B. Complete these sentences with either a direct object or a predicate nominative. Then identify each verb as transitive or intransitive.

11. The United States bicycle team passed the _____.
12. All the team members were _____.
13. One member wore a _____.
14. Hal's bicycle is a _____.
15. The United States team won the _____.

C. 16. Write the paragraph that your teacher will now dictate to you.

Apply

D. 17.–26. Write ten sentences about the Olympics. Use an action verb followed by a direct object in five sentences. Use a linking verb followed by a predicate nominative in five sentences.

LANGUAGE REVIEW

Action Verbs and Linking Verbs   pages 134–137

Copy these sentences. Draw one line under the action verbs and two lines under the linking verbs.

1. Rome is a city of contrasts.
2. Ancient ruins stand beside plush, modern hotels.
3. The Colosseum and the Arch of Titus were once in the center of ancient Roman activity.
4. Now taxis, cars, and buses surround these historic ruins.
5. Such heavy traffic sometimes surprises even modern Romans.

Helping Verbs   pages 138–139

Copy these sentences. Underline each main verb and circle each helping verb.

6. Mexico City is considered a wonderful place to live.
7. It has become one of the fastest-growing cities in the world.
8. Every week hundreds of people are moving there.
9. In the past many people had lived in hotels.
10. Now the Mexicans are building houses for newcomers.

Principal Parts of Regular and Irregular Verbs   pages 140–145

Copy these sentences and underline the verbs. After each sentence write which principal part was used.

11. Renée and her parents flew to Paris on their vacation.
12. Renée had always dreamed of the Champs Elysées.
13. The Eiffel Tower amazed her with its beauty.
14. One day Renée and her parents ate lunch at a sidewalk cafe.
15. Renée had eaten her *quiche.*
16. Renée knew some French words.
17. She asks her dad a question in French.
18. Her dad answered the question.
19. "I have already chosen something for you in that store."
20. Later Renée wore her special dress.

Present, Past, Future, and Present Perfect Tenses   pages 146–149

Copy these sentences and underline the verbs. After each sentence write which tenses were used.

21. Many people think Rio de Janeiro is the capital of Brazil.
22. Years ago, however, several leaders chose another capital.
23. Then they began an entirely new city. It soon grew very large.
24. They have given the name *Brasilia* to the new capital.
25. Visitors will often travel to Brasilia on their vacations.

Verb Complements   pages 150–151

Copy these sentences. Draw one line under all action verbs and two lines under all linking verbs. Then circle any complements and identify each as a direct object or a predicate nominative.

26. Hamilton is the capital of Bermuda.
27. England rules the country and oversees the government in the city of Hamilton.
28. Restaurants, shops, and public buildings line Front Street, Hamilton's main road.
29. Cars are luxuries in Bermuda; even Hamilton business executives drive mopeds.
30. The loveliest sights in Bermuda are the beaches of clean pink and white sand.
31. Bermuda has few sources of fresh water.
32. The people collect rain water on the roofs of their houses.

Applying Verbs

33.–42. Write ten sentences about a state capital in the United States or the capital of a European, African, or South American country. Use at least five action verbs and five linking verbs. Vary your tenses, and use verb complements wherever possible.

STUDY SKILLS

Lesson 10: Understanding the Parts of a Book

Jim had especially enjoyed "Ransom," one of the stories in his literature book. Where in the book might he find the name of a volume of stories by the same author?

Think and Discuss

Not all the information in a book comes from the large main section, or body. The front and back sections also contain a great deal of useful material. Study this list of the parts of a book and the information each contains.

- The **title page** includes the title of the book, the author, the publisher, and the city of publication.
- The **copyright page** tells when the book was published. It sometimes includes the titles of other books from which material was reprinted by permission. This is the *acknowledgments* section.
- The **table of contents** lists each unit, chapter, story, or section in the order in which it appears in the book.
- The **body** contains the message or lessons in the book.
- The **glossary** is a brief dictionary at the back of the book. It lists words from the book that might be unfamiliar. It is arranged in alphabetical order.
- The **index** lists each section or topic in the book in alphabetical order and includes the page numbers on which it can be found.

Where would you find the publication date of a book? Which two sections are in alphabetical order?

Practice

A. Answer the questions based on these sample pages.

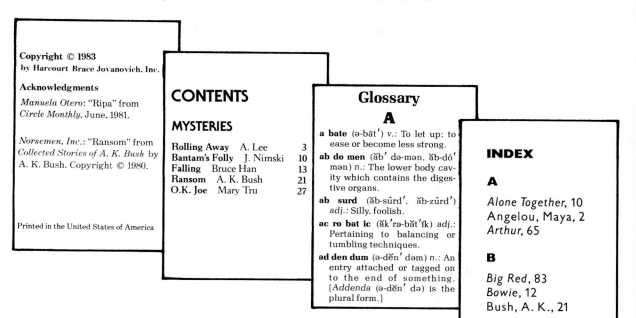

Copyright © 1983
by Harcourt Brace Jovanovich, Inc.

Acknowledgments

Manuela Otero: "Ripa" from
Circle Monthly, June, 1981.

Norsemen, Inc.: "Ransom" from
Collected Stories of A. K. Bush by
A. K. Bush. Copyright © 1980.

Printed in the United States of America

CONTENTS

MYSTERIES

Rolling Away	A. Lee	3
Bantam's Folly	J. Nimski	10
Falling	Bruce Han	13
Ransom	A. K. Bush	21
O.K. Joe	Mary Tru	27

Glossary

A

a bate (ə-bāt′) *v.*: To let up; to ease or become less strong.

ab do men (ăb′ də-mən, ăb-dō′ mən) *n.*: The lower body cavity which contains the digestive organs.

ab surd (ăb-sûrd′, ăb-zûrd′) *adj.*: Silly, foolish.

ac ro bat ic (ăk′rə-băt′ĭk) *adj.*: Pertaining to balancing or tumbling techniques.

ad den dum (ə-děn′ dəm) *n.*: An entry attached or tagged on to the end of something. [*Addenda* (ə-děn′ də) is the plural form.]

INDEX

A

Alone Together, 10
Angelou, Maya, 2
Arthur, 65

B

Big Red, 83
Bowie, 12
Bush, A. K., 21

1. What company published Jim's book?
2. When was the book printed?
3. Under what section heading are the five stories listed?
4. On what page is the story "Ransom," which Jim liked?
5. Name the title and author of the book Jim wanted.
6. How many syllables are in the word *abdomen*?
7. How many pronunciations does *abdomen* have?
8. What part of speech is the word *abate*?
9. According to the index, on what page does the selection called *Bowie* begin?
10. How many index entries begin with *A*?

Apply

B. 11. Take your math or English book and list what it includes under front and back material. Briefly describe what information each section or page has to offer.

Lesson 11: Skimming and Scanning

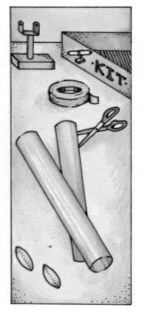

Jason found a book called *Projects You Can Put Together for Next to Nothing.* Interested, he looked over the table of contents. Then he turned to the chapter on simple telescopes for the supplies he would need to build one.

Think and Discuss

The two skills Jason used in thumbing through the projects book are known as **skimming** and **scanning.** To *skim* is to look at material in order to note its general subject, its divisions, and its major headings. To *scan,* on the other hand, is to look quickly at a particular passage, searching for *key words.* If, like Jason, you were trying to find out how to build a simple telescope, you would scan for words such as *eyepiece, base, mirror, lens,* and so on. Would you skim or scan to find this information?

1. materials for building a robot
2. the information covered in a book about airplanes
3. your name in a list of the members of your class

Practice

A. Study this sample table of contents. Answer the questions by skimming.

1. How many units are covered in the sample?
2. How many chapters are in Unit 5?
3. What is the title of Unit 5, Chapter 2?
4. What kinds of objects are discussed in Unit 5?
5. Which unit contains a chapter on how to build a clubhouse?

B. Read the questions that follow this section of a telephone book page. Answer the questions by scanning.

McManus Peter and Sally 71 Speare	821-5896
MacNeil Catherine MD 35 Madison St	838-3437
Manganaro Maria Mrs. 67 State St	845-0205
Milly's Dress Shop 40 Lincoln Rd	838-5650
Mountaindale Hospital Newcastle St	838-8000
Mountaindale School Boscobel Rd	838-7500
Murray D 138 Cliffside Dr	821-6927
Murray William 22 Maple Lane	845-1893

6. Which listing covers two people?
7. Which number would you use to call Dr. MacNeil?
8. Where is the hospital located?
9. Which *Murray* lives on Maple Lane?
10. Whose number is 845-0205?

Apply

C. 11.–12. Skim the first page of an almanac. Write the titles of the main sections listed on that page. Then scan the almanac to find and write the names of the governor and lieutenant governor of your state.

COMPOSITION

Lesson 12: Prewriting

Summarizing the Plot for a Book Report

Ilona was talking with Tom about a book report she was writing. "I *never* have trouble describing the main characters or giving my opinion," Ilona sighed. "But when I try to tell about the plot, I either write *everything* that happened or practically nothing at all!"

"I know," grumbled Tom. "I have the same problem. I never know *what* to put down for the plot."

Think and Discuss

Summarizing plots need not be a difficult task. What happens in nearly every story? The main character has a problem. He or she works through the trouble, trying one thing, then another to solve it. By the end of the book, the problem is gone. Here is a brief form that will help you summarize the plot for most works of fiction.

- Main character's problem: _____
- Things he/she does to try to solve it: 1. _____
                                          2. _____
- Other characters who help or hinder: 1. _____
                                          2. _____
- Most exciting event in the story: _____
- <u>Hint</u> about how problem is solved: _____

If the book you are reading varies from this format, use the items that fit, and substitute another category for any one that is not appropriate. The entire plot summary can be done, if you wish, in a single paragraph.

Using the summarizing form, how might you describe the plot of a simple children's story such as *Cinderella* or *The Three Bears*? How might you summarize *Treasure Island*?

How to Summarize a Plot

1. **Tell what the main character's problem is. If there is more than one main character and they all have problems, concentrate on the problem of only one character.**
2. **Tell what the character does to solve the problem. If too many things happen, select only one or two important events.**
3. **Mention how one or two other characters get involved in the problem.**
4. **Tell the climax, or high point, of the story, but do not give away the solution to the character's problems. Hint at it instead.**

Practice

A. Copy the form from page 158 onto a sheet of paper. Fill in the form to summarize the plot of *Jack and the Beanstalk* or *The Tortoise and the Hare.*

Apply

B. Now you can try your hand at summarizing a plot on your own.

Choose a Book

- Select a book that you really enjoyed, one that you think your audience would also like.
- Be sure that the book has at least one main character.

Choose Your Audience

- Decide which person or group you will share your book with. You might want to share it with a friend, a relative, a teacher, or some of your classmates. The subject matter of the book itself may help you decide who your audience should be.

Summarize the Plot

- Follow the model on page 158. For now, simply fill in the form. Later you will work your notes into a paragraph.
- Remember that the summarizing form you have been using is a *guide.* Change it whenever necessary to suit the type of book you will be using for your report.
- Keep your responses as simple and as short as possible without losing important details.

Review Your Work

- Look over your summarizing form. Think about your book.
- Have you captured the main idea of the book?
- Do the incidents you selected reflect the most important event?
- Save your form for the Apply exercise in Lesson 13.

Lesson 13:   Composing
Writing a Book Report

Akako read *The Door in the Wall,* a novel by Marguerite de Angeli. She wanted to tell her class about it. She decided that a good way to share the book with the class would be through writing a book report. Read the book report she wrote.

The Door in the Wall was written by Marguerite de Angeli. The story takes place in England during the Middle Ages. The times are often unhappy, for England is at war. A terrible disease called the plague is spreading in its cities. Excitement and happiness still exist, however, as a young boy, Robin, soon finds out.

When this novel begins, Robin's father, Sir John de Bureford, has gone off to fight in the wars. Robin's mother, Lady Maud, has been asked to serve the Queen. Robin is left with the household servants. Then Robin comes down with a mysterious disease. He finds that he cannot move his legs. When the plague strikes the household, Robin is left with no one to care for him.

Robin is rescued by Brother Luke, a monk who brings Robin to live with him. Brother Luke tells Robin, "Thou has only to follow the wall far enough and there will be a door in it." Robin is not sure what Brother Luke means, but he gladly goes with him just the same. The monks take care of Robin, and soon he is able to get around on crutches. Then a message from Sir John urges Robin to go to the castle of Sir Peter de Lindsay with Brother Luke and John—go—in—the—Wynd, a minstrel, as guides. They have many adventures, both on the way to the town of Lindsay and after they arrive. When the town is attacked by the enemy, it is up to Robin to save it.

I really liked The Door in the Wall. I felt that Marguerite de Angeli's characters were real people. What I liked best about the book, however, was following along with Robin and seeing how he learns to live with his handicap. As he discovered what it meant to find "the door in the wall," I discovered it too.

Think and Discuss

A book report tells the writer's opinion about a book. A book report should allow another reader to decide whether or not he or she wants to read it.

Akako's book report contains all the proper information. Akako gives the title, author, and setting of the novel in the first paragraph. It is there that she introduces the most important character from the novel as well. The second and third paragraphs tell the story of *The Door in the Wall*. Notice that Akako does not tell everything that happens. For example, much of the story is covered by sentences such as "They have many adventures." Akako also did not give away the ending of the novel. Why do you think she left out that piece of information?

What sentence gives Akako's opinion of *The Door in the Wall?* Akako did not end her report with that sentence; instead, she explained *why* she felt that way. In your book reports, always explain your feelings about the book.

How to Write a Book Report

1. **Write the title and author of the book. Underline the title.**
2. **Include the names of the most important characters.**
3. **Explain the time and place (the setting) of the story.**
4. **Tell about one or two events in the story.**
5. **Give your opinion and a reason for your opinion.**

Practice

A. Answer these questions about Akako's book report.

1. What is the book's title? Who wrote it?
2. Who is the main character?
3. What does the title of the book really mean?

4. Write one important event that Akako mentions in her report.

5. Why should a book report not give the entire story, ending and all, of a book?

Apply

B. Follow these guidelines as you put your notes into paragraph form.

Write the Introduction to the Report

- The first part always includes the title, author, setting, and main characters of the book.

Write Your Plot Summary

- Follow the order of your summarizing form.
- The first item on your form would make a good topic sentence.
- The other items will be the basis for detail sentences.

Write an Opinion Statement

- The last part of your book report should tell whether or not you enjoyed the book. One or two reasons for your opinion would make a good conclusion.

Review Your Report

- Reread your work. Be sure all the parts of a good book report have been included.
- Check to see whether your report captures the central idea of the book.
- Be sure that you did not give away the ending of the book.
- Save the report for revising in Lesson 14.

A Challenge

Imagine that you have just read a book about an eleven-year-old student who accidentally went to the moon with three U.S. astronauts. Write a book report about it that will have your classmates wishing such a book were real.

Lesson 14: Revising

Editing and Proofreading a Book Report

Editing and Proofreading Marks

≡ capitalize

⊙ make a period

∧ add something

⌄, add a comma

ᵛᵛ ᵛᵛ add quotation marks

⤴ take something away

◯ spell correctly

¶ indent the paragraph

/ make a lowercase letter

∿ transpose
tr

Marta wrote a book report on *The House of Dies Drear.* As she wrote, however, she forgot about some of the guidelines for writing a book report. What are they?

Think and Discuss

Here is Marta's report and the changes she made.

The action in *The House of Dies*
by Virginia Hamilton
Drear, takes place in a small Ohio
Town. Everything seemed strange as
thomas and his family moved into
their
there new home⊙ thomas knew that
the house had once been part of the
underground railroad, which had
helped escaping slaves. He was
amazed
amazzed and fritened, however, by
frightened
its sliding walls, secret Passages,
and Tunnels. Strange things
happened almost immediately as
became convinced
Thomas, thought that the old
, Mr. Pluto,
caretaker, was trying to drive
his family
them away. The House of Dies Drear is one of
the most interesting and exciting
books I have ever read.

Revising for **content** is making sure that all the information required is actually *in* your report. By adding the name of the author and her opinion of the book, Marta completed the information required by the guidelines. Notice that she changed *thought* to *became convinced* because the new words were more specific. The same is true of changing *them* to *his family* and adding the caretaker's name.

Marta also made some changes in mechanics. What did she do to show she needed to add capital letters to some words? How did she remind herself to remove some capital letters? How did she indicate words that were misspelled?

Marta's plot summary needs improvement. How would you change it?

How to Revise a Book Report

Editing

1. Check your report to be sure you have included the title, author, setting, and characters.
2. Be sure you have written a complete plot summary.
3. Be sure you have included your opinion of the book and reasons to support your opinion.
4. Be sure your sentences flow smoothly from one to the next. Check the transitional expressions in your plot summary.

Proofreading

5. Correct all mistakes in spelling, punctuation, and mechanics.
6. Be sure you indented the first word of your paragraph.

Practice

A. Rewrite Marta's book report, making all the corrections she marked on her original copy.

B. This is a book report about an *imaginary* book. Add whatever information is necessary to complete all the guidelines for writing a book report. Write the report in final form.

   The Folly of the River is the story of a young girl who lives during the Middle Ages. A small river winds its way through the reeds and the underbrush near her home. Because no other children live in her area, she spends hours and hours at the water's edge. Eventually she learns to speak to the river in its own language. The river tells her an important secret.

C. Be sure that the paragraph you rewrote in Practice A is correct. Study it carefully, noting capital letters and punctuation. Then put the paper away and write the paragraph again as your teacher dictates it.

Apply

D. Reread the book report you wrote for Lesson 13.

   ### Edit Your Report
   - Check your **content.** Use items 1–3 in the blue box on page 165 as a guide.
   - Check your **style.** Item 4 in the blue box on page 165 may help.

   ### Proofread Your Report
   - Follow the points in items 5 and 6 on page 165. If you have quoted any material directly from the book, be sure it is enclosed in quotation marks.
   - Copy your report onto a clean sheet of paper.

Writing Titles

- Underline the titles of books, newspapers, TV shows, magazines, movies, record albums, musical compositions, and plays. In printed material these appear in italic type.

  <u>Ghosts I Have Been</u>, <u>Cleveland Plain Dealer</u>, <u>Time</u>, <u>Star Wars</u>

- Place titles of songs, stories, articles, chapters, and poems in quotation marks.

  ''The Star Spangled Banner,'' ''The Open Window,'' ''Old Ironsides''

- Capitalize the first word and all other important words in a title.

  <u>The Lion, the Witch and the Wardrobe</u>

Copy these sentences. Punctuate them correctly.

1. My favorite book is a wrinkle in time.
2. The orchestra is playing the song moon river.
3. This issue of natural history is very interesting.
4. Shall we see alice in wonderland this afternoon?
5. My sister watches city news roundup on TV.
6. Your copy of the book facts about ants is missing.
7. Where is that article how to build a birdhouse?
8. Earline calls her story frankenstein rides a horse.
9. Our carrier delivers the news tribune every day.
10. Guadalupe bought the record album the wizard of oz.
11. Sakura memorized the poem hold fast your dreams.
12. My father is reading the novel war and peace.
13. His cousin is appearing in the play our town.
14. How many times have you seen the movie star wars?
15. The violinist is practicing the work called afternoon of a faun.

LITERATURE

Lesson 15: Reading Myths

Imagine that you lived thousands of years ago. Every day you saw natural events that you could not explain. Thunder and lightning, sunrise and sunset, and the changes of season were all great mysteries. To explain some of these things, you might have made up a story.

Think and Discuss

Myths are stories that were created hundreds of years ago. They served as explanations for events that occur in the world around us. For a long time people knew very little about the scientific reasons for events in the world.

In myths, early people created a system of gods and goddesses who looked like humans, but lived forever and had great powers. Read this myth about Demeter and Persephone to find out what natural event is explained.

Demeter and Persephone

Ingri and Edgar Parin D'Aulaire

Persephone was the daughter of Demeter, goddess of the harvest, and her mother loved her so dearly she could not bear to have her out of her sight. When Demeter sat on her golden throne, her daughter was always on her lap; when she went down to earth to look after her trees and fields, she took Persephone. Wherever Persephone danced on her light feet, flowers sprang up. She was so lovely and full of grace that even Hades, who saw so little, noticed her and fell in love with her. He wanted her for his queen, but he knew that her mother would never consent to part with her, so he decided to carry her off.

One day as Persephone ran about in the meadow gathering flowers, she strayed away from her mother. Suddenly, the ground split open and up from the yawning crevice came a dark chariot drawn by black horses. At the reins stood grim Hades. He seized the terrified girl, turned his horses, and plunged back into the ground.

With the frightened girl in his arms, Hades raced his horses down, away from the sunny world. Down and down they sped on the dark path to his underground palace. He led weeping Persephone in, located her beside him on a throne of black marble, and decked her with gold and precious stones. But the jewels brought her no joy. She wanted no cold stones. She longed for warm sunshine and flowers and her golden-haired mother.

Above, on earth, Demeter ran about searching for her lost daughter, and all nature sorrowed with her. Flowers wilted, trees lost their leaves, and the fields grew barren and cold. In vain did the plow cut through the icy ground; nothing could grow while the goddess of the harvest wept. People and animals went hungry, and the gods begged Demeter again to bless the earth. But she refused to let anything grow until she had found her daughter.

Bent with sorrow, Demeter turned into a gray old woman. She returned to the meadow where Persephone had vanished and asked the sun if he had seen what had happened. But he said no, dark clouds had hidden his face that day. She wandered around the meadow, and after a while she met a youth whose name was Triptolemus. He told her that his brother, a swineherd, had seen his pigs disappear into the ground and had heard the frightened screams of a girl.

Demeter now understood that Hades had kidnapped her daughter, and her sorrow turned to anger. She called to Zeus and said that she would never again make the earth green if he did not command Hades to return Persephone. Zeus could not let the world perish, and he sent Hermes down to Hades, bidding him to let Persephone go. Even Hades had to obey the orders of Zeus, and sadly he said farewell to his queen.

Joyfully, Persephone leaped to her feet, but as she was leaving with Hermes, a hooting laugh came from the garden. There stood the gardener of Hades, grinning. He pointed to a pomegranate from which a few of the kernels were missing. Persephone, lost in thought, had eaten the seeds, he said.

Then Hades smiled. He watched Hermes lead Persephone up to the bright world above. He knew that she must return to him, for she had tasted the food of the dead.

When Persephone again appeared on earth, Demeter sprang to her feet with a cry of joy and rushed to greet her daughter. No longer was she the sad old woman, but a radiant goddess. Again she blessed her fields and the flowers bloomed anew and the grain ripened.

"Dear child," she said, "never again shall we be parted. Together we shall make all nature bloom." But joy was soon changed to sadness, for Persephone had to admit that she had tasted the food of the dead and must return to Hades. However, Zeus decided that mother and daughter should not be parted forever. He ruled that Persephone had to return to Hades and spend one month in the underworld for each seed she had eaten.

Every year, when Persephone left her, Demeter grew sad, nothing grew, and there was winter on earth. But as soon as her daughter's light footsteps were heard, the whole earth burst into bloom. Spring had come. As long as mother and daughter were together, the earth was warm and bore fruit.

Demeter was a kind goddess. She did not want people to starve during the cold months of winter when Persephone was away. She lent her chariot, laden with grain, to

Triptolemus, the youth who had helped her to find her lost daughter. She told him to scatter her golden grain over the world and teach people how to sow it in spring and reap it in fall and store it away for the long months when again the earth was barren and cold.

Remember This

1. **A myth is a story that explains natural events.**
2. **Myths feature gods and goddesses.**
3. **Gods and goddesses have great powers and live forever.**
4. **Gods and goddesses often symbolize natural objects or events.**
5. **Myths often teach common-sense lessons that are still valid today.**

Practice

A. Copy these sentences. Complete each with the correct answer.

1. This myth explains the coming of _____.
   a. floods   **b.** winter   **c.** meteors   **d.** clouds
2. Demeter was the goddess of _____.
   a. horses   **b.** nymphs   **c.** the harvest   **d.** summer
3. In this myth, winter occurs because _____.
   a. Demeter is sad   **b.** Zeus is angry
   c. the sun goes out
4. In this myth, spring comes back when _____.
   a. Hades laughs   **b.** flowers bloom
   c. Persephone returns
5. In this myth, winter lasts _____.
   a. a few months   **b.** one year   **c.** underground
   d. three days

B. Using the myth of Demeter and Persephone, answer these questions.

6. Give one example of the supernatural powers of Hades.
7. How do you know that Demeter's powers were great?
8. The characters in nature myths often resemble the powers they have over the earth. How do both Demeter and the earth change when Persephone is absent?
9. The main characters in myths often *symbolize,* or stand for, various happenings in nature. Explain how Persephone was a *symbol* of spring.
10. Give an example of how both Hades and his kingdom *symbolize* death.

Apply

C. Get ready to write a myth of your own.

Prewriting
- Select a topic like high and low tides, phases of the moon, rain, or some other natural event.
- Choose an audience for your myth.
- Think of a possible mythological explanation for your topic.
- Think of various ways in which the gods or goddesses could be involved in your explanation.
- List several explanations. Circle the one you like best.

Composing
- Using the details you have noted, develop a nature myth around your topic. Have the characters symbolize natural events.

Revising
- When you are finished writing, read your myth. Be sure it makes sense.
- Check that the events in your myth are in a logical order.

- Check that your myth moves smoothly from introduction to conclusion.
- Check for proper spelling, punctuation, and mechanics.
- Copy your revised myth onto a clean sheet of paper.

A BOOK TO READ

Title: Among the Dolls
Author: William Sleator
Publisher: E. P. Dutton

The last thing Vicky wanted was an ugly old antique dollhouse for a birthday present. She had counted on a ten-speed bicycle. Slowly, though, she felt the almost magnetic pull of the toy. At first the dolls played nicely with each other as Vicky moved them about. Then the nastiness began. To Vicky's horror, her own life began to change too! Her usually gentle mother scolded and nagged the girl for her lack of friends and her grades that had begun to drop lately. The worse her own life became, the worse the dolls behaved. Then it happened. . . .

About to take the daughter doll out of the dollhouse, Vicky felt dizzy and closed her eyes for a minute. When she opened them, she was *inside* the dollhouse! "You are small and helpless now, I see," said the aunt doll softly. Her painted smiling mouth did not move at all, and it was more terrifying than anything Vicky had ever seen. Too late, Vicky realized that whatever happened in the tiny house was reflected in her own real family. What could she do?

This is a chilling story with an unusual plot. The black-and-white pictures by Trina Hyman match the mood exactly.

UNIT TEST

● **Action Verbs and Linking Verbs**   pages 134–137

Copy these sentences. Underline the action verb(s) or linking verb(s) in each sentence. Write *A* after each sentence with an action verb and *B* after each sentence with a linking verb.

1. Most of Africa's rivers rise in the highlands and flow to the seas.
2. The Nile, an African river, is the longest in the world.
3. The Nile travels 4,187 miles northward to the Mediterranean Sea.
4. The Congo and the Niger are the next longest rivers in Africa.
5. These two rivers empty into the Atlantic Ocean.

● **Helping Verbs and Main Verbs**   pages 138–139

Copy these sentences. Underline each main verb and circle each helping verb.

6. Africa's waterfalls are considered one of its loveliest features.
7. These spectacular waterfalls have slowed Africa's development.
8. Waterfalls have made travel difficult in many areas.
9. Nevertheless, it is believed that they will produce much power.
10. Until now, few African waterfalls have been used for this purpose.

● **Principal Parts of Regular and Irregular Verbs**   pages 140–145

Copy these sentences. Choose the correct principal part of the verb in parentheses ( ).

11. The height of Africa's Mount Kilimanjaro has been (measure, measured) at 19,340 feet.
12. Ice and snow have always (covered, cover) Mount Kilimanjaro.
13. Few plants can (grow, grew) there except on its lower slopes.
14. Roderigo has (chose, chosen) to write a report on the geography of Africa.
15. He will (know, known) a great deal about Africa when he has (finish, finished).

16. Roderigo's grandfather (serve, served) in Africa during World War II.

17. Roderigo's grandfather had (swam, swum) in Lake Tanganyika; Roderigo (says, say) that he will also (swim, swum) there someday.

18. Many years from now Roderigo will (take, took) his trip to Africa.

19. When he has (grow, grown) up, he will (fly, flew) there and (begin, began) his travels.

20. For now he will simply (write, written) his paper on Africa while he (thinks, thought) about the future.

● **Verb Tenses**   pages 146–149

Write sentences using the verb form in parentheses ( ).

21. he (*fly*, future)   **22.** Arthur (*drink*, past)
23. you (*know*, past)   **24.** she (*wear*, present perfect)
25. it (*freeze*, future)   **26.** they (*speak*, present)
27. we (*sing*, past)   **28.** I (*give*, present perfect)
29. he (*laugh*, present)   **30.** you (*catch*, future)

● **Verb Complements**   pages 150–151

Copy these sentences. Label each underlined verb *transitive* or *intransitive*. Then label any verb complements *PN* for predicate nominative or *DO* for direct object.

31. Africa <u>is</u> one of the warmest continents in the world.

32. Its climate <u>combines</u> heat with too much or too little rain.

33. Heavy tropical rains <u>batter</u> the Guinea coast and the Congo basin.

34. Some areas <u>receive</u> 150 inches (3.75 m) of rain a year.

35. The Sahara, however, <u>is</u> the driest part of the African continent.

● **The Parts of a Book**   pages 154–155

Copy these sentences. Complete each with a correct book part.

1. The _____ contains definitions of unfamiliar words used in the book.

2. The _____ lists items or chapters in the book in the order in which they are presented.

3. The _____ contains the place and date of the book's publication.

4. The _____ lists items in the book in alphabetical order.

5. The name of the book and its author are printed on the _____.

● **Skimming and Scanning**   pages 156–157

Decide whether each person should skim or scan to find the information he or she wants. Write *skim* or *scan* on your paper.

6. Jack is leafing through a biography of Henry Ford to find out the name of his first mass-produced car.

7. Maria wants to find her aunt's phone number in the local telephone directory.

8. Jack found a book called *The Only Way to Train a Dog.* He wants to know whether there is a chapter on training guide dogs.

● **Prewriting, Composing, and Revising — Book Report**

pages 158–166

1. Choose a book that you enjoyed. Copy this form on your paper. Fill in the form to summarize the plot of your book.

Main character's problem: _____

Things he/she does to try to solve it: _____

Other characters who help or hinder: _____

Most exciting event in the story: _____

Hint about how problem is solved: _____

Then write a book report on the book you chose. Include information for each of the five guidelines for writing a book report. Edit and proofread your report.

● **Mechanics Practice**   page 167

Write correctly these sentences that contain titles.

2. Today's new york times carries an article called the cascade mountains, a new american playground.

3. Do you like the song we've only just begun?

4. Carl Sandburg's poem fog is one of my favorites.

5. Pat is reading the short story the open window.

6. Have you watched upstairs, downstairs on TV?

● Reading Myths   pages 168–173

Read this myth. Then answer the questions that follow.

During the early years of rule by the gods and goddesses of Nimyar, the hours of the day were ruled by Arcite. The world was still very new and was completely covered with a heavy mist. Because the mist was so cold and damp, the people of earth complained to Rontag, king of the gods.

"We cannot work, we cannot eat, we cannot sleep with these damp clouds covering the land. We are tired of living like this," they groaned.

"The people are right," Rontag decided. "I must do something to help them." So he sent for Arcite.

Arcite arrived at Rontag's palace with his two daughters, Daia and Nita. "How can I help you, Lord Rontag?" he asked.

"See here, Arcite," Rontag answered. "You are the god of the hours. You must do something to take away this gray mist that covers the people. Give them change and warmth."

Immediately Daia and Nita agreed to take Rontag's work upon themselves. Arcite gave Daia a magic golden rope to carry, and he gave Nita a silver one. Then the girls flew straight up into the mist.

The girls wandered through space, marveling at the stars and planets scattered across the heavens. Finally Daia found a hot golden star which she tied with her rope and pulled after her toward Nimyar. Nita found a small silver planet that glowed with a soft, sweet light. She tied her silver rope around it and followed her sister.

As soon as the hot golden star reached the earth's atmosphere, the damp mist cleared, and the people rejoiced. The cool silver planet kept the star's heat from becoming too great.

Rontag and Arcite congratulated the two girls on their work and put them in permanent charge of the heavens. Arcite decreed that Daia's golden star would rule the world every 12 hours and that this period would be called *day*. Nita's soft silver planet would glow for the other 12 hours, and that time would always be called *night*.

1. What natural happening does this myth describe?
2. What were the golden star and the silver planet?
3. Of what did the people complain to Rontag?
4. How did the gods and goddesses in this myth prove that they had supernatural powers?
5. Of what were Daia and Nita *symbols*?

MAINTENANCE and REVIEW

Sentences   pages 2–11

Copy these sentences. Next to each write *declarative, interrogative, imperative,* or *exclamatory.* Then write whether it is in *natural word order* or *inverted word order.* Draw one line under all simple subjects and two lines under all simple predicates.

1. In the southwest Pacific Ocean lies the Philippines.
2. More than 7,000 islands are a part of this country.
3. What is the capital of the Philippines?
4. Manila, on the island of Luzon, was founded in 1571.
5. The city has been called "The Pearl of the Orient."
6. What a beautiful place Manila must be!
7. Manila produces sugar, soap, and coconut oil.
8. Manila's most important product, however, is abaca, a fiber.
9. How do people use this fiber?
10. Abaca can become rope, rugs, and cloth.

Paragraphs   pages 40–47

11.–15. Copy this paragraph. Underline the topic sentence. Do not copy any sentences that do not belong.

You may know February as the month in which Abraham Lincoln and George Washington were born, but many other important people were born in February. Thomas Edison was born on February 11, 1847. Novelists Charles Dickens and Jules Verne have February birthdays, as do poets Langston Hughes, Henry Wadsworth Longfellow, and Edna St. Vincent Millay. February, a cold month, brings snow to many parts of the country. "Buffalo Bill" Cody was born on February 26, 1846, and "Babe" Ruth was born on February 6, 1895. On February 21, 1972, Richard M. Nixon became the first American President to visit China. Susan B. Anthony, Enrico Caruso, Charles A. Lindbergh, Galileo, and W.E.B. Du Bois are among the other famous people born in February.

Common and Proper Nouns   pages 90–91

16.–30. Reread sentences 1–10. Copy 4 proper nouns and 11 common nouns that appear in those sentences.

Noun Plurals and Possessive Nouns   pages 92–93, 96–97

Write the plural and possessive forms of these nouns.

31. boy   **32.** dress   **33.** baby   **34.** Alberto
35. woman   **36.** Alex   **37.** tank   **38.** fish

Verbs   pages 134–139

39.–48. Reread the exercises entitled "Sentences" and "Paragraphs." Copy five main verbs and their helping verbs. Then copy three action verbs and two linking verbs.

Principal Parts of Verbs   pages 140–145

Write the principal parts of these verbs.

49. take   **50.** talk   **51.** catch   **52.** begin
53. ring   **54.** wear   **55.** lift   **56.** choose

Verb Tenses   pages 146–149

Copy these sentences, using the correct tense of the verb in parentheses ( ). Use at least once each of the four tenses you have learned. Next to each sentence, write the name of the tense.

57. This pond always _____ in December.   (freeze)
58. _____ your father _____ with us later, Patwin?   (skate)
59. I _____ these warm gloves in town last weekend.   (buy)
60. _____ everybody _____ the good news on the radio?   (hear)
61. It _____ later tonight.   (snow)
62. How many pairs of gloves _____ you _____ so far?   (buy)
63. I _____ already _____ two pairs this winter.   (lose)
64. _____ you _____ care of your new pair now?   (take)

Direct Objects and Predicate Nominatives   pages 150–151

65.–70. Reread the exercises entitled "Sentences," "Paragraphs," and "Verb Tenses." Copy three direct objects and three predicate nominatives that appear in those exercises.

5

LANGUAGE
Learning About
Adjectives and Adverbs

STUDY SKILLS
Combining
Word Parts

COMPOSITION
**Writing
Descriptions**

LITERATURE
**Reading Lyric
Poetry**

Have you ever tried to describe a scene to someone? If you have, you know that you need to picture the scene in your mind. Close your eyes and picture a scene that contains waterfalls, flowers, shrubs, and trees. After you have a clear picture in your mind, open your eyes and look at the photograph on the left. Did you picture the same scene as the one in the photograph? You probably did not because you were not given all the details about that specific scene.

Look at the picture again. What details might you add to the word *flowers?* Choices such as *bright, tall, brilliant, red, scarlet,* and *willowy* all describe the flowers. As you know, these words are *adjectives.* Adjectives help readers form clear pictures in their minds. How does the water tumble? You might have used an adverb such as *smoothly* to answer that question. Adverbs also make writing vivid and interesting.

In this unit you will be studying not only about adjectives and adverbs but also about prefixes, suffixes, and roots. You will use your knowledge of adjectives and adverbs to write descriptive paragraphs. Finally you will read lyric poems and use them as models for composing your own descriptive lyric poem.

Now turn the page and start describing!

◀ *Tropical foliage, Burney Falls in California*

LANGUAGE

Lesson 1: Understanding Common, Proper, and Predicate Adjectives

Read these sentences. Notice how the addition of the underlined words gives a clear picture.

1. A horse gallops along the shore.
2. A <u>black</u> <u>Arabian</u> horse gallops along the <u>rocky</u> shore.
3. The waves break upon the coast.
4. The waves, <u>icy</u> and <u>gray</u>, break upon the <u>English</u> coast.

Think and Discuss

The underlined words in each sentence above are **adjectives.** Adjectives tell something about nouns. The words *black* and *Arabian* describe the noun *horse.* They change, or modify, the idea of a horse by telling what it is like. The word *rocky* modifies the noun *shore.* Which noun is modified by the words *icy* and *gray*? Which noun is modified by the word *English*?

> ● An **adjective** is a word used to modify a noun or pronoun. It answers the questions *what kind, which one, whose, or how many.*

Most adjectives come directly *before* the nouns they modify. The **articles** *a, an,* and *the,* for example, always do this. Sometimes, however, adjectives will *follow* these nouns. Look back at sentences 2 and 4. Do the underlined adjectives come before or after the nouns they modify?

Some adjectives are formed from proper nouns. These adjectives are called **proper adjectives.** All other adjectives are called **common adjectives.**

> • A **proper adjective** is formed from a proper noun. It begins with a capital letter.

Some proper adjectives are formed from proper nouns that name places. These proper adjectives are sometimes formed by adding *n* or *an* to the proper noun. Proper adjectives for *Africa, Asia,* and *Australia* are *African, Asian,* and *Australian.* Other proper adjectives require different spellings as in these examples.

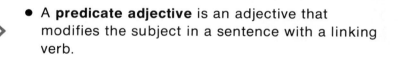

China — Chinese Denmark — Danish France — French
Greece — Greek Israel — Israeli Norway — Norwegian
Peru — Peruvian Switzerland — Swiss Thailand — Thai

Adjectives can also be connected by linking verbs to the nouns they modify. When they are used as complements, they are called **predicate adjectives.**

> • A **predicate adjective** is an adjective that modifies the subject in a sentence with a linking verb.

Predicate adjectives usually follow linking verbs. When sentences are in inverted order, however, the predicate adjectives come *before* their linking verbs. Read these examples of sentences in both kinds of order.

5. The cave was dark.
6. Dark was the cave.
7. The grass was cool and wet.
8. Cool and wet was the grass.

Which word modifies the noun *cave* in sentences 5 and 6? Which words are predicate adjectives in sentences 7 and 8?

Practice

A. Rewrite each sentence correctly, capitalizing each proper adjective. Then circle the common adjectives.

1. The jockey, angry and upset, had lost a lucky greek coin.
2. The quiet trainer spoke gently to the gruff owner.
3. "She's a fine rider," he said, pointing to the korean girl.
4. The chestnut arabian stallion looked like a winner.
5. The tired, gallant horse had won two european races.

B. Copy each sentence. Underline the predicate adjectives. Circle the word that is modified.

6. From a distance, the crowd seemed noisy.
7. We were anxious to see who would win.
8. A thousand fans became nervous and tense.
9. The jockey looked familiar.
10. Happy were the friends of the winner.

C. Complete these sentences with predicate adjectives.

11. At the start of the race we were _____.
12. The training seemed _____ and _____.
13. _____ were our hopes.
14. The weather became _____ for the race.
15. Our horse looked _____.

Apply

D. Write the proper adjectives formed from these proper nouns. Then use each proper adjective in a sentence.

16. Spain   17. Mexico   18. Peru   19. China

Write a sentence containing a predicate adjective for each linking verb on this list.

20. am   21. are   22. was
23. were   24. had been   25. seem
26. look   27. become   28. could be

Lesson 2: Comparing with Adjectives

Notice how the adjective *deep* is used in the following sentences.

1. The Atlantic Ocean is <u>deep</u>.
2. The Pacific Ocean is <u>deeper</u> than the Atlantic.
3. The Pacific is the <u>deepest</u> ocean in the world.

Think and Discuss

Most adjectives have three forms. These three forms are called the three **degrees of comparison.** They are the **positive degree,** the **comparative degree,** and the **superlative degree.** In sentence 1 the adjective is in the positive degree. The sentence simply makes a statement about the Atlantic Ocean. In the second sentence the adjective is in the comparative degree. How many things does the adjective *deeper* compare? In the third sentence the adjective is in the superlative degree. How many things are compared by the adjective *deepest*?

> - The **positive degree** of an adjective is used when only one thing is described.
> - The **comparative degree** of an adjective is used when two things are compared.
> - The **superlative degree** of an adjective is used when three or more things are compared.

The comparative and superlative degrees of most one-syllable adjectives are formed by adding *er* and *est* to the positive form. In words of one syllable, when the final consonant is preceded by a vowel, double the final consonant before adding an ending. For one-syllable adjectives that end in *e,* drop the *e* before adding comparative and superlative endings. Read the examples on the following page.

Positive	Comparative	Superlative
small	smaller	smallest
big	bigger	biggest
nice	nicer	nicest

To form the comparative and superlative degrees of adjectives that end in a consonant and *y*, add *er* and *est* after changing the *y* to *i*.

Positive	Comparative	Superlative
dry	drier	driest
funny	funnier	funniest
lonely	lonelier	loneliest

Most adjectives of three or more syllables require *more* and *most* or *less* and *least* to form the comparative and superlative degrees.

Positive	Comparative	Superlative
enjoyable	more enjoyable	most enjoyable
enjoyable	less enjoyable	least enjoyable

The degrees of comparison of some adjectives are formed in special ways.

Positive	Comparative	Superlative
good	better	best
bad	worse	worst
many	more	most

Practice

A. Copy these adjectives. Next to each write its degree of comparison.

1. brighter
2. least capable
3. saddest
4. more worthy
5. simple
6. happier
7. worse
8. most thrilling
9. shiny

B. Write the comparative and superlative forms of these adjectives.

10. skillful   11. joyous   12. lovely
13. cheerful   14. strong   15. friendly
16. tough   17. good   18. successful

C. Rewrite each of these sentences. Use the correct form of the adjective in parentheses ( ).

19. The blue whale is _____ than an elephant. (large)
20. A storm at sea is _____ than a storm on land. (dangerous)
21. People who exercise regularly are usually _____ than those who do not. (healthy)
22. An ocean cruise is the _____ vacation of all. (good)
23. A dolphin is _____ than a sea snail. (intelligent)
24. Whales sing _____ songs. (beautiful)
25. They are _____ to humans than eels are. (friendly)

Apply

D. **26.–30.** Write three sentences using the comparative degrees of *quick, dependable,* and *efficient.* Write two sentences using the superlative degrees of *talkative* and *valuable.*

To Memorize

Hope is a thing with feathers
That perches in the soul,
And sings the tune without the words,
And never stops at all.

Emily Dickinson

1. To what does the poet compare hope?
2. How are these two things alike?

Lesson 3: Understanding Adverbs

Read these sentences.

1. In 1529, 234 sailors sailed <u>bravely</u> from Spain.
2. Eighteen returned three years <u>later</u>.
3. All were glad to be <u>back</u> in Spain.
4. They had experienced <u>very</u> bad times.

What question does each of the underlined words answer?

Think and Discuss

The underlined words in sentences 1–4 are **adverbs.** They modify verbs, adjectives, and other adverbs. In sentence 1, for example, *bravely* modifies the verb *sailed* by answering the question *how.* In sentence 3, *back* acts as an adverb modifying the verb *to be.* It answers the question *where.* The adverb *very* in sentence 4 modifies the adjective *bad.* It states to what degree or to what extent the times were bad. What word does *later* modify in sentence 2? What question does it answer?

> • An **adverb** is a word that modifies a verb, adjective, or other adverb. It answers the questions *how, when, where,* and *to what extent.*

Adverbs that modify verbs can be placed either before or after the verbs. Those that modify adjectives and adverbs, however, usually come before the words they modify.

Read these examples of adverbs that answer each of the four questions.

How?—brightly, kindly, well, quietly
When?—now, later, tomorrow, first
Where?—here, there, away, nearby
To what extent?—very, mostly, quite

Practice

A. Copy these sentences. Underline the adverbs and circle the word or words they modify.

1. Ferdinand Magellan's crew circled the globe completely.
2. Magellan sailed on the ship *Trinidad*, which was well equipped.
3. During the day it was fairly simple for the other ships to follow the *Trinidad*.
4. Magellan prepared carefully for nighttime sailing.
5. At night the *Trinidad* carried a brightly burning light called a *farol*.

B. Copy these sentences. Then write whether the underlined adverb tells *how, when, where,* or *to what extent*. Write whether the word it modifies is a verb, an adjective, or an adverb.

6. The other ships could follow the farol <u>easily</u> on the darkest night.
7. <u>Occasionally</u> Magellan would set another light beside the farol.
8. <u>Then</u> all the other ships lit a single light.
9. Magellan counted the lights to make sure the entire fleet was <u>there</u>.
10. It was a <u>very</u> easy method to use.

Apply

C. 11.–20. Write a paragraph about a historical or imaginary ocean voyage. Use ten different adverbs in your paragraph.

Lesson 4: Comparing with Adverbs

Which of these sentences compares one action with another?

1. You and I laugh loudly.
2. I laugh louder than you do.

Think and Discuss

Adverbs have degrees of comparison just as adjectives do.

> - The **positive degree** of an adverb is used when only one thing is described.
> - The **comparative degree** of an adverb is used when two things are compared.
> - The **superlative degree** of an adverb is used when three or more things are compared.

The comparative and superlative degrees of most one-syllable adverbs and a few two-syllable adverbs are formed by adding *er* and *est* to the positive form. Remember to change *y* to *i* if the adverb ends in a consonant and *y*. The comparative and superlative of most adverbs that end in *ly* or that have two or more syllables are formed by adding *more* and *most* or *less* and *least*.

Positive	Comparative	Superlative
soon	sooner	soonest
early	earlier	earliest
calmly	more calmly	most calmly
quietly	less quietly	least quietly

A few adverbs have special forms.

Positive	Comparative	Superlative
well	better	best
little	less	least
much	more	most

Some adverbs cannot be used to make comparisons. Some of these are: *too, never, always, not, here,* and *there.*

Practice

A. Copy these adverbs and write their degrees of comparison.

1. soon
2. best
3. more
4. more carefully
5. neatly
6. earlier
7. least swiftly
8. anxiously
9. fastest
10. less gently
11. nearer
12. recently

B. 13.–24. Write the other degrees of each adverb in Practice A.

Apply

C. 25.–35. Write a paragraph about an imaginary contest you have entered. Use at least eleven adverbs in different degrees of comparison.

HOW OUR LANGUAGE GROWS

Hundreds of words have been made using the names of people. The word *sandwich* was named for the *Earl of Sandwich.* Thanks to the scientist *Louis Pasteur,* we have *pasteurized* milk. Did you ever eat beef *Stroganoff?* You can thank the nineteenth-century Russian diplomat *Count Paul Stroganoff* for this delicious dish named after him.

1. Look up these words in a dictionary or encyclopedia. Find out which people gave their names to them.

   a. peach melba   **b.** guppy   **c.** dunce

2. Many flowers and trees have been named after people. Use your dictionary to find out where these words come from.

   d. fuchsia   **e.** magnolia   **f.** sequoia redwood   **g.** Douglas fir

Lesson 5: Using Adjectives and Adverbs

Read these sentences.

1. I did a <u>good</u> job on this painting.
2. I paint <u>well</u>.
3. Are you <u>well</u> enough to work?

Which of the underlined words are adjectives? Which are adverbs?

Think and Discuss

Words can often be used as different parts of speech. *Well,* for example, can be either an adjective or an adverb, depending on its job in a sentence. In sentence 2 *well* is an adverb answering the question *how.* In sentence 3, however, it is a predicate adjective that means "healthy." It modifies *you* and follows the linking verb *are.* The word *good* is always an adjective.

Look at these sentences.

4. We had an <u>early</u> class, and we finished <u>early</u>.
5. Our <u>fast</u> runner ran <u>fastest</u> in the race.

When *early* modifies the noun *class,* it is an adjective. When it modifies the verb *finished,* it answers the question *when* and is an adverb. How are the forms of *fast* used in sentence 5?

The word *not* is a negative adverb. Whenever you use it in a sentence, be sure to combine it with positive words as in these examples.

6. I did <u>not</u> finish <u>anything</u> today.
7. I did<u>n't</u> go <u>anywhere</u>.

Using the words *nothing* and *nowhere* instead of *anything* and *anywhere* would have resulted in two negative words in the same sentence.

Sometimes short sentences containing adjectives and adverbs can be combined into a single, longer sentence. How have sentences 8 and 9 become sentence 10?

8. This painting is bright and colorful.
9. It looks good on my wall.
10. This bright, colorful painting looks good on my wall.

Practice

A. Copy these sentences. Write whether the underlined words are adjectives or adverbs.

1. The patient instructor taught clearly.
2. A new student listened attentively.
3. Some large paintings were completed today.
4. Arlene cleaned her favorite brush carefully.
5. My oil painting is hanging there.

B. Use *good* or *well* to complete each sentence below.

6. My painting looks _____.
7. It was a _____ day for me.
8. Yesterday I felt ill, but today I feel _____.
9. My instructor paints really _____.
10. He also gives _____ advice.

C. Combine each set of sentences into one sentence.

11. a. I painted a seascape.   b. The seascape was beautiful.
    c. I painted it yesterday.
12. a. My aunt uses paints.   b. They are oil paints.
    c. She uses them well.
13. a. I will try my new paints.   b. My paints are acrylic.
    c. I will try them outside.

Apply

D. 14.–23. Write sentences using *any, anywhere, anything, anybody, anyway* with the adverb *not*. Write sentences using *no, nowhere, nothing, nobody, never.*

LANGUAGE REVIEW

Common, Proper, and Predicate Adjectives   pages 182–184

Copy these sentences. Draw one line under all common adjectives and two lines under all proper adjectives. Circle any predicate adjectives.

1. Edwin Herbert Land is the inventor of the instant camera.
2. In high school he was a brilliant student.
3. During his busy college years Land started a small business.
4. He made a glare-free plastic sheet; he called it a Polaroid filter.
5. Most carmakers were not interested in Polaroid windshields.
6. So Land used his clever invention in sunglasses.
7. By 1945 Land's small American company had earned 15 million dollars.
8. Land's business soon grew larger.
9. His employees were talented and eager.
10. Before long, European and South American stores were ordering Polaroid sunglasses.
11. Land became very successful.
12. His idea for a new camera was creative and inspired.

Comparing with Adjectives   pages 185–187

Complete these sentences with the correct degree of comparison of the adjective in parentheses ( ).

13. Land began his _____ invention, the instant camera, in the 1940's. (important)
14. Land had been taking _____ photographs of his family. (many)
15. His daughter Jennifer was _____ than Land himself was. (impatient)
16. She wanted to see a _____ photo that Land had just snapped. (beautiful)
17. Land thought that the idea of an instant camera was the _____ one he had yet worked on. (interesting)

Adverbs   pages 188–189

Copy these sentences. Underline all the adverbs.

18. An almost unknown woman, Augusta Rogers, was an inventor.
19. Rogers had grown very cold riding in unheated automobiles.
20. She quickly invented an auto heater that did not need fire.
21. Her invention was first used in Brooklyn, New York.
22. Later Rogers's heater was installed in new cars.

Comparing with Adverbs   pages 190–191

Complete these sentences with the correct degree of comparison of the adverbs in parentheses ( ).

23. An auto spark arrester was Rogers's _____ planned invention. (carefully)
24. Her next invention, a folding chair, was _____ designed. (beautifully)
25. Her last invention was _____ accepted than the chair. (eagerly)
26. It was a net canopy that was _____ against mosquitoes. (effective)
27. The _____ thing about Augusta Rogers was that she completed all these inventions in only four years. (amazing)

Using Adjectives and Adverbs   pages 192–193

Combine each group of sentences into a single longer sentence.

28. Janna was tired. She was unhappy. She waited for the train.
29. She had missed the first train. It was the early train.
30. She decided to invent a wristwatch alarm. She decided suddenly.
31. Later, Janna was upset to learn that wristwatch alarms had already been invented. She was disappointed.
32. Nevertheless, Janna bought a wristwatch alarm and was happy. She was contented.

Applying Adjectives and Adverbs

33.–42. Write ten sentences about something you might invent. Use adjectives and adverbs to describe it.

STUDY SKILLS

Lesson 6: Understanding Prefixes

1. Joanne said, "My brother Andy is so <u>irresponsible</u>!"
2. "No, he's not," I said. "He's just <u>independent</u>."

What do both of the underlined words have in common?

Think and Discuss

A **base word** is a complete word that has no syllables attached to it. Often new words are made from base words plus other syllables. If those syllables are placed *before* the base word, they are known as **prefixes.**

> • A **prefix** is a syllable or syllables added to the beginning of a word to change its meaning.

The base word of the underlined adjective in sentence 1 is *responsible.* Adding the prefix *ir,* which means *not,* changes the meaning to *not responsible.* What is the base word in sentence 2? How does the prefix change it? Study this chart of prefixes.

Prefix	Meaning	New Word
bi	two, twice	<u>bimonthly</u>
dis	away, off, lack of, not	<u>displease</u>
ex-	former	<u>ex-mayor</u>
extra	outside of, beyond	<u>extraordinary</u>
fore	before, in front, ahead	<u>foreground</u>
il	not (often before *l*)	<u>illegal</u>
im	not (often before *m*)	<u>imbalance</u>
in	not	<u>incomplete</u>
ir	not (often before *r*)	<u>irregular</u>

Prefix	Meaning	New Word
mis	badly, wrong, not	<u>mis</u>understand
non	not	<u>non</u>sense
over	too much, above	<u>over</u>eat
post	after	<u>post</u>war
pre	before	<u>pre</u>heat
re	back, again	<u>re</u>trace
semi	half of, partly	<u>semi</u>circle
tri	three	<u>tri</u>cycle
un	not	<u>un</u>clear
un	the opposite of	<u>un</u>lock

Practice

A. Write these words on your paper. Circle each prefix. Write the definition of each word.

1. bicycle
2. misuse
3. dissatisfied
4. improper
5. nonpoisonous
6. forewarn
7. semiannual
8. illegible
9. overdo

B. Match these prefixes and base words to make new words. Write the new words.

Prefix	Base Word
10. semi	view
11. tri	manageable
12. pre	movable
13. re	final
14. im	appear
15. un	angle

Apply

C. **16.–25.** Write as many words as you can that begin with the prefix *un*. Then check a dictionary to see how many are correct. Write ten sentences using at least one of your words in each.

Lesson 7: Understanding Suffixes

Read these sentences.

1. This melon is certainly <u>sweet</u>.
2. I have never tasted such <u>sweetness</u> before.

How are the underlined words different?

Think and Discuss

You have already learned that syllables added to the front of base words can change their meaning. Syllables added to the *ends* of base words, however, can change both their *meaning* and their *part of speech*. For example, the word *sweet* in sentence 1 is an adjective modifying the noun *melon*. In sentence 2, however, the word *sweetness* is a noun used as the direct object of the verb *tasted*. *Sweetness* means "the quality of being sweet." The ending *-ness* that changes the part of speech of the word *sweet* is a **suffix**.

> • A **suffix** is a syllable or syllables added to the end of a base word. A suffix changes the base word's *part of speech* and sometimes changes its *meaning*.

Study this chart of common suffixes.

	Suffix	Base Word	New Word
	able	depend (verb)	depend<u>able</u>
	ible	suggest (verb)	suggest<u>ible</u>
Adjective-	ful	power (noun)	power<u>ful</u>
Forming	ish	child (noun)	child<u>ish</u>
Suffixes	less	help (noun)	help<u>less</u>
	ous	danger (noun)	danger<u>ous</u>
	y	dirt (noun)	dirt<u>y</u>

Suffix	Base Word	New Word
ance	attend (verb)	attend<u>ance</u>
ence	depend (verb)	depend<u>ence</u>
er	farm (verb)	farm<u>er</u>
or	act (verb)	act<u>or</u>
ion	direct (verb)	direct<u>ion</u>
tion	reduce (verb)	reduc<u>tion</u>
ity	humid (adjective)	humid<u>ity</u>
ty	certain (adjective)	certain<u>ty</u>
ment	appoint (verb)	appoint<u>ment</u>
ness	gentle (adjective)	gentle<u>ness</u>
self	one (noun)	one<u>self</u>

Noun-Forming Suffixes applies to the group above.

en	thick (adjective)	thick<u>en</u>
n	wide (adjective)	wide<u>n</u>

Verb-Forming Suffixes applies to the group above.

ly	swift (adjective)	swift<u>ly</u>

Adverb-Forming Suffix applies to the group above.

Practice

A. Copy these words. Circle the suffix and underline any base words that change before the suffix is added. Write the original base word.

1. hunter
2. Spanish
3. healthy
4. acceptance
5. valueless
6. humanity
7. correction
8. strengthen
9. believable
10. government
11. joyful
12. creation

B. 13.–24. Copy the words in Practice A. Next to each write the definition, and tell how the new word differs *in use* from the original base word.

Apply

C. 25.–30. Write six words formed from base words and suffixes. Use each one in a sentence of your own.

Lesson 8: Understanding Roots

What do the words in each row have in common?

1. biology   geology   psychology
2. kilogram   kilometer   kilowatt

Think and Discuss

You already know how to add prefixes or suffixes to base words in order to form new words. **Roots** are like base words in that you can add prefixes, suffixes, and even other roots or base words to them. They are unlike base words in that they are only *word parts*, not whole words.

> • A **root** is a word part that can be combined with prefixes, suffixes, base words, and other roots to form new words.

Study this chart of roots and base words.

Root/Base Word	Meaning	New Word
aud, audio	hear	auditor
auto	self	automatic
bio	life	bionic
geo	earth	geometry
gram, graph (y)	write	telegram
kilo	thousand	kilowatt
log, logy	study of	psychology
meter	measure	centimeter
micro	small	microsurgery
multi	many	multimedia
phone, phono	hear	telephone
photo	light	photograph
scope, scopy	see	periscope
therm, thermo	heat	thermal
tele	far	television

Using the chart, give the definitions of *biology* and *geography*.

Practice

A. Copy these words. Draw a line between each word part.

1. microscope
2. kilometer
3. telegraph
4. microphone
5. phonograph
6. geology
7. autograph
8. telescope
9. autobiography
10. thermometer
11. audiometer
12. microbiology

B. 13.–24. Copy the words in Practice A. Find each word in the dictionary and write its meaning.

C. 25. Write the paragraph that your teacher will now read aloud.

Apply

D. 26.–37. Write twelve sentences using the words in Practice A.

A Challenge

Make a word-search puzzle using prefixes, roots, and suffixes. Write the words or word parts you used underneath the puzzle. Exchange puzzles with a classmate. Circle prefixes in blue, suffixes in red, and roots in green. When you are both finished, check each other's work to be sure all the words and word parts are correct.

COMPOSITION

Lesson 9:   Prewriting

Brainstorming for Descriptive Words

Sam's class was preparing to write descriptive paragraphs. They decided to work together on the planning stage, although each student would later write his or her own description. For a topic, they chose a stretch of ocean beach that they had all visited many times. What other steps would they work on together?

Think and Discuss

For a description, Sam's classmates needed **descriptive words** that appealed to their senses. They set up a diagram that looked like this one.

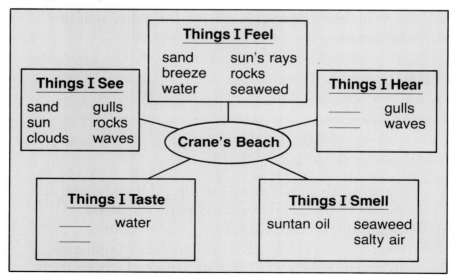

What other words might be added to the diagram? Why might some items be listed under more than one sense?

The next step was to take each item and list as many words as possible to describe them. Here is a partial list of words from the class's brainstorming session.

Things I Feel	Things I Hear

sun's rays: burning
      warm—pleasantly
      scorching
	gulls: shriek
	      call
	      swoop
	      swish
	      aw-k-k

breeze: cool
      refreshing—like
        lemon ice
      light
      teasing
      chilly
	waves: crash—mightily
	      roar—like
	        distant thunder
	      hiss—angrily?
	      break
	      foam

Notice that the class came up with verbs, adverbs, adjectives, and even some comparisons. As they considered each item on their lists, they limited themselves to descriptive words that appealed to each of the senses. Why, for example, would they not add *glistening* or *indigo blue* to the list of words describing the waves? What descriptive words might you list next to *seaweed* under the heading "Things I Smell"?

How to Brainstorm Descriptive Words

1. **Make a diagram or chart of the five senses. List the items from the scene you are describing that appeal to each sense.**
2. **Consider separately each object or item listed under a particular sense. Write as many words as you can to describe each one.**
3. **List descriptive words for each item that appeal *only* to the sense you are working on.**
4. **Add vivid comparisons to help your audience experience the scene as you did.**

Practice

A. Use the cluster of objects under "Things I See" from the first diagram. List as many descriptive words as you can under each item. Use the second diagram as a model.

B. Follow the directions for Practice A, but use the objects under "Things I Taste" and "Things I Smell."

Apply

C. Set up your own descriptive paragraph.

Choose Your Topic

● Choose a scene that you know well, a place that has made a strong impression on you. In remembering a particular picnic spot, for example, you might recall the smell of grilling hamburgers, the crackling of the fire, and the many different shades of green in the trees and grass.

● If you have many possibilities to choose from, select the one that you can best relive in your mind.

Choose Your Audience

● You might want to write your paragraph for a friend, who shared the experience or scene with you, or for a stranger, who is unaware that the place exists.

Brainstorm Your Details

● Follow the diagrams in your book. Remember to list *as many* descriptive words as you can. Do not worry about how good they are.

Review Your Work

● Look over your word lists one at a time. Circle the words that describe most vividly each scene. If new words occur to you while you are reading, add them to your lists.

● Save your work for the Apply exercise in Lesson 10.

Lesson 10:   Composing
Writing Descriptive Paragraphs

Read this paragraph.

The soft, white clouds and the bright, clear sky had been losing ground all afternoon. In from the east rolled huge, dark storm clouds that took over the area like an advancing army. Suddenly everything grew still. The cool breeze that had rustled the leaves was gone. The sparrows stopped chirping in the garden. A faint, greenish glow hung over the horizon, warning all to take cover. The storm was only seconds away!

What does this paragraph describe? To which of your senses does this description appeal?

Think and Discuss

Paragraphs that **describe** should appeal to the senses of the reader. That is, they should allow the reader to *see, feel, hear, taste,* and *smell* the object or scene described. However, you need not appeal to all five senses in one paragraph. In fact, you may want to concentrate on only one or two.

To appeal to the senses, the writer must choose precise, or exact, words. The adjectives *soft, white, bright,* and *clear* that describe the summer sky before the storm are balanced by the adjectives *huge* and *dark*. These words describing the storm clouds are given added power when the clouds are mentioned as *rolling* across the sky. Together with the phrases *had been losing ground* and *like an advancing army*, the *rolling* storm clouds were meant to make you think of enemy tanks. The storm is pictured as a powerful army "taking over" the bright blue summer sky.

Another aid in writing descriptive paragraphs is to combine adjectives and adverbs to make them modify a single word. Putting two or even three modifiers together can be very effective if it is not overdone. When two modifiers are put together as in *soft, white* and *faint, greenish,* a comma or the joining words *and, or,* and *but* usually connect them. If three modifiers are used, the first and second are separated by a comma and the second and third by a comma plus the word *and.*

Finally, as in other paragraphs, vary your sentences. In the example about the storm, sentences 3, 4, and 5 are shorter than the rest, and sentence 2 is written in inverted order. All of these touches help make your paragraph more interesting.

How to Write a Descriptive Paragraph

1. **Think about your scene and the overall impression it had on you. Your whole paragraph should build up the same effect.**
2. **Write an introductory sentence that sets the stage for your description. The sentence need not be a topic sentence of the type you wrote for other paragraphs.**
3. **Write detail sentences that support your topic and reinforce the feelings you have about it.**
4. **Use specific words to make your scene come alive.**
5. **Try to use two or more descriptive words in a sentence.**
6. **Vary your sentences in length, type, and structure.**

Practice

A. Read this paragraph. Then answer the questions.

The first sign that the storm had started was a sudden gust of wind. Stronger and stronger it grew, until young trees were bent almost double by its force. Then the rain began. Driven by the wind, it beat down the grass and whipped leaves off the trees. Whistling through tree branches, wind and rain lashed out, striking rocks and trees like icy knives. Surprised by its sudden, wild start, I stood at my window wondering at the storm's fearful power.

1. Which words in the paragraph appeal to your sense of *sight*?
2. Which words appeal to your sense of *touch*?
3. Which words appeal to your sense of *hearing*?
4. Which sentence helps give the paragraph *variety*?
5. Which single *quality,* or *feature,* of the storm is expressed in this paragraph?
6. Give an example of two modifiers separated by the word *and.* What word do they both modify?
7. Give an example of two modifiers separated by a comma. What word do they both modify?

B. Copy this paragraph. Add descriptive words and proper punctuation where needed.

Half an hour passed, and the **8.** _____ storm began to die down. The wind became a **9.** _____ **10.** _____ breeze, and the rain softened to a **11.** _____ patter. Once again the young trees stood **12.** _____ and **13.** _____. Gradually the **14.** _____ clouds scattered, and patches of **15.** _____ **16.** _____ and **17.** _____ sky showed through. **18.** _____ the sun appeared, **19.** _____ at first but gathering strength with every **20.** _____ moment. At last the sparrows returned.

C. Copy each sentence, replacing the underlined general adjective with two specific adjectives.

21. As the sun continued to shine, the <u>wet</u> streets became dry.
22. <u>Pretty</u> flowers turned their petals to the clear blue sky.
23. <u>Big</u> trees swayed gently in the breeze.
24. An <u>interesting</u> bird hopped quickly along the white picket fence.
25. Even the <u>dull</u> paint on the old house seemed to sparkle.

Apply

D. Reread the word lists you made in Lesson 9. Add any other words that come to you as you read. Get ready to write a descriptive paragraph.

Write an Introductory Sentence
- This sentence may simply describe the first object in your scene. However, be sure to give your audience a general idea of your topic.

Write Detail Sentences
- Support your topic. You might want to arrange your details in time or space order, or you might want to give a general impression. Be sure that all details contribute to your scene.
- Use words from your word lists. Vary the types of sentences you write.
- Try to leave your audience feeling the same way you did when you experienced the scene for the first time.

Review Your Work
- Go back and check for specific words.
- Take out any words that do not contribute to the general impression you want to make.
- Check to see whether you can combine any descriptive words.
- Save your paragraph for revising in Lesson 11.

Lesson 11: Revising

Editing and Proofreading Descriptive Paragraphs

Nina Young Bear wrote a paragraph about a painting she had seen. Here is her revised paragraph.

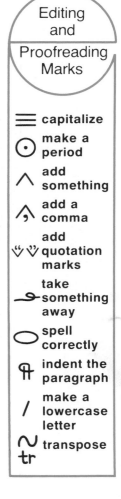

Editing and Proofreading Marks

≡ capitalize

⊙ make a period

∧ add something

⌄ add a comma

ᵛᵛ ᵛᵛ add quotation marks

⤷ take something away

◯ spell correctly

¶ indent the paragraph

/ make a lowercase letter

∿ transpose
tr

> *Last week I saw a* ~~picture~~ **painting at** *in the* ~~art gallery~~ **Seabury** ~~it was by a~~ **the Dutch** *modern artist* **Vonk** *from Holland.* *A bowl of* **brightly** ~~colored~~ *daisies* ~~was on~~ **sat** **small, dark** *a table. The flowers* **yellow and** **cheerful,** *stood out* ~~against~~ *the* **deep shadows** ~~darkness~~ *behind them. As I* ~~looked~~ **gazed** *at the* ~~picture~~ **painting,** *I* ~~got the feeling of~~ **could almost feel a** *stillness broken by the bright color of the yellow* **blooms** ~~flowers~~*.*

Think and Discuss

Nina's descriptive paragraph appeals mainly to the sense of *sight*. Which descriptive words in the revised paragraph help you "see" the painting in your mind?

Even after adding words that would appeal to her reader's senses, Nina knew that she could be still more exact. For this reason she changed *picture* to *painting, was* to *sat, looked* to *gazed*, and *flowers* to *blooms*. She sensed that the phrase *got the feeling of* sounded awkward, so she changed that as well. Why are the words *deep shadows* better than the noun *darkness*?

Nina's first sentence was a run-on, so she broke it into two short sentences. Then she changed *from Holland,* which describes the artist, to the proper adjective *Dutch* and added the artist's name. She kept variety in mind when she added her descriptive adjectives. How are the two new adjectives that modify *table* in sentence 3 different from those in sentence 4 that modify *flowers*?

How to Revise Descriptive Paragraphs

Editing
1. Check your paragraph for *completeness.*
2. Be sure you have appealed to several senses.
3. Make sure you have used specific words.
4. Check for sentence variety, including combinations of two or more descriptive words separated by commas.

Proofreading
5. Check for correct spelling, punctuation, and mechanics. Check especially for commas used to separate descriptive words.

Practice

A. Rewrite Nina's revised paragraph in final form.

B. When your corrected paragraph from Practice A is completed, study it carefully. Then put it away and write the paragraph as your teacher dictates it.

Apply

C. Reread the paragraph you wrote in Lesson 10.

Edit Your Paragraph
- Check your **content.** Items 1 and 2 in the blue box above may help.
- Check your **style.** Use items 3 and 4 in the same blue box as a guide.

Proofread Your Paragraph
- Correct all errors in spelling, punctuation, and mechanics.
- Copy your paragraph onto a clean sheet of paper.

MECHANICS PRACTICE

Punctuating Adjectives and Adverbs

- Capitalize proper adjectives.

  Alain speaks the English and French languages.

- Use commas to separate words in a series.

  European, Australian, and African students came to our school.

Rewrite these sentences adding capital letters and commas.

> Buona sera, signore e signori.

1. My friend Diane is tall blond and blue eyed.
2. She is of french-canadian descent.
3. She studied in Connecticut Ohio and Washington D.C.
4. Diane is a lawyer a writer and a gourmet cook.
5. Another friend named Elvira is an english teacher.
6. Elvira is brazilian, but she studied in american schools.
7. She speaks the portuguese spanish and english languages.
8. Elvira teaches english literature in a brazilian school.
9. My friend Tino is an italian waiter.
10. I have other friends who speak the greek polish and hungarian languages.
11. George, for example, comes from a greek family.
12. He loves his greek homeland and visits it often.
13. Clara has never met her hungarian relatives.
14. Dot speaks the polish english and czech languages.
15. Diane George Clara and Dot come from varied backgrounds.
16. All of these american citizens are my good friends.
17. European african and asian people often speak many languages.
18. Many french people can speak the english german and italian languages in addition to their own.
19. Many chinese people speak the russian and japanese languages.
20. Being able to speak one two or three other languages is a wonderful accomplishment.

LITERATURE

Lesson 12: Understanding Imagery in Lyric Poetry

Read this poem.

January

The days are short,
　　The sun a spark
Hung thin between
　　The dark and dark.

Fat snowy footsteps
　　Track the floor.
Milk bottles burst
　　Outside the door.

The river is
　　A frozen place
Held still beneath
　　The trees of lace.

The sky is low.
　　The wind is gray.
The radiator
　　Purrs all day.

John Updike

What pictures does the poet help you to see in this poem?

Think and Discuss

The poem "January" is a good example of a **lyric poem.** A lyric poem expresses a poet's feelings, usually in a brief, songlike manner. The subject matter usually includes nature, love, or sadness. It *describes* people and things rather than tells a story about them. Often, though not always, it has a definite rhythm and rhyme. Finally, to help the poet express feelings, he or she makes great use of figures of speech.

Figures of speech are devices, or aids, by which the poet makes his or her feelings clear. Through them the poet presents images, or pictures, to help the reader see as the poet does. Study these definitions.

A **simile** is a comparison of two unlike things. The words *like* or *as* are used to make the comparison. "The fire burned as brightly as the sun" is a simile. It compares the fire to the sun by stating that both burn brightly.

A **metaphor** is also a comparison. Unlike similes, however, metaphors do not use *like* or *as.* Instead, they state that one person or thing *is* another. "Her hands were icicles" is a good example of a metaphor.

When the same *beginning letter* is repeated in several nearby words, this is called **alliteration.** In the poem "January," "bottles burst" is an example of alliteration.

Assonance is a repeating of the same *vowel sound* in several nearby words. In the third verse of "January," the short /i/ sound in *river, is,* and *still* is an example of assonance.

Consonance is a repeating of the same *consonant sound* in several nearby words. (The consonants do *not* have to be exactly alike, but they must make the same *sound.*) In the third verse of "January," the words *is, frozen,* and *trees* all contain the /z/ sound.

Besides having so many figures of speech, what other qualities of a lyric poem does "January" express? How do you think the poet feels about January?

Practice

A. Read this poem. Answer the questions in sentences.

Fog

The fog comes
on little cat feet.

It sits looking
over harbor and city
on silent haunches
and then moves on.

Carl Sandburg

1. What is Sandburg describing?
2.–3. What two things is Sandburg comparing?
4.–5. Does Sandburg use a *simile* or a *metaphor* to make the comparison? How can you tell?

B. Read this poem. Then copy and complete the sentences.

Velvet Shoes

Let us walk in the white snow
    In a soundless space;
With footsteps quiet and slow,
    At a tranquil pace,
    Under veils of white lace.

I shall go shod in silk,
    And you in wool,
White as a white cow's milk,
    More beautiful
    Than the breast of a gull.

We shall walk through the still town
    In a windless peace;
We shall step upon white down,
    Upon silver fleece,
    Upon softer than these.

We shall walk in velvet shoes:
    Wherever we go
Silence will fall like dews
    On white silence below.
    We shall walk in the snow.

Elinor Wylie

6. One example of a *simile* in the poem is _____.
7. An example of a *metaphor* in the poem is _____.
8. An example of *alliteration* is _____.
9. An example of *assonance* is _____.
10. An example of *consonance* is _____.

C. Read this poem. Then copy and complete the sentences.

Spring Thunder

Listen. The wind is still,
And far away in the night—
See! The uplands fill
With a running light.

Open the doors. It is warm;
And where the sky was clear—
Look! The head of a storm
That marches here!

Come under the trembling hedge—
Fast, although you fumble,
There! Did you hear the edge
Of winter crumble?

Mark Van Doren

11. The poet shows feelings of _____ in this poem.
12. In "Spring Thunder" the poet appeals to the reader's senses of _____, _____, and _____.
13. The scene pictured in this poem is _____.
14. In every verse, the _____ and _____, _____ and _____ lines rhyme.
15. The subject matter of the poem is _____.
16. The "running light" in the first verse is _____.
17. The poet compares the oncoming storm to _____.
18. The /s/ sounds in *listen* and *still* as well as the /l/ sounds in *listen, still, uplands, fill,* and *light* are examples of _____.
19. Although the words *clear* and *here* are spelled differently, they have the same vowel sound. They are examples of _____.
20. There are at least _____ people in this poem watching the storm. The reader can tell because _____.

D. Read this poem. Think about the images or pictures the poet wants you to see. Then answer the questions that follow.

Serve Me a Slice of Moon

Serve me a slice of moon
on a hot summer day.
A
nice
ice
slice
that rustles like taffeta
against my teeth —
and trickles winter through me
drop by drop.
Serve me a slice of moon
on a hot summer day —
with just a dab
of deep,
dark
shivery shadows
on top.

Marcie Hans

21. The poet never makes a direct comparison in this poem. Yet the poem makes you think of something cool and delicious. What is it? (Think of what you would like to have a slice of on a hot summer day.)
22. What does the poet mean by saying that the slice of moon "trickles winter through me"?
23. Find a simile. What two things are compared?
24. Find at least one example of alliteration in the poem.
25. Find a good example of assonance.
26. How does the assonance help the poet to express how *refreshing* a slice of moon would be?

Apply

E. Try your hand at writing a short lyric poem of your own.

Prewriting

- Plan your poem the same way that you planned your descriptive paragraph. Remember that you want to present a sharp, clear, vivid picture in words. You want your audience to feel the same way you did when you had the experience.
- Choose a topic that you know well and that made a strong impression on you. You may get some topic ideas from the poems in this lesson.
- Brainstorm for words as you did in Lesson 9.

Composing

- Do not be concerned about the format of your poem. It does not have to rhyme. It does not have to *sound* poetic. It should sound natural, like ordinary speech.
- Write a rough draft. Perhaps your poem will look more like a descriptive paragraph at the start. This is fine.
- As you write, make every word count. Take out any word that does not contribute to your overall impression.
- Tell your audience how you feel about the topic. Did the experience make you *glad, angry, contented, sad, uneasy, thrilled,* or *awed*? Try to use words that convey one of these impressions.

Revising

- Look back over your work. Divide your "sentences" or lines into phrases. Write each phrase on a separate line, as Marcie Hans did in "Serve Me a Slice of Moon." One line of poetry might even be a single word.
- Wherever you can, use a figure of speech to make an image sharper. However, do not force any into your poem.

- If you wish, add rhyming words to your poem as in "Spring Thunder" or "January." Again, do not force it. Some poems sound better unrhymed.
- Reread your poem. When you are satisfied with it, give your poem a title.
- Copy your revised poem onto a clean sheet of paper.

A BOOK TO READ

Title: **My Side of the Mountain**
Author/Illustrator: Jean George
Publisher: E. P. Dutton

Young Sam Gribley lived in an apartment in New York City with his mom and dad, four sisters, and four brothers. Then one lovely May morning Sam left New York to live by himself in the woods in the Catskill Mountains. All he took was a penknife, a ball of cord, an ax, forty dollars, and some flint and steel.

My Side of the Mountain is the story of how Sam lived by himself in his home in a hemlock tree. It is an exciting account of Sam's experiment in being completely on his own. Through the diary Sam kept, we learn how he tamed a wild falcon and how he tracked deer that had been left by hunters. We learn how he made himself deerskin clothing and how he gathered berries and nuts to store for the winter. We also meet some of Sam's friends: Bando, the college professor who Sam thinks is an escaped convict, and the Baron, a weasel who lives nearby. We meet Frightful, the trained falcon, Jessie Coon James, the raccoon who digs mussels for them, and many others.

Jean George wrote and illustrated the story of Sam. Her pictures show a special feeling for nature during the changing seasons of the year. *My Side of the Mountain* is a good book for anyone who enjoys camping and the outdoors.

5 UNIT TEST

● **Adjectives**   pages 182–184

Copy these sentences. Then write the letter that correctly answers the question following each one.

1. Ben and his sister Lucy decided to have an amusing scavenger hunt. The word *amusing* is **a.** a proper adjective **b.** a common adjective **c.** not an adjective.

2. In a scavenger hunt, people search for many objects on a written list. The adjectives in this sentence are **a.** *hunt, many,* and *written* **b.** *scavenger, many,* and *objects* **c.** *scavenger, many,* and *written.*

3. The first person to find all the objects on the list wins a special prize. Among the adjectives in this sentence are **a.** *first* and *list* **b.** *first* and *special* **c.** *first* and *prize.*

4. Lucy included French bread, Italian salami, and Spanish olives. There are **a.** five **b.** three **c.** four proper adjectives in this sentence.

5. Other objects were a Canadian dime, a pink towel, a plastic bottle, and a fluffy slipper. Of the describing adjectives in this sentence, there are: **a.** one proper and four common **b.** two proper and three common **c.** one proper and three common adjectives.

Copy these sentences. Underline all the predicate adjectives.

6. Lucy was glad when Ben offered to help with the list.
7. Both became silly as they added an inner tube and a Halloween mask.
8. Other objects were added until Ben and Lucy felt satisfied.
9. They were excited as they made nine more copies of the list.
10. Their friends were amused and eager when they heard about the scavenger hunt.

Adverbs   pages 188–189

Copy these sentences. Underline all the adverbs.

11. Quickly and carefully the ten friends began their search.
12. Enrico immediately found the salami in his own refrigerator.
13. Soon Sally had located a slipper and a nearly empty jar of olives.
14. Suzanne politely asked a garage owner for an inner tube.
15. Bob could not carry a rake, an inner tube, and a yardstick very well, so he carefully hid them until he could return.

Comparing with Adjectives and Adverbs   pages 185–187, 190–191

Copy these sentences. Use the correct degree of comparison of the adjectives and adverbs in parentheses ( ).

16. Judy was the _____ hunter at first. (successful)
17. She had searched _____ than any of the others. (carefully)
18. Before long, Bob was the _____ of all. (messy)
19. He was covered with burrs from _____ crossing a field. (carelessly)
20. Roosevelt looked the _____ ; he was wearing the Halloween mask he had found, a huge bear head! (silly)

Using Adjectives and Adverbs   pages 192-193

Combine each group of sentences into a single longer sentence.

21. Enrico soon grew tired. He was also hungry.
22. He began to eat the salami he had found. It was delicious salami.
23. Anna soon found a toothbrush. It was yellow. It was moldy.
24. Now she was looking for a rake. She was looking here. She was looking there.
25. She shouted happily, finding one at last. Her shout was loud.

Prefixes, Roots, and Suffixes   pages 196-201

Copy these words. Draw one line under each prefix and two lines under each suffix. Then circle all roots or base words.

1. unusual	2. neighborly	3. disappearance
4. forecaster	5. immortalize	6. untruthfulness
7. telescope	8. telegrapher	9. irresponsible
10. graphology	11. predictable	12. awaken
13. imperishable	14. semitropical	15. miscalculation

● Prewriting, Composing, and Revising—Descriptive Paragraphs

pages 202–210

1. Think of a place you have seen. Make a chart to tell what things you felt, saw, heard, tasted, and smelled there. Then write words to describe each item. (List only descriptive words that appeal to the sense under which the item appears on your chart.) Use your notes to write a paragraph describing the place you have seen. Revise your paragraph. Be sure it includes words and phrases that appeal to the senses. After you proofread your work, rewrite your paragraph in final form.

● Mechanics Practice   page 211

Copy these sentences. Add capital letters and commas.

2. Do you know any greek latin or french stories that have been translated into the english language?

3. Homer was a greek poet and storyteller.

4. Aesop phaedrus and la fontaine wrote fables for greek latin and french literature.

5. How many writers composed fables in the chinese japanese and russian languages?

6. Many nations have long colorful and interesting histories.

7. Did you know that the spanish french and english explored the united states before it was a nation?

8. Today many of our streets cities and natural features have names from european languages.

9. Places in the middle of our country have norwegian german and polish names.

10. Many american families have ancestors who were from ireland africa and china.

11. Our country's pioneers were brave daring and inventive.

12. Of course, the american indians were here before any other settlers.

13. The navajo hopi and apache are only three of the many indian groups still living in the southwest.

14. Some american indians live in New Mexico Arizona and Texas.

15. In the southeast american indian groups can be found in Florida.

16. The seminole indians are one of the largest groups in the state.

Read these three lyric poems. Then write answers to the questions.

Red

All day
across the way
on someone's sill
a geranium glows
red bright
like a
tiny
faraway
traffic light.

Lilian Moore

The Toucan

Tell me who can
Catch a toucan?
Lou can.

Just how few can
Ride the toucan?
Two can.

What kind of goo can
Stick you to the toucan?
Glue can.

Who can write some
More about the toucan?
You can!

Shel Silverstein

Text of "The Toucan" from
WHERE THE SIDEWALK ENDS:
The Poems and Drawings of Shel
Silverstein. Copyright © 1974
by Snake Eye Music, Inc.
Reprinted by permission of
Harper & Row, Publishers, Inc.

Flashlight

My flashlight tugs me
through the dark
like a hound
with a yellow eye,

sniffs
at the edges
of steep places,

paws
at moles
and rabbits
holes,

points its nose
where sharp things
lie asleep—

and then it bounds
ahead of me
on home ground.

Judith Thurman

1. Which two poems contain similes?
2. Which poem's /s/ and /z/ sounds show examples of consonance?
3. Which poem is almost all assonance? Name its vowel sounds.
4. Which poem reveals the best example of rhyme?
5. All three poems express feelings about something in nature. Which one, however, is a bit different from most lyric poems? Why?
6. Which poem's /ow/ sound shows assonance? What vowels make this sound?
7. Copy an example of a simile. What two things are compared?
8. Which "sharp things" "lie asleep" in the poem "Flashlight"?
9. What is the "yellow eye" of the hound in Judith Thurman's poem?
10. Which poem reveals alliteration in its /g/ sounds?

6

LANGUAGE
Learning About Pronouns

STUDY SKILLS
Building Vocabulary Skills

Look quickly at the photograph on the left. What is the first thing you see? Now look more carefully. What else do you notice? Think about the picture. What do you think happened before the picture was snapped? What might happen next? Make up a story.

As you made up your story, did you keep using the words *dog* and *bird,* or did you sometimes use the words *it, he,* or *her* instead? If you used words such as *it, he,* or *her,* you were using *pronouns.* In this unit you will study the different kinds of pronouns. You will also learn how to use pronouns correctly.

Can you spot a spot on either animal? What is unusual about that sentence? Of course, the word *spot* is used in two different ways. Words such as *spot* are called homographs. You will be learning about homographs, homophones, and compound words. A compound word joins two words together. What compound word is formed from the names of the animals in the picture?

When you made up your story about the picture, you had to think of your details. In this unit you will study a way to plan and organize details for writing short stories. You will read the short story "Father Wakes Up the Village" and use it as a model for writing your own short story.

Now turn the page to see what happens next!

◀ *An unusual friendship between two animals*

LANGUAGE

Lesson 1: Understanding Pronouns and Antecedents

Which words in sentence 1 does <u>their</u> replace?

1. Jennifer and Royal waited for Jennifer and Royal's turn in the arena.
2. Jennifer and Royal waited for <u>their</u> turn in the arena.

Think and Discuss

Sentences are much less awkward when **pronouns** are used in place of some of the nouns. Pronouns take the place of nouns and always refer to them and agree with them. The nouns to which they refer are their **antecedents.**

> • A **pronoun** is a word that takes the place of a noun. The noun to which a pronoun refers is its **antecedent.**

Read these sentences.

3. Jennifer stroked Royal's neck to calm Royal.
4. Jennifer stroked Royal's neck to calm <u>him</u>.

The underlined word in sentence 4 is a pronoun. Pronouns vary according to the way they are used. Study this chart.

Singular	Plural
I, me, my, mine	we, us, our, ours
you, your, yours	you, your, yours
he, she, it, him,	they, them, their,
her, his, hers, its	theirs

How might sentence 5 be improved with pronouns?

5. Jennifer worried about Royal's front leg, but Royal's front leg did not bother Royal.

Practice

A. Copy these sentences. Underline the pronouns. Draw an arrow from each pronoun to its antecedent.

1. Jennifer and Royal waited their turn.
2. When the signal was given, it startled Royal.
3. Royal reared onto his hind legs.
4. Jennifer calmed Royal by patting him.
5. Jennifer and Royal did their routine, and people clapped for them.
6. Royal knew that he had done a good job.
7. Jennifer was proud of her beautiful horse.

B. Copy these sentences. Replace the underlined nouns and phrases with pronouns.

8. People congratulated Jennifer and Royal on Jennifer and Royal's performance.
9. Royal won a blue ribbon for Royal's looks.
10. The judges awarded a prize to Jennifer because Jennifer had handled Royal so well.
11. Jennifer always knew that Jennifer could ride horses.
12. Royal had been given to Jennifer when Royal was only a year old.
13. Jennifer had received Royal for Jennifer's ninth birthday.
14. Now Jennifer and Royal ride whenever Jennifer and Royal can.
15. Royal knows that Royal has a good home.

Apply

C. 16. Write a paragraph about an animal you might like to have for a friend. Underline all the pronouns.

Lesson 2: Understanding Subject Pronouns

Read these sentences.

1. Alan and Betsy went to the concert together.
2. Alan and she went to the concert together.

How is sentence 2 different from sentence 1?

Think and Discuss

Pronouns may be used in place of any nouns. When pronouns replace nouns used as **subjects,** however, only certain forms are correct. Study these **subject pronouns.**

Singular	Plural
I	we
you	you
he, she, it	they

Subject pronouns are often used by themselves in place of nouns. Sometimes, however, when more than one subject is involved, pronouns replace one or both nouns. In sentence 2 the pronoun *she* replaces the noun *Betsy.* Notice that the subject pronoun form is used because it is part of the subject. Which pronoun might be used to replace the noun *Alan?*

Subject pronouns are also used after linking verbs. That is, only a subject pronoun may follow a form of the verb *be* or any other linking verb. Study these sentences.

3. The cellists were John and Angela.
4. Angela said, "The cellists were he and I."

The subject pronouns *he* and *I* in sentence 4 replace the nouns *John* and *Angela* from sentence 3. The subject pronouns are used because they follow a linking verb. Whenever *I* is used with a noun or another pronoun, always remember to put *I* last.

Practice

A. Copy these sentences. Underline the subject pronouns.

1. Classical music is beautiful when it is played well.
2. Betsy says she likes Mozart's *Jupiter Symphony.*
3. She attends concerts whenever she can.
4. She also likes Beethoven because he is so dramatic.
5. Alan prefers Chopin because he likes the piano.

B. Replace these underlined words with subject pronouns.

6. Betsy and <u>Alan</u> love classical music.
7. <u>Betsy and Alan</u> go to concerts often.
8. <u>One day Betsy</u> said to Alan, "Why don't <u>Alan</u> and <u>Betsy</u> go to the Beethoven concert next week?"
9. "<u>The concert</u> should be exciting."
10. "Good," said Alan. "<u>Betsy and Alan</u> will go."

Apply

C. 11.–20. Write ten sentences about a piece of music you like. Use one subject pronoun in each sentence.

HOW OUR LANGUAGE GROWS

Fifteen percent of our everyday words come from Latin, the language of the ancient Romans. Many have interesting histories. *Secure* comes from *sine cura* which means "without care," and thus "safe." A *missile* is "something that has been sent." *Salary* comes from the Latin word *sal* which means "salt." That is because Roman soldiers were paid in salt. Eventually *salary* became the word for "money that is earned by working."

Use a standard dictionary to answer these questions.

1. Which Latin words gave us *cabbage, calendar,* and *money?*
2. Which English words do we get from *extremus* and *intendo?*

Lesson 3: Understanding Object Pronouns

Read these sentences.

1. Laughing Ludmilla outsmarted the robbers.
2. Laughing Ludmilla outsmarted them.
3. Laughing Ludmilla taught them a lesson.

Which pronouns in sentences 2 and 3 replace a noun in sentence 1?

Think and Discuss

You have already seen that subject pronouns can replace nouns used as subjects or predicate nominatives. **Object pronouns** can replace nouns used as direct objects or indirect objects.

- A **direct object** is a word that receives the action of a verb.
- An **indirect object** is a word that tells to whom or for whom something is done.

In sentence 2, for example, *them* receives the action of the verb *outsmarted*. It is a direct object. In sentence 3 *them* tells to whom the lesson was taught. It is an indirect object. Look at this chart of object pronouns.

Singular	Plural
me	us
you	you
him, her, it	them

Notice that the forms of object pronouns are different from those of subject pronouns. Whenever you replace a noun used as a direct object or as an indirect object, be sure that you choose the right form from this chart.

Practice

A. Copy these sentences. Underline direct object pronouns once and indirect object pronouns twice.

1. *Laughing Ludmilla and the Missing Map* tells the story of a stolen map and how Ludmilla finds it.
2. Ludmilla knows who the robbers are, and she follows them.
3. Her classmates give her no encouragement.
4. "Detectives are serious," they say. "We can't treat you like a real detective."
5. This was true; when troubles surrounded her, Ludmilla always laughed.
6. But Ludmilla thought, "I will give them a reason to take back their words."
7. Soon she sees one of the robbers and follows him.

B. Copy these sentences, completing each with an object pronoun. Write *direct object* or *indirect object* to show how each is used.

8. The second robber is a woman who has been waiting in a cave. Ludmilla recognizes _____.
9. The first robber says to the second robber, "I have the map," and gives _____ a folded paper.
10. Hiding nearby, Ludmilla hears _____.
11. "I must trick _____; they must give _____ the map," she thinks.
12. Suddenly the robbers turn and see _____.
13. Ludmilla runs away, thinking, "I must outrun _____."
14. One robber cries, "That girl has seen _____! If she gets to the police, she will give _____ our names."
15. As the robbers chased _____, Ludmilla laughed.

Apply

C. 16.–25. Finish the story of Laughing Ludmilla. Use at least ten object pronouns in your story.

Lesson 4: Understanding Possessive and Reflexive Pronouns

How are the underlined words used in these sentences?

1. The Turgeons are taking <u>their</u> vacation.
2. They bought <u>themselves</u> plane tickets to Paris.
3. The best seats on the plane are <u>theirs</u>.

Think and Discuss

Pronouns that show ownership are called **possessive pronouns.** Pronouns that refer to the subject of a sentence are called **reflexive pronouns.** Study these charts.

Possessive Pronouns That Modify Nouns		Possessive Pronouns That Are Complements	
Singular	**Plural**	**Singular**	**Plural**
my	our	mine	ours
your	your	yours	yours
his, her, its	their	his, hers	theirs

Reflexive Pronouns	
Singular	**Plural**
myself	ourselves
yourself	yourselves
himself, herself, itself	themselves

Sentence 1 contains a possessive pronoun that modifies the noun *vacation.* Sentence 3 contains a possessive pronoun used as a complement after the linking verb *are.* Sentence 2 contains a reflexive pronoun used as an indirect object.

> • **Possessive pronouns** take the place of possessive nouns.
> • **Reflexive pronouns** end in *self* or *selves.* They always refer to the subject of the sentence.

Practice

A. Copy these sentences. Underline each possessive pronoun once and each reflexive pronoun twice.

1. Mr. Turgeon unpacked his luggage immediately; Mrs. Turgeon unpacked hers later.
2. They treated themselves to dinner and a show in Paris.
3. Later Mrs. Turgeon bought her husband a suit.
4. Soon the Turgeons repacked their luggage.
5. Before long they found themselves in London.
6. Mrs. Turgeon reminded herself about her camera.
7. A friendly Englishman took their pictures.

B. Complete these sentences with possessive and reflexive pronouns. Underline each possessive pronoun once and each reflexive pronoun twice.

8. In London Mrs. Turgeon treated _____ to a new dress.
9. Mr. Turgeon surprised _____ wife with a necklace.
10. "We should treat _____ to a Shakespeare play," said Mr. Turgeon. "_____ tickets are still good."
11. "I'd like to see Spain later, Emile," said Mrs. Turgeon. "What is _____ opinion?"
12. "I agree," he answered. "Let's get _____ tickets tomorrow."
13. But the airline people said, "All _____ seats are taken."
14. That night Mrs. Turgeon returned to the hotel and said, "Don't upset _____, Emile. I've chartered _____ plane."
15. "I'm lucky," replied Mr. Turgeon. "_____ wife is a pilot. She can fly us to Spain _____!"

Apply

C. 16.–25. Write a paragraph about the Turgeons' flight to Spain. Use at least five possessive pronouns and five reflexive pronouns.

Lesson 5: Using Pronouns Correctly

Name the pronouns in sentences 1–3. How is each used?

1. The rocket sent us higher and higher.
2. We were traveling to the planet Zircon.
3. The scientists had chosen David and me.

Think and Discuss

Subject and **object pronouns** are the two pronoun forms that are most often confused. Pronouns used as subjects or as predicate nominatives should always follow the forms you studied in Lesson 2. Pronouns used as direct and indirect objects should be those studied in Lesson 3. Always ask yourself how a particular pronoun is used before you decide which form is correct in a sentence.

Contractions, shortened forms of words, may involve pronouns. Remember to place the apostrophe where the letters of one word are left out so that two or more words can be put together. Study these examples.

I'll = I will	we've = we have
you've = you have	he's = he is, he has

Form contractions for *we will, you had,* and *they have.*

When combining two or more short sentences using pronouns, be sure to choose only pronoun forms from the proper lists. Tell why each of these underlined pronouns is correct. (Note that Donna is the speaker.)

4. This seat is David's. This seat is Donna's.
   These seats are <u>ours</u>.
5. The navigator is David. The captain is Donna.
   The navigator and captain are <u>he</u> and <u>I</u>.
6. The scientists gave David orders. The scientists gave Donna orders.
   The scientists gave <u>him</u> and <u>me</u> orders.

Practice

A. Copy these sentences and underline the pronouns. After each sentence, write whether the pronouns are *subject, object, possessive,* or *reflexive* pronouns.

1. I landed on Zircon with the crew.
2. Harry gave me a map of the area.
3. David did not trust himself alone.
4. He took Harry along to explore the hills.
5. The only leader left was I.
6. David and Harry planted our flag.
7. Zircon was now officially ours.

B. 8.–14. Write each of the pronouns in Practice A. Then write how each was used in the sentence.

C. Write contractions for these phrases.

15. I have	**16.** you are	**17.** she would	**18.** it will
19. we had	**20.** they had	**21.** they will	**22.** he would

D. Combine each pair of sentences into a single sentence. Replace the underlined nouns with pronouns.

23. The crew gave David a cheer. The crew also gave Harry a cheer.
24. Then David explored the underground caverns. Donna (the speaker) explored too.
25. David brought back some rocks. Donna (the speaker) found some water.
26. The rocket returned the leaders (including the speaker) to Earth. The rocket returned the crew as well.
27. The crew (including the speaker) brought President Clancy the plants. The crew (including the speaker) also brought the rocks and the water sample.

Apply

E. 28.–35. Write a paragraph about a space trip you might take someday. Use at least eight pronouns.

LANGUAGE REVIEW

Pronouns and Antecedents   pages 226-227

Copy these sentences. Underline each pronoun and draw an arrow from the pronoun to its antecedent.

1. Phillip decided that he would build a snow fort.
2. When Jan and Una saw Phillip, they offered to help him.
3. The girls worked with the snow as if it were bricks and stones.
4. Una made the fort a semicircle; she gave it curving walls.
5. As the fort grew larger, the three friends were proud of their work.

Subject Pronouns   pages 228–229

Copy these sentences. Underline all pronouns used as subjects.

6. Phillip and the girls decided that they would make windows in the fort's curved walls.
7. They would be small on the outside and larger on the inside of the fort.
8. Jan began digging into the walls; it was hard work.
9. She made the opening wide on her side and narrowed it as she came closer to the outside wall.
10. It was just as Phillip had planned it.

Object Pronouns   pages 230–231

Copy these sentences. Underline all pronouns used as direct objects.

11. The fort continued to grow; Phillip named it Fort Courage.
12. Soledad and Kijika saw the fort and asked if they could build it too.
13. Later three other friends started a new fort and named it Fort Fantastic.
14. Anne and David joined them in their work.
15. Both groups were so proud of their forts that they would not ruin them in a snowball fight.

Copy these sentences. Underline all pronouns used as indirect objects.

16. Kijika had an idea; he gave it much thought.
17. "Let's build a bridge between the forts. It will give us something else to do," he said.
18. Soledad wrote a message to the others. "Give them this," she told Jan.
19. When Anne read Kijika's idea, she said to Jan, "Tell him we agree!"
20. The bridge was begun; Phillip wanted to give it a name.

Possessive and Reflexive Pronouns   pages 232–233

Complete these sentences with possessive pronouns.

21. "After all, the project was _____ idea," said Phillip.
22. "Well, it is _____ project now," answered Rose.
23. "We all worked on it," said David. "_____ name should be Friendship Bridge."
24. "The original idea was _____, Phillip," said Chim. "Do you like _____ name?"
25. "Yes, I do," answered Phillip quietly. "_____ project should be a friendly one."

Complete these sentences with reflexive pronouns.

26. Rose saw a ledge that needed fixing; "I'll do it _____," she thought.
27. "Be careful, Rose!" called Chim. "Don't hurt _____!"
28. Suzanne suddenly saw Rose fall. "Come here, everyone," she called. "Rose has hurt _____!"
29. "No, I'm not hurt," answered Rose. "I've just scared _____."
30. "Our project is beautiful," everyone agreed when it was finished. "And we did it all by _____."

Applying Pronouns

31.–40. Write ten sentences about a winter experience you have had. Draw one line under the subject pronouns and two lines under the direct object pronouns.

STUDY SKILLS

Lesson 6: Understanding Homophones and Homographs

Read sentence 1 aloud. How are the two underlined words different? Read sentence 2. What do the underlined words mean? In what other ways are they different?

Think and Discuss

The words *flour* and *flower* sound alike but have different meanings and different spellings. They are called **homophones.** One of the problems with homophones is that one word is often used for another. The words *to, two,* and *too* all sound alike, but each word has a different meaning. Look at the sentences below.

3. Move *to* the right.   (to = in the direction of)
4. *Two* noblemen rode by.   (two = a pair)
5. Some servants rode by *too.*   (too = also)

Words that are spelled alike but have different meanings and sometimes different pronunciations are called **homographs.** Which sentence at the top of the page uses homographs? Here are two more examples.

6. Line up in single *file.*   7. *File* your nails.

238   VOCABULARY/USAGE: Homophones and Homographs

> - **Homophones** are words that sound alike but have different spellings and meanings.
> - **Homographs** are words that are spelled alike but have different meanings and sometimes different pronunciations.

Practice

A. Copy the following sentences. Underline the homophone that correctly completes each one.

1. The theater featured (two, too, to) short films.
2. I went (two, too, to) the end of the line.
3. Were you there (two, too, to)?
4. May I have (two, too, to) tickets?
5. Give the money (two, too, to) the cashier.

B. Copy the following sentences. Underline the homophone that correctly completes each one.

6. The battle (scene, seen) was a deserted (plane, plain) near a mighty castle.
7. The (steal, steel) lances glistened in the (son, sun).
8. There were (eight, ate) (knights, nights) in armor.
9. Each (road, rode) a horse along the dusty (road, rode).
10. (Won, One) of them wore (for, four) gold stars.

C. Write a sentence using each of these homophones.

11. know/no
12. groan/grown
13. pear/pair
14. tail/tale
15. roll/role
16. toe/tow

Apply

D. Write a sentence using each of these homographs. Use your dictionary to find the meanings of the words. Write the meaning you have used after the sentence.

17. staple
18. cuff
19. mold
20. fawn
21. close
22. lead
23. record
24. wind

Lesson 7: Understanding Compound Words

What do all of these words have in common?

lighthouse   junior high school   merry-go-round

Think and Discuss

Some words are made of two or more words put together. These are called **compound words.** Many compounds are simply written as single words such as *jellyfish, milestone,* and *freeway.* Others, however, appear as separate words that are considered as one. Examples of these compound words are *science fiction* and *cash register.* A third kind of compound is connected by hyphens as in the words *baby-sitter* and *jack-of-all-trades.*

- A **compound word** consists of two or more words used as a single word.
- A **closed compound** is a compound made of two words written together as one.
- An **open compound** is a compound in which the words are written separately.
- A **hyphenated compound** is a compound connected by hyphens.

Which kind of compound word is each of the three examples at the beginning of this lesson?

Practice

A. Copy these sentences. Underline each compound word.

1. Howard Carter discovered the age-old tomb of King Tutankhamun in 1922.
2. Tut was a nine-year-old boy when he became pharaoh.

3. Tut was the son-in-law of the famous pharaoh Akhenaton, who worshiped the sun.
4. When Tut died at 18, he was buried in a rocky tomb in the so-called Valley of the Kings.
5. English scientists digging for objects from ancient Egypt found a staircase in some rocks.
6. They dug down into a buried tomb and opened up a treasure chest full of jewels, gold, and artwork.
7. King Tut's mummy was found surrounded by all the household things he would need during his afterlife.

B. Use these numbered words to make ten new compounds.

8. high	9. sun	10. self	11. cottage	12. full
13. eye	14. steam	15. know	16. main	17. news

Apply

C. 18.–32. Make a list of five closed compounds, five open compounds, and five hyphenated compounds. Write a sentence for each.

To Memorize

What is once loved   Take it home
You will find   In your mind
Is always yours   And nothing ever
From that day.   Can take it away.

Elizabeth Coatsworth

1. What does the poet mean when she tells you to take something home in your mind?
2. Think of some people or things that you have loved. How do you feel when you think about them, even when they are not with you?

COMPOSITION

Lesson 8:   Prewriting

Developing a Short Story Through Its Main Character

Read this summary of a short story.

> When Randy was 12, his mother got a job that required her to work long hours. As a result, Randy had to spend much time baby-sitting for his sister Susie. At first he resented not being able to spend more time with his friends. Gradually, however, his attitude changed. He heard little Susie say her first word. He helped her learn to walk. He began to understand, how children think and learn. Randy eventually realized that he was enjoying his work with Susie.

Think and Discuss

People change and grow through the experiences they have. How did Randy feel about baby-sitting when his mom first got her job? How did he change as time passed?

Not all experiences lead to changes like Randy's. Yet in fiction, as in real life, characters and events evolve, or change, together. You can use this fact to advantage when you are planning a story.

As a class exercise, make up a character. Then think of a problem for the character to face. As he or she deals with the problem, show how the character develops. What difficulties might stand between the character's problem and its solution? How might other characters help or hinder?

Here is a simple diagram you can use to show how character and plot grow together.

Main character: Randy Acheson, 12 years old
Problem: Randy must baby-sit for his little sister, and he does not like it.
Outcome: Randy will solve his problem.

Beginning	Middle	Ending
Randy's mother gets a job. Randy has to take care of Susie. Randy is resentful. He struggles to control his negative feelings.	Susie says her first word. She "discovers" closets. She learns to walk. Randy is amazed. Randy learns to amuse Susie with books and building blocks. He begins to enjoy his job.	Randy's mother has a week of vacation. She is happy to see how well Randy works with Susie.

Notice that this diagram concentrates on only a few events in the story. As each event happens, however, you can see how the character changes, grows stronger, and eventually overcomes his problem. What other events might you use to show how Randy changes?

How to Develop Character and Plot

1. **Choose a character. Give the character a problem to solve.**
2. **Decide whether the character will succeed or fail with the problem.**
3. **Make a diagram like the one on this page. Plan the beginning and ending.**
4. **Fill in the middle of the diagram. Show how the character grows and changes.**

Practice

A. Copy this diagram onto a sheet of paper. Add events to the middle section showing how the character develops.

Beginning	Middle	Ending
Melissa wants to learn sign language to communicate with her nonhearing friend, Robert.		Melissa has learned sign language so well that her other friends ask her to teach them also.

B. Make a diagram showing some true or imaginary event that might be suitable for a story.

Apply

C. Now prepare a diagram for a story of your own.

Choose a Character
● Yow will probably find it easy to model a character after someone you know.

Give the Character a Problem
● Think of a problem for your character to face. It should be something difficult but still solvable.

Make a Diagram
● Fill in the beginning and end of your diagram.
● Think of intermediate steps as you did in the Practice exercise. These steps will make up the middle of your story.

Review Your Work
● Look over your diagram. Do the intermediate steps show how your character grows and changes? Replace any steps that do not illustrate this.
● Save your work for the Apply exercise in Lesson 9.

Lesson 9:   Composing
Writing a Short Story

A short story has a **beginning,** a **middle,** and an **ending.** An interesting beginning will make a reader want to read the entire story. Read this story beginning.

Horse Crazy

Denise Drews was horse crazy. She read every horse book she could find. Models of ponies, palominos, and thoroughbreds cluttered her bedroom. Her walls were covered with horse pictures, and horse dreams filled her head. More than anything, Denise wanted to have a horse of her own.

Gazing sadly out her bedroom window, Denise tried to imagine a horse grazing in the grass by the garage. It wasn't easy to do. Her father had just told her for the fiftieth time that the yard was much too small for a horse. The neighbors would complain. Her mother had just told her that a horse was too much responsibility. It would cost a fortune just to feed it.

"Ask for a reasonable pet," Mr. Drews said.

"What about a puppy or a kitten?" Mrs. Drews suggested.

But Denise didn't want a puppy or a kitten. She was horse crazy!

Think and Discuss

The beginning of a story introduces three story elements—the **setting,** the **characters,** and the **plot.** The setting tells when and where a story takes place. What setting is mentioned at the beginning of this story? The people (and animals) in a story are the characters. What three characters appear in the first paragraphs of "Horse Crazy"? The important events in a story form the plot.

A plot often contains an unexpected event or a problem that a character must solve. What problem does Denise face in the story?

In the middle of the story, the plot becomes more important. The story writer orders the events of the plot in a way that creates interest, suspense, or excitement. These events build up to a high point called the **climax** of the story. This is often the point of greatest suspense. Read the middle of "Horse Crazy."

That Saturday was the last time Denise asked for a horse. Three weeks went by, and not once did Denise ask for the impossible. Mr. and Mrs. Drews wondered if Denise had outgrown her interest in horses.

Then one day out at the golf course, Mr. Drews saw his old friend, Bill Friday.

"I saw Denise out riding that big palomino of hers again today," said Mr. Friday. "He certainly is a beautiful animal, but he must have cost a fortune!"

"Palomino?" said Mr. Drews. "It couldn't have been Denise you saw. She doesn't have a—"

"Oh, it was Denise, all right," said Mr. Friday. "We stopped and talked about her horse."

That same day in a supermarket, Mrs. Drews saw her neighbor, Mrs. Garcia.

"That's such a cute pony Denise has," said Mrs. Garcia. "I see her riding it all the time in the park. She rides a white mare too. Did you buy her both?"

"A pony and a horse?" said Mrs. Drews. She was so surprised she didn't know what else to say.

What events in the middle of "Horse Crazy" happen unexpectedly? What effect does this have on the reader?

A story should have a satisfying ending. The ending should reveal the solutions to any problems that the characters have faced. The ending should also include an explanation for any unexpected events that happened in the story. Read the ending to "Horse Crazy."

That night, Mr. and Mrs. Drews were waiting at the door for Denise to get home. They had a lot of questions about palominos and ponies. No sooner had Denise walked into the living room than the questioning began.

"Denise, you don't have a big palomino, do you?" Mr. Drews asked.

"He's one of my favorite horses," Denise replied, with a twinkle in her eye.

"Do you have a pony and a white mare too?" Mrs. Drews wanted to know.

"Two ponies," said Denise, "a white mare, and two brown ones."

Mr. Drews was confused. Mrs. Drews was amazed. Denise smiled at her astonished parents and started to explain.

"Mrs. Fox up at the stables knows I love horses, so she asked me if I would help out on weekends. When the owners are away, I have to exercise the horses, so I get to ride all I want."

Mr. and Mrs. Drews looked at each other in relief.

"So you don't want a horse anymore?" they asked.

"Maybe someday," said Denise, "but right now, six are enough!"

At the beginning Denise's problem was that she wanted a horse. She knew that her parents would not help her solve the problem, and she was on her own. How did she take charge of the situation? How did she grow and change?

> **How to Write a Short Story**
>
> 1. **Plan your story in advance. Decide on a beginning, a middle, and an ending.**
> 2. **Write the beginning of the story. Give names to the characters. Decide on the setting. Tell what problem the main character faces.**
> 3. **Write the middle of the story. Show how your main character grows and changes.**
> 4. **Write the ending of the story. Show how the problem is solved (or not solved). Be sure that all details are explained.**

Practice

A. Answer these questions about the story "Horse Crazy."

1. Which minor character did Mr. Drews talk to briefly?
2. What was the setting in which he talked to this man?
3. Which minor character is mentioned but never actually appears in the story as it is now?
4. Other words for the beginning, the middle, and the ending of a story are *introduction, complication,* and *resolution.* Using a dictionary and the information you already have about the parts of a story, tell how these three terms are appropriate.
5. What was the setting for the ending of the story?

B. Write a short paragraph for "Horse Crazy" that can be placed after the beginning section. Describe how Denise gets her job at the stables and tell how this makes her feel. Use these suggestions.

6. Write one sentence that describes the setting of Fox's Stables.
7. Write one sentence that describes Mrs. Fox.
8. Write two sentences in which Mrs. Fox tells Denise that she needs help in the stables.
9. Write two sentences in which Denise suggests a solution to the problem.
10. Write two sentences that describe how Denise reacts when Mrs. Fox tells her that she can have the job.

Apply

C. Reread the diagram you prepared in Lesson 8. Now you will develop your ideas into a story.

Write the Beginning
- Follow the guidelines in the blue box on page 248.
- Remember that this is your rough draft, or copy, of the story. Concentrate on putting your *ideas* on paper; do not worry about anything else.

Write the Middle
- Here you should concentrate on the events that make your character develop. Follow the items you wrote in your diagram.

Write the Ending
- Follow your diagram and the guidelines on page 248. Tie up all the loose ends.
- Be sure to show how your character has changed. You might even want to add a surprise ending.

Review Your Work
- Reread the rough, or first, draft of your story. Check to see that it makes sense.
- Save the story for additional work in Lesson 10.

Lesson 10: Composing
Writing Dialog in a Story

Find the exact words of the characters in this story.

Mr. Jones walked into a restaurant and was astonished to see a dog about to pay his bill.

"Let me see," said the dog to the cashier. "I owe you $1.20 for the sandwich, 55 cents for milk, and 35 cents for the apple. That comes to exactly $2.00."

The dog paid the cashier and left.

Mr. Jones exclaimed, "I don't believe it! That's the smartest dog I've ever seen!"

"Oh, he's not so smart," replied the cashier. "He can't even add right."

Think and Discuss

The exact words of a speaker are called a **direct quotation.** Quotation marks are used to show where a direct quotation begins and ends. How does the writer begin the first word of each quotation? Notice how commas and periods are used in the model dialog along with the quotation marks. There are three speakers in the story—Mr. Jones, the dog, and the cashier. How does the writer show when a new speaker is beginning to talk?

How to Punctuate Direct Quotations

1. **Use a comma to separate direct quotations from the rest of the sentence.**
2. **When a direct quotation is interrupted, do not begin the second part with a capital letter unless it is a new sentence.**
3. **When a direct quotation is a question or exclamation, place the question mark or exclamation point inside the quotation marks.**
4. **Begin a new paragraph when the speaker changes.**

Practice

A. Rewrite the following sentences, adding correct punctuation.

1. I don't like sherbet said Sonia icily.
2. Ice cream she added coolly is all right, though.
3. Mommy! cried Baby Bird Daddy just fell into the teapot.
4. Well answered Mrs. Bird he just has to learn not to fly off the handle like that!
5. Was that your dog asked Alice that jumped through the screen door?
6. Yes I answered and he really strained himself when he did it.
7. Why asked Sally do elephants paint their toenails red?
8. So that they can hide in cherry trees replied Jane.
9. How are the fish in this lake? Mr. Brown asked an unhappy-looking fisherman.
10. Well said the fisherman I drop them a line twice a day, but so far I've had no replies.
11. I knew that Lydia was a light sleeper said Corinne
12. I was surprised however to see her bed hanging from a chandelier
13. Three sardines saw a submarine look out shouted one
14. What is it asked the second sardine
15. Relax said the third sardine it's only a can of people

B. **16.** Rewrite this story, adding punctuation and beginning new paragraphs wherever necessary.

Walking down the street one day, I met a man coming out of a house. He had a black eye and a bloody nose, and he was holding his arm as if it hurt. His hair and suit were a terrible mess, and he was covered with dust from head to foot. Looks like you just had an argument with a truck I remarked. No he replied it was only a vacuum cleaner. I accidentally stepped on the bag, and the whole thing just exploded. Well, that explains the dust I answered but how did you hurt your face and arm? When I stepped on the vacuum cleaner bag, the cover popped off and hit me in the face he explained, looking a bit foolish. The explosion startled the dog who bit me, and here I am. Well I remarked, shaking my head sadly, that's what happens when you leave the vacuum cleaner lying around the house. You should have put it away when you finished cleaning. Why the man asked in surprise. I only came here to ask for directions to State Street!

Apply

C. Reread the rough draft of your story. Now you will add some dialog.

Add Dialog to Your Introduction
● Dialog always makes a story more interesting. You may want to have your main character discuss his or her problem with a friend. Try to make your quotations sound like real speech.

Add Dialog to the Middle and Ending
● Characters often reveal themselves through their speech. A character who makes trouble grumbles frequently and never agrees with what others have to say. A good character, however, offers advice and help.
● Show how your main character struggles with the problem. Have the character talk to others about it.
● Use dialog at the end of the story to show how your main character resolves the problem.

Review Your Work
● Read your story again. How does it sound with conversation added? Do the words sound natural?
● Save the draft of your story for the Apply exercise in Lesson 11.

Lesson 11: Composing

Making Transitions Within and Between Paragraphs

An received a postcard from her friend Bian, who was at camp. Raindrops had blurred some of the words, but the message was still clear.

> Dear An,
>   What a night! ~~[blurred]~~ I got lost in the woods alone. ~~[blurred]~~ a strange shadow scared me. Guess what it was--only a scarecrow! ~~[blurred]~~ I was so scared that I started to run. In doing this I tripped over my flashlight and skinned my knees. ~~[blurred]~~ I got back to camp.
>   Your friend,
>   Bian

Think and Discuss

The words that were blurred on An's postcard were **transitional expressions.** You learned a few of them in your lesson on time-order paragraphs. These words connect ideas so that your reader can see the relationship between one sentence or paragraph and the next.

The first transitional word on the postcard might have been *first.* This would indicate that Bian was planning to relate some events in the order in which they happened. What might the next one be?

To begin her next sentence, Bian probably chose a word like *Yet* or *But.* Such a word depends on the first sentences for its meaning and at the same time introduces the actions in the next few sentences. What might Bian's last transitional expression have been?

Transitional words, however, are not used to show only time relationships. Study these transitional expressions.

- Expressions that show **similar ideas** are: *and, also, too, likewise, in the same way.*
- Expressions that show **contrasting ideas** are: *but, however, in contrast, on the other hand.*
- Expressions that give **additional information** are: *furthermore, in addition, too, moreover.*
- Expressions that show **the result** of an action are: *therefore, as a result, nevertheless.*
- Expressions that give **a choice** are: *either . . . or, or, neither . . . nor.*

Other transitional expressions that may be useful are *for example* and *in fact.*

Unless they are very short, transitional expressions are usually set off by commas. If they begin a sentence, a comma is usually placed *after* the transitional words.

1. The scarecrow had frightened me. <u>However</u>, I soon felt calm again.

If transitional words occur within a sentence, commas are placed *before* and *after* the words.

2. The scarecrow had frightened me. Soon, <u>however</u>, I felt calm again.

A few exceptions to the rule about commas are the words *and* and *but,* and the expressions that give a choice. Commas may also be omitted after single, introductory time words.

3. The scarecrow had frightened Kuni <u>and</u> me. <u>Neither</u> he <u>nor</u> I calmed down quickly.

> **How to Use Transitional Expressions**
> 1. **Use transitional expressions to show relationships between sentences.**
> 2. **Use transitional expressions to show relationships between paragraphs.**
> 3. **Set off most transitional expressions with commas.**

Practice

A. Copy these sentences. Underline the transitional expressions and punctuate them correctly.

1. I am no camper. Nevertheless I will try it out.
2. In fact I said those very words to Tom last week.
3. Therefore we packed our supplies and headed for the woods.
4. He was whistling happily. In contrast I was filled with dread.
5. First of all I was stung by a bee.
6. As a result I had a huge bump on my nose and my left eye was swollen.
7. Moreover I tripped on a rock and fell into the river.
8. Tom on the other hand was dry and unhurt.
9. Therefore he could not understand why I wanted to go home.
10. He did however agree to stop and camp for the night.

B. 11.–15. Copy this paragraph, completing it with the proper transitional words and punctuation.

Putting up a tent is easy. (First, Then) select a level spot. (Finally, Then) lay the tent out and make sure it is flat. Make sure the tent door faces the right direction too. (Next, Second) pound in the stakes at the four corners and secure the tent ropes. (After that, Before) crawl into the tent and put up the center pole. Pound in the rest of the stakes. (Finally, Third) cross your fingers and hope it doesn't rain too hard.

C. Copy these sentences, adding transitional expressions of your own.

16. It might rain hard.
17. Your tent might float away.
18. This is probably what will happen.
19. You will probably have to hike to the nearest town.
20. A helicopter might come along and rescue you.

Apply

D. Look over the draft of your short story again. Get ready to refine its development by using transitional expressions.

Add Transitional Expressions Within Paragraphs
● Add a transitional word or expression wherever needed to show relationships between ideas.

Add Transitional Expressions Between Paragraphs
● Be sure that movement *between* paragraphs is clear. In the story "Horse Crazy," note how transitions like *then one day* and *That same day in a supermarket* move the action along.

Review Your Work
● Look over your story one more time. Be sure that it is complete.
● Be sure your ideas flow smoothly from one to the next.
● Save the story for revision in Lesson 12.

A Challenge

Create a crossword puzzle using transitional words, the names of the parts of a short story, and any other new words from Lessons 8 through 11. The more words you can fit into your puzzle, the better it will be.

Lesson 12: Revising

Editing and Proofreading Short Stories

Study the revising Marcia did on this story.

Editing and Proofreading Marks

The Ice–Skating Ghost

tr People always claimed the skating rink was haunted. (Until last week, I never believed it.) The ghost was supposed to be a woman wearing an old–fashioned dress and ice skates.

Last Saturday, my friend Inge asked, will you take pictures of me figure skating? I think you're such a good photographer. "I'd love to," I said. We went down to the rink on Monday night. ~~I remember it was Monday because my social studies paper was due that day.~~ Inge and I waited till the rink emptied out. Then I shot (two) rolls of film. ~~Well, not quite two rolls.~~ By the time we were almost finished, the empty rink was starting to feel eerie. "Hurry up and do that axel so we can go home!" I said.

We walked out of the rink I took the last pictures, and caught the bus home. What a shock I had when I printed those pictures. I didn't get a chance to develop the film for three days. On one photo, skating right beside Inge, was the ice–skating ghost. We hadn't seen her with our eyes, but the camera had picked her up!

Proofreading Marks key:

- ≡ capitalize
- ⊙ make a period
- ∧ add something
- ⋏ add a comma
- ⌄⌄ add quotation marks
- ⟋ take something away
- ◯ spell correctly
- ¶ indent the paragraph
- / make a lowercase letter
- ∿ tr transpose

Think and Discuss

To give your writing unity and coherence, your sentences must follow one another in a logical way. You might have to delete, add, or move sentences around.

In revising, Marcia took out two sentences and moved two sentences. She also made spelling and punctuation corrections. Look at the marks in the box on page 257. Which mark did Marcia use to take out a sentence? Which mark shows where a new paragraph begins? How does Marcia show that a sentence should be moved from one part of the story to another?

How to Revise a Short Story

Editing
1. **Read over what you have written. Be sure that the whole story makes sense.**
2. **Check the beginning of the story. Be sure that the beginning introduces the characters, the plot, and the setting.**
3. **Check the middle of the story. Be sure that it develops the plot and shows the main character growing and changing.**
4. **Check the ending of the story. Be sure that it resolves the problem of the story in a satisfactory way.**
5. **Add any dialog that will make the story more interesting.**
6. **Add transitional expressions to link sentences and paragraphs.**

Proofreading
7. **Correct all mistakes in spelling, punctuation, or other mechanics.**
8. **Be sure the first sentence of each paragraph is indented.**
9. **Check the format of your dialog.**

Practice

A. 1. Rewrite Marcia's story. Make each of the changes that Marcia has indicated.

B. Rewrite these three very short stories by adding, changing, or taking away sentences for unity and coherence. Add proper punctuation as well, paying special attention to the conversation.

2.   While visiting a classroom in our neighborhood one day, a police officer stopped to answer a question for a six-year-old boy. Taking a look at his uniform, the little boy asked are you a police officer? Yes he answered, then continued giving his talk. Again the little boy raised his hand and said my mother told me that if I ever needed help, I should ask the police. Is that right? It just so happens that we have an excellent police force. Yes, that's right the officer answered. Well, then the little boy asked, holding out his foot will you please tie my shoe?

3.   I was out for a walk by the lake one day when I saw a boy walking out of the water. The lake was known as Lake Soggybottom, and it had something to do with an old legend. Anyway, the boy came walking out of the water with an angry and disgusted look on his face. He was clothed and wet. How did you come to fall into the lake I asked him sympathetically. Who came to fall into the lake he asked. I didn't come to fall in. I came to fish. Then I realized that the boy had misunderstood my question.

4. My friend Janet once attended a party at which there were several important people from her company. The company was called H. S. Gref and Company, Inc. after the name of the founder. During dinner Janet happened to mention the name *Gordon.* Knowing that the important person on her other side did not know who Gordon was, she explained, Gordon is one of our cats. *One* of the cats? How many cats do you have asked the person. Seven. There's Gordon, Ted, Agatha, Mohammed, Cecily . . . said Janet, proceeding to name all seven. Then she added there's Caroline, the dog. The important person was surprised that she had so many animals, so the person politely asked do you have any children? Oh, yes answered Janet proudly we have a boy and a girl—named Spot and Puff.

C. 5. Be sure that the story you rewrote for Practice A is correct. Then study it well. Write the story again as your teacher dictates it to you.

Apply

D. Find the draft of your short story with all the additions you made. Get ready to put it into final form.

Edit Your Story
- Check your **content.** Use guidelines 1–4 in the blue box on page 258.
- Check your **style.** Items 5 and 6 in the same blue box may help.

Proofread Your Story
- Use items 7–9 in the blue box as a guide. Go back to Lesson 10 if necessary to check the rules for punctuating dialog.
- Write or type your story for the last time. Congratulations on your work!

MECHANICS PRACTICE

Using Quotation Marks, Hyphens, Apostrophes, and Commas

- Use quotation marks to show where the speaker's exact words begin and end. Start a new paragraph for each new speaker.

  "Do you know the difference between a mailbox and a swimming pool?" asked Fred.

  "No, I don't," Harriet replied.

  "Then I am certainly not going to let you mail any more of my letters," said Fred with a laugh.

- Use hyphens correctly in compound words.

  Irene is a Greek-speaking American citizen.

- Use an apostrophe when forming a contraction.

  he will—he'll   she is—she's   they are—they're

- Add commas to transitional elements in sentences and paragraphs.

  First of all, you shattered my glasses with that high note. I think, therefore, that you should take up stamp collecting.

A. Write these compound words correctly.

1. major-general   **2.** mother in law   **3.** steel-worker
4. bass-viol   **5.** editorinchief   **6.** sky scraper
7. townhouse   **8.** Seeing Eye dog   **9.** coveredwagon

B. 10. Write this story correctly. Use commas, apostrophes, and quotation marks. Begin new paragraphs where needed.

A lonely worm had been trying to find a friend for weeks and weeks. After a long search he found one in the very garden where he lived. Hello he said. Ive never seen you before. Well then you havent looked around very much said his new friend. Why do you say that asked the first worm. Because the second worm laughed Im your other half.

LITERATURE

Lesson 13: Understanding the Parts of a Short Story

Think about the short story you just completed. What three main parts did it have?

Think and Discuss

The short story is well named. It is short, sometimes only one or two pages long. It is also a story, with a setting, characters, and a plot.

"Father Wakes Up the Village" is a selection from Clarence Day's novel *Life with Father*. Each of its chapters, however, is a story in itself. In this selection, Father, who will do nothing in any way but his own, shakes up a sleepy town. As you read, decide where the beginning, the middle, and the end of the story occur.

Father Wakes Up the Village
Clarence Day

One of the most disgraceful features of life in the country, Father often declared, was the general carelessness of small village store owners. He said he had supposed that such men were interested in business, and that that was why they had opened their shops and sunk capital in them. But no, they never used them for anything but gossip and sleep.

Usually, when Father talked this way, he was thinking of ice. He strongly objected to spending even one day of his life without a glass of cold water beside his plate at every meal. There was never any difficulty about this in our home in the city. A great silver ice-water pitcher stood on a counter all day, and when Father was home its outer surface was frosted with cold.

One of the first summers that Father ever spent in the country, he rented a furnished house in Irvington on the Hudson, not far from New York. It had a garden, a stable, and one or two acres of woods. He took a train for New York every morning at eight-ten, after breakfast. He got back between five and six, bringing anything special we might need along with him, such as a basket of peaches from the city, or a fresh package of his own private coffee.

Things went well until one day in August the iceman didn't come. It was hot, he and his horses were tired, and he hated to come to us anyhow because the house we had rented was perched up on top of a hill. He said afterward that on this particular day he had not liked the idea of making his horses drag the big ice wagon up that sharp and steep road to sell us fifty cents' worth of ice. Besides, all his ice was gone anyhow—the heat had melted it on him. He had four or five other good reasons. So he didn't come.

Mother got so worried about what Father would say that she decided to send to the village. There was no telephone, of course. There were no motors. She would have liked to spare the horse if she could, for he had been worked hard that week. But as this was a crisis, she sent for Morgan, the coachman, and told him to bring up the cart.

We arrived at the little town after a while and I went into the Coal & Ice Office. An old clerk was dozing in a corner, his chair tilted back and his chin resting on his shirt front. I woke this clerk up. I told him about the problem at our house.

He hunted around his desk a few minutes, found his chewing tobacco, and said, "Well, sonny, I'll see what I can do about it."

I thanked him very much, as that seemed to me to settle the matter. I went back to the cart, and we drove slowly home.

Mother was sitting out on the porch. I said the ice would come soon now. We waited.

It was a long afternoon.

At five o'clock, Brownie was hitched up again. The coachman and I drove back to the village. We had to meet Father's train. We also had to break the bad news to him. He would have no ice-water for dinner.

The village was as sleepy as ever, but when Father arrived and learned what the situation was, he said it would have to wake up. He told me that he had had a long, trying day at the office, and he was completely worn out. But if any iceman imagined for a moment he could behave in that manner, he, Father, would take his head off. He marched into the Coal & Ice Office.

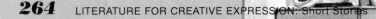

When he came out, he had the clerk with him, and the clerk had put on his hat and was vainly trying to calm Father down. He was promising that he himself would come with the ice wagon if the driver had left. He would deliver all the ice we could use, and he'd be there inside an hour.

The clerk went off toward the stables to hitch up the big horses. Father waited till he'd turned the corner. Then Father marched to the butcher's.

After nearly a quarter of an hour, the butcher and his helper came out, carrying what seemed to be a coffin, wrapped in a black raincoat. It was a huge cake of ice.

Father got in, in front, sat on the box seat beside me, and took up the reins. We drove off. The coachman was on the rear seat, sitting back-to-back to us, keeping the ice from sliding out with the calves of his legs. Father went a few doors up the street to a little furniture shop and got out again.

I went in the shop with him this time. I didn't want to miss any of this performance. Father began by demanding to see all the man's iceboxes. There were only a few. Father selected the largest he had. Then, when the sale seemed arranged, and when the owner was smiling broadly with pleasure at this sudden windfall, Father said he was buying that refrigerator only on two conditions.

The first was that it had to be delivered at his home before dinner. He added that he dined at six-thirty, and that there was no time to waste.

The shopkeeper gave in.

The second condition, which was then put to him firmly, was staggering. Father announced that the icebox must be delivered to him full of ice.

The man said he was not in the ice business.

Father said, "Very well then, I don't want it."

The man said that it was an excellent icebox.

Father made a short speech. It was the one that we had heard so often at home about the carelessness of village store owners, and he put such strong emotion in it that his voice rang through the shop. He closed it by saying, "An icebox is of no use to a man without ice. If you haven't the sense to sell your goods to a customer who wants them delivered in condition to use, you had better shut up your shop and be done with it. Not in the ice business, hey? You aren't in business at all!" He marched out.

The dealer came to the door just as Father was getting into the cart, and called out anxiously. "All right, Mr. Day, I'll get that refrigerator filled for you and send it up right away."

Father drove quickly home. A thunderstorm seemed to be brewing and this had waked the horse up, or else Father was putting some of his own supply of energy into him. I saw that Morgan was looking kind of desperate, trying to sit in the correct position with his arms folded while he held in the ice with his legs. The big cake was continually slipping and sliding around under the seat and doing its best to plunge out. It had bumped against his calves all the way home. They must have got good and cold.

A little later, after Morgan had unharnessed and hurriedly rubbed down the horse, he ran back to help us boys break the cake of ice up, push the chunks around to the back door, and cram them into the icebox while Father was dressing for dinner.

Then the iceman arrived.

The old clerk was with him, like a guard in charge of a prisoner. Mother stepped out to meet them and at once gave the iceman the scolding that had been waiting for him all day.

The clerk asked how much ice we wanted. Mother said we didn't want any now. Mr. Day had brought home some, and we had no room for more in the icebox.

The iceman looked at the clerk. The clerk tried to speak, but no words came.

Father put his head out of the window. "Take a hundred pounds, Vinnie," he said. "There's another box coming."

A hundred-pound block was brought into the house and heaved into the washtub. The ice wagon left.

Just as we all sat down to dinner, the new icebox arrived full.

Mother was annoyed. She said, "Really, Clare!" crossly. "Now what am I to do with that piece that's waiting out in the washtub?"

Father chuckled.

She told him he didn't know the first thing about keeping house, and went out to the laundry to tackle the problem.

Father's soul was at peace. He dined well, and he had his coffee served to him on the porch. Father took a deep breath of the sweet-smelling air and smoked his evening cigar.

"Clarence" he said, "King Solomon had the right idea about these things. 'Whatsoever thy hand findeth to do,' Solomon said, 'do thy darnedest.'"

Later I heard Father saying contentedly on the porch, "I like plenty of ice."

Briefly describe the plot of the story. Who are the main characters?

Remember This

1. **A story has three main parts.**
2. **The <u>introduction</u> (the beginning) gives the background, setting, and characters of the story.**
3. **The <u>complication</u> (the middle) presents the problem in the story and shows how the characters try to solve it. The complication continues up to the highest point of interest, or climax, of the story.**
4. **The <u>resolution</u> (the end) shows the outcome of the problem.**

Nearly all short stories have these three parts. Sometimes, however, an author will omit the resolution on purpose to leave readers in suspense. Sometimes, too, when a story begins in the middle of some exciting action, the background material will be held off for a few lines. A proper introduction with all necessary information, however, always appears near the beginning.

Practice

A. Write the answers to these questions.

1. What information does the introduction give?
2. Early in the complication, Clarence, the young son, goes to town to try to settle his family's problem. What were the results of his efforts?

3. The second part of the complication deals with Father's efforts to solve the problem. What were the results?

4. The high point, or climax, of the story usually ends the complication. What is the climax of this story?

5. Why is it necessary for the son to fail in getting Father's ice?

Apply

B. Try adding a scene to the short story you just read.

Prewriting
- Decide where in the story you want the new scene to occur.
- Decide what will take place. Try to make it amusing. Follow the format you used in Lesson 8.

Composing
- Write your scene in paragraph form. Add dialog wherever it will add interest to your work.

Revising
- Follow the guidelines from the blue box on page 258.
- Copy your scene onto a clean sheet of paper.

A BOOK TO READ

Title: **The Saturdays**
Author/Artist: Elizabeth Enright
Publisher: Holt, Rinehart & Winston

This book is about the four Melendy children—Mona, Rush, Randy, and Oliver—and their Saturday adventures in New York City. This book will take you all over one of the most fascinating cities in the world as you share the excursions of the Melendy children. You may be happy to know that the author, Elizabeth Enright, has written a whole series about the adventures of this delightful family.

6 UNIT TEST

● **Pronouns and Antecedents**   pages 226–227

Read each pair of sentences. Write the letter of the pronoun that correctly completes each *second* sentence.

1. Walruses usually live on ice floes. Sometimes however, **a.** we, **b.** us, **c.** they come to shore.
2. The name *walrus* has an interesting history. **a.** It, **b.** Them, **c.** You means "whale horse."
3. One male walrus weighed 3,000 pounds. **a.** You, **b.** She, **c.** He was 12 feet long.
4. A mother walrus teaches her calf to swim. **a.** They **b.** She, **c.** Us dives underwater with the baby on her back.
5. On long trips, the calf rides on the mother's back. **a.** Them, **b.** It, **c.** We seems comfortable traveling like this.

● **Understanding Subject Pronouns**   pages 228–229

Write each sentence. Choose the correct pronoun.

6. Onida and (I, me) are on the softball team.
7. It was (she, her) who saw the accident.
8. The three best pitchers are Shada, Dena, and (I, me).
9. No, it was not (we, us) who won the championship.
10. It was (I, me) who lost that game.

● **Object Pronouns**   pages 230–231

Copy these sentences. Choose the pronouns used as direct objects.

11. The largest penguins, scientists tell (we, us), are emperor penguins.
12. People first discovered (they, them) in Antarctica.
13. Admiral Byrd had one for a pet; he wrote about (he, him) often.
14. A friend told (I, me) that the emperor's neck is gold.
15. I told (she, her) that the emperor's back is black and that its chest is the color of rich cream.

270   TEST: Unit 6

Rewrite each sentence. Replace the indirect object nouns with pronouns.

16. You gave the trash collectors my best suit!
17. Bea baked Ben some biscuits and beans.
18. I handed Kiwa the hot potato.
19. Bruce offered the moose juice.
20. Mother cheerfully gave Laura all my musical instruments.

● Possessive and Reflexive Pronouns   pages 232–233

Write each sentence. Underline the possessive pronouns.

21. Marge gave her cold to Amy and Ted.
22. Leo and Kiku gave their full attention to the talking cow.
23. What I like about the room is its diamond-shaped windows.
24. Billie Jo, I don't want your autograph on the new ball.
25. This alligator is mine.

Copy these sentences. Circle the correct reflexive pronoun to complete each.

26. Is Jack talking to (himself, hisself) again?
27. I can't serve all you people right now, so why don't you just help (yourself, yourselves).
28. I gave (ourselves, myself) a headache by doing somersaults and standing on my head all afternoon.
29. Did they lose (theirselves, themselves) in the House of Mirrors again?
30. Does Grace still believe it (herself, themselves)?

● Pronoun Usage   pages 234–235

Rewrite these sentences. Substitute the correct pronoun contractions for the underlined words. Choose the correct object pronoun in parentheses ( ).

31. He is going to give (we, us) a lecture for being late.
32. They have given (I, me) an idea!
33. She is teaching (they, them) Morse code.
34. I am bringing (she, her) a pet monkey.
35. You will find (he, him) by the wishing well.

Homophones and Homographs   pages 238–239

Copy these pairs of words. Next to each group write whether the words are homophones or homographs.

1. whole/hole
2. bass/bass
3. lead/lead
4. meat/meet
5. convict/convict
6. herd/heard
7. bear/bear
8. rain/reign
9. time/thyme

Compound Words   pages 240–241

Write these compound words correctly.

10. lowspirited
11. meadow lark
12. German-shepherd
13. freeforall
14. ear phone
15. oysterbed
16. bottle neck
17. editorinchief
18. boxinggloves
19. post master
20. sisterinlaw

Prewriting, Composing, and Revising — Short Story

pages 242–260

1. Prepare to write a short story. Choose two characters and a setting for the story. The plot can be a simple problem that one of the characters manages to solve. On your paper, draw this diagram to plan your story.

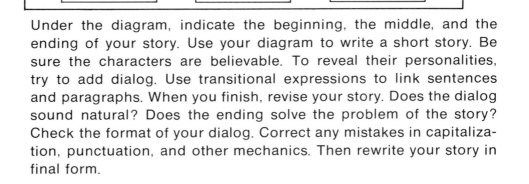

Beginning	Middle	Ending

Under the diagram, indicate the beginning, the middle, and the ending of your story. Use your diagram to write a short story. Be sure the characters are believable. To reveal their personalities, try to add dialog. Use transitional expressions to link sentences and paragraphs. When you finish, revise your story. Does the dialog sound natural? Does the ending solve the problem of the story? Check the format of your dialog. Correct any mistakes in capitalization, punctuation, and other mechanics. Then rewrite your story in final form.

Copy these sentences. Add the proper punctuation.

2. Doc said the absent minded professor you have to help me
3. What can I do for you, Professor asked the doctor
4. It's my memory said the professor I can't remember anything anymore
5. First of all how long has this been going on asked the doctor
6. How long has what been going on asked the professor
7. Now said the governor is the time for all good men to come to the aid of the party
8. I think however said the mayor that I will vote for the other party
9. I am a Greek speaking American citizen said Mr. Andropoulos proudly
10. Why asked Ann does the sea roar all night
11. You'd roar too said Sue if your bed were full of crabs and sand

● **Reading a Short Story**   pages 262–269

Copy these sentences. Imagine they are taken from a short story. Label each *introduction, complication,* or *resolution,* depending on the section of the story from which each might have been taken.

1. Georgia went into the living room and said to her mother, half smiling, "Why did you hide my presents so well this year?"
2. Georgia felt happy even though she knew she had lost the argument. "Nothing is better," she thought, "than being really surprised on your birthday."
3. Georgia coaxed some more. "Please, Mom, don't be mean. Tell me where my presents are hidden!"
4. A few days before her birthday, Georgia Crane started searching through the house for her birthday presents.
5. Mrs. Crane became so annoyed that she stopped her work and declared, "All right! You can have your presents now, but don't expect anything else on your birthday. Decide."
6. Georgia searched in all the familiar hiding places. She looked in the closets, under the bed, and up in the attic.

MAINTENANCE and REVIEW

Nouns and Pronouns   pages 90–93, 96–97, 226–235

Copy these sentences. Underline the nouns and pronouns. Above each, tell how it is used in the sentence.

1. Winter is often a beautiful season.
2. Crisp, white snow covers the hills and valleys.
3. Many animals hibernate and avoid the season's hardships.
4. Other animals make themselves nests but sometimes leave them.
5. The windswept hills and frozen lakes offer them little food.

Verbs   pages 134–145

6.–10. Copy the verbs from sentences 1–5. After each verb, write whether it is an *action* verb or a *linking* verb and whether it is *transitive* or *intransitive*.

Verb Tenses   pages 146–149

Copy these sentences. Underline the verbs. After each sentence write the tense of the verb you underlined.

11. Inside the house we keep a roaring fire ablaze.
12. The temperature outside will go down again tonight.
13. This morning Jan piled plenty of logs by the hearth.
14. We have used many of them already.
15. Tonight Don will trudge outside for more wood.

Adjectives and Adverbs   pages 182–193

Copy these sentences. Underline each adjective and adverb. Draw an arrow from each adjective or adverb to the word it modifies.

16. Frosty, white patterns appear on the windows.
17. Eager children always wipe them away to see the glorious world outside.
18. The more ambitious children build forts; the lazier ones watch gleefully.

19. The sun is bright overhead.

20. The crisp snow, however, does not melt because the air is so cold.

Plurals, Abbreviations, and Contractions   pages 92–95, 234–235

Form plurals from the first set of words, abbreviations from the second, and contractions from the third.

21. mouse **22.** candy **23.** sled **24.** hello **25.** proof
26. berry **27.** fox **28.** path **29.** inch **30.** fish

31. Avenue **32.** Ohio **33.** Doctor **34.** Senator **35.** River
36. Wyoming **37.** Hawaii **38.** Street **39.** January **40.** February

41. will not **42.** he would **43.** I have **44.** it is **45.** cannot
46. you will **47.** we had **48.** would not **49.** she is **50.** is not

Paragraphs   pages 40–47

51. Copy these paragraphs. Underline the topic sentences. Cross out any sentences that do not belong. At the end of each paragraph, tell how it was developed.

The trees in my front yard glisten with ice and clink together when the wind stirs their branches. On the white snow below, birds and squirrels hop about after the seeds and bread crumbs I have thrown for them. My house is small but it is warm inside. Beyond the front yard a cleared lake waits for skaters to glide over its smooth surface, laughing and calling to one another. A sparrow just hopped onto my windowsill looking for breakfast. Far away, the blue hills glow with a somber light, eager for the life-giving touch of spring. From my front porch to the distant hills, nature is caught in the harsh but beautiful grip of winter.

Juanita's grandparents, Señor and Señora Acevedo, decided to come to the United States to live. Their house was too large, anyway, since their children had married and moved away. Now Juanita is one of the happiest people I know. She loves having her grandparents nearby, and listens for hours to their stories of beautiful Spain. She says that she wishes all of her classmates could be as lucky as she is.

LANGUAGE
Learning About
Connecting Words

STUDY SKILLS
Drawing Logical
Conclusions

COMPOSITION
Writing
Compositions

LITERATURE
Reading Humorous
Literature

Study the photograph on the left. Pretend you are swimming with the diver in the picture. Describe what you see as you explore the underwater regions.

When you first looked at the photograph, perhaps you thought, "Oh, what a beautiful picture!" Do you know what part of speech *oh* is? It is an interjection. You will be learning about interjections, conjunctions, and prepositions in this unit.

Think hard for a minute. Would you really want to swim underwater with the diver in the picture? When you answer that question, you are stating an opinion. What are the reasons for your opinion? Suppose you said, "I like swimming underwater because everyone likes it." Is this statement logical? Why or why not? When you state an opinion, you want to be sure that it is based on logical reasoning. In this unit you will learn how to identify logical reasoning. You will learn the difference between a fact and an opinion. You will also learn how to organize paragraphs into a composition that states and supports an opinion.

When you read the humorous essay "Dogs That Have Known Me," you will learn the author's opinion of dogs. Then you will use the essay as a model for a humorous composition of your own.

Turn the page and dive into the unit!

◀ *Diver observing a sea urchin in Maui, Hawaii*

LANGUAGE

Lesson 1: Using Prepositions and Prepositional Phrases

Read these sentences.

1. Into the lower bunk jumped Frank.
2. Mike was already in the upper bunk.

Which word in sentence 1 shows the relationship between Frank's jumping and the lower bunk?

Think and Discuss

Words that show relationships between a noun or pronoun and some other word in a sentence are called **prepositions.** The noun or pronoun that *follows* the preposition is the **object of the preposition.** In sentence 1, *into* is the preposition and *bunk* is the object. The words *the lower* come between them. Together, the four words form a **prepositional phrase.** In sentence 2, *in* is the preposition and *bunk* is its object. Which words make up the prepositional phrase?

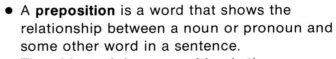

- A **preposition** is a word that shows the relationship between a noun or pronoun and some other word in a sentence.
- The **object of the preposition** is the noun or pronoun that follows the preposition. One or more words may come between the preposition and its object.
- A **prepositional phrase** is a group of words that begins with a preposition and ends with a noun or pronoun as the object of the preposition.

Here is a list of common prepositions. Make up a sentence of your own using two of them.

about	above	across	after	against
along	among	around	at	behind
below	beneath	beside	between	beyond
by	down	during	except	for
from	in	inside	into	near
of	off	on	onto	outside
over	past	to	through	under
up	upon	with	within	without

Practice

A. Copy these sentences. Circle the preposition in each.

1. Frank stayed at Mike's house.
2. They told stories about ghosts and other creepy things.
3. Then it was time for bed.
4. Mike climbed into the upper bunk.
5. Frank jumped onto the lower bunk.

B. Copy these sentences. Draw one line under each preposition and two lines under its object.

6. Beside Mike lay his cat Fleur.
7. Fleur crept under Mike's covers.
8. Mike thought a ghost had sneaked into his bed.
9. Frank heard a shout from the upper bunk.
10. He saw Fleur race across the room.

Apply

C. **11.–20.** Finish the story of Frank, Mike, and Fleur. Write ten sentences with at least one preposition in each. Circle your prepositional phrases.

Lesson 2: Using Prepositional Phrases as Adjectives and Adverbs

Read these lines of poetry by Carl Sandburg.

In the morning hours, in the dawn,
The sun puts out the stars of the sky . . .

Find three prepositional phrases in these lines.

Think and Discuss

A **prepositional phrase** can be used as an adjective, and it can also be used as an adverb. Adjectives modify nouns and pronouns. They answer the questions *what kind, which one, whose,* and *how many.* Adverbs modify verbs, adjectives, and other adverbs. They answer the questions *how, when, where,* and *to what extent.*

In Carl Sandburg's lines of poetry, which words are modified by prepositional phrases? What questions do the prepositional phrases answer? Here is another line of poetry by Sandburg.

Remember all paydays of lilacs and songbirds;

The prepositional phrase *of lilacs and songbirds* modifies the noun *paydays.* It answers the question *what kinds.* What part of speech is it?

Explain how the two prepositional phrases are used as adverbs in these lines by Nikki Giovanni.

in the springtime the violets
grow in the sidewalk cracks . . .

Practice

A. Copy these sentences. Underline each prepositional phrase and draw an arrow to the word it modifies. Tell whether it is used as an adjective or as an adverb.

1. Carl Sandburg's house stands in Galesburg, Illinois.
2. The poet's typewriter sits on an old table.
3. In his poetry Sandburg praised the Midwest.
4. He wrote many poems about working people.
5. He also wrote a biography of President Lincoln.

B. Copy these sentences. Add prepositional phrases used as adjectives to complete each sentence.

6. I would like to read a biography _____.
7. Sometimes I listen to records _____.
8. Poetry _____ is my favorite.
9. Poetry books are in the literature section _____.
10. Many poems are _____.

C. Copy these sentences. Add prepositional phrases used as adverbs to complete each sentence.

11. Nikki Giovanni wrote the lines about springtime used _____.
12. _____ Nikki Giovanni reveals deep feelings.
13. She is a black poet who writes _____ of black people.
14. A record album called *Truth Is on Its Way* is sold _____ that feature poetry records.
15. _____ Nikki Giovanni reads her poetry accompanied by gospel music.

Apply

D. 16.–25. Write ten sentences about a writer or writers whose work you admire. Use at least one prepositional phrase in each sentence. Write whether your prepositional phrases are used as adjectives or adverbs.

Lesson 3: Understanding Appositives

Read these sentences.

1. Janet and Rita's bicycle, a tandem, is slow but fun.
2. Jennie's new ten-speed bicycle, "Spitfire," is sleek and fast.

What kind of bicycle are Janet and Rita riding? What is the name of Jennie's bicycle?

Think and Discuss

Sentences often contain words or groups of words that explain or identify nouns or pronouns in the sentence. These words are called **appositives.** An appositive follows the noun or pronoun it identifies. Find the appositive in this sentence.

3. Baron von Drais, a German, invented one of the first bicycles.

The appositive is *a German.* It identifies the nationality of Baron von Drais.

> • An **appositive** is a noun or phrase that is placed next to another noun or pronoun in order to tell more about it.

Notice that appositives are set off from the rest of the sentence by commas. One comma marks the beginning of the appositive. The other marks where the appositive ends. If the appositive is the last word in the sentence, the proper end punctuation follows it. Read this model sentence that has an appositive at the end.

4. One of the first bicycles was invented by Baron von Drais, a German.

Practice

A. Copy these sentences. Underline the appositive in each one. Circle the noun or pronoun that the appositive explains or describes.

1. The first bicycles, wooden structures with iron wheels, were called *boneshakers.*
2. The *ordinary*, a bicycle with a huge front wheel, was popular in the 1880's.
3. Horse owners, critics of bicycles, said that the invention was dangerous.
4. The invention of brakes, helpful stopping devices, made bicycles much safer.

1884

5. John Dunlop, an Irish veterinarian, invented the air-filled tire.
6. This tire, a piece of garden hose, was filled with air and put on his son's bicycle.
7. Its advantages, speed and comfort, outweighed the problems of flat tires and blowouts.

1888

8. Another improvement, lightweight steel tubing, made the bicycle even faster.
9. The bicycle business, a source of wealth for manufacturers, grew quickly.

10. By the beginning of the twentieth century, most Americans, adults and children, wanted bicycles.

1890's

B. 11. Write the paragraph that your teacher will now dictate to you.

Apply

C. 12. Write a paragraph about a bicycle or another kind of wheeled vehicle you would like to own. Describe it, using at least three appositives in the paragraph. If you wish, you may "invent" a fantasy machine that carries you into another space or time.

The modern bicycle

Lesson 4: Understanding Interjections

Both of these sentences contain the word *oh*. Which of the two expresses stronger feeling?

1. Oh! You frightened me.
2. Oh, I'm sorry. I didn't mean to.

Think and Discuss

Some words are used to express feelings. These words are called **interjections**. Interjections are punctuated in two different ways. A strong interjection is usually followed by an exclamation point. The sentence that comes after it begins with a capital letter. A mild interjection is followed by a comma, and the first word after it is not capitalized unless it is a proper noun or the word *I*.

> • An **interjection** is a word used to express feeling.

Read this list of common interjections.

ah	aha	alas	bravo	eek
hurray	oh	oops	ouch	pssst
ssh	ugh	well	whew	wow

Which interjections express surprise or pleasure? Which express unpleasant feelings?

Practice

A. Copy these sentences. Underline the interjection in each.

1. Oh, I understand.
2. Oops! I slipped.
3. Ouch! My toe hurts.
4. Well, just lean on me.
5. Oh! Get a doctor.
6. Whew! We're in time.
7. Well, that's a good idea.
8. Ah, I see the sign.

B. Copy these sentences, capitalizing and punctuating correctly.

9. Eek something just bit me on the nose.
10. Oh did you see what it was?
11. Ssh it's coming back again.
12. Aha there it is now.
13. Pssst can you see it?
14. Wow I think it's a bat.
15. Ugh I hope you're wrong.

Apply

C. 16.–25. Write ten sentences using interjections. Imagine that you are at an amusement park and are trying all the rides for the first time. Vary your sentences between strong and mild interjections.

HOW OUR LANGUAGE GROWS

Sports and games are very important to many people. The word *sport* comes from the Middle English word *disporten* meaning "to amuse yourself." The word *game* comes from the Old English word *gaman,* which means "amusement." In addition to being fun and exercise, sports are also a source of many words and expressions.

Look at these phrases from baseball. We use them as figures of speech: *touching base, out in left field, throw a curve,* and *off base.* Football is another source of colorful expressions. It is full of such figures of speech as *running interference, getting signals crossed,* and *in a huddle.*

1. List three figures of speech used in another sport.
2. What do these expressions mean both on and off the field?

Lesson 5: Understanding Conjunctions

Read these sentences.

1. This is my notebook. 2. This is my record book.
3. These are my notebook and my record book.

How are the books held together in the picture? How are the words held together in the sentence?

Think and Discuss

Words that join other words or groups of words in a sentence are called **conjunctions.** The most common conjunctions are *and, but,* and *or.* These are **coordinating conjunctions,** conjunctions that join words or groups of words of equal importance. In sentence 3, for example, the coordinating conjunction *and* joins the words *my notebook* and *my record book,* two compound nouns preceded by *my.*

> • A **conjunction** is a word that joins words or groups of words.
> • A **coordinating conjunction** joins words or groups of words of equal importance in a sentence.

Coordinating conjunctions join words or phrases that are the same part of speech and that do the same kind of job in each sentence. This is called **parallel structure.** How do coordinating conjunctions achieve parallel structure in these two sentences?

4. June gets rubber bands from her dad or from the store.
5. Ken likes thin rubber bands, but Jane likes thick ones.

Practice

A. Copy these sentences. Circle the conjunction in each sentence. Then underline the words, phrases, or short sentences that are joined by each conjunction.

1. Rubber bands can be made from natural or synthetic materials.
2. Manufacturers first make a rubber hose or tube.
3. These hoses are different colors and different sizes.
4. Some machines cut the bands, and other machines package them.
5. Rubber bands are used in industry and in the home.
6. The post office once used string, but now it uses rubber bands.
7. Rubber bands are used on braces for teeth and on huge shipping crates.
8. Dentists need tiny bands, but shippers need giant bands.
9. Eventually, most bands are broken or lost.
10. One manufacturer lists two thousand uses for bands, but most people know only a few.

Apply

B. Copy these sentences. Make each sentence longer by adding a coordinating conjunction and another sentence.

11. About 25 million pounds of rubber bands are sold in the United States every year, _____.
12. No one is sure what happens to all the old bands, _____.
13. Some bands are imported, _____.
14. Save rubber bands, _____.
15. One youngster made rubber bands into a ball weighing four pounds, _____.

Lesson 6: Combining Sentences with Conjunctions

Rosita wrote this paragraph about words that begin with the letters *sn.*

```
Words that begin with sn are snooty. They are
snide too. No one likes the word snob. No one likes
the word snipe. When I say snooty, my nose hurts.
When I say sniveling, my nose hurts. I would never
snore or sneer. I would like to be snug, though.
```

Later Rosita combined the sentences in her paragraph.

```
Words that begin with sn are snooty and snide.
No one likes the word snob or snipe. When I say
snooty and sniveling, my nose hurts. I would never
snore or sneer, but I would like to be snug.
```

Think and Discuss

The conjunctions that Rosita used, *and, or,* and *but,* have different meanings. They express different relationships between the words and sentences they join.

The conjunction *and* expresses **addition.** A word or phrase that follows *and* adds to what has gone before.

1. Snakes live in lakes. Snappers live in lakes.
   Snakes *and* snappers live in lakes.

The conjunction *but* expresses **contrast.** Whatever follows *but* shows a change from what has gone before.

2. A sneaky snob snivels. A snarling snob snaps.
   A sneaky snob snivels, *but* a snarling snob snaps.

Two short sentences have been combined here, and a comma is placed before the conjunction.

The third conjunction, *or,* expresses a **choice.** A word, phrase, or sentence following *or* gives another possibility.

3. Snoops live under stoops. Snoops live in coops.
   Snoops live under stoops *or* in coops.

When you combine words, phrases, or sentences with conjunctions, decide whether you wish to show addition, contrast, or choice. Then choose the conjunction that makes this clear. Your new sentences should be parallel in structure.

Practice

A. Make one sentence out of each pair below. You will be combining words, phrases, or complete sentences. Each new sentence should show the meaning given in parentheses ( ).

1. That snob snapped my snorkel.
   That snob snapped my snowshoe.   (addition)
2. The sneak snared my snapshot.
   He didn't snare my sneakers.   (contrast)
3. You can't sneer at snapping turtles.
   You can't snarl at snapping turtles.   (choice)
4. The snipes can snub me.
   They can't snoop around my snapdragons.   (contrast)
5. The snappers are sniveling.
   The snowbirds are sniveling.   (addition)
6. Snuffy snoozes. He never snores.   (contrast)
7. The snare could be in the snapbeans.
   The snare could be under the snails.   (choice)
8. Avoid the snark at the snack bar.
   Make it snappy.   (addition)
9. The snob sneezed all winter.
   The snob sniffled all winter.   (addition)
10. Don't snap at the snowman's snout.
    He will snicker at your snazzy cap.   (choice)

Apply

B. 11. Write a paragraph using as many *sn* words as you can think of or find in the dictionary. Use the conjunctions *and, or,* and *but* in your sentences.

LANGUAGE REVIEW

Prepositions and Prepositional Phrases   pages 278–279

Copy each sentence. Circle the preposition and underline its object.

1. People like to read about mysterious happenings.
2. Monsters and dragons are part of our history.
3. The interest in UFOs is no exception.
4. The UFO craze began during the late 1940's.
5. It quickly spread around the world.

Prepositional Phrases Used as Adjectives and as Adverbs   pages 280–281

Copy each sentence. Underline the prepositional phrase. Draw an arrow to the noun or verb each phrase modifies.

6. Newspapers reported sightings of flying saucers.
7. Some writers wrote stories without facts.
8. The public wanted to know the truth about UFOs.
9. Air Force investigators gathered information on UFOs.
10. They talked to pilots who had seen things of great size.
11. The Air Force investigations began in 1947.
12. They did not end until 1969.
13. The Air Force reported that swamp gas, weather balloons, and air bubbles were seen in the sky, not UFOs.
14. Plane lights, satellites, clouds, and birds were often in the area where "UFOs" had been seen.
15. Not every sighting was explained with ease, however.

Appositives   pages 282–283

Copy each sentence. Underline each appositive. Circle the noun that the appositive explains or describes.

16. One Air Force investigation, Project Blue Book, examined 9,265 UFO reports.
17. The Air Force identified the natural causes for about 8,600 reports, more than 90 percent.

18. The Air Force officers, an open-minded group, examined each report in detail.
19. Researchers and scientists, mostly professors at universities, were allowed to examine the Air Force records.
20. The findings of the scientists, a book-length report, did much to question belief in UFOs.

Interjections   pages 284–285

Copy each sentence. Underline the interjection. Then add the correct punctuation after the interjection.

21. Look is that a UFO?
22. Hmmm it's hard to tell.
23. Oh it's coming closer.
24. Yes and it does look strange.

Conjunctions   pages 286–287

Copy these sentences. Circle each conjunction. Underline the words, phrases, or sentences that are joined by each one.

25. UFO sightings come and go in waves.
26. UFOs are not reported for a while, and people forget them.
27. Then a report appears on TV or in the newspapers.
28. People think satellites or reflections are flying saucers.
29. Normally, people would not even have noticed these things, but now some people are sure that they are UFOs.

Applying Conjunctions

Combine each pair of sentences with a conjunction. Use the conjunction that shows the meaning given in parentheses ( ).

30. UFOs have been studied for years.
    Very little information of value has resulted.   (addition)
31. Some people claim that they have seen space creatures.
    Some say they have talked with them.   (choice)
32. These close encounters are difficult to believe.
    These close encounters are impossible to prove.   (addition)
33. Fewer people are interested in UFOs today.
    Some organizations still believe that creatures from space are trying to reach earth.   (contrast)

STUDY SKILLS

Lesson 7: Understanding Analogies

In which ways are these pairs of words alike?

1. daffodil, iris   **2.** peach, plum   **3.** starfish, clam

Think and Discuss

Whenever you try to figure out what several things have in common, you are making an **analogy**. Analogies show the relationships between things, and being able to understand them is an important thinking skill.

You have already used analogies to some extent in writing your paragraphs of comparison and contrast. In tests, however, analogies are often presented as two pairs of objects. To measure your thinking ability, one member of one pair is usually missing. Once you can figure out the relationship between the objects in the complete pair, you can reason what the missing object must be. Read this model analogy.

4. FINGER **is to** HAND **as** toe **is to** _____.

Since you know that a *finger* is one of the five digits, or extensions, of the hand, it is easy to reason that a toe has that same relationship only with a *foot*. A kind of shorthand used to show such relationships looks like this.

5. FINGER : HAND :: toe : foot

The dots in heavy type in model 5 perform the same job as the words in heavy type in sentence 4. Complete these analogies.

6. EYE : SIGHT :: nose : _____.
7. BREAD : SANDWICH :: bark : _____.

Practice

A. Write the relationship that exists between each pair of items.

1. leaf, tree
2. robin, bird
3. white, snow
4. Anna, girl
5. burn, fire
6. cold, ice

B. Copy these analogies, completing each with the *most exact* answer.

7. FISH : WATER :: bird :
   a. egg   **b.** worm   **c.** sky
8. LEG : ANKLE :: arm :
   a. wrist   **b.** finger   **c.** hand
9. TADPOLE : FROG :: caterpillar :
   a. worm   **b.** bird   **c.** butterfly
10. BODY : HEART :: car :
    a. gasoline   **b.** engine   **c.** seats
11. KNIFE : STEEL :: candle :
    a. wax   **b.** wick   **c.** birthday cake

Apply

C. 12.–15. Write four analogies. Exchange them with a classmate, and try to solve each other's analogies.

To Memorize

Swift things are beautiful:
Swallows and deer,
And lightning that falls
Bright-veined and clear. . . .

Elizabeth Coatsworth

1. Why does the poet describe lightning as "bright-veined"?
2. What swift things besides those in the poem are beautiful?

Lesson 8: Understanding Fact and Opinion

Here is a short quiz. You should be able to complete the sentences very easily.

1. The date today is _____.
2. The only month with fewer than 30 days is _____.
3. Of the four seasons, _____ is the most colorful.

Compare your answers with those of your classmates. On which ones did you all agree?

Think and Discuss

When you read something that can be *proven true or false,* you are reading a **fact.** When you read something that tells what someone *thinks or believes,* you are reading an **opinion.** An opinion cannot be proven true or false. Which sentence is which in 4 and 5?

4. Fireworks are often part of July Fourth celebrations.
5. July Fourth is the highlight of the summer.

Sometimes certain words show that an opinion is being given, such as *surely* or *certainly.* Most of the time, however, it takes careful reading to tell fact from opinion, since opinions are sometimes worded to sound like facts. Are these facts or opinions?

6. These Mother's Day cards are the best money can buy.
7. It will certainly rain on Mother's Day.
8. It will surely rain on Labor Day too.
9. It rained on Mother's Day and Labor Day last year.

Practice

A. Copy these sentences. Write *opinion* for each sentence that states an opinion and *fact* for each sentence that states a fact.

1. There are 12 months in a year.
2. All months should have the same number of days.
3. February is the shortest month of the year.
4. December is the happiest month of the year.
5. Colorful leaves make autumn the loveliest season.
6. Leap Year brings good luck.
7. Halloween falls on October 31 every year.
8. A winter without snow will be disappointing.
9. A winter without snow is certain to be wonderful.
10. May 24 is someone's birthday.

B. Read this paragraph and list all the opinions in it.

We need to celebrate more holidays. After all, we observe Washington's and Lincoln's birthdays. We should observe John Quincy Adams's birthday as well. Adams was born on July 11 and eventually became America's sixth President. December 17 should be a holiday too. This date marks the Wright brothers' first successful flight which took place near Kitty Hawk, North Carolina. December 17 should be celebrated as National Kitty Hawk Day!

Apply

C. Choose one of the following topics and write a brief paragraph about it. Include at least two facts and two opinions about the topic in your paragraph.

your school playground   scary movies
burned toast   blue jeans

Lesson 9: Reasoning Logically

Helen and David were helping with the weekly food shopping. In one aisle, David suddenly exclaimed, "I'm going to try this *Fanfare*. A commercial says it's the top-selling cere l now. It must be good."

"Don't do that!" answered Helen. "That's not a logical reason for buying anything!"

Why do you think Helen reacted the way she did?

Think and Discuss

Logic is the science of reasoning correctly. The error in reasoning that David made is a common one on which advertisers often rely to sell their products. It is called **an appeal to the people.** When an advertisement states, for example, that 50 million families buy *Fanfare* cereal, people are impressed. Like David, they see the product in a store, remember the ad, and buy it too. Yet they fail to realize that the cereal's advertised popularity does not prove that it is *good.* Moreover, most people never even question the truth of the illogical claim.

Sometimes advertisers use the reverse of the best-seller idea. If a product does not sell well, they say that it appeals only to a select few, those who really recognize quality, for example. Some people, wanting to be known as having good taste, begin to buy the product. The promoters win again!

Another error in reasoning that advertisers use is **begging the question,** which means to assume that something has been proved true. Suppose, for example, that the promoters of *Fanfare* cereal wanted people to believe *Fanfare* could make them physically fit. Their slogan might be, "Why wait any longer to enjoy total fitness with *Fanfare*?" At first the message makes sense. Few people would put off the chance to become totally fit so easily. One who reasons logically, however, will think,

"Wait a minute! No one has *proved* that *Fanfare* can make me fit." The advertisers had hoped people would take for granted a claim the company could not possibly prove!

A careful thinker will always listen closely to any form of persuasion. Such a person accepts only statements that have been proved true by logic.

Practice

A. Copy these examples of persuasion. After each, write whether the statement uses logical or illogical persuasion.

1. Anyone with a sense of value will appreciate *Teenie Tennis Shoes*. Buy a pair today.
2. How much longer are we going to accept such waste in our city government?
3. All my friends are allowed to go camping this weekend. I should be allowed to go too!
4. My family has been buying *Whoopee Waffle Mix* for years. The waffles have always been good. Whoopee must be a quality-conscious company.
5. It is obvious that Sue Simmons will not be a good class president. Vote for Judy Johnson instead.

B. 6.–10. Use the examples of persuasion from Practice A. For each illogical statement, write the type of error in reasoning used, and explain how you knew that it was illogical.

Apply

C. 11.–15. Use newspapers and magazines to find five printed examples of illogical persuasion. On a separate sheet of paper, explain why each statement is illogical. Then write a logical statement to replace each illogical one.

COMPOSITION

Lesson 10:   Prewriting

Generating Ideas for a Composition of Opinion

Kareem was struggling with a plan for a composition of opinion. "I always have trouble choosing a topic," he thought glumly. "What can I possibly write about?"

What subjects might make good topics for a composition of opinion? Why?

Think and Discuss

To write a composition of opinion, think about preferences you have. Think about your clothes, for example. Do you have a shirt that you like better than the others? Why? Think about school—courses that you are taking now or that you will take soon. Which one do you think will prove most valuable to you? Why?

Kareem thought about the various areas of his life. "I have *plenty* of things to write about," he realized. "I think I'll do a composition on speed skating and why I enjoy it so much!" To help sort out his most important reasons, Kareem made a diagram like this.

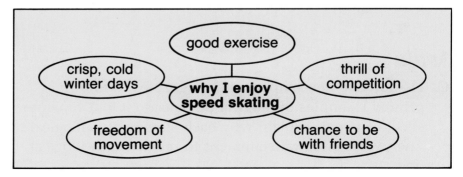

What other reasons might Kareem add to this diagram? Suppose you had to choose three reasons for your composition. Which three would you use? Why? Would your choices be different if you were writing the composition for your health teacher? What if you were writing for your best friend?

How to Plan a Composition of Opinion

1. **Think about your daily life—your school, friends, pastimes.**
2. **Choose a topic that you feel strongly about, either *for* or *against*.**
3. **Make a diagram. Put your chosen topic in the middle.**
4. **List around the central topic the reasons for your opinion.**
5. **Think about your reasons. Consider the audience for whom you are writing.**
6. **Choose the three reasons that mean the most to you and that will appeal most to your audience.**

Practice

A. Use these topics for the center circles in four diagrams. Complete the diagrams with your own reasons.

1. why I like living in _____
2. why someday I might like to live in _____
3. why someday I would like to be a _____
4. why the best thing I will do this year is _____

B. Make two opinion-reason diagrams of your own. You may choose your own topics or select two from those on the next page.

- why I enjoy (skiing, gymnastics, or another sport)
- why I would like to take part in the space program
- why our forests and wetlands should be preserved

Apply

C. Get ready to plan your composition of opinion.

Choose Your Topic

- Select something that you feel strongly about and that would make an interesting composition.

Choose Your Audience

- Decide whom you want to read your composition. The reasons you choose to support your opinion may be guided in part by your audience.

Make a Diagram

- This will help you to evaluate your reasons and choose the ones that are best. Follow the guidelines in the blue box on page 299.

Choose the Three Best Reasons

- Three reasons will make a solid composition, not too sketchy and not too long.
- If you plan one paragraph to discuss each reason, you will have just enough room for an intelligent explanation.
- Number your three chosen reasons in the order of their importance. It is always a good idea to save your best reason for last. It is the one that your audience will surely remember.

Review Your Work

- Look over your diagram. Have you chosen a worthwhile topic? Have you selected the three best reasons to support your opinion?
- If another reason should occur to you, think about it in relation to the reasons you have already chosen. If it is a good one, replace the weakest reason in your diagram with the new one.
- Save your work for the Apply exercise in Lesson 11.

Lesson 11:   Composing
Writing a Composition of Opinion

George really likes to cook. Both his parents are excellent cooks, and George learned early to enjoy making good food. In a composition George explains why he loves his hobby.

Think and Discuss

The kind of composition George wrote is called a **composition of opinion.** Such writing gives the reasons for one's beliefs, often with the hope of persuading others to share that opinion.

A composition of any kind has three main parts: an **introduction,** a **body,** and a **conclusion.** The introduction, the first paragraph or paragraphs, should tell the writer's purpose or state the main idea of the composition. The introduction should also arouse the interest of the reader. Here is the introduction of George's composition.

    Can you tell the difference between a pudding and
    a mousse? Can you tell chicken cacciatore from
    chicken florentine? Can you make a perfect soufflé?
    I can, and I enjoy every minute I spend in the
    kitchen. I think cooking is fun for many reasons.

One of the best ways to get someone interested in what you write is to ask questions. This is especially true if the questions are unusual or if the reader can recognize the terms used but not know the answers. Can you think of other ways to arouse interest?

The body of the composition follows the introduction. In the body the writer organizes and presents information that supports his or her opinion. The body usually contains several paragraphs, each of which develops one of the writer's points. The paragraphs should flow together smoothly, making easy transitions that keep the writing coherent. Here is the body of George's composition.

First of all, I enjoy learning new things, especially when I can get involved in the process and try my own hand at it. This does not mean that I have no disasters as I learn. The first time I spent $2.65 of my own money for special cake ingredients, I burned the cake. Yet, even through the disaster I did learn, and I haven't burned a cake since then.

Next I enjoy the challenge of working at something that is usually done by adults. I like to prove that I can follow a recipe as well as an experienced grownup can, and achieve the same--or better-- results. The first time I worked out a shortcut for making a strawberry soufflé, I felt like Julia Child at her best!

Finally, and maybe best of all, I enjoy eating what I cook. I don't have much time for cooking on school days with football or Little League and homework to do. On the weekends, however, I am the only 11-year-old on my block who gets to eat fettuccine al pesto, insalata romagna, lemon sole, and mousse au chocolat--all made with my own two hands. The delicious aromas in the kitchen are made even better when I sit down to a great meal that I have cooked myself!

One of the good things about the body of George's composition is that he gave examples to support each of his points. Not only are they interesting—and humorous at times—but they prove the sincerity and earnestness of George's belief. What transitional expressions did George use to tie his paragraphs together? What other expressions might he have used?

The conclusion of a composition of opinion should summarize the points mentioned in the body or end it in some other suitable way. Here is the conclusion of George's composition.

Yes, I enjoy cooking. My walnut pudding is just as good as my walnut mousse. I still need practice on my chicken cacciatore before it's as good as my chicken florentine. My strawberry soufflé, however, is a real treat! Perhaps someday I'll be one of the world's great chefs!

Since George had begun his composition by asking about various dishes, he thought it would be a good idea to round it off by mentioning the same dishes again. The exclamation in the final sentence reveals George's great enthusiasm for his hobby and further supports the reader's conclusion that George is sincere. How else might he have finished his composition?

How to Write a Composition of Opinion
1. **Write an introduction. Tell what your opinion is. You may want to ask a question to catch your reader's interest.**
2. **Write the body of your composition. Allow one paragraph for each supporting reason.**
3. **Tie your paragraphs together with well-chosen transitional expressions.**
4. **Write a conclusion to let your readers know that you have finished.**

Practice

A. Answer these questions about a composition of opinion.

1. What are the three parts of a composition?
2. What does the writer of a composition of opinion attempt to do?
3. What information does the first part of a composition contain?
4. What goes into the second part of a composition?
5. How does a writer decide how many paragraphs should make up the second part of the composition?
6. How can the writer keep the composition flowing smoothly?
7. What information does the last part of a composition contain?
8. What simple plan might help the writer to organize the composition in an orderly way?

Apply

B. Read over your opinion and the reasons you chose to support it. Use this material to write your composition.

Write Your Introduction

● Think of an interesting beginning to catch your reader's attention and interest.

Write the Body of Your Composition

● Follow the numbered order you decided on in Lesson 10. Remember that your most important or strongest reason should be mentioned last.

● Use the information in the blue box on page 303 to help you.

Write Your Conclusion

● You might want to sum up your reasons or answer any questions you asked in your introduction. An interesting statistic or an exclamation at the end of your composition will also be remembered by your reader.

Review Your Work

● Reread your composition. Check for transitional expressions to keep your work coherent.

● Save your work for revising in Lesson 12.

A Challenge

Make three sets of five index cards. Write an adjective and a noun (such as *frilly hats*, *open-toed shoes*, or *burned meatloaf*) on each card of the first set. On the second set, write on each card "I like it/them because . . ." and finish each sentence with a humorous twist (such as, "They hurt my feet" or "I can't see without them"). On the third set, write on each one, "I don't like it/them because . . ." and finish each sentence with another humorous twist.

Put all the cards of each kind together. Then choose one from each deck and write a composition of opinion on the results of your draw.

Lesson 12: Revising

Editing and Proofreading a Composition of Opinion

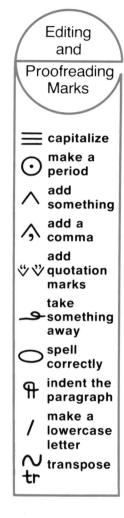

Garnetta wrote a composition of opinion about Bermuda and its people. The composition form, however, gave her some trouble. What are the three parts of a composition?

Think and Discuss

Here is the introduction to Garnetta's paper and the changes she made on it.

> When my parents took me to Bermuda last Fall, all I *expected* (exspected) was an extra two weeks of vacation. My *appreciation of Bermuda and its people* idea about the trip was changed *,however, came to understand spirit* when I got into the (spirt) of the (iland) *island* on the *wonderful* second day. Bermuda is a nice place, and I *have three good reasons for thinking so.*

Garnetta's friend Christine reminded her that the introduction is supposed to arouse interest. Garnetta's words, however, were vague. By changing *My idea about the trip* to *My appreciation of Bermuda and its people* helped a great deal. Not only are her new words more specific, but they suggest to her reader the aspects of Bermuda that she will discuss.

To further aid the reader, Garnetta added *and I have three good reasons for thinking so* to the end of her introduction. These words make it clear that Garnetta is writing a composition of *opinion.*

Once she felt satisfied that her introduction did what it was supposed to do, Garnetta went back and made some changes in style and grammar. Explain the changes that Garnetta made.

How to Revise a Composition of Opinion

Editing

1. Check that you have included the three parts of a composition: introduction, body, and conclusion.
2. Be sure that you have explained each reason for your opinion in a separate paragraph.
3. Check the order in which you listed your reasons. The most important one should be mentioned last so that your audience will remember it.
4. Take out any material that does not directly concern your topic. Keep your composition unified and coherent.
5. Think about your audience. Be sure you have defined any terms that your reader may not know or that are confusing.
6. Check for effective use of transitional expressions between sentences and paragraphs.

Proofreading

7. Correct all errors in spelling, punctuation, and mechanics.
8. Be sure you indented the first word of each new paragraph.

Practice

A. Rewrite Garnetta's introduction as it should appear in the final draft.

B. On the next page you will find three paragraphs taken from the body of Garnetta's composition. They have already been marked for changes in grammar and punctuation. As you recopy each paragraph, make any changes you feel are necessary in the way she presents her ideas.

My second reason for liking Bermuda so much ~~are~~ is
the people. Two-thirds of them are natives of ~~african~~
african descent, ~~decent~~ and the other third are mostly from England,
the country that administers the ~~iland~~ island. The ~~british~~
governor has several ~~municiple~~ municipal buildings in Hamilton,
the capital, although St. George was the capital long
ago. Many ~~ceremonys~~ ceremonies and parades are still held in st.
George because of its ~~hysterical~~ historical importance to the
~~iland~~ island.

I love the food of Bermuda. You may not think
that an ~~iland~~ island so close to the united States and
governed by England could have ~~specal~~ special food. The
~~Bermudans~~ Bermudians make a ~~specal~~ special fish stew that is delicious.
Everyone should also take the Glass bottom Boat
tour, which is ~~alot~~ a lot of fun.

~~Finly~~ Finally Bermuda is the most beautiful ~~iland~~ island I
have ever seen. Long, unspoiled beaches of pink sand
~~strech~~ stretch for miles in the warm sunshine. The Clear,
aqua-blue waters are a joy to ~~swimers~~ swimmers, fishers,
and sailors alike. Soft tropical ~~brezes~~ breezes ~~bring~~ waft the
odors of ~~jasmin~~ jasmine and honeysuckle throughout the ~~iland~~ island.
As if this natural beauty were not enough, the
~~inhabitents~~ inhabitants keep Bermuda sparkling clean.

C. Originally Garnetta's composition had included the
next paragraph about things to see in Bermuda. She
took it out, however, when she realized that it did not
support the main idea of her composition. Rewrite the
paragraph so that if she wanted to, Garnetta could
include it.

Bermuda's aquarium features fish that live in the surrounding ocean waters. Their botanical garden includes native plants as well as those grown in other semi-tropical regions. Devil's Hole is a natural fish pond. Caves, water carnivals, and a perfume factory are other things that visitors to Bermuda might want to see.

D. When you have completed Practice A and you know that it is correct, study it well. Pay close attention to the punctuation, some of which you have just learned in this unit. Then put your corrected paper away and rewrite the paragraph as your teacher dictates it.

Apply

E. Reread your composition of opinion. Now you may revise it and put it into final form.

Edit Your Composition

● Check your **content.** Use items 1–4 in the blue box on page 306 to help you.
● Check your **style.** Use items 5 and 6 in the blue box as a guide.

Proofread Your Composition

● Follow guidelines 7 and 8 in the same blue box. Check punctuation of appositives, interjections, and any special uses of prepositional phrases.
● Copy or type your revised composition onto a clean sheet of paper.

MECHANICS PRACTICE

Using Commas and Exclamation Points in Sentences

- Use commas to set off introductory or transitional expressions.

  Nevertheless, I want to build a sundial.

- Use commas to set off appositives from the rest of the sentence.

  The sundial, a simple clock, is of no use on rainy days.

- Use a comma after two or more prepositional phrases at the beginning of a sentence.

  In the darkness at night, we can't use the sundial either.

- Use a comma after a mild interjection.

  Well, that should just about do it.

- Use an exclamation point after a strong interjection.

  Wow! We're an hour late for the show.

Add commas and exclamation points to these sentences.

1. In the course of an average day a person breathes 3,500 gallons (13,300 L) of air.
2. Ouch A bee just stung me on one of my ten toes.
3. A gorilla one of the great apes can't swim.
4. Say do you know what is unusual about hummingbirds?
5. No I don't.
6. Hummingbirds tiny brightly colored birds fly backwards!
7. Next let me tell you something interesting about dolphins.
8. Oh what is that?
9. The dolphin a small-toothed whale sleeps with one eye open.
10. On the subject of eyes most people blink 13 times a minute.
11. Your little sister however blinks only 7 times a minute.
12. Did you know that Albert a person in perfect health drinks 8 glasses of water a day?
13. Well that explains why he sloshes when he walks.
14. Wow You certainly are silly.
15. On top of everything else I'm a comedian too.

LITERATURE

Lesson 13: Reading Humorous Literature

Compositions like the ones you and your classmates wrote in this unit may have many different subjects. They may have different purposes and may be of different lengths. All compositions, however, have the same three parts. What are they?

Think and Discuss

Not all compositions follow the rules you learned as closely as some do. **Humorous compositions,** or essays, are often informally organized and sometimes may seem to wander, but that is usually part of their humor. The language in such works is generally informal. Moreover, the author frequently exaggerates, but this is done to make a point—and to get a laugh.

As you read this humorous composition, try to decide where its three parts begin and end. Be on the lookout for any of the elements of humor already mentioned. Also, watch for others that may occur to you as you are reading.

Dogs That Have Known Me

Jean Kerr

I never meant to say anything about this, but the fact is that I have never met a dog that didn't have it in for me. You take Kelly, for instance. He's a wire-haired fox terrier and he's had us for three years now. I wouldn't say that he was terribly handsome but he does have a very nice smile. What he doesn't have is any sense of fitness. All the other dogs in the neighborhood spend their afternoons yapping at each other's heels or chasing cats. Kelly spends his whole day, every day, chasing swans on the millpond. I don't actually worry because he will never catch one. For one thing, he can't swim. Instead of settling for a simple dog-paddle like everybody else, he has to show off and try some complicated overhand stroke, with the result that he always sinks and has to be fished out. Naturally, people talk, and I never take him for a walk that somebody doesn't point him out and say, "There's that crazy dog that chases swans."

Another thing about that dog is that he absolutely refuses to put himself in the other fellow's position. We have a pencil sharpener in the kitchen and Kelly used to enjoy having an occasional munch on the plastic cover. As long as it was just a nip now and then, I didn't mind. But one day he simply lost his head and ate the whole thing. Then I had to put it up high out of Kelly's reach. Well, the scenes we were treated to—and the sulking! In fact ever since, he has been eating things I know he doesn't like just to get even. I don't mean things like socks and mittens and paper napkins, which of course are delicious. Lately he's been eating plastic airplanes, suede brushes, and light bulbs. Well, if he wants to sit under the piano and make low and loving growls over a suede brush just to show me, okay. But frankly I think he's lowering himself.

Time and again I have pointed out to Kelly that with dogs who are looking for a finer, lighter chew—it's bedroom slippers two to one. I have even dropped old bedroom slippers here and there behind the furniture, hoping to tempt him. But the fact is, that dog wouldn't touch a bedroom slipper if he was starving.

The first dog I remember well was a large black and white mutt that was part German shepherd, part English sheepdog, and part collie — the wrong part in each case. We called him Ladadog from the title by Albert Payson Terhune. He was a splendid dog in many respects, but I'm afraid he was a bit of a social climber. He used to pretend that he was just crazy about us. I mean, if you just left the room to comb your hair he would greet you on your return with lickings, pawings, and tail-waggings. And a longer separation — let's say you had to go out on the front porch to pick up the mail — would set Ladadog off into such a demonstration of thanksgiving that we used to worry for his heart.

However, all this sentiment disappeared the moment he stepped outside. I remember we kids used to spot him on our way home from school, chasing around the Parkers' lawn with a cocker spaniel friend of his, and we'd rush over to him with happy squeals of "Laddy, oleboy, oleboy, oleboy," and Ladadog would just stand there looking slightly pained and distinctly cool. It wasn't that he cut us dead. He nodded, but it was with the remote air of a celebrity saying, "Of course I remember you, and how's Ed?"

We kept making excuses for him and even worked out an elaborate explanation for his behavior. We decided that Ladadog didn't see very well, that he could only recognize us by smell and that he couldn't smell very well in the open air. However, the day came when my mother met Ladadog in front of the A & P. She was wearing her new brown coat with the beaver collar, and, lo and behold, Ladadog greeted her with joy and rapture. After that we just had to face the truth — that dog was a snob.

He also had other peculiarities. For instance, he saved lettuce. He used to beg for lettuce and then he would store it away in the cellar behind the coalbin. I don't know whether he was saving up to make a salad or what, but every so often we'd have to clean away a small, soggy lump of decayed vegetation.

And every time the phone rang he would run from wherever he was and sit there beside the phone chair, his tail thumping and his ears bristling, until you'd make some sort of an announcement like "It's just a wrong number" or "Eileen, it's for you." Then he would immediately disappear. Clearly, this dog had put a call in to someone, but we never did figure out to whom.

Come to think of it, the dog that gave us the most trouble was a beagle named Murphy. As far as I'm concerned, the first thing he did wrong was to turn into a beagle. I had seen him bounding around in a pet-shop window, and I went in and asked the man, "How much is that adorable fox terrier in the window?" Did he say, "That adorable fox terrier is a beagle"? No, he said, "Ten dollars, lady." Now, I don't mean to say one word against beagles. They have rights just like other people. But it is a bit of a shock when you bring home a small ball of fluff in a shoebox, and three weeks later it's as long as the sofa.

Murphy had a habit that used to leave us open to a certain amount of criticism from our friends who were not dog-lovers. He never climbed up on beds or chairs or sofas. But he always sat on top of the piano. In the beginning we used to try to pull him off of there. But after a few noisy scuffles in which he knocked a picture off the wall, scratched the piano, and smashed a lamp, we just gave in — only to discover that, left to his own devices, he hopped up and down as delicately as a ballet dancer. We became quite used to it, but at parties at our house it was not unusual to hear a guest remark, "I think I see a big dog on the piano."

It's not just our own dogs that bother me. The dogs I meet at parties are even worse. I don't know what I've got that attracts them; it just doesn't bear thought. My husband swears I rub chopped meat on my ankles. But at every party it's the same thing. I am sitting with a group in front of the fire when all of a sudden the large mutt of the host appears in the archway. Then, without a single bark of warning, he hurls himself upon me. My stockings are torn before he finally settles down peacefully in the lap of my new black dress. I blow out such quantities of hair as I haven't swallowed and glance at my host, expecting to be rescued. He murmurs, "Isn't that wonderful? You know, Brucie is usually so distant with strangers."

Nowadays if I go anywhere I just ask if they have a dog. If they do, I say, "Maybe I'd better keep away from him — I have this bad allergy." This does not really charm the lady of the house. But it is safer. It really is.

What was the funniest characteristic, or quality, of each of the dogs that have known Jean Kerr? Some of the elements of humor found in essays like Jean Kerr's are in this list. Can you think of any others?

1. informal vocabulary
2. informal organization
3. exaggeration

Remember This

1. **Humorous literature is usually <u>informally organized</u>.**
2. **Humorous literature often involves <u>exaggeration</u> for the effect it produces on the reader.**
3. **Humorous literature usually contains <u>informal vocabulary</u>.**

Practice

A. Write the answers to these questions.

1. Copy the single sentence that acts as the introduction to the composition.
2. Where does the body of the composition end?
3. A conclusion is supposed to end the composition "in a suitable way." Explain how this conclusion is suitable.
4. Give one example of informal vocabulary in this composition.
5. Give one example of exaggeration in this composition.
6. Why might this composition be called "informally organized"?
7. Copy one example in which a dog seems to be given human qualities by the author.
8. How does the author feel about dogs? Explain your opinion.

Apply

B. Suppose that someone has given you one of these gifts for your birthday.

- a model of the Eiffel Tower five feet (1.5 m) high
- a hundred helium-filled balloons
- a life-sized stuffed toy hippopotamus

Write a humorous paragraph or short composition in which you explain how you handle the gift and put it to good use.

Prewriting

- Choose your topic and your audience.
- Make a list of the possible uses for your gift. The more amusing and exaggerated the better.
- As the basis for your work, choose one or two of the uses you listed.

Composing

- In the first part of your work, explain what the gift was. Then describe your reaction to it and tell how you moved it to the place where you would keep the gift permanently. Make your description amusing.
- In the remainder of your work, explain the use you have found for your gift. Again, make it as amusing as possible. Exaggerate.

Revising

- Read your work. Does it make sense? Are your descriptions amusing?
- Check your vocabulary. Always substitute specific words for general ones. In this case, check for words and comparisons that will make your audience laugh.
- Check for informal language and organization. Remember that guidelines for more formal writing are relaxed in humorous work.
- Check your spelling, punctuation, and mechanics. Even humorous work should be correctly written.
- Copy your humorous composition onto a clean sheet of paper.

A BOOK TO READ

Title: **How Did We Find Out About Black Holes?**
Author: Isaac Asimov
Publisher: Walker & Company

What is a black hole? When a star collapses, its pull of gravity is so intense that not even light can escape it. It shows up as a "hole" in space—a spot from which no light comes.

Isaac Asimov goes into detail in this book about why stars collapse, why and how black holes are formed, and how astronomers can detect them.

7 UNIT TEST

● **Prepositions and Prepositional Phrases**   pages 278–279

Copy each sentence. Label each preposition *A* and each object of the preposition *B*.

1. The first ice skates were made from bone.
2. They were invented in the ninth century.
3. Later, these bone skates were replaced by wooden skates.
4. People in Holland, Sweden, Norway, and Russia used skates often.
5. Ice skates were transportation during the long, cold winters.

● **Types of Prepositional Phrases**   pages 280–281

Copy each sentence. Underline the prepositional phrase used as an adjective. Circle the noun it modifies.

6. Iron skates were a big improvement over the old wooden skates.
7. Steel clip-on skates with straps later became popular.
8. Colonists from Europe brought ice skates along when they left their native lands.
9. During the nineteenth century, ice skating was an important form of recreation here.
10. The game of ice hockey cannot be played unless people skate.

Copy each sentence. Underline the prepositional phrase used as an adverb. Circle the verb it modifies.

11. Ice hockey originated in Canada; today, however, hockey fans can be found in nearly every country.
12. Professional hockey teams are based throughout the United States and Canada.
13. Hockey games are won with speed and accuracy.
14. Hockey demands both strength and stamina at all times.
15. The number of indoor skating rinks is growing everywhere by leaps and bounds.

Appositives   pages 282–283

Copy these sentences. Underline each appositive. Circle the noun that the appositive describes or explains.

16. Figure skating, a most graceful but demanding sport, grows in popularity every year.
17. Jackson Haines, an American, invented the sport in the 1860's; now, however, we cannot imagine that it once did not exist.
18. Sonja Henie, an Olympic champion, did much to popularize it during the 1930's.
19. Her ice carnival, a popular American amusement, toured the United States during these years.
20. Dick Button, an outstanding American skater, won fourteen figure-skating championships.

Interjections   pages 284–285

Copy these sentences. Underline each interjection. Then add the correct capitalization and punctuation after the interjection.

21. Hmm I think Roger is going to pass the puck.
22. Wow he passed it to me by mistake.
23. Well I guess I'd better take a shot.
24. Bravo that was a great shot.
25. Hurray I scored the winning goal.

Conjunctions   pages 286–287

Copy these sentences. Circle each conjunction. Underline the words, phrases, or sentences that are joined by it.

26. The first roller skates were designed and invented in 1789 by Joseph Merlin, a musician.
27. He put them on and skated to a fancy costume party, playing his violin as he went.
28. He had a good time at the party, but he forgot one thing, something that he always regretted later.
29. Once he started to go fast, Merlin didn't know how to slow or stop the skates!
30. He crashed into a huge mirror, breaking it and his violin; in fact, he nearly broke both his legs.

● Combining Sentences with Conjunctions   pages 288–289

Combine each pair of sentences with a conjunction. Use the conjunction that shows the meaning given in parentheses.

31. Roller skating has always been popular.
Today it is more popular than ever.   (contrast)

32. Today's skates are more comfortable than ever before.
Today's skates are easier to handle than ever before.   (addition)

33. Outdoors, the new wide polyurethane wheels hug the sidewalks.
Outdoors, the new wide polyurethane wheels hug the road.   (choice)

● Analogies   pages 292–293

Copy these analogies. Complete each with the most exact answer.

1. FEATHERS : OWL   : :   fur :
   a. coat   **b.** squirrel   **c.** person

2. DEN : BEAR   : :   burrow :
   a. rabbit   **b.** lion   **c.** spider

3. WATER : LAKE   : :   ice :
   a. lake   **b.** glacier   **c.** ice skates

4. ANGLE : SQUARE   : :   arc :
   a. triangle   **b.** line   **c.** circle

● Fact and Opinion   pages 294–295

Write *opinion* or *fact* for each sentence.

5. Some of the first roller skates were made from ice skates.

6. These early skates had wooden rollers, not wheels.

7. They looked strange and felt awkward.

● Reasoning Logically   pages 296–297

Write whether each statement is logical or illogical. If illogical, write the type of error in reasoning used.

8. Join the top athletes. Drink *Ready Set Go* orangeade.

9. Why not enjoy your most relaxing vacation on Play Island?

10. Marge, aren't you going to the game? Everyone else is.

1. Make a diagram giving your opinion about one of these topics. Include four reasons for your opinion.

   ■ birthdays (other people's)
   ■ rainy days
   ■ birthdays (your own)
   ■ space travel

   Use your diagram to write a composition of opinion explaining how you feel about your chosen topic. When you revise your work, be sure that all three parts of the composition are included. Check your spelling and punctuation. Then rewrite your composition in final form.

● **Mechanics Practice**   page 309

Copy these sentences. Add commas and exclamation points wherever necessary.

2. Aha I saw you drink that extra carton of milk.
3. At the beginning and middle of every day I drink extra milk.
4. At the end of every day I think about what I have eaten.
5. In addition I check to be sure I've had all my vitamins.
6. Say I bet you'll be like Wilma Rudolph the great runner.
7. Oh I'd rather be like Lena Horne the great singer instead.

● **Humorous Literature**   pages 310–317

Read these sentences taken from one of Erma Bombeck's newspaper columns. Write whether each came from the *introduction,* the *body,* or the *conclusion.*

1. The grass is brown and doesn't need cutting.
2. Did you realize that August is the only "No Holiday" month on the calendar?
3. But thank goodness for August—everyone's time to lie back and be grateful that there is absolutely no occasion to rise to.
4. It's too late to diet for bathing suits and it's too early to diet for the Christmas parties.
5. It's too hot to cook. It's too humid to let your hair grow.

LANGUAGE
Building Sentences

STUDY SKILLS
Preparing Reports

Do you have a favorite sport? Look at the picture on the left. What might this girl's favorite sport be? Describe the action in the photograph.

When people first begin to participate in a sport, they usually have much to learn. Do you think this is the first time the girl in the picture has ridden a horse? What are the reasons for your answer? Being able to control a horse as it jumps hurdles is a difficult task. The girl in the picture had to prepare herself properly. When she first began riding, she had to learn the correct way to mount a horse. What other things might she have had to learn before she was prepared for jumps?

Writers have to prepare themselves too. They cannot sit down and write a report without first learning everything they can about a topic. In this unit you will study how to prepare a good research report. You will learn how to take notes, develop an outline, organize a bibliography, and write a first draft. If you prepare carefully, writing a research report should seem as easy to you as jumping hurdles seems to a good rider.

Finally you will study some narrative poetry as you prepare to write an original narrative poem.

Now turn the page and start clearing hurdles!

◀ *Rider and horse clearing a hurdle*

LANGUAGE

Lesson 1: Understanding Compound Subjects and Predicates

Read these sentences.

1. Blue whales and humpback whales swim in all the oceans of the world.
2. Whales swim in the water but rise to the top to breathe.

Name the simple subject and predicate of both sentences. What is unusual about the subject of sentence 1 and the predicate of sentence 2?

Think and Discuss

Most of the sentences you have worked with until now have had only one simple subject and one simple predicate. Many sentences, however, involve more than one person performing a single action. Others involve one person who performs two or more actions. These are examples of compound elements in sentences.

- A **compound subject** consists of two or more subjects that have the same predicate.
- A **compound predicate** consists of two or more predicates that have the same subject.

The coordinating conjunctions *and, but,* and *or* usually join compound subjects and predicates. Commas are also used to connect such subjects and predicates when there are more than two in a single sentence.

Read these sentences.

3. Whales, humans, and mice are all mammals.
4. Newborn whale calves swim, rise, and dive with their mothers.

How are commas combined with coordinating conjunctions to join the compound subjects and predicates in sentences 3 and 4?

Practice

A. Copy these sentences. Underline all compound subjects once and all compound predicates twice.

1. Toothed whales and baleen whales are the two major kinds of whales.
2. A whale's huge body produces heat and keeps it warm.
3. Lampreys, barnacles, and other parasites sometimes attach themselves to whales.
4. A whale's bones are spongy and contain oil.
5. The flippers of a whale balance the creature and keep it level.

B. Copy these sentences. Use commas where necessary.

6. Whales sharks and manta rays feed on plankton.
7. The blue whale the fin whale and the humpback whale are all called tubed whales.
8. Tubed whales swim all over the world feed in the North and South Poles but often return to warm waters.
9. The blue whale grows longer than a railroad car stands higher than a house and is larger than a dinosaur.
10. The playful humpback whale leaps somersaults and splashes in the water.

Apply

C. 11.–20. Locate the subject *whales* in an encyclopedia. Then write ten sentences about whales. Include at least five compound subjects and five compound predicates.

Lesson 2: Understanding Clauses

Study these sentences.

1. Jane was on time to meet us.
2. Alicia looked at her watch anyway.
3. Jane was on time to meet us, but Alicia looked at her watch anyway.

How did sentences 1 and 2 become sentence 3?

Think and Discuss

Until now you have been dealing with words, phrases, and short sentences that you have joined to make longer sentences. The two sentences that have been joined to make up sentence 3 are called **clauses.** A clause is a group of words that has its own subject and predicate.

Some clauses can stand alone, and others cannot. This lesson will concentrate on those that *can.* Clauses that can stand alone, that is, those that express a complete thought, are called **independent clauses.** A simple sentence, having its own subject and predicate, and expressing a complete thought, has the same form as an independent clause.

> - A **clause** is a group of words that contains a subject and a predicate and is used as part of a sentence.
> - An **independent clause** is a clause that expresses a complete thought and can stand alone.

Look back at sentence 3. If you took away the comma and the coordinating conjunction, what would be left? What punctuation would make them two separate sentences?

Practice

A. Copy these sentences. Underline the independent clauses.

1. Alicia's father is a pilot, and he flies an L-1011 jet.
2. We visited him at the airport, and we saw his plane.
3. All the instruments amazed me, but Mr. Conlan is used to them.
4. The body of the jet was huge, and we were impressed.
5. Two in our group had flown before, but everyone was eager to fly in Mr. Conlan's plane.
6. After an hour we left the airport, but we did not go home.
7. Instead, we went to a bakery, and we watched Jane's dad at work.

B. Rewrite these sentences. Add punctuation and conjunctions to make new sentences with two independent clauses each.

8. Mr. Milici is a baker he loves his job.
9. We watched him make cannoli he let us ice some eclairs.
10. Afterward we rode a bus to the harbor it took an hour.
11. We were too late to see Denise's mother the harbor master told us to wait.
12. He said we could wait on the dock we could go to the snack bar for a sandwich.
13. Later we saw Denise's mom we were glad of it.
14. Mrs. Carey is a tugboat pilot she was guiding a huge ocean liner to port.
15. We enjoyed our day visiting parents at work we plan to visit others very soon.

Apply

C. 16.–25. Imagine that you are visiting a friend's mother or father at work. Write a paragraph in which you explain what he or she does. Use at least ten independent clauses in your paragraph.

Lesson 3: Understanding Compound Sentences

Read these sentences written for a report about rivers.

1. Rivers were once the chief means of transportation.
2. They remain important passages today.

How many clauses are in each of these sentences?

Think and Discuss

You know that every sentence must express a complete thought. Some sentences, like 1 and 2 above, express only *one* complete thought. These sentences are called **simple sentences.** A simple sentence has one complete subject and one complete predicate. They have the same form as independent clauses.

Now read this sentence. Notice that the two simple sentences, or independent clauses, are joined.

3. Rivers were once the chief means of transportation, and they remain important passages today.

This sentence expresses *two* complete thoughts. It is a **compound sentence.** What are the two complete thoughts? Which word joins them? Which mark of punctuation comes before the conjunction *and*?

Here are three more compound sentences. Notice the conjunction in each one.

4. Rivers can build up deltas, or they can cut valleys through mountains.
5. Rivers move forward, but they also move gradually sideways.
6. Swift rivers often cause trouble for farmers; their currents carry rich topsoil away from the fields.

What is omitted when the comma is replaced by a semicolon as in sentence 6?

> ● A **compound sentence** is made up of two independent clauses joined by a comma and a conjunction or by a semicolon.

To identify a compound sentence, first look for a semicolon or the conjunctions *and, or,* or *but.* Then see if the semicolon or conjunction joins two independent clauses. Do not confuse a simple sentence that has a compound subject or predicate with a compound sentence.

Practice

A. Copy only the compound sentences. If a sentence is not compound, write *not compound.*

1. Rivers can be harnessed, and they are a cheap source of power.
2. Rainwater can enter a river, or it can disappear into the ground.
3. Heavy rains anywhere in the country can cause flooding.
4. Rivers may have scanty flows, or they may surge with too much water.
5. People build dams, but rivers can wash them away.

B. Add another independent clause to each of these independent clauses to make five compound sentences. Use semicolons in two compound sentences.

6. The flood plain is part of a river's natural flow.
7. Powerful rivers can cut away their banks.
8. People can build on a flood plain.
9. Flood plains may be dangerous.
10. Floods destroy homes and businesses.

Apply

C. 11.–20. Write ten compound sentences of your own about a real or imaginary body of water. Join the clauses of three of your sentences with semicolons.

Lesson 4: Understanding Subject-Verb Agreement

Compare these sentences. The simple subjects are underlined once. The verbs are underlined twice.

1. Aiyana sews a square for the quilt.
2. The children sew squares for the quilt.

In each sentence the verb is *sew*. But the form of the verb in sentence 1 is different from the form in sentence 2. Which subject is singular? Which subject is plural?

Think and Discuss

You know that words can be singular or plural. This quality is called **number.** Singular verbs are used with singular subjects. Plural verbs are used with plural subjects. In sentence 1, for example, both the subject and the verb are singular. In sentence 2 both the subject and the verb are plural. Subjects and verbs that are used together correctly are said to **agree.** Read this sentence.

3. Lian and Rick have patches for the quilt.

Name the compound subject. Does the verb agree?

> • Every verb must **agree** with its subject in **number.**

Practice

A. Copy these sentences. Use the correct verb.

1. Mr. Carl, the art teacher, (has, have) begun a project.
2. Groups of students (designs, design) squares for a quilt.
3. The theme of the quilt (is, are) the four seasons.
4. Juana, Ezra, and Tika (has, have) ideas for squares.
5. First they (sketches, sketch) their ideas on paper.

6. Each student (presents, present) an idea to Mr. Carl.
7. Then each student (chooses, choose) a square to sew.
8. Juana, Ezra, and Tika (wants, want) red squares.

B. Copy these sentences. Use the correct verb. Tell whether the subject and verb are singular or plural.

9. Mr. Carl's students (finishes, finish) the quilt.
10. They (displays, display) it in the auditorium.
11. Parents, teachers, and students (examines, examine) it.
12. The quilt (causes, cause) a sensation.
13. All the parents (raves, rave) about the design.
14. Someone (calls, call) the newspaper about the project.
15. The next day a reporter (arrives, arrive) at school.

Apply

C. 16. Finish the story of the quilt by telling what was in the newspaper article.

HOW OUR LANGUAGE GROWS

Everyone hears sounds a little differently. In English we describe the sound of a dog as *woof-woof* or *arf-arf* or *bow-wow*. A Japanese dog, on the other hand, says *wung-wung*, while an Italian dog says *bu-bu.* German dogs say *wau-wau*, and Vietnamese dogs say *gaugau.*

If you get hurt, you will probably yell *ouch!* In France people yell *aie!* In Italy they will yell *aio!* and in Mexico they yell *ay!* The word *crash* is *kling* to the Danes, *krats* to the Finns, and *hua-la-la* to the Chinese.

1. Using a foreign language dictionary, find out what sound a ringing telephone makes in Greece and Italy—or in two other countries of your choice.
2. How would the Japanese and the Finns—or people from two other countries—say *ouch*?

Lesson 5: Understanding Varied Sentences

Renée wrote these two sentences. Which is better and why?

1. A refreshing breeze sprang up.
2. During the night a refreshing breeze sprang up and rustled the leaves.

Think and Discuss

Longer sentences are not always better sentences. However, good longer sentences offer more information than do short ones. In addition, words can be added and rearranged with more imagination in a longer sentence. Look at sentence 1, for example. It makes a simple statement. Sentence 2, however, presents added information and varies the structure of the original sentence. By adding a prepositional phrase at the beginning and an extra verb and object at the end, the writer has achieved greater interest.

Read these guidelines for more interesting sentences.

How to Make Your Sentences More Interesting

1. **Begin with one or two prepositional phrases.**
2. **Use a compound subject or a compound predicate.**
3. **Write a compound sentence.**
4. **Add to an independent clause a clause that cannot stand alone.**
5. **Add an appositive.**
6. **When writing conversation, include the name of the person to whom the subject is speaking.**

The last suggestion involves what is called **direct address.** Like appositives, names used in direct address must be set off by commas. Moreover, a comma must follow two introductory prepositional phrases, the first clause in a compound sentence, and an introductory clause that cannot stand alone. Look at these examples.

3. At dawn on the next day, the sky was clear.
4. The haze had lifted, and the air was crisp and cool.
5. Mary, look at the mallard, the duck with the shiny green head.
6. While he is swimming, the other ducks are resting on the grass.

Why are commas used in these sentences?

Practice

A. Copy these sentences. After each, tell how the original underlined sentence has been made more interesting.

1. At the water's edge three ducklings searched for insects.
2. The mother duck, the one standing nearby, watched over her ducklings.
3. The sun came up, and a cool breeze stirred the water of the lake.
4. About nine o'clock in the morning, the children came out to play.
5. As they ran and jumped, the ducks watched them.

B. Add interesting phrases or clauses to these sentences. Add proper punctuation.

6. The children ate lunch.
7. They swam in the lake.
8. The breeze died down.
9. The children went into the house for dinner.
10. The sun set.

Apply

C. 11. Write a paragraph describing a happy spring or summer day. Add extra phrases or clauses to all but one of your sentences.

LANGUAGE REVIEW

Compound Subjects and Predicates   pages 324–325

Copy these sentences. Draw one line under all compound subjects. Draw two lines under all compound predicates. Add commas where needed.

1. A killer whale steers and stops with its flippers.
2. With its teeth the whale can grasp rip and tear food.
3. Dolphins belugas and gray whales are hunted by killer whales.
4. Fact and fiction are often combined in stories about killer whales.
5. Some killer whales have been tamed and perform for audiences.
6. Whales travel in packs and hunt in groups.

Clauses   pages 326–327

Copy these sentences. Underline each clause. Circle any conjunctions that join clauses.

7. You will learn about many careers over the next few years.
8. We take some careers for granted.
9. Journalists write for newspapers and magazines, or they work at radio and television stations.
10. Go to a theater, and you will see another career — acting.
11. Computer science employs many people and continues to grow.
12. Someday you must choose your own career.

Compound Sentences   pages 328–329

Copy these sentences. After each one, write whether it is simple or compound. If the sentence is compound, circle the conjunction that joins the simple sentences.

13. The weather is turning warmer, but no one wants to go swimming.
14. The campers have planned a Racing Day, and they are now completing their preparations.
15. The events will be running races and swimming relays.

16. Contestants can enter the swimming relays in the morning, or they can choose the running races in the afternoon.
17. Anya and Ramona will team up for the swimming relay.
18. They have been practicing every afternoon this week and stand a good chance of winning.
19. A picnic is planned for 5:30 P.M., but the awards ceremony will not take place until 8:15.

Subject-Verb Agreement   pages 330–331

Copy these sentences, using the correct verb in parentheses ( ).

20. Marionettes (is, are) puppets controlled from above the stage by strings held by the puppeteer.
21. Both the very young and the very old (enjoys, enjoy) traditional marionette shows.
22. The marionette that you wish to buy (comes, come) in a number of sizes.
23. All the marionettes in a play (has, have) special roles.
24. Some puppeteers (practices, practice) the complex movements of their marionettes for hours each day.

Varied Sentences   pages 332–333

Follow the directions in parentheses ( ) to rewrite these sentences.

25. The performers did not appear frightened. (Add a prepositional phrase.)
26. Ms. Baker had rehearsed with the cast each afternoon. (Add an appositive.)
27. The cast knew what to do. (Add a clause.)
28. The star was a little nervous. (Add a clause.)
29. The drama unfolded. (Add two prepositional phrases.)
30. The audience applauded warmly. (Add a prepositional phrase and a clause.)

Applying Sentence Building

31.–40. Write ten sentences about something that you would like to build. Use compound subjects or·predicates in two of your sentences, and make three other sentences compound. Vary your sentences in as many ways as you can.

STUDY SKILLS

Lesson 6: Taking Notes

Kele's family decided to buy a dog. Kele was chosen to find out more about poodles. In a library book he found this information.

Poodles. Poodles originated in Germany. They are very intelligent and easy to train. Poodles come in three sizes—toy, miniature, and standard. Toys are under 10 inches (40 cm) high; miniatures are 10 to 15 inches (40 to 60 cm) high; and standards are over 15 inches (60 cm) high. The coat of a poodle is curly and sheds very little.

How could Kele remember these facts to tell his family?

Think and Discuss

Note taking is a useful way of recording information. You probably take notes every day. For example, when you write your homework assignments or jot down a telephone number, you are taking notes.

Note taking will help you to remember facts when you read. It is especially important in helping you to remember facts as you prepare to write a report. To take notes, begin by writing the main subject of the material. What is Kele's main subject? Then jot down all the details that are important to remember. You do not need to use complete sentences when you take notes—using key words and phrases is an acceptable part of note taking. Read Kele's notes at the top of the next page.

Read the notes that Kele took.

Poodles
Intelligent, easy to train
Three sizes: Toy (under 10 in. or 40 cm)
Miniature (10-15 in. or 40-60 cm)
Standard (over 15 in. or 60 cm)
The Book of Dogs

Why do you think that Kele did not make note of the fact that poodles originated in Germany?

How to Take Notes

1. **Include important facts and details.**
2. **Use key words and phrases.**
3. **Record the name of the book or magazine from which you are taking the information.**
4. **Use simple, clear abbreviations to save time.**
5. **Be sure your notes are accurate and readable.**

Practice

A. Read this paragraph about collies. Then, using the guidelines in this lesson, take notes on the paragraph.

Collies. Collies are friendly, playful, and easy to train. Many collies have been trained to herd sheep. Collies come in two varieties: rough coat and smooth coat. The rough coat is more beautiful but is also more difficult to groom. A grown collie stands about 25 inches (1 m) high. *The Book of Dogs*

Apply

B. You will soon be writing a real research report. Talk to your teacher about possible topics. Then do some research and prepare note cards.

Lesson 7: Preparing a Bibliography

Marjorie was taking some notes. As she studied her note cards, she realized that the material she was using had come from a number of sources. How can Marjorie make her readers aware of the titles of books and magazines she has used?

Think and Discuss

A **bibliography** is an important part of a research paper. It gives credit to the original author of the information you used. At the same time it lists the sources so that interested readers can find more material on the topic. Study these entries from Marjorie's bibliography. Note the order of the information. Pay special attention to capitalization and punctuation.

Book
Hamilton, Edith. Mythology. Boston: Little, Brown & Co., 1942.

Magazine article
Banta, Corinne. "Gods and Goddesses: Exploring Greek Mythology." English Journal, September 1977, p. 57.

Article in an encyclopedia
Littleton, C. Scott. "Mythology." The World Book Encyclopedia, vol. 13, pp. 813–31. Chicago: World Book-Childcraft International, Inc., 1980.

Each bibliographic entry lists the author, title, and publication information. When the author's name does not appear, the title comes first. Encyclopedia and magazine entries give both the title of the article and the name of the source in which it appears.

If you study other bibliographies, you will sometimes see the names of two authors. Both authors will be listed last name first. If the book or article bears the name of an editor instead of an author, its bibliographic entry will contain the abbreviation ''ed.'' If an article appears on several pages spread throughout the book or magazine, you will see the abbreviation ''ff'' after the first page on which it appears. In a finished bibliography all entries will be listed in alphabetical order.

Practice

A. 1. Write the three bibliographic entries in this lesson in proper order.

B. Reread the bibliographic entries in this lesson; then answer these questions.

2. In what city was *Mythology* printed?

3. Who is the author of the article entitled ''Mythology''?

4. Who publishes *The World Book Encyclopedia?*

5. When did the article entitled ''Gods and Goddesses: Exploring Greek Mythology'' appear?

6. What mark of punctuation follows the city of publication for books and encyclopedias?

7. How many pages does the encyclopedia article cover?

Apply

C. 8. Using correct form, write the bibliographic information for three of the sources you are using in your own research report.

COMPOSITION

Lesson 8: Prewriting
Making an Outline

Marjorie had to write a research report on a topic of her choice. She had chosen "Strange Creatures of Mythology" as her topic, and she had taken a good set of notes. Now she was ready to organize them.

Think and Discuss

The best way to organize your material is by writing an outline that contains main ideas and important details. Study the outline Marjorie wrote.

I. Introduction
II. Evil male creatures
    A. Typhon
    B. Minotaur
III. Evil female creatures
    A. Gorgons (Medusa)
    B. Sphinx
IV. Good creatures
    A. Chiron
    B. Phoenix
V. Conclusion

Each roman numeral stands for the main idea of a paragraph. Each capital letter stands for a detail that supports the main idea. Notice that each entry is brief, begins with a capital letter, and is parallel in structure to the other entries. Parallel structure means that your entries must be similar in wording. In Marjorie's outline, for example, all the letter entries are names of creatures, and all the numeral entries are more general nouns.

Practice

A. Rewrite this part of an outline about plants found in Greek mythology.

I. Flowers
A. hyacinth
B. anemone
C. sunflower
II. Other Plants in Greek Mythology
A. laurel
B. Syrinx became a reed.

Apply

B. Reread the notes you made for your research report. You will use these notes to make an outline.

Choose Your Main Ideas
- From your notes pick three important ideas.
- Use a roman numeral for each main idea.

Choose Important Details
- For each main idea write at least two important details.
- Use a capital letter for each important detail.

Review Your Work
- Reread your outline. Be sure that your entries are parallel.
- Save your outline for the Apply in Lesson 9.

Lesson 9:   Composing

Writing a Rough Draft from an Outline

Marjorie's outline entitled "Strange Creatures of Mythology" had been highly praised by her teacher. As a result, Marjorie was very enthusiastic about beginning her research report. What advice might you give Marjorie as she prepares the **rough draft,** or copy, of her work?

Think and Discuss

The rough, or first, draft of a report is useful for one reason: It helps the writer put ideas on paper. In her rough draft, Marjorie did not have to worry about the *form* of her work—paragraph indentation, spelling, punctuation, and so on. The only thing she needed to concentrate on was *content*.

First Marjorie arranged her note cards to follow the order of her outline. Then, with her notes on one side of her desk and her outline on the other, she began to write her introduction.

The **introduction** of a research report tells the reader what the topic is. Often, however, the writer includes an extra sentence or two to arouse the reader's interest. Marjorie's extra sentences would give a brief description of one of the creatures in Greek mythology. Her description of the Hydra, she hoped, would present such a fearsome picture that her reader could not help but read the entire report.

The **body** of Marjorie's report would include all the information she had written in her outline under *II, III,* and *IV*. Each section listed under a particular roman numeral would have its own paragraph in the report. Each creature would be mentioned in the order in which it appeared on the outline. What might be a good reason for writing a rough draft in this way?

The **conclusion** of Marjorie's report, like her introduction, would be one paragraph long. Rather than summarize what she had already presented, Marjorie planned to mention three other creatures in this paragraph. The brief description given, she hoped, would encourage her readers to explore the topic more fully on their own. Why might writing final details in this manner be an excellent way to end a report?

How to Write a Rough Draft

1. **Keep your note cards and your outline next to you at all times while you write.**
2. *Follow your outline.* **This is your most important rule. Do not add anything to your rough draft that is not on the outline. Do not leave out anything.**
3. **Plan to write one paragraph for each roman numeral on your outline.**
4. **Write an** *introduction* **that will arouse your reader's interest. Write a** *conclusion* **that will make your reader remember your report.**
5. **Concern yourself only with** *content* **at this point. You will refine your work later.**

Practice

A. Suppose you had made the notes and the partial outline that you see on this page and the next for one paragraph in the body of a report. Write the paragraph, using the notes for information and the outline for order.

Outline

III. Birdlike creatures
   A. Griffin
   B. Harpy

Notes

Griffin: had head and wings of an eagle and body of a lion; lived in far north of Greece; guarded treasure of gold from the one-eyed Arimaspians, who kept trying to steal it

Harpy: was half bird and half woman; stole food from victims; left horrible smell; tormented blind King Phineas; finally driven away by sons of north wind

Apply

B. Find your notes, your outline, and your partial bibliography. Now write a rough draft of your report.

Write Your Introduction
● Tell what your research report will be about.
● Include a detail to arouse your reader's interest.

Write the Body of Your Report
● Follow your outline. Use guidelines 2, 3, and 5 in the blue box on page 343.

Write Your Conclusion
● There are many ways to end a report. You might summarize or suggest ideas for further study.

Review Your Work
● Check your rough draft against your outline. Be sure that you have included everything you planned. Take out anything that does not belong.
● Check the *order* of your draft. The points mentioned should be in the same order as in the outline.
● Save your draft for the Apply in Lesson 10.

A Challenge

Imagine that your favorite fictional character is real. Make up an outline in which you use the character's appearance, interests, and goals as the main ideas. List detail entries. Then write a rough draft about the character from your outline.

Lesson 10: Composing
Writing a Research Report

Marjorie's rough, or first, draft looked good. Her notes had been both thorough and accurate. She had followed her outline point by point. What other work could be done on her report before its final revision?

Think and Discuss

Here is a copy of the research report that Marjorie completed. As you read, compare each idea that she presents with the points listed on her outline in Lesson 8. Notice first of all how her introduction captures the reader's attention.

Picture a huge serpent with nine heads and a poisonous bite in every set of teeth! This frightful creature was the Hydra, one of the strange beings found in ancient mythology. In this report you will meet several creatures in all their horrible shapes and sizes. You will even meet a few who proved useful or friendly to humans.

Why did Marjorie begin her research report with an exclamation? Marjorie opened her report with a colorful description, then continued with the promise of more in the rest of the report. At the same time she cleverly involved the reader in her words by asking him or her to picture the creature she was describing. Once this is done, she can move on to the body of her report. Here she will present the three groups of creatures she has listed in her outline.

Read the body of Marjorie's report.

Typhon was a giant with a hundred dragon heads and a body covered with serpents. He was taller than the tallest mountain, and fire blazed from all his dragon mouths. Zeus, father of the gods, finally conquered Typhon with his thunderbolts. The Minotaur, in contrast, had the head of a bull and the body of a man. He lived in a labyrinth, or maze, on the island of Crete, and he was killed by Theseus, Duke of Athens.

Not all the famous monsters were male. The Gorgons, for example, were three sisters with serpents for hair, claws made out of brass, and staring eyes. Medusa, the only Gorgon who was mortal, was conquered by the Greek hero Perseus. The Sphinx was a monster with the head of a woman, the body of a dog, and the paws of a lion. She lived outside the city of Thebes, and after many years she was killed by the prince Oedipus.

A few of the strange creatures of mythology were not evil. The Centaurs were a group of creatures half man and half horse. Chiron, a Centaur, was known for his goodness. He taught humans the use of herbs as medicines and instructed the Greek heroes in the arts. The Phoenix, finally, was a bird of great beauty that lived for 600 years in the Arabian desert. Whenever it neared the end of its normal life, it was burned on a funeral pyre and then rose, young again, from its ashes.

A careful writer, Marjorie kept to her outline and did not allow herself to wander to other subjects. Her wise use of transitional expressions such as *in contrast, for example,* and *finally* helped her report run smoothly. Where transitional expressions did not seem quite right, she wrote a whole sentence that joined what she had already said with what she was about to say.

Now read the conclusion of Marjorie's report.

    This report could not possibly describe all the
creatures of mythology. Some are evil and some are
good, but all of them are interesting. Anyone who
would like to learn more about these creatures might
start with the mythology books by Bulfinch and Edith
Hamilton. Pegasus, the winged horse, Cerberus, the
three-headed dog of Hades, and the Chimera, a
fire-breathing monster, are just a few of the beings
that will keep you reading for hours.

Marjorie used two clever devices in her conclusion. By
naming three more creatures, she aroused her reader's
curiosity again. She also gave a suggestion for further study.

How to Write a Research Report

1. **Look over your rough, or first, draft. Add any material that you may have forgotten from your outline. Take out anything that you did not intend to include.**
2. **Read every paragraph in your rough draft individually. Go back and add transitional expressions or transitional sentences wherever they would help your coherence.**
3. **Complete your bibliography. Be sure it contains entries for every reference work you used. Be sure each entry is in the correct form.**
4. **Give your research report a title.**

Practice

A. Write the answers to these questions.

1. What was the purpose of Marjorie's research project?
2. What was the purpose of her introduction?
3. What was the purpose of the body of her report?
4. What was the purpose of her conclusion?
5. What kept Marjorie from wandering off her subject?

Apply

B. Reread the rough draft of your research report. Make a few refinements in your work.

Check for Unity and Coherence

- Study your draft. Check to see that every sentence in every paragraph is related to your topic. This will ensure unity in your report.
- As you read, insert transitions that will make your work flow smoothly. Add material both *within* and *between* paragraphs. This will contribute to coherence.

Complete Your Bibliography

- Remember that you prepared only a partial bibliography in Lesson 7. Add any reference not previously listed.
- Write your sources in alphabetical order by the authors' last names.

Review Your Work

- Be sure you included all the information you meant to include.
- Be sure your transitions are appropriate.
- Be sure your bibliography is in order.
- Save your report for revising in Lesson 11.

To Memorize

Most of us spend more time fixing the blame than fixing the problem.   *Anonymous*

1. Which is easier to do: blame someone or something for causing a problem, or solve the problem?
2. Which is more practical in the long run? Why?

Lesson 11:   Revising

Editing and Proofreading a Research Report

Study the revising Marjorie did on these sentences.

> *tr* [Scylla and Charybdis] the monsters] lived near the
> *strait* ~~straight~~ that ~~seperates~~ *separates* Sicily and Italy. Scylla had
> the head of a beautiful maiden. √Whenever a ship
> passed in this channel, the barking dogs reached out
> *grasp*
> to ~~grab~~ six sailors and devour them. Scylla's body, *tr*
> *Her*
> ~~you see,~~ was composed of the heads and necks of six
> horrible barking dogs.

Think and Discuss

The revising Marjorie did to these sentences helped the *development* of her paragraph. By changing the last sentence into the third sentence, she made her ideas follow logically. What was wrong with the original order?

When you edit for **development,** you check that your sentences progress logically. When you edit for **content,** you check that everything you had planned is actually there. You also check to see that you do not have too much information.

The sentences on Scylla and Charybdis, for example, had once been part of Marjorie's third paragraph. When she checked her first version of the report, however, she realized that the paragraph was too long. As a result she removed it from her outline and her finished report.

Editing and Proofreading Marks

≡ capitalize

⊙ make a period

∧ add something

∧̆ add a comma

ᵛᵛ add quotation marks

~~take something away~~

◯ spell correctly

¶ indent the paragraph

/ make a lowercase letter

∼ transpose
tr

How to Revise a Research Report

Editing

1. Be sure each sentence in your report relates to your topic.
2. Be sure your sentences and paragraphs are linked with appropriate transitions.
3. Be sure that you have included introductory and concluding paragraphs. Be sure that you have a paragraph for each main point in the body of your report.
4. Be sure that you have defined any unfamiliar word in your report.

Proofreading

5. Correct mistakes in spelling, punctuation, and mechanics. Pay particular attention to the format of your bibliography.

Practice

A. 1. Rewrite Marjorie's sentences about Scylla as they should appear in final form.

Apply

B. You will now revise your research report.

Edit Your Report

- Check your **content.** Use guidelines 1–3 in the blue box above to help you.
- Check your **style.** Follow guideline 4 in the same blue box.

Proofread Your Report

- Make corrections in spelling, punctuation, and mechanics. Use item 5 in the same blue box as a guide.
- Write or type your report on clean paper.

MECHANICS PRACTICE

Capitalizing and Punctuating Outlines and Sentences

- Use a comma and a conjunction or use a semicolon in compound sentences.

   I feel lazy today, and I want to do something different.
   Let's go to the beach; it should be sunny today.

- Capitalize the letters of important subsections and the first word of every part of an outline.

   A. Put up a sun umbrella

- Indent in outlines; use periods after numbers and letters.

   I. How to get a tan
      A. Put on some light sunscreen lotion

- Use commas and quotation marks to set off direct quotations.

   Jane said, "Why do I need a sunscreen?"

- Use quotation marks in chapter titles and in titles of short stories.

   Chapter 8 is entitled "Burning to a Crisp."

A. 1.–14. Write this mixed-up outline correctly.

   A. Soil washed away in severe storms I. Kinds of rain C. Earth cleansed B. Soft rain A. Moisture content in soil increased C. Floods caused B. Reservoirs' levels raised B. Reservoirs endangered D. Downpour III. Harmful effects C. Driving rain A. Drizzle II. Beneficial effects D. Mud slides started

B. Rewrite these sentences, adding the correct punctuation.

15. I want to go to the beach but is it going to rain?
16. Don't worry the paper says sunny and warm.
17. All right, we'll go but let me get my book.
18. This is a book about weather one chapter is called Beach Weather.
19. I'm going swimming but don't put the book away.
20. We don't need the book Arnold it just started to rain.

LITERATURE

Lesson 12: Recognizing Stories in Verse

Answer these questions based on material you have already learned.

1. What are the parts of a short story?
2. What does the first part of a story do?
3. How is a poem different from a short story?

Think and Discuss

Some poems offer the best features of poems and stories together. Like other poems, they have rhythm and rhyme, express emotion, and often use figures of speech. Like short stories, on the other hand, they have a setting, characters, and a plot. Sometimes they also have an introduction, a complication, and a resolution. These poems are called **narrative poems,** or poems that tell a story.

This poem, "The Walrus and the Carpenter," was written by Lewis Carroll, the author of *Alice's Adventures in Wonderland.* The setting is the seashore; the main characters are the Walrus and the Carpenter, a strange but amusing pair, and a group of talking oysters. Although much of the conversation seems to be nonsense, notice how the Walrus and the Carpenter achieve what they set out to do.

The poem is humorous, at least from the Walrus's and the Carpenter's points of view. As you read, note the lines that are especially humorous, and try to figure out just what makes them so.

The Walrus and the Carpenter

1

The sun was shining on the sea,
    Shining with all his might;
He did his very best to make
    The billows smooth and bright—
And this was odd, because it was
    The middle of the night.

2

The moon was shining sulkily,
    Because she thought the sun
Had got no business to be there
    After the day was done—
"It's very rude of him," she said
    "To come and spoil the fun!"

3

The sea was wet as wet could be,
    The sands were dry as dry,
You could not see a cloud, because
    No cloud was in the sky;
No birds were flying overhead—
    There were no birds to fly.

4

The Walrus and the Carpenter
    Were walking close at hand;
They wept like anything to see
    Such quantities of sand.
"If this were only cleared away,"
    They said, "it would be grand!"

5

"If seven maids with seven mops
    Swept it for half a year,
Do you suppose," the Walrus said,
    "That they could get it clear?"
"I doubt it," said the Carpenter,
    And shed a bitter tear.

6

"O Oysters, come and walk with us!"
    The Walrus did beseech.
"A pleasant walk, a pleasant talk,
    Along the briny beach;
We cannot do with more than four,
    To give a hand to each."

7

The eldest Oyster looked at him,
    But never a word he said;
The eldest Oyster winked his eye,
    And shook his heavy head—
Meaning to say he did not choose
    To leave the oyster-bed.

8

But four young Oysters hurried up,
  All eager for the treat;
Their coats were brushed, their faces washed,
  Their shoes were clean and neat—
And this was odd, because, you know,
  They hadn't any feet.

9

Four other Oysters followed them,
  And yet another four;
And thick and fast they came at last,
  And more, and more, and more—
All hopping through the frothy waves,
  And scrambling to the shore.

10

The Walrus and the Carpenter
  Walked on a mile or so,
And then they rested on a rock
  Conveniently low;
And all the little Oysters stood
  And waited in a row.

11

"The time has come," the Walrus said,
  "To talk of many things:
Of shoes—and ships—and sealing-wax—
  Of cabbages—and kings—
And why the sea is boiling hot—
  And whether pigs have wings."

12

"But wait a bit," the Oysters cried,
  "Before we have our chat;
For some of us are out of breath,
  And all of us are fat!"
"No hurry!" said the Carpenter.
  They thanked him much for that.

13

"A loaf of bread," the Walrus said,
    "Is what we chiefly need;
Pepper and vinegar besides
    Are very good indeed—
Now, if you're ready, Oysters dear,
    We can begin to feed."

14

"But not on us!" the Oysters cried,
    Turning a little blue.
"After such kindness, that would be
    A dismal thing to do!"
"The night is fine," the Walrus said,
    "Do you admire the view?"

15

"It was so kind of you to come!
    And you are very nice!"
The Carpenter said nothing but
    "Cut us another slice.
I wish you were not quite so deaf—
    I've had to ask you twice!"

16

"It seems a shame," the Walrus said,
    "To play them such a trick,
After we've brought them out so far,
    And made them trot so quick!"
The Carpenter said nothing but
    "The butter's spread too thick!"

17

"I weep for you," the Walrus said;
    "I deeply sympathize."
With sobs and tears he sorted out
    Those of the largest size,
Holding his pocket-handkerchief
    Before his streaming eyes.

18

"O Oysters," said the Carpenter,
    "You've had a pleasant run!
Shall we be trotting home again?"
    But answer came there none—
And this was scarcely odd, because
    They'd eaten every one.

Lewis Carroll

Now that you have read the poem, explain what makes this poem humorous.

Two of the most noticeable features of this poem are rhythm and rhyme. **Rhythm** is a regular pattern of stressed, or accented, syllables. They give the poem its beat. **Rhyme** is a regular pattern of similar sounds that usually occurs at the ends of lines. Read this verse from "The Walrus and the Carpenter."

"The time has come," the Walrus said,   a
    "To talk of many things: b
Of shoes—and ships—and sealing-wax—   c
    Of cabbages—and kings—   b
And why the sea is boiling hot—   d
    And whether pigs have wings."   b

You know that certain words in a sentence are more important than others. You know too, that some syllables of words are stressed, or accented, more than other syllables. Applying this idea to the verse, you can place an *accent mark* (') on the words or syllables that receive the greatest stress. Look at the accent marks on the verse. How many accented syllables are in the first line? How many are in the second? Where are these patterns repeated?

Look at the verse again. Which lines rhyme? When you want to show the **rhyme scheme,** or *pattern of rhyme,* you use letters, beginning with *a.* The word *said,* therefore, is labeled *a,* and any word that rhymes with *said* at the end of a line is also labeled *a.* The last word in the second line, *things,* does not rhyme with *said,* so it is given the letter *b,* and so on. The completed rhyme scheme for this verse is *a, b, c, b, d, b.* Why would the word *wax* be labeled *c* and the word *hot* be labeled *d*?

Now consider the poem as a story. The *introduction,* the first five verses, presents the two major characters and gives the setting. When the Walrus asks the Oysters to join him for a walk, the *complication* begins. What *problem* is presented in the complication?

The *climax,* the last part of the complication and the high point of the story, gives at least a partial answer to the problem. In the climax the Walrus and the Carpenter sit down to lunch, an act that seems to upset the Oysters. Only bread, butter, pepper, and vinegar are mentioned, however, so if anything else is on the menu, the reader does not know it yet. Verses 14 through 17 make up the climax.

The *resolution,* which ends the poem, is verse 18. As in a short story, it gives the final answer to the problem that arose in the complication.

Since "The Walrus and the Carpenter" is written in verses and has a definite rhythm and rhyme, it has the qualities of a poem. Yet, since it has an introduction, a complication, and a resolution, it is also a story.

Practice

A. Read this narrative poem. Then answer the questions that follow.

Godfrey Gordon Gustavus Gore

Godfrey Gordon Gustavus Gore—
No doubt you have heard the name before—
Was a boy who never would shut a door!

The wind might whistle, the wind might roar,
And teeth be aching and throats be sore,
But still he never would shut the door.

His father would beg, his mother implore,
"Godfrey Gordon Gustavus Gore,
We really do wish you would shut the door!"

Their hands they wrung, their hair they tore;
But Godfrey Gordon Gustavus Gore
Was deaf as the buoy out at the Nore.

When he walked forth the folks would roar,
"Godfrey Gordon Gustavus Gore,
Why don't you think to shut the door?"

They rigged out a Shutter with sail and oar,
And threatened to pack off Gustavus Gore
On a voyage of penance to Singapore,

But he begged for mercy, and said, "No more!
Pray do not send me to Singapore
On a Shutter, and then I will shut the door!"

"You will?" said his parents; "then keep on shore!
But mind you do! For the plague is sore
Of a fellow that never will shut the door,
Godfrey Gordon Gustavus Gore!"

William Brighty Rands

1. Copy the first verse of the poem. Place accent marks on the syllables or words that should be stressed in each line.
2. Look at the first verse you copied. What pattern does the rhyme show?
3. Which verses serve as the introduction?
4. Who are the main characters?
5. Which verses make up the complication?
6. What is the problem expressed by the complication?
7. What is the climax of the story?
8. Which verses make up the resolution?
9. Which figures of speech can you find in this poem?
10. How has the poet used exaggeration effectively?

Apply

B. Try writing a narrative poem of three verses with four lines to a verse.

Prewriting
● Choose the setting, characters, and plot.
● Decide what should be included in the introduction, the complication, and the conclusion.
● List any words that will help you describe the characters and their actions.

Composing

- Write the first verse. You may wish to make each verse rhyme although that is not necessary.
- After you have introduced the character and setting, develop the action of the poem. Continue to use the same rhyme scheme as in the first verse.
- Be sure you bring the action to a climax. Be humorous if you wish.
- Write a resolution for the narrative.

Revising

- Read the whole poem aloud to be sure it makes sense.
- Hear the sound of the poem. Change any lines that do not carry the rhythm or mood of the poem.
- Be sure to give your poem a title that will capture your audience's interest.
- Copy your poem onto a clean sheet of paper.

A BOOK TO READ

Title: **A Dancer's World**
Author: Margot Fonteyn
Publisher: Alfred A. Knopf

Dame Margot Fonteyn, a world-renowned ballerina, has written this book to share her vast knowledge of the world of ballet with young dancers and their parents. The book includes advice on dance schools, opportunities for male dancers, and descriptions of life in a ballet company. There is also a chapter written by Dame Margot's mother, describing what it is like to live with a devoted dancer. The book gives a first-hand view of life as ballerina — a very difficult, but a very rewarding career.

8 UNIT TEST

● **Compound Subjects and Predicates**   pages 324–325

Number your paper from 1 to 5. Next to each number write the letter
that tells you what the underlined words are. Use this code.

a. compound subject   **b.** compound predicate
c. complete subject   **d.** complete predicate

1. <u>Gas</u> and <u>oil</u> are forms of petroleum.
2. Petroleum, in various forms, <u>powers automobiles and heats homes</u>.
3. <u>The great state of Texas</u> is an oil-producing area.
4. <u>Oil is moved overland by pipelines and is carried across the sea
   by tankers</u>.
5. <u>Oil spills</u> <u>kill</u> fish and <u>destroy</u> beaches.

● **Clauses**   pages 326–327

Copy these sentences. Underline each clause.

6. Many flowers are pollinated by insects.
7. Insects visit flowers to drink nectar, and their legs pick up the
   flowers' pollen.
8. They are attracted to bright-colored, fragrant flowers.
9. Insects pollinate flowers, but so does the wind.
10. Hay fever is caused by wind-carried pollen.

● **Compound Sentences**   pages 328–329

Copy these sentences. After each one, write whether it is *simple* or
compound.

11. Honeybees die after stinging, but wasps can sting again and again.
12. Dark and bright colors attract both bees and wasps.
13. Yellow jackets are aggressive wasps, and they are easily angered.
14. A wasp nest may be found in fallen leaves or a dead log.
15. You can walk away from a bee or wasp, but you should never
    thrash at it.

Subject-Verb Agreement   pages 330–331

Copy these sentences, using the present tense of each verb in parentheses ( ).

16. Photography _____ a popular hobby.   (be)
17. Marcia and Toby _____ to become professional photographers. (want)
18. A candid photo _____ a subject's personality.   (reveal)
19. Photographs of an important event _____ part of history. (become)
20. Albums or picture frames _____ your favorite pictures.   (display)

Varied Sentences   pages 332–333

Study the underlined words that have been added to each of these simple sentences. Then write whether that group of words is a *prepositional phrase,* a *clause,* or an *appositive.*

21. The state flower of Alaska, the forget-me-not, grows wild throughout the state.
22. The mountain laurel is also called the spoonwood, and it blossoms in early summer.
23. The violet comes in many shades of purple, yellow, and white.
24. The goldenrod is mistakenly blamed for hay fever, but it is really a healing plant.
25. The wood of the hawthorn tree was valued by the pioneers.

Notes   pages 336–337

1. Using the information in "Compound Subjects and Predicates" from the first exercise in this Unit Test, make a set of notes about petroleum.

Bibliographies   pages 338–339

Put each of these bibliographic entries into the proper form.

2. *Writer's Digest.* August 1981, pp. 36–39 "Action! Action! Action!" by Cynthia Graham.
3. Joan Lowery Nixon's novel *The Kidnapping of Christina Lattimore.* New York, 1979, by Harcourt Brace Jovanovich, Inc.
4. "Diving," an article on pages 200–202 of vol. 5 of *The World Book Encyclopedia,* by Micki King Hogue. 1980. Chicago: World Book-Childcraft International, Inc.

● Outlines   pages 340–341

Copy this part of an outline. Use correct capitalization, punctuation, and indentation, and make sure that your points are parallel in structure.

The Moon
I. the moon reflects light
A. source of light
B. phases of moon
II. tides
A. relation to moon
B. frequency
III. eclipses

● Prewriting, Composing, and Revising — Research Report
pages 340–350

1. Use these notes and this part of an outline to make a rough draft of a paragraph for a research report.

<u>Time</u>: American Indians calculated time of events by number of "moons"; the words *month* and *Monday* are from *mona,* an Anglo-Saxon word for *moon*
<u>Mythology</u>: Roman moon goddess Diana; hunted with crescent moon for bow and moonbeams for arrows

IV. How the Moon Influenced People
A. Time
B. Mythology

Then write your paragraph as it would appear as part of a research report. Include transitional expressions if needed. Revise your paragraph and write it in final form.

● Mechanics Practice   page 351

Add commas, semicolons, or quotation marks where needed in these sentences. Add capital letters where necessary.

2. I recently read an article called exploring england s canals.
3. These artificial waterways cover some 2500 mi. (4022 km) and they reach from london to liverpool.

362   TEST: Unit 8

4. The canals were begun as part of the industrial revolution the first one opened in 1761.
5. The article says today, the cruising waterways have become pathways to peace and pleasure for millions of boaters.
6. Waterways are important in history think of the many times that rivers influenced it.
7. If julius caesar had not crossed the rubicon river the course of roman history might have been very different.
8. Once caesar was across the river he said the die is cast.
9. That meant that he had made his move he could not turn back again.
10. The tigris and euphrates two famous historical rivers helped shape early civilization.
11. This article the cradle of civilization tells about the tigris and the euphrates.
12. The early egyptians could not have lived without the nile river.
13. Well now said marie i think that the seine river in paris is important there could be no left bank area without the seine.
14. Now that you mention it answered rose the early american settlers couldn't have brought their goods to market without the mississippi river.
15. This chapter called the waterways of history mentions all those and more.

● Stories in Verse   pages 352–359

Copy and complete each statement.

1. The _____ of a narrative poem identifies character and setting.
2. A _____ poem tells a story.
3. Like a _____, a narrative poem has characters and a plot.
4. _____ is a regular pattern of accented syllables.
5. _____ is a regular pattern of similar sounds at the ends of lines.

Copy and mark the rhythm and rhyme scheme on this verse.

Don't let him know she liked them best,
    For this must ever be
A secret, kept from all the rest,
    Between yourself and me.

Communication is an important part of everyone's life. How is the state trooper in the photograph communicating? Listening well and speaking clearly are necessary for effective communication. What might happen if the dispatcher did not listen carefully to the words of the state trooper?

This unit will focus on communicating effectively. You will learn about listening and speaking in class, at meetings, and during interviews. You will study how to make introductions and present oral reports. Look at the photograph again. What might happen if the state trooper did not choose the most accurate words for what he wants to transmit? Choosing effective words is another skill that you will study in this unit.

When the state trooper returns to headquarters, he will have to write a report. It is likely that he will use formal language in his report. When you write, sometimes formal language is needed, while at other times informal language will do. In this unit you will learn how to decide whether to use formal or informal language when you write letters. You will read some letters that author E. B. White wrote to some sixth graders, and you will write some letters of your own.

So turn the page and communicate!

◀ *A state trooper using communication in his work*

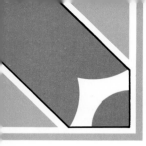

LANGUAGE

Lesson 1: Listening in Class

Paul had just received a corrected test paper from his teacher. He had not done well, and he showed his paper to Miki. Miki studied it for a moment and then said, "Why, Paul, you didn't follow directions. Didn't you listen to what Mr. Lenski was saying?"

"I guess not," admitted Paul.

Think and Discuss

Developing good listening skills is important in many areas of your life, but perhaps nowhere is it more practical than in the classroom. You must listen in class each day. In particular, many of your tests require you to follow your teacher's instructions. People who do well in school are usually those who listen well.

Follow these guidelines when you listen in class.

How to Listen Well in Class

1. **Keep your mind on what the speaker is saying.**
2. **Listen for main ideas, which are often expressed in key terms or phrases.**
3. **Make mental pictures of points to remember.**
4. **Take brief notes to help you remember details.**
5. **If you do not understand what has been said, ask for an explanation.**

When you listen to test instructions, realize that there are certain terms that tell you what kind of test you are taking. They will tell you what your job as the test taker is.

Study this list of terms.

Compare: Show how two or more things are alike.
Describe: Create a word picture.
Define: Give the meaning.
Explain: Tell how or why.

Practice

A. Study these sentences. Copy *only* those that give helpful tips for listening in class.

1. Sharpen your pencil while the speaker is talking.
2. Listen for key terms or phrases.
3. Ask about anything you do not understand.
4. Think about what the speaker is wearing.
5. Keep your notes short and to the point.
6. Listen for the order in which things should be done.
7. Write down everything you hear.

B. 8. Listen carefully as your teacher reads aloud a set of instructions. Follow the instructions.

Apply

C. 9. Working with a partner, take turns reading aloud the directions from one of your textbooks. Practice listening to directions and following them carefully.

To Memorize

Little things make perfection, but perfection is no little thing.

Michelangelo

How does attention to little things help to create perfection? How might this saying apply to someone such as Michelangelo, a great artist? How might it apply to you?

Lesson 2: Conducting a Meeting

Read this part of the beginning of a meeting.

Reiko Arimitsu: This afternoon's meeting of the Drama Club will now come to order. Arthur Hartmann, will you please read the minutes of our last meeting?

Arthur: At the meeting of April 12, Inge Sonntag announced that we had collected $205.50 from tickets to our spring play. After expenses were met, we were left with a balance of $134.82. Lydia Stamos moved that we use the money to buy scripts and makeup. Sheila Harrison seconded the motion, and it was approved unanimously.

Reiko: Thank you, Arthur. Since there is no old business, let's go to our first item of new business. We will need a new club vice-president because Ron Karas is moving to Texas this summer. Are there any nominations?

Bridget O'Connor (raising her hand and addressing the chair): Madam chairperson.

Reiko: Yes, Bridget?

Bridget: I would like to nominate Agnes Petrelli.

Who is in charge of this meeting? What is Arthur's job? Who is the club treasurer?

Think and Discuss

Class and club meetings will run efficiently if a certain order is followed. The proper order of a meeting is called **parliamentary procedure.**

The Drama Club meeting follows parliamentary procedure. Reiko, the **chairperson,** ran the meeting. Arthur, the **secretary,** took notes, called **minutes.** At the beginning of every meeting, the secretary reads the minutes from the previous meeting. Some meetings include special reports from other members. Who had given a special report at the previous meeting of the Drama Club?

When other people wish to speak at a meeting, they must be **recognized.** Who asked to be recognized at the Drama Club meeting? Any suggestion for action or discussion is called a **motion.** Motions must be **seconded,** or suggested by two people, before they can be discussed or voted on. Who had seconded a motion in the previous meeting of the Drama Club?

Practice

A. Copy and complete these sentences.

1. The proper order of a meeting is called _____ .
2. The _____ runs the meeting.
3. The notes, or _____ , of the meeting are recorded by the _____ .
4. People who wish to speak must ask to be _____ .
5. A _____ , or suggestion for action or discussion, cannot be acted upon until it has been _____ .

B. Copy the opening of the Drama Club meeting. Write the rest of the meeting according to these directions.

6. Have Reiko ask for someone to second the nomination; have Olga DeVries second it.
7. Have the names of Roberto Padilla and Dena Bluehouse placed in nomination and seconded.
8. Have Lydia address the chair and move that the nominations be closed; have Inge second the motion.
9. Have Reiko ask Arthur to record the votes. Have Arthur announce the winner.
10. Have Reiko welcome the new vice-president and declare the meeting closed.

Apply

C. 11. Imagine that you are a member of the Senate in ancient Rome. What might happen in one of your meetings? Working with other members of your class, write a meeting and present it to the class.

Lesson 3: Making Introductions

Alexa brought her younger brother, Mark, to visit the nursing home where she does volunteer work. When Alexa saw Mrs. Lafayette in the hall, she realized that the woman did not know who Mark was. What should she do?

Think and Discuss

Introductions allow strangers to meet one another. You can show courtesy for others by introducing them when they are in a new situation. Alexa, for example, might have greeted Mrs. Lafayette and then said, "Mrs. Lafayette, this is Mark, my brother. He is nine years old, and he is in the fourth grade at Nesbitt Elementary School. Mark, I would like you to meet Mrs. Lafayette, the woman who has taught me all those new songs I have been singing lately."

Follow these guidelines for making introductions.

How to Make Introductions

1. If you are introducing a younger person to an older person, mention the older person's name first.
2. If you are introducing a person to a group, mention the name of the group first.
3. If the person being introduced is standing, you should also stand.
4. If the other person offers to shake hands, you should respond.
5. If you are being introduced, you should respond to the introduction with an answer such as "Hello" or "How do you do?" and the person's name.
6. If you are introducing other people, you should put them at their ease by telling each person a little about the other.

When you introduce older people to younger people, or a group to a new person, you should keep your language fairly formal. You can be more casual when you make introductions to people close to your own age. If Alexa wanted to introduce Mark to her classmate, B. G., she would make an introduction like this: "B. G., this is Mark, my ten-year-old brother. Mark, this is B. G., who plays right field on our school baseball team."

Practice

A. Write these introductions so that they will be more courteous.

1. "Hiya, Dan. This is my mom."
2. "I don't know anyone here. Who are you?"
3. "Shake hands with my aunt, Jackie. She's from North Dakota."
4. "Peggy, this is my grandfather."

B. Write an introduction for each of these situations.

5. Introduce the captain of the high school football team to your great aunt Agatha.
6. Introduce Sharri, a classmate, to your mother.
7. Introduce your three best friends to the police chief.
8. Introduce Joyce Reynolds, a reporter for the *Harristown Post,* to your English class.
9. Introduce your twin and yourself to your new teacher.
10. Introduce your grandparents, who are visiting from Arizona, to Grete, an exchange student at school.

Apply

C. 11. Write an introduction that will allow two historical characters to meet one another, such as Christopher Columbus and George Washington or Galileo and Julius Caesar.

Lesson 4: Interviewing

Francine needed some information about how a large building is cared for. She found an expert in her own school—Mr. Powell, the school custodian. How will she get the information she needs?

Think and Discuss

An excellent way to get firsthand information on a topic is by **interviewing** someone who has experience in that area. Reporters for newspapers and television often conduct interviews and ask questions to help them gather information. You, too, can use interviews when you prepare an oral or written report. Keep these guidelines in mind.

How to Conduct an Interview

1. **Make arrangements by writing or calling to request an interview. Set a convenient time and place.**
2. **Prepare several appropriate questions in advance.**
3. **Record what is said. Use a tape recorder if one is available, or take clear, complete notes.**
4. **Ask further questions if the answers you receive are not clear or specific.**
5. **Thank the person for the interview.**

Preparing appropriate questions is especially important. Because Francine's purpose is to learn about the care of a large building, she will ask Mr. Powell questions about his work. She will not ask how many children he has.

Practice

A. Imagine that you are to conduct an interview to learn about the career of a magician. You will be talking to a well-known magician. Copy *only* those questions that would be appropriate for your interview.

1. What is the largest object that you have ever made disappear on stage?
2. Do you like pizza?
3. Have you studied with other magicians?
4. How old were you when you first became interested in magic?
5. What is your hat size?
6. What is the most difficult part about performing in front of a large audience?
7. Did you ever have a trick fail on stage? What did you do?

Apply

B. 8. Interview someone in your school. Set up an appointment, prepare a list of appropriate questions, and take careful notes.

HOW OUR LANGUAGE GROWS

How's your Spanish? Because you know English, you may know more Spanish than you think you do.

We use many words in English that came from Spanish. *Hacienda, fiesta,* and *sombrero* are some good examples. We use other Spanish words that have become so common in our language that we consider them English. Some examples are *bonanza, burro, cargo, siesta,* and *patio.* These words are spelled the same in Spanish as in English. Many other words are slightly different in spelling: *lasso* (English), *lazo* (Spanish); *ranch* (English), *rancho* (Spanish).

1. Which English words came from these Spanish words?

cafetería	guitarra	cacao	batata
hamaca	tabaco	mestengo	castaneta

2. Think of three other Spanish words that we use.

Lesson 5: Presenting an Oral Report

Most people are not comfortable giving oral reports until they have had much practice giving them. The way to be as comfortable as possible, however, is to be well prepared.

Think and Discuss

Many of the techniques that you learned to help you prepare written reports are also useful in preparing **oral reports.** For example, in both cases you begin by choosing a topic that interests you. To choose an appropriate topic, you must keep the length of the report in mind. In both cases you do research, make note cards, and prepare an outline.

After that point, however, the two kinds of reports become somewhat different. When you prepare for an oral report, write your outline on a new set of note cards. Copy both the main ideas and the supporting details, and leave room to fill in any details that you must report exactly, such as statistics and direct quotations. When you present an oral report, you speak from an outline—an outline that contains only key words and phrases, not every word.

Once you have transferred your outline to note cards, practice your report, beginning with an interesting introduction. Talk about the major ideas in the order in which you have outlined them. Finish your oral report with a summary of your main points and add an interesting conclusion. You may find it helpful to practice in front of a mirror or to record your report so that you can watch and listen for any changes you need to make.

When the time comes to give your report, take your place confidently. Look at your audience and wait until they are ready to give you their full attention. As you speak, follow these guidelines.

> **How to Present an Oral Report**
>
> 1. Speak directly to the audience, referring to your notes for details.
> 2. Speak clearly, loudly, and with expression.
> 3. Give an introduction that will capture the attention of your audience.
> 4. Discuss each major topic of your outline in order, and report your details correctly.
> 5. Throughout your oral report, try to make "eye contact" with members of the audience.
> 6. Summarize the main ideas at the end.

Practice

A. Make an outline for an oral report based on the interview you conducted in the previous lesson, or use the outline you prepared for your research report in Unit 8. Transfer the outline to note cards, and practice giving the report.

Apply

B. Give the oral report that you have prepared. Have the class comment on your presentation.

A Challenge

Imagine that you are living in a world colony on a distant Earth satellite in the year 2500. Invent a letter, number, or letter-and-number code that can be used to send messages from one world colony to another. Then write a brief message in the code (about the length of a telegram) asking for supplies of food and rocket parts from the colony of Inter-Euro II. Keep these points in mind.

1. How would the message be sent?
2. Who would receive your message?
3. What "address" would you use?

LANGUAGE REVIEW

Listening in Class   pages 366-367

Imagine that you are taking a test about ancient Egypt. Your teacher includes these instructions. Write in your own words what each instruction means.

1. Compare the life of an ancient Egyptian farmer to the life of a farmer in modern America.
2. Define *sarcophagus* and *scarab.*
3. Describe a pyramid.
4. Explain the importance of the Nile River to ancient Egyptians.

Meetings   pages 368-369

Copy the list of words in the first column. Next to each word, write its definition from the second column.

5. minutes
6. motion
7. parliamentary procedure
8. secretary
9. recognize
10. chairperson

a. give permission to speak
b. proper order of a meeting
c. person in charge of the meeting
d. person who takes notes
e. suggestion for action or discussion
f. notes of a meeting

Introductions   pages 370-371

Decide whether these statements about introductions are true or false. Copy the true statements. Revise the false statements so that they will be true; then copy them.

11. You must always shake hands when you meet someone.
12. If you introduce a younger person to an older person, you should mention the older person's name first.
13. If you introduce a new person to a group, you should mention the person's name first.
14. If the person being introduced to you is standing, you would look up from your seat and smile warmly.
15. "How do you do?" is a proper response to an introduction.

Interviews   pages 372- 373

Put these steps for an interview in proper order.

16. Arrive with a list of appropriate questions.

17. Thank the person for the interview.

18. Record the interview or take careful notes.

19. Call or write to request an interview.

20. Ask additional questions if an answer has been unclear.

Oral Reports   pages 374–375

21.–25. Read this story about Deacon and his oral report. Then list five things he might have done to improve it.

   Deacon decided to give an oral report on World War II. Although he knew that the topic was long, he figured he could give his presentation in five minutes if he talked very quickly. After he had finished his research, he prepared an outline. Standing in front of the mirror with a sheet of paper in his hands, he read through his outline—once.

   When the time came to give his speech, Deacon stood in front of the class and read from his outline in a flat voice. At first he was too afraid to look at the audience. As he got into the body of his report, however, he began to relax. Soon he became quite expressive—in fact, by the time he reported on some of the major battles of the war, he was waving his hands in the air and jumping up and down to make the class realize how exciting these battles had been.

Applying Listening and Speaking

26. Imagine that your pen pal from Kansas is visiting you. Write an introduction for him to your friends and write a brief report that he might give about life on a farm.

27. Now that you know what to listen for in *class,* list five things you should listen for in taking a message over the phone.

28. You have been asked to help the first-grade teacher at your school. While she is working with one group of students, you must dictate a spelling test to the rest. Write a simple set of directions that will enable the children to head and number their papers correctly.

STUDY SKILLS

It is very clear that the two children had opposite reactions to the movie that they saw. However, the word *interesting* doesn't really tell you much about the movie. Let's suppose the movie is a comedy. The words *amusing* and *hilarious* would tell more than the word *interesting*. Do *amusing* and *hilarious* have similar meanings? Can you think of another word for *amusing*?

Think and Discuss

Look again at the sentences above. The words *interesting* and *boring* have opposite meanings. Words that have contrary, or opposite, meanings are called **antonyms.** Can you think of another antonym for *boring*? Name another antonym for *interesting*.

Words that have the same or similar meanings are called **synonyms.** You can improve your speech and your writing by learning synonyms and antonyms. If you cannot think of synonyms or antonyms for certain words, use your dictionary.

> • **Synonyms** are words that have similar meanings.
> • **Antonyms** are words that have opposite meanings.

Practice

A. Number your paper from 1 to 10. After each number write whether the pair of words are antonyms or synonyms.

1. wise/foolish
2. truthful/honest
3. fast/rapid
4. small/tiny
5. remember/forget
6. sad/elated
7. smile/grin
8. glad/sorry
9. clear/transparent
10. dislike/enjoy

B. Copy these words. Then write one synonym and one antonym for each.

11. fast
12. harmful
13. faithful
14. begin
15. slender
16. sad
17. generous
18. darkness
19. hate

C. Copy these sentences below. Use a different synonym in place of each underlined word.

20. It was a good meal in a good restaurant.
21. We had a nice table with a nice view.
22. There were big drawings on the big menu.
23. The bread was warm.
24. My dinner was great.
25. We left the large waiter a large tip.

Apply

D. 26. Make a bridge of words from bad to good. First find as many words as you can that suggest some degree of *badness*. Arrange them in order from those meanings *most* to *least* bad. Then find and arrange words that suggest *goodness,* from *least* to *best*.

Lesson 7: Using the Thesaurus

Anna Red Cloud wrote this sentence in a report.

The sickness pulverized Cora's health.

She could not understand why her teacher had put a question mark next to the word *pulverized.* Do you know what is wrong with it?

Think and Discuss

Anna's class had been studying ways to make their writing more precise. They had been using the **thesaurus,** a book that contains thousands of synonyms for common English words. In the thesaurus Anna had already found dozens of synonyms to use. In sentence 1, however, she had selected a word that did not quite fit. Look up *destroy* in your thesaurus, and see if you can find a better synonym than *pulverize.*

Anna checked the word *pulverize* in her dictionary and found that it meant "to break into fine pieces; crush into dust." At once she realized that a sickness cannot *pulverize* a person's health. She had chosen a synonym with the wrong **shade of meaning** for her sentence.

A **shade of meaning** is a slight difference in meaning between two similar words. Anna's thesaurus listed *demolish, dynamite, shatter, torpedo,* and *raze* in addition to *pulverize* as synonyms for *destroy.* Would any of these have been appropriate in Anna's sentence? Which synonyms for *destroy* would be most suitable for these sentences?

1. The explosion <u>destroyed</u> every window in the house.
2. The apartment house was <u>destroyed</u> to make room for a new condominium.

Practice

A. Read the following entry from a thesaurus and write answers to the questions below. Use your dictionary to look up any word you do not understand.

> **guide,** *noun* 1. conductor, director; 2. leader, mentor; 3. pilot
> **guide,** *verb* 1. conduct, direct, escort; 2. lead; 3. pilot; 4. steer, usher

1. In what two ways can the word *guide* be used?
2. Which word means the same as *conductor*?
3. Which word means "one who flies a plane or guides a ship"?
4. Which synonym for the verb *guide* means "to lead someone to a theater seat"?
5. Which synonym for the verb *guide* means "to lead a band or orchestra"?

B. Copy the following sentences. Write the best synonym for *guide* in each one.

6. The *guide* on the train showed us where to sit.
7. Rafael asked to *guide* my sister Anjelica to the dance.
8. The mountain climbers hired Olaf to *guide* the way to the top of the mountain.
9. Ms. Wong, my father's history teacher, was his *guide* during his college years.
10. A police officer in Rome *guided* us to the right street.

Apply

C. 11.–20. Look up the words *master* and *honor* in the thesaurus. Write ten sentences. Use a synonym with a different shade of meaning in each one.

COMPOSITION

Lesson 8: Prewriting

Conveying an Impression Through Tone

While touring California, Lucinda and her mother had to have their car's air conditioner fixed. Later each wrote a letter home. Read these sentences.

---

1. Since the air conditioner is still under warranty, I expect your company to reimburse me for the cost of the work that was done on it.

---

2. She was awfully angry when the garage worker charged her for fixing the air conditioner. She's writing to the dealer to get her money back!

Which sentences are from Lucinda's letter? Which are from her mother's? What differences do you see?

Think and Discuss

Tone is the overall impression built up in a piece of writing by the words used in it. Often a writer decides to use one word instead of another, depending on the *purpose* for the writing or the *audience* for whom the writing is intended. Which of the sentences on the next page did Lucinda write to her great aunt Sophie? Which sentence did she write to her friend Jane?

> 3. We had such a pleasant visit that I will always remember it as a wonderful part of our trip.

> 4. We had a dynamite time – the place was lit up like the Fourth of July, and Rock Salt was so loud that the roof nearly caved in!

Sometimes a writer chooses words with certain shades of meaning because he or she wants to give a particular impression. One rainy day during the trip, Lucinda, her mother, and her brother Ray each wrote letters home. This is how each described the rain.

Lucinda's letter	Mother's letter	Ray's letter
dripped	cooled	hammered
drenched	refreshed	rumbled
drizzled	washed clean	whipped
misted	soothed	poured
swamped	renewed	crashed
flooded	sprinkled	battered
washed away	revived	beat down
soaked	bathed	drummed
deluged	freshened	roared

What was Lucinda's attitude toward the rain? How did her mom feel about it? With what aspect of the rain was Ray most impressed?

When you are writing, decide what kind of impression you want to give. Choose words with shades of meaning that suggest that attitude. Remember that your purpose and audience will also determine your tone.

Practice

A. These sentences come from two letters. Copy the sentences. Next to each one, write *formal* or *informal,* depending on the tone.

1. The place was as dry as a bone; I carried a canteen wherever I went.

2. Baja was so hot that going out was like walking into an oven!

3. We would also appreciate receiving a city map and, if possible, a diagram of the transit system.

4. Walking into the motel every night, we felt like wilted vegetables being put into the refrigerator!

5. We hope you can suggest a moderately priced hotel that is not too far from the downtown area.

6. I had lots of fun on the cable cars.

B. Lucinda liked the cool, moist air of San Francisco, but Ray preferred warmer, dryer Southern California. Write ten words that Lucinda might use to describe

San Francisco. Then write ten words that Ray might use to describe Southern California. Use a thesaurus or other word book.

Apply

C. In the following lessons, you will be writing for varied *purposes* and *audiences.* You will write at least one friendly letter and one business letter.

Choose Your Topics

- Decide what you will write about in your friendly letter. Then choose a topic for a business letter. Select subjects you know about personally so that you will not have to do any research.

Choose Your Purpose and Audience

- Decide to whom you will write each letter and the reasons you have for writing them.

Select a Tone for Each Letter

- Decide how you feel about your friendly letter topic. Write one word that most clearly describes the impression you want to make.
- You know that a business letter should be formal and businesslike. However, depending on your purpose, choose a word that will describe your tone. (For example, are you *complaining, requesting,* or *ordering?*)

Make Word Lists to Establish Your Tone

- Think about each letter. Make a list of words that you might use in your friendly letter. Make another list for your business letter.

Review Your Work

- Look over each list. Do all the words reflect your purpose and audience? Do all the words establish the tone you want to create? Take out any words that do not belong.
- Save your word lists for the Apply exercises in Lessons 9 and 10.

Lesson 9:   Composing

Writing a Friendly Letter

Read this letter Artie wrote to a friend he met last summer while he was on vacation.

Heading
Sender's address

> *1645 Pearse Road*
> *Trenton, New Jersey 08608*
> *April 28, 19--*

Dear Sam, ←——— Greeting

Body

> *Do you remember last summer when I told you that my baseball team is always in last place? Well, we have just won three games.*
>
> *How is your team doing? What's your batting average so far?*
>
> *Write soon and tell me all the news. Can you visit me in June?*

Closing ——→ *Your friend,*

Signature ——→ *Artie*

Think and Discuss

A letter written to a friend to send greetings and news is called a friendly letter. Thank you notes, invitations, and other kinds of social notes are friendly letters that are written for a specific purpose.

A friendly letter is organized into five main parts: the *heading, greeting, body, closing,* and *signature.* How many paragraphs does Artie's letter have? Notice that Artie tells Sam his good news in the first paragraph. Then he asks Sam some questions about himself. What is the purpose of Artie's third paragraph?

Here is how Artie addressed the envelope for his letter.

Artie Underhill
1645 Pearse Road
Trenton, N J 08608

Sam Overton
64 West Lane
Columbus, OH 43201

Notice that there are two addresses on the outside of the envelope. The sender's address is written in the upper left corner and the receiver's address is written in the middle of the envelope just below the center. Why is the sender's name placed on the envelope? Both addresses contain the state abbreviation and a ZIP code, a number placed directly after the city and state. Why are ZIP codes so important? When a letter is ready to be mailed, a stamp is placed in the top right corner.

How to Write a Friendly Letter

1. Write your address and the date in the upper right corner of the letter.
2. Write the greeting under it and to the left.
3. Write the body in paragraph form. Tell your friend some news about yourself. Ask your friend something about his or her life.
4. Use words that suit your purpose and audience. Be sure your tone reflects the way you feel about your news.
5. Write your closing and your signature in a line with your heading.
6. Address your envelope correctly.

Practice

A. Rewrite this letter in correct form. Label the parts of the letter. Make an envelope, using your address for that of the receiver.

1825 Main Street Pittsburgh PA 15208 May 14, 19-- Dear Alyson I almost can't believe that there are only six weeks left until vacation. Our teachers are trying hard to help us finish this year's work. I guess they want to make sure we are all well prepared for junior high. When is your last day of school? Will you be going to camp this summer? Please write and let me know so we can make our plans. Say hello to your family for me. your friend Connie

Apply

B. Reread your notes and the list of words you made for your friendly letter in Lesson 8.

Write the Heading and Greeting of Your Letter
- Use your own address and today's date.
- Follow the model on page 386.

Write the Body
- Look over the notes you made on the purpose of your letter. Tell your friend your news.
- As you write, refer to your list of tone words. You may also use words that are not on your list if they reflect the same feeling as the others.

Write the Closing and Signature
- Follow the model on page 386.

Address the Envelope
- If you do not know your friend's address, you may make up an address.
- Use the model on page 387 as a guide.

Review Your Work
- Reread your completed letter. Be sure your vocabulary gives the impression you intended.
- Save your letter for revising in Lesson 11.

Lesson 10:   Composing

Writing a Business Letter

Read the following business letter.

Heading	4 Washington Square New York, New York 10003 April 13, 19—

American Shirt Co.
7777 South Market Street **Inside address**
Chicago, Illinois 60617

Dear Sir or Madam: ⟵ **Greeting**

   On March 5, 19—, I ordered a sequined
T shirt, size <u>medium</u>, catalog order number
TC–815 M. I enclosed a money order for $9.95,
which included postage and handling charges.
   On April 12 the shirt arrived, but it was a
size <u>large</u>. I am sending it back to you and
would appreciate your sending one in the size
ordered. If you cannot fill my order, please
refund my money by return mail.   **Body**

Closing ⟶ Sincerely yours,
Signature ⟶ *Judith McAllister*
             Judith McAllister

Why did Judith write to the store instead of telephoning?

Think and Discuss

   A **business letter** is written to accomplish a specific
business purpose. The letter from Judith to the shirt
company is a letter of *complaint.* For what other purposes
might you write a business letter?
   Before writing a business letter, collect all your facts
and list them in the most logical order you can. Keep your
language simple and clear. Look at each part of Judith's
letter. In what ways is a business letter different from a
friendly letter?

Practice

A. Write the following letter of *request* in correct form.

950 Briar Circle Minneapolis, MN 55420 Apr. 20, 19-- Ms. Alice Shore, Director, Camp Tiana, St. Louis MO 63103 Dear Ms. Shore I will be visiting in St. Louis this summer and may be attending your camp. Please send me some information on your programs. I am interested in gymnastics. Thank you for your help. Sincerely Ramon Ortega.

Apply

B. Read the list you prepared for a business letter.

Write Your Heading, Inside Address, and Greeting

● Follow the model on page 389.

Write the Body of Your Letter

● Think about your purpose for writing. Use words from your list that reflect the proper tone.

Write the Closing and Signature

● Follow the model on page 389.

Address the Envelope

● The format is the same as for the friendly letter.

Review Your Work

● Reread your letter. Does it have a formal tone?

● Save your letter for revising in Lesson 11.

Lesson 11: Revising
Editing and Proofreading Letters

Notice the changes Sandy made in this letter.

64 West Lane
Cleveland, Ohio 44114
~~Marc~~ *March* 12, 19--

~~U.S. Dept.~~ *United States Department* of Energy
Washington, D.C. 20025

Dear Sir *or Madam*:

In June our school will be having its first ~~one of a kind~~ science fair. I plan to do ~~something~~ *a project* on solar heating. ~~I would like you to~~ *Please* send me any ~~freebies~~ *free information* you may have. I would ~~be~~ *appreciate* ~~glad in~~ receiving it soon.

gratefully,
Sandra Darcy
~~Sandy~~
Sandra Darcy

Think and Discuss

Most of Sandy's changes involved her use of specific words. Why did she change *something* to *a project*? What was wrong with her use of *freebies*? How does the word *appreciate* improve the letter? Why did she change *I would like you to*? What corrections did Sandy make to her headings? Why? What improvement did Sandy make to her greeting? Sandy needed to make a change in her signature. Why? Explain any other changes she made.

Practice

A. Rewrite Sandy's letter. Include all the changes that she marked.

Apply

B. Reread both your letters. Follow these guidelines to revise them.

Edit Your Letters

- Check your **content.** Use items 1 and 2 in the blue box above.
- Check your **style.** Use items 3 and 4 in the same blue box to help you.
- Be sure you consider both your purpose and audience as you edit for content and style.

Proofread Your Letters

- Use guideline 5 in the blue box. Be sure you have spelled all names and addresses correctly.
- Write or type clean copies of both letters.

MECHANICS PRACTICE

Capitalizing and Punctuating Letters

- Capitalize names of streets, towns, cities, states, countries, organizations, and buildings.

  > Girl Scouts of America

- Use a comma in an address to separate the city and the state or the city and the country.

  > Union Springs, Alabama

- Use a comma between the day and the year in a date.

  > April 8, 19--

- Use a comma after the greeting in a friendly letter and after the closing in any letter.

  > Dear Ken,   Your friend,

- Use a colon after the greeting in a business letter.

  > Dear President Wilson:

Rewrite this letter in correct form.

35 forest street old tappan new jersey 07675 august 13 19-- action clay company boomerang building 700 lexington avenue new york new york 10017 gentlemen i have not yet received the special deluxe set of clay number 605 that i ordered from your company two months ago i have the canceled check for $11.07 which i sent with my order so i know that my letter arrived please send my merchandise within one week or refund my money thank you for your attention to this request sincerely michael milo

Copy these sentences adding capital letters and punctuation.

1. Why is one of the important dates in history june 15 1215?
2. King john of england signed the Magna Carta then
3. It was signed in runnymede england.
4. Now tell me what happened on march 15 44 AD
5. That was the day on which Julius Caesar was killed in rome.

LITERATURE

Lesson 12: Reading the Letters of Famous People

The letters of famous people are often interesting to read. They usually show that no matter how famous such people are, the writers have the same thoughts and feelings that you do.

Think and Discuss

The writer E. B. White spent most of his life writing essays and novels. Two of his best-known books for young people are *Stuart Little* and *Charlotte's Web.* E. B. White wrote many letters to all kinds of people. This letter was written to a group of sixth-graders whose teacher had sent him some of her students' compositions.

North Brooklin, ME
May 20, 1973

Dear Sixth-Graders:

Your essays spoke of beauty, of love, of light and darkness, of joy and sorrow, and of the goodness of life. They were wonderful compositions. I have seldom read any that have touched me more.

To thank you and your teacher Mrs. Ellis, I am sending you what I think is one of the most beautiful and miraculous things in the world—an egg. I have a goose named Felicity and she lays about forty eggs every spring. It takes her almost three months to accomplish this. Each egg is a perfect thing. I am mailing you one of Felicity's eggs. The insides have been removed—blown out—so the egg should last forever, or almost forever. I hope you will enjoy seeing the great egg and loving it. Thank you for sending me your essays about being somebody. I was pleased that so many of you felt the beauty and goodness of the world. If we feel that when we are young, then there is great hope for us when we grow older.

Sincerely,
E. B. White

In his letter Mr. White told the students about his goose named Felicity. What connection do you see between Mr. White's feelings about Felicity's egg and his feelings about the students' compositions?

Now read this letter. E. B. White wrote it to a girl who had asked him a question about his book *Stuart Little.*

North Brooklin, ME
February 4, 1974

Dear Jill:

Thanks for your letter—I was very glad to get it. And it is nice to know that you are interested in my stories.

"Stuart Little" is the story of a quest, or search. Much of life is questing and searching, and I was writing about that. If the book ends while the search is still going on, that's because I wanted it that way. As you grow older you will realize that many of us in this world go through life looking for something we can't quite name. In Stuart's case, he was searching for the bird Margalo, who was his ideal of beauty and goodness. Whether he ever found her or not, or whether he ever got home or not, is less important than the adventure itself. If the book made you cry, that's because you are aware of the sadness and richness of life's involvements and of the quest for beauty.

Cheer up—Stuart may yet find his bird. He may even get home again. In the meantime, he is headed in the right direction, as I am sure you are.

Sincerely,
E. B. White

How is the theme, or main idea, of this letter similar to that of the first letter you read?

> **Remember This**
>
> 1. Letters show the writer's thoughts and feelings.
> 2. The letters of famous writers may reveal how they view the characters in their books.
> 3. The letters of famous writers may also reveal their interest in their readers.

Practice

A. Write the answers to these questions.

1. Why do you think Mr. White wrote to the class?
2. Why did he send one of Felicity's eggs to them?
3. What connection do you see between the egg's lasting "almost forever" and the students' compositions?
4. One of the qualities of a good writer is the ability to see beauty in the simplest things—and then to express it in an understandable way. How did Mr. White communicate his feelings about a simple egg?
5. Some people think that great writers have to use big, important-sounding words. After reading Mr. White's letter, tell why you agree or disagree with this belief.

B. Write the answers to these questions.

6. What question do you think the girl asked Mr. White in the second letter?
7. What was Mr. White's answer?
8. What reason did Mr. White give for ending the book the way he did?
9. From reading E. B. White's letter, tell in your own words what his purpose was for writing *Stuart Little.*
10. Mr. White said that we go through our lives searching for something—often something we can't quite name. In your own words, try to express *one* good or beautiful thing for which you might spend your life searching.

Apply

C. You may not agree that an egg is beautiful. What is beautiful to you? Write a letter to a friend. Tell your friend about some simple thing that has brought you both beauty and happiness.

Prewriting

- You already know your purpose and audience. Now you must choose the topic of your letter.
- Make a list of words that apply to your topic and reveal your attitude.

Composing

- Write your letter. Follow the model on page 386 and the guidelines on page 387.

Revising

- Check the tone of your letter. Be sure that it is consistent.
- Check your spelling, punctuation, and mechanics.
- Copy your letter onto a clean sheet of paper.

A BOOK TO READ

Title: **P.S. Write Soon.**
Author: Colby Rodowsky
Publisher: Franklin Watts

In young Tanner's world she seemed the one person out of place. The McLean family all excelled at everything they tackled. The clumsy leg brace, the result of an auto accident, made Tanner feel worse. She wrote glowing, untrue letters to Jessie Lee, her friend in Virginia.

When her favorite brother returned home with a new bride, Tanner tried every mean tnck to make Cheryl uncomfortable, while her letters to Jessie grew more and more outlandish. The conclusion of this story is very touching. This is a wonderful story for those who sometimes feel less than perfect.

UNIT TEST

● **Listening in Class**   pages 366–367

Write the letter of the answer that best completes each of these statements.

1. When listening in class, it is **a.** not necessary to take notes; **b.** helpful to take notes; **c.** impolite to take notes.
2. It is a good idea to listen **a.** for key words; **b.** to every word; **c.** for unimportant details.
3. It is never wrong to **a.** interrupt the speaker; **b.** ask questions; **c.** ask a classmate what was said.
4. Listening to the *order* in which test directions are given is **a.** not important as long as you understand the question; **b.** difficult and unnecessary; **c.** often important.
5. If you are asked to *compare* two statements on a test, this means to **a.** match items from two groups; **b.** give the meaning of the items; **c.** show how the statements are alike.

● **Conducting a Meeting**   pages 368–369

Copy these sentences, correctly completing each one.

6. A suggestion for a particular action made during a meeting is called a _____.
7. The person who conducts the meeting is the _____.
8. The rules according to which a meeting is conducted are called _____.
9. The _____ takes notes on what happens at the meeting.
10. The notes from the meeting are called _____.

● **Making Introductions**   pages 370–371

Copy each statement and label it *true* or *false.*

11. When introducing two people, you should say the names of both people.
12. You should never introduce yourself to a group.

13. When you introduce a younger person to an older person, it is courteous to say the name of the older person first.
14. It is good to include something about each person when you make an introduction.
15. If you introduce yourself, you should tell something about yourself.

● **Interviewing**   pages 372–373

Copy each statement and label it *true* or *false.*

16. You should never tell the purpose of your interview.
17. It is rude to take notes when you conduct an interview.
18. Questions should be prepared ahead of time.
19. Interviews can supply good information for school reports.
20. Only famous people can be interviewed.

● **Oral Reports**   pages 374–375

Copy each statement and label it *true* or *false.*

21. You should always memorize an oral report.
22. A speaker should never refer to notes when talking to an audience.
23. A speaker should interest the audience in the topic.
24. A speaker should look at the audience.
25. A speaker should appear confident and at ease.

● **Synonyms and Antonyms**   pages 378–379

Copy these words. Write one synonym and one antonym next to each one.

1. damp	2. huge	3. sharp
4. chilly	5. cry	6. finish
7. foolish	8. rise	9. tasty
10. soft	11. tall	12. find
13. crawl	14. nervous	15. remember

● **The Thesaurus**   pages 380–381

16.–20. Look up the word *rough* in a thesaurus. Write five sentences using synonyms for *rough.* Each synonym should have a different shade of meaning.

● **Prewriting, Composing, and Revising — Friendly Letter and Addressing an Envelope** pages 382–388, 391–392

1. Make a list of ten words that you might use in a letter to a cousin or a friend, telling how you feel about vacationing in the mountains with your family. Use your list of words to write a friendly letter. Be sure to include the five main parts. Edit your letter for tone. Proofread it for spelling, capitalization, and punctuation. Rewrite your letter in final form. Then, on a separate sheet of paper, draw an envelope and address it to your cousin or friend. Remember to add the ZIP code.

● **Prewriting, Composing, and Revising — Business Letter and Addressing an Envelope** pages 382–385, 389–392

2. Choose one of these topics for a business letter.

   - receiving a beginner's magic kit without an instruction book
   - writing for information about a school you would like to attend
   - answering a letter offering you a newspaper route
   - discussing why you would like to hang a poster about the school play in the local market

   Depending on your topic, decide whether your business letter's purpose will be to complain, explain, persuade, inform, request, or thank. Think of words you might use in your letter and list them. Remember to use words that suggest the right tone. Write down any other ideas that you might use in your letter. Next make up a company or person to whom you will address your letter. Use your word list and your other notes to write your business letter. Be sure you include all the parts of a business letter. You should also include all the information needed and yet keep to the point. Revise your letter. Does its language describe your attitude about the topic? If not, take out any words or expressions that do not belong. Check for errors in spelling, punctuation, and other mechanics. Then rewrite your letter in final form.

● **Mechanics Practice** page 393

Punctuate these letter parts correctly.

3. Houston Texas 77060   4. dear jack   5. Dear mayor greene
6. your classmate   7. May 19 19--   8. toledo ohio 43613

9. dear sir   **10.** regretfully   **11.** dear general
12. 2 holly rd   **13.** 5 clay st   **14.** beazley inc
15. ames IA 50010   **16.** sincerely   **17.** dear sue

Punctuate these addresses and dates correctly.

18. 6212 chatwood terrace
portland oregon 97220
may 15 19--

19. senator mary mc queeny
senate office building
washington dc 20005

20. joe harper
8 silver lane drive
schaumburg illinois 60193

21. 3130 hamlet lane
dallas texas 75220
september 24 19--

22. joan murray polanski
2299 bush street
bound brook new jersey 08805

23. 6 pineboard drive
walpole massachusetts 02081
february 15 19--

24. raymond michaels
1308 walker avenue
sanford florida 32771

25. 30 valley road
new york new york 10028
december 3 19--

● **Reading Letters**   pages 394–397

Copy these statements and label each *true* or *false*.

1. Letters reveal the private personality of the sender.
2. Letters of famous people are always formal.
3. Letters can give a picture of life at the time they were written.
4. Well-written letters can be a form of literature.
5. Famous people are too busy to write letters to students.
6. The letters of famous people show that the writers are very much like the rest of us.

MAINTENANCE and REVIEW

Sentences   pages 2–11, 326–329

Read these sentences. Write the numbers of those that are simple, then the numbers of those that are compound. Tell how many clauses there are altogether.

1. Mary McLeod Bethune was a remarkable woman.
2. She was born in South Carolina, and as a girl she picked cotton.
3. She wanted an education, and she worked hard at many difficult jobs.
4. A woman in Colorado paid some of her school expenses.
5. Mary McLeod Bethune attended college in Chicago, but she returned to the South to teach.
6. She heard about some poor children in Florida and felt sorry for them.
7. With a dream—and less than $2.00—she began a school in Daytona Beach.
8. Bethune College joined Cookman Institute in 1923.
9. Many students have graduated from Bethune-Cookman College.
10. President Franklin D. Roosevelt gave Mary McLeod Bethune an important position in the National Youth Administration, and she became a frequent guest at the White House.

Paragraphs   pages 40–47

11.–20. Write sentences 1–10 in paragraph form. Draw one line under each simple or compound subject and two lines under each simple or compound predicate. What is the topic sentence of the paragraph?

Common and Proper Nouns   pages 90–91

21.–35. Using sentences 1–10, copy nine common nouns and six proper nouns.

Verbs   pages 134–149

Write the principal parts of these verbs. Follow this example.

to wear: wear(s), wore, (have, has, had) worn

Then use each verb in a sentence. Next to each sentence, write the tense of the verb you used.

36. to sell   **37.** to grow   **38.** to go
39. to ride   **40.** to swim   **41.** to think

Adjectives, Adverbs, and Pronouns   pages 182–193, 226–235

42.–55. Turn to "Demeter and Persephone," the myth found in this book. Copy seven adjectives, four adverbs, and three pronouns that appear in that myth.

Prepositions   pages 278–281

56.–60. Copy five prepositional phrases from the paragraph that you wrote about Mary McLeod Bethune. Next to each one, write the word it modifies.

Conjunctions   pages 286–289

Copy these sentences. Underline all conjunctions or punctuation that replaces them, and circle the words or groups of words that each connects.

61. The state of Wyoming is ninth in size but forty-ninth in population.
62. Wyoming has been nicknamed "The Equality State"; its women were the first in the country to vote, hold public office, and serve on juries.
63. Did Wyoming become a state in 1890 or in 1891?
64. Wyoming is famous for the beauty of its Rocky Mountains, and I hope to go there and visit them some day.

Listening and Speaking   pages 372–373

65.–70. Imagine that you are going to interview for your class a character from a book you have enjoyed. Write an appropriate introduction and five questions you would ask during the interview.

SENTENCE DIAGRAMING

Diagrams are pictures that help explain something. To explain how sentences are put together, sentence diagrams are made. They show how the parts of a sentence relate to one another.

The Simple Subject and Verb *pages 6–7*

The first step in diagraming a sentence is to draw a base line. Then find the verb in the sentence. Write it on the right-hand half of the line.

Johnny Appleseed walked through the wilderness.

	walked

Next, find the simple subject of the sentence. Ask yourself: "Who or what *walked*?" Johnny Appleseed walked. *Johnny Appleseed* is the subject of the sentence. Write this on the left-hand side of the line. Draw a vertical line between the subject and the verb, making sure it crosses the base line.

Johnny Appleseed	walked

When the verb contains more than one word, the whole verb phrase is written on the line.

Johnny Appleseed	was walking

Practice

Diagram the simple subjects and verbs in these sentences.

1. This quiet man's real name was John Chapman.
2. He wandered for hundreds of miles on foot.
3. On his route he planted apple seeds.
4. Soon apple tree seedlings were sprouting.
5. Today this man is remembered as Johnny Appleseed.

Natural and Inverted Word Order *pages 10–11*

In most sentences the subject comes first and then the predicate follows. This is **natural word order.**

> Johnny Appleseed wandered through the woods.

Sometimes, however, the word order is reversed, and the verb comes before the subject. This is **inverted word order.**

> Through the woods wandered Johnny Appleseed.

Sentence diagrams are meant to show how the parts of a sentence relate to one another. They do *not* show word order. The subject *always* comes before the verb in a sentence diagram. Therefore, both sentences above would be diagramed the same way.

Johnny Appleseed	wandered

However, the first word in a sentence — and all other capitalized words — remain capitalized in a sentence diagram. Compare these sentences and their diagrams.

Deer ran through the forest.

Deer	ran

Through the forest ran deer.

deer	ran

Practice

These sentences may be in natural or inverted word order. Find and diagram the simple subjects and verbs in these sentences.

1. Under the trees ran a quiet brook.
2. Dappled shadows played across the brook's surface.
3. Fish of all kinds swam in the clear waters.
4. On the banks turtles were sunning themselves.
5. Overhead glided clouds of every shape and description.

The Four Types of Sentences *pages 2–3*

Below are the four types of sentences. The simple subject and the verb have been diagramed in each one.

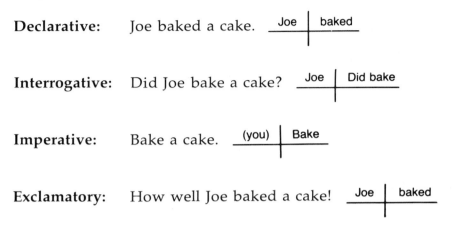

Declarative: Joe baked a cake. | Joe | baked |

Interrogative: Did Joe bake a cake? | Joe | Did bake |

Imperative: Bake a cake. | (you) | Bake |

Exclamatory: How well Joe baked a cake! | Joe | baked |

In the interrogative sentence the subject often comes between the two parts of a verb. In the diagram the subject comes first followed by the whole verb phrase. The first word in the sentence is left capitalized.

In an imperative sentence the subject is usually not stated. It is understood to be *you*. This is diagramed by writing *(you)* for the simple subject.

Practice

Diagram the simple subject and verb in each sentence.

1. Buy more flour to make a carrot cake.
2. Will you eat dinner after this?
3. You have eaten a piece of carrot cake already.
4. How much you ate!
5. You must eat all of your vegetables at dinner.
6. Did Beth eat too much cake?
7. Beth devoured most of all.
8. How I love cake!
9. Carrot cake is my favorite.
10. Why did you use nuts as a topping?

Direct Objects *pages 150–151*

The sentence diagrams so far have contained only the simple subject and verb of a sentence. Now another sentence part will be added: the **direct object.** When a noun or pronoun follows an action verb and receives the action of the verb, that word is a direct object.

> Tourists write postcards.

Tourists is the subject, or what the sentence is about. The verb *write* tells what the subject is doing. The noun *postcards* answers the question "Tourists write *what?"* *Postcards* is the direct object. The sentence is diagramed like this.

Tourists	write	postcards

Notice that the vertical line between the verb and the direct object stops at the base line. Here is another example.

Subj. Verb   Dir. Obj.
 ↓   ↓   ↓
Buses carry passengers.

Buses	carry	passengers

Practice

Find and diagram the simple subject, verb, and direct object in each of these sentences.

1. His camera takes sharp pictures.
2. The officer directed the bus through the traffic jam.
3. Drivers everywhere honked their horns impatiently.
4. The shrill noise filled the village square.
5. Passengers on the bus clicked their cameras again and again.
6. The tourists would remember this trip for a long time.
7. They wrote postcards to their friends.
8. Everyone enjoyed the experience.
9. Suitcases contain souvenirs.
10. Does your camera contain film?

Possessives and Articles *pages 182–184, 232–233*

Possessive nouns and pronouns often come before other nouns to show ownership. The **articles** *a, an,* and *the* always signal a noun. Possessives, articles, and nouns are shown in this sentence diagram.

Ian's sister found her books.

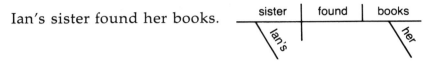

The possessives and articles are written on slanting lines under the nouns they modify. Here is another example.

The girl is reading her book.

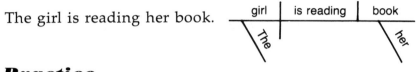

Practice

Diagram all the words in these sentences.

1. The notebook's pages fluttered.
2. The drawing showed Jan's dog.
3. Keith's notebooks covered the desk.
4. Bob's message arrived.
5. Was that his message?

Indirect Objects *pages 230–231*

Indirect objects always tell to whom or for whom something is done. In a diagram the indirect object is placed on a horizontal line below the verb, with a slanting line joining it to the verb. Here is an example.

Li gave Cara the book.

Cara is the indirect object, because Li gave the book *to her.* Notice that indirect objects appear only in sentences that have **direct objects.**

Practice

Diagram all the words in these sentences.

1. Tom gave Lucille his binoculars.
2. The class gave her a party.
3. Ricardo lent Lucy a pencil.
4. The coach offered Lawanda the pitcher's position.
5. John's mom bought him a sweater.

Predicate Nominatives *pages 150–151*

Predicate nominatives follow linking verbs. The subject and the predicate nominative refer to the same person or thing in a sentence. In diagraming, the predicate nominative is written on the base line after the verb. The line separating the predicate nominative from the verb is slanted toward the subject of the sentence.

Mrs. Wong is a teacher.

She became the principal.

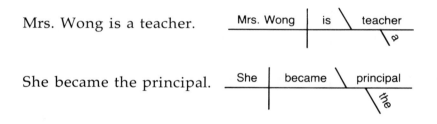

Practice

Diagram all the words in these sentences.

1. The principal is Mrs. Wong.
2. Her office had been the teachers' room.
3. My sister became the twins' friend.
4. Did the man become an engineer?
5. Heather's flower was a rose.
6. Gwendolyn is a lawyer.
7. John became a pianist.
8. John is Gwendolyn's brother.

Adjectives   *pages 182–184*

An **adjective** is a word that can modify a noun or pronoun. In a diagram these adjectives are placed on slanting lines under the words they modify.

The back stairs creak.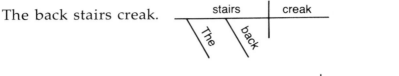

The new telephone is ringing.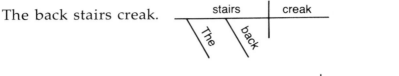

Practice

Diagram these sentences.

1. Linda's small gray puppy has disappeared.
2. The unhappy child shouted the dog's name.
3. Soft, sad whimpers were heard.
4. A warm, tiny tongue licked Linda's right hand.
5. Happy Linda hugged her little friend.

Predicate Adjectives   *pages 183–184*

Predicate adjectives are treated like predicate nominatives. They are placed on the base line after the linking verb and are separated from the verb with a line slanting toward the subject.

Heidi is intelligent.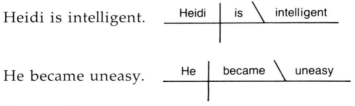

He became uneasy.

Practice

Diagram these sentences.

1. The pillow looks soft.
2. Are you hungry?
3. The child seems honest.
4. Kai's dress is lovely.

Adverbs   *pages 188–189*

Most **adverbs** add to the meaning of verbs. In a sentence diagram adverbs are placed beneath the words they modify.

The sun shone brightly.

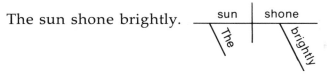

Remember that a sentence diagram does *not* show word order. An adverb is placed beneath the word it modifies, even if the two words are separated in the sentence. The adverb *not* is shown like any other adverb.

The sun did not shine yesterday.

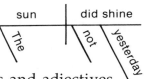

Some adverbs modify other adverbs and adjectives. They often answer the question *to what extent?* To show this relationship, diagram like this.

A very large fish then surfaced quite suddenly.

An adverb modifying a predicate adjective looks like this.

The fish was very silvery.

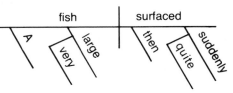

Practice

Diagram these sentences.

1. Read the thermometer carefully.
2. We certainly want warm weather badly.
3. The citrus farms were badly damaged.
4. Luckily the crops were not totally destroyed.
5. Soon newspapers reported the event.

Prepositional Phrases *pages 278–279*

A **prepositional phrase** is made up of a preposition, its object, and its modifiers. It can modify a verb in the same way that an adverb does. In this sentence the prepositional phrase *into the room* modifies the verb *hurried*. It is used as an adverb.

The printer hurried *into the room.*

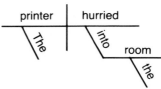

A prepositional phrase can also modify a noun in the same way that an adjective does. In this sentence *of newspapers* modifies the noun *stack*. It is used as an adjective.

The stack *of newspapers* is heavy.

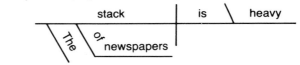

Practice

Diagram these sentences.

1. The presses run for several hours.
2. The type for the presses is made of metal.
3. A sheet of newsprint goes into the press.
4. Stop the presses for a news flash!
5. Did Meda finish the story about the flood before the deadline?
6. The newspaper for today landed on the front porch.
7. Meda's story appeared on the first page.
8. The mayor of Crystal City congratulated Meda at the courthouse.

Conjunctions   *pages 284–287, 326–329*

The connecting words *and, but,* and *or* are **conjunctions.** They join words, phrases, or sentences together. Here are diagrams of several sentences involving conjunctions.

Compound Subject: John and Malcolm raided the refrigerator.

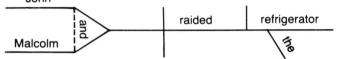

Compound Predicate: They ate the pears and drank milk.

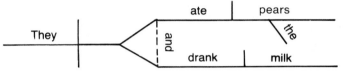

Compound Sentence: The bakery on the corner closed, but we bake our own bread.

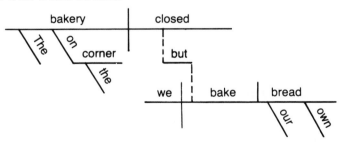

Practice

Diagram these sentences.

1. The clerk stacked the shelves and swept the floor.
2. The baseball gloves and tennis balls were sold.
3. Customers in line grumbled and complained.
4. Stu bought skis, and Jan bought skates.
5. The busy salesclerk wrapped my package but forgot the bow.

 **REVIEW HANDBOOK**

Sentences

GRAMMAR

sentence

declarative
sentence

interrogative
sentence

imperative
sentence

exclamatory
sentence

- A **sentence** is a group of words that expresses a complete thought. It begins with a capital letter and ends with a punctuation mark.   *(pages 2–3)*

  Saturn is the second largest planet.

- A **declarative sentence** makes a statement. It ends with a period.   *(pages 2–3)*

  Home computers are becoming very popular.

- An **interrogative sentence** asks a question. It ends with a question mark.   *(pages 2–3)*

  When does the second semester begin?

- An **imperative sentence** makes a request or gives an order. It ends with a period.   *(pages 2–3)*

  Sign on the dotted line.   Please pass the salt.

- An **exclamatory sentence** shows surprise or strong feeling. It ends with an exclamation point.   *(pages 2–3)*

  You just won first prize!   The house is on fire!

Practice

Copy these sentences. Add capital letters and punctuation where needed. After each sentence write which of the four sentence types it is.

1. the spacecraft transmitted pictures of Saturn
2. what is the largest planet in our solar system
3. the spacecraft Voyager 2 passed Saturn in 1981
4. what a spectacular view of the planet this is
5. look at Saturn through this telescope
6. is it true that Saturn has a flat moon
7. the ringed planet has at least 13 moons

Clauses and Sentence Types

- A **clause** is a group of words that contains a subject and a predicate and is used as part of a sentence. *(pages 326–327)*

  <u>The train will arrive soon.</u>

- An **independent clause** is a clause that expresses a complete thought and can stand alone. *(pages 326–327)*

  <u>The picnic was canceled</u> because the weather was bad.

- A **simple sentence** contains one independent clause. *(pages 328–329)*

  Dana jogs every morning.   She keeps fit.

- A **compound sentence** is made up of two independent clauses joined by a comma and a conjunction or a semicolon. *(pages 328–329)*

  <u>Joe likes football</u>, but <u>Dave prefers baseball</u>.

clause

independent clause

simple sentence

compound sentence

Practice

A. Copy these sentences. Draw one line under each independent clause.

1. The sky darkened, and the hikers looked for shelter.
2. They were annoyed because they had no rain gear.
3. They saw a tall tree; it could provide shelter.
4. They did not head for it.

B. Copy these sentences. Draw one line under each independent clause. Label each sentence *simple* or *compound.*

5. Benjamin Franklin experimented with lightning.
6. He attached a key to a kite string, and he flew the kite in a thunderstorm.
7. Lightning struck the kite; the key sparked!
8. Franklin had learned a great lesson.

Subjects and Predicates

complete subject
- The **complete subject** is all the words that make up the subject of a sentence. *(pages 4–5)*

  The flock of Canadian geese flew south.

complete predicate
- The **complete predicate** is all the words that make up the predicate of a sentence. *(pages 4–5)*

  The singer strained to reach the high note.

simple subject
- The **simple subject** is the key word or words in the complete subject of a sentence. *(pages 6–7)*

  The old metal bridge gets icy in winter.

simple predicate
- The **simple predicate** is the key word or words in the complete predicate of a sentence. *(pages 6–7)*

  The dog waited impatiently for its dinner.

compound subject
- A **compound subject** consists of two or more subjects that have the same predicate. *(pages 324–325)*

  The seniors and juniors have exams today.

compound predicate
- A **compound predicate** consists of two or more predicates that have the same subject. *(pages 324–325)*

  The wind shrieked and howled fiercely.

***you* (understood)**
- *You* **(understood)** is the subject of an imperative sentence. *(pages 8–9)*

  (You) Do not park by the fire hydrant.

Practice

Copy these sentences. Draw one line under the complete subject and two lines under the complete predicate.

1. The loud music blared from station WWTR.
2. The driver of the bus called to the owner of the radio.
3. "Turn that radio off, sir."
4. The music lover left at the next stop.

Nouns

- A **noun** is a word that names a person, place, or thing. *(pages 90–91)* **noun**

- A **common noun** names *any* person, place, or thing. It is a general word that begins with a small letter. *(pages 90–91)* **common noun**

  sea   letter   child   carpenter

- A **proper noun** names a *particular* person, place, or thing. A proper noun begins with a capital letter. *(pages 90–91)* **proper noun**

  Abigail Adams   Santa Fe   Halloween

- A **singular noun** names *one* person, place, or thing. *(pages 92–93)* **singular noun**

  boy   town   sandwich   street

- A **plural noun** names *more than one* person, place, or thing. *(pages 92–93)* **plural noun**

  girls   cities   highways   lunches

Practice

A. Copy each noun. Label it *common* if it is a common noun and *proper* if it is a proper noun.

1. Florida
2. carrots
3. building
4. judge
5. Lincoln Memorial
6. courage
7. Missouri River
8. canyon
9. August

B. Copy each noun. Label it either *S* (for *singular*) or *P* (for *plural*).

10. children
11. Jupiter
12. kittens
13. libraries
14. China
15. oxen
16. geese
17. radio
18. foxes
19. peace
20. horn
21. teeth

Noun Plurals

plural noun

- Form the plural of most nouns by adding an *s*. Add *es* to nouns that end in *z, s, x, sh,* or *ch*. *(pages 92–93)*

  letter — letters   crash — crashes

- If a noun ends in *y* with a vowel before it, add an *s*. If the noun ends in *y* with a consonant before it, change the *y* to *i* and add *es*. *(pages 92–93)*

  bay — bays   penny — pennies

- To form the plural of nouns that end in a vowel and *o*, add only an *s*. For some nouns that end in a consonant and *o*, add *es*. *(pages 92–93)*

  rodeo — rodeos   echo — echoes

- To form the plural of most nouns ending in *f* or *fe*, change the *f* to *v* and add *es*. For others, add an *s*. *(pages 92–93)*

  life — lives   wolf — wolves   chef — chefs

- The plurals of some nouns are formed by a vowel change within the singular form. Others are the same in both the singular and plural. *(pages 92–93)*

  goose — geese   tooth — teeth   sheep — sheep

- Form the possessive of a singular noun by adding an apostrophe and an *s*. Form the possessive of a plural noun that ends in *s* by adding an apostrophe only. Otherwise, add an apostrophe and *s*. *(pages 92- 93)*

  Gus's dog   girls' books   women's chorus

Practice

Copy each noun. Next to it write its plural form.

1. sky
2. child
3. film
4. fox
5. radio
6. man
7. thief
8. story
9. key
10. torch
11. buzz
12. calf

Complements

- A **complement** completes the meaning of the verb.   **complement**

    Sheila caught the <u>baseball</u>.

- A **direct object** follows an *action* verb and receives its   **direct**
  action.   *(pages 150–151)*   **object**

    Arletta paddled the <u>canoe</u>.

- An **indirect object** tells to whom or for whom something   **indirect**
  is done.   *(pages 230–231)*   **object**

    We gave the <u>twins</u> a birthday present.

- A **predicate nominative** follows a *linking verb* and tells   **predicate**
  what the subject is.   *(pages 150–151)*   **nominative**

    Dr. Gonzales is my <u>dentist</u>.

- A **predicate adjective** is an adjective that modifies the   **predicate**
  subject in a sentence with a linking verb.   *(pages 183–184)*   **adjective**

    The salad is <u>delicious</u>!

Practice

A. Copy each sentence. Draw one line under the direct
object and two lines under the indirect object.

1. The town awarded Reynaldo a scholarship.
2. They gave him the award last Thursday.
3. Reynaldo wrote the council a letter of appreciation.
4. All Reynaldo's friends offered him congratulations.

B. Add predicate nominatives or predicate adjectives
to these sentences.

5. The ostrich is the _____ of the bird world.
6. Ostriches are so _____, however, that they cannot fly.
7. The huge bird looks _____.
8. Its speed on land, however, is _____.

Verbs

verb
● A **verb** expresses action or being. *(pages 134–135)*

action
verb
● An **action verb** expresses physical or mental action. *(pages 134–135)*

climbed hit dreamed supposes

linking
verb
● A **linking verb** links, or joins, the subject of a sentence with a word or words in the predicate. *(pages 136–137)*

transitive
verb
● **Transitive verbs** are action verbs that are followed by direct objects. *(pages 150–151)*

intransitive
verb
● **Intransitive verbs** include all linking verbs and any action verbs that are not followed by direct objects. *(pages 150–151)*

main
verb
● The **main verb** is the verb that expresses the action or being. *(pages 138–139)*

is <u>running</u> have <u>learned</u> are <u>singing</u>

helping
verb
● The **helping verb** is the verb that helps the main verb express its action. Most helping verbs are forms of *be*, *have*, and *do*. *(pages 138–139)*

<u>are</u> thinking <u>has</u> won <u>does</u> swim

Practice

Copy each verb. Label it *action verb* or *linking verb* as well as *transitive* or *intransitive*.

1. Baseball is a favorite American sport.
2. Thousands of fans watch it each year.
3. Television stations carry the Big League games.
4. Larry's TV set broke.
5. He was quite sad all week.
6. He could not watch the big game.
7. His father bought tickets to the game.
8. Larry was happy again.

Regular and Irregular Verbs

- The three basic forms of a verb are its **principal parts.** These are the **present,** the **past,** and the **past participle.** The past and past participle of regular verbs are formed by adding *d* or *ed* to the present form. *(pages 140–141)*

principal parts

regular verbs

Present	Past	Past Participle
talk(s)	talked	(have, has, had) talked

- The past and past participle of **irregular verbs** are not formed by adding *d* or *ed* to their present forms. Their past and past participles are formed in a variety of ways, as shown on this chart. *(pages 142–145)*

irregular verbs

Present	Past	Past Participle
begin(s)	began	(have, has, had) begun
break(s)	broke	(have, has, had) broken
bring(s)	brought	(have, has, had) brought
catch(es)	caught	(have, has, had) caught
choose(s)	chose	(have, has, had) chosen
come(s)	came	(have, has, had) come
do(es)	did	(have, has, had) done
drink(s)	drank	(have, has, had) drunk
eat(s)	ate	(have, has, had) eaten
find(s)	found	(have, has, had) found
fly(ies)	flew	(have, has, had) flown
freeze(s)	froze	(have, has, had) frozen
give(s)	gave	(have, has, had) given
go(es)	went	(have, has, had) gone
grow(s)	grew	(have, has, had) grown
know(s)	knew	(have, has, had) known
ride(s)	rode	(have, has, had) ridden
ring(s)	rang	(have, has, had) rung
run(s)	ran	(have, has, had) run
say(s)	said	(have, has, had) said

Present	Past	Past Participle
sell(s)	sold	(have, has, had) sold
sing(s)	sang	(have, has, had) sung
speak(s)	spoke	(have, has, had) spoken
swim(s)	swam	(have, has, had) swum
take(s)	took	(have, has, had) taken
tear(s)	tore	(have, has, had) torn
think(s)	thought	(have, has, had) thought
wear(s)	wore	(have, has, had) worn
write(s)	wrote	(have, has, had) written

Practice

Complete each sentence with the past or past participle of the verb in parentheses ( ). Write the sentences.

1. Lynn _____ to her desk and sat down. (go)
2. She _____ to write a thank you letter. (begin)
3. "What should I say first?" she _____. (think)
4. "I know I should have _____ sooner." (write)
5. "I have _____ one excuse after another." (find)
6. Lynn _____ her pen from her desk. (take)
7. She _____ her words carefully. (choose)
8. Then, dissatisfied, she _____ up the paper. (tear)
9. She _____ annoyed with herself. (grow)
10. Then, determined, she _____ again. (try)
11. The words _____ more easily this time. (come)
12. At last she had _____! (finish)
13. "Finally, I have _____ it!" she thought. (do)
14. Then she _____ at her watch in disbelief. (look)
15. "How time has _____!" she said to herself. (fly)
16. "I _____ I'd write to Ann too," Lynn remarked. (say)
17. "This letter is easier to write," she _____. (think)
18. Lynn _____ a clean sheet of paper. (find)
19. She _____ a long letter about her friends. (write)
20. "I did this in ten minutes," she _____. (think)

Verb Tenses

- The time expressed by a verb is its **tense.** *(pages 146–147)*   **tense**

    listens   listened   will listen   has listened

- The **present tense** expresses action that is taking place   **present**
now. *(pages 146–147)*   **tense**

    The pitcher <u>throws</u> the ball.

- The **past tense** expresses action that took place at *some*   **past**
definite time in the past. *(pages 146–147)*   **tense**

    When the game <u>was</u> over, we <u>went</u> home.

- The **future tense** expresses action that will take place   **future**
at *some time in the future.* *(pages 146–147)*   **tense**

    Our plane <u>will land</u> soon.   Dad <u>will meet</u> us.

- The **present perfect tense** expresses action that took   **present**
place at *some indefinite time in the past* or that began in   **perfect**
the past and is *still going on.* *(pages 148–149)*   **tense**

    The band <u>has been playing</u> a long time.

Practice

Copy the verb(s) from each sentence. After each verb write
present, past, future, or *present perfect* to identify its tense.

1. Stingrays belong to the same fish family as sharks.
2. A stingray will use its poisonous tail for defense.
3. The ray used its long barbed tail like a whip.
4. Many people have made needles from stingray barbs.
5. Stingrays feed on shellfish, clams, and small fish.
6. A stingray digs for clams with its fins.
7. The presence of a stingray has always meant danger.
8. Stingray barbs release poison.
9. Stingrays lived in prehistoric times.
10. Undoubtedly we will find more stingray fossils.

Adjectives

adjective
- An **adjective** is a word that modifies a noun or pronoun. It answers the questions *what kind*, *which one*, *whose*, or *how many*. *(pages 182–184)*

  The <u>two</u> <u>tiny</u> kittens peeked into the <u>open</u> bag.

common adjective
- A **common adjective** is a simple descriptive word. It is not capitalized unless it begins a sentence. *(pages 182–184)*

  <u>Brilliant</u> flowers make a <u>spectacular</u> display.

proper adjective
- A **proper adjective** is formed from a proper noun. It begins with a capital letter. *(pages 182–184)*

  The suit is made of <u>English</u> tweed.

positive degree
- The **positive degree** of an adjective is used when only *one* thing is described. *(pages 185–187)*

  The <u>mysterious</u> stranger disappeared.

comparative degree
- The **comparative degree** of an adjective is used when two things are compared. *(pages 185–187)*

  Chicago is <u>larger</u> than Miami.

superlative degree
- The **superlative degree** of an adjective is used when *three or more* things are compared. *(pages 185–187)*

  Bruce is the <u>youngest</u> of the four brothers.

Practice

Copy these sentences. Underline the adjectives. Do not underline the articles *a, an,* and *the*. Tell which degree of the adjective is used.

1. It was the brightest, loveliest day of the summer.
2. I walked two miles down the shady road.
3. The road was longer than I had thought.
4. A light breeze carried the fresh scent of sweet clover.

Adverbs

- An **adverb** is a word that modifies a verb, adjective, or other adverb. It answers the questions *how*, *when*, *where*, and *to what extent.* *(pages 188–189)*

  adverb

  > The dog barked <u>loudly</u>.   (modifies verb *barked*)
  > The sun is <u>very</u> bright.   (modifies adjective *bright*)
  > The snail moved <u>quite</u> fast.   (modifies adverb *fast*)

- The **positive degree** of an adverb is used when only *one* thing is described.   *(pages 190–191)*

  positive degree

  > The deer ran <u>swiftly</u>.

- The **comparative degree** of an adverb is used when *two* things are compared.   *(pages 190–191)*

  comparative degree

  > Steve left <u>earlier</u> today than he did yesterday.
  > Greg writes <u>more carefully</u> than Josh does.

- The **superlative degree** of an adverb is used when *three or more* things are compared.   *(pages 190–191)*

  superlative degree

  > Of all the players, Bill tried the <u>hardest</u> to win.
  > This car runs <u>most economically</u> of all.

Practice

Copy these sentences. Underline the adverbs. Draw an arrow to the word that the adverb modifies. Tell which degree of the adverb is used.

1. The guinea pig slowly munched the lettuce.
2. My guinea pig eats faster than yours does.
3. Your guinea pig, however, runs more quickly than mine.
4. Sarah's pet moves most quickly of all.
5. Guinea pigs swiftly alert each other to danger.
6. In such moments they whistle loudly.
7. This guinea pig responds more intelligently than most.
8. He must learn faster than the others.

Pronouns

pronoun, antecedent
- A **pronoun** takes the place of a noun. An **antecedent** is the noun to which a pronoun refers. *(pages 226–227)*

    The plants needed water. <u>They</u> were wilted.

subject pronoun
- A **subject pronoun** acts as the subject of a sentence or a predicate nominative. *I, you, he, she, it, we,* and *they* are subject pronouns. *(pages 228–229)*

    <u>I</u> read the book. The winner was <u>she</u>.

object pronoun
- An **object pronoun** can be a direct or indirect object or the object of a preposition. *Me, you, him, her, it, us,* and *them* are object pronouns. *(pages 230–231)*

    Carl saw <u>him</u> yesterday.   (direct object)

possessive pronoun
- A **possessive pronoun** takes the place of a possessive noun. *My, your, his, her, our, their, its, mine, hers, yours, ours,* and *theirs* are possessive pronouns. *(pages 232–233)*

    That book is <u>mine</u>. <u>My</u> name is on <u>its</u> cover.

reflexive pronoun
- **Reflexive pronouns** end in *self* or *selves*. The words *myself, yourself, himself, herself, itself, ourselves, yourselves,* and *themselves* are reflexive pronouns. *(pages 232–233)*

    Why don't you give <u>yourself</u> a vacation?

Practice

Copy the pronouns from these sentences. After each one write its antecedent in parentheses (   ).

1. Jenny gave Ben a letter and asked him to mail it.
2. Jenny told her brother Ben, "I will do you a favor too."
3. Ben told Jenny, "Fine, you can mow the lawn for me."
4. Jenny answered, "I will do it."
5. Ben commented, "Then you and I will be even."

Prepositions

- A **preposition** is a word that shows the relationship between a noun or pronoun and some other word in a sentence. *(pages 278–279)*

    The wastebasket is <u>beside</u> the desk.

- A **prepositional phrase** is a group of words that begins with a preposition and ends with a noun or pronoun as the **object of the preposition.** *(pages 278–279)*

    Put the paper <u>in the drawer</u>.

- Prepositional phrases can modify nouns or pronouns, as adjectives do. They can also modify verbs, adjectives, or adverbs, as adverbs do. *(pages 280–281)*

    The book <u>on the table</u> is mine.   (modifies *book*)
    We looked <u>inside the tent</u>.   (modifies *looked*)

- The following are commonly used prepositions: *at, by, in, for, from, of, off, on, up, above, after, around, before, behind, between, below, during, except, over, through, to, under, until, without.* *(pages 278–279)*

preposition

prepositional phrase, object of the preposition

Practice

Copy these sentences. Draw one line under each prepositional phrase and two lines under the object of the preposition.

1. The sun sank slowly behind the hills.
2. A coyote's howl could be heard in the distance.
3. An owl sat on a branch, waiting for darkness.
4. The bird slept by day and hunted at night.
5. The owl spotted a mouse beneath it scampering away.
6. The mouse escaped into a burrow.
7. A rabbit sat by a tree and scratched behind one ear.
8. Then it thumped its hind foot on the ground.
9. The owl turned its head in the direction of the sound.
10. It did not go after the rabbit, however.

Interjections and Conjunctions

interjection
- An **interjection** is a word used to express feeling. *(pages 284–285)*

  <u>Oh!</u> What a surprise.

conjunction
- A **conjunction** is a word that joins words or groups of words. *(pages 286–287)*

  Animals <u>and</u> plants are living things.

coordinating conjunction
- A **coordinating conjunction** joins words or groups of words that are of equal importance in a sentence. Common coordinating conjunctions are: *and*, *or*, *but*. *(pages 286–287)*

  We can go by train <u>or</u> bus.
  Carla waited for Sue, <u>and</u> Anne waited for Peg.

Practice

A. Copy these sentences. Underline the interjections.

1. Goodness! I did not expect a birthday present.
2. Say! That is a big package.
3. Hmm, what can it be?
4. Wow! It is just what I always wanted!

B. Copy these sentences. Underline the coordinating conjunctions.

5. You can take the train and the plane.
6. The trip to Hackensack and Hoboken sounds like fun.
7. You may go to a travel agency to buy your ticket, or you may wait to buy it at the airport.
8. Be sure to take your toothbrush and your pajamas, but do not pack too much.
9. Have a good time, and send us a letter or a postcard.
10. You will have fun and see many sights, but you will be glad to come home.

Paragraphs

- A **paragraph** is a series of sentences that develops a single topic. The topic on which the paragraph is based is its **main idea.** *(pages 40–42)*
- A **topic sentence** is one that expresses the main idea of a paragraph. *(pages 43–44)*
- A **detail sentence** supports the topic sentence by adding details. *(pages 43–44)*

paragraph, main idea

topic sentence

detail sentence

Practice

A. Read this paragraph. Then answer the questions.

The North and South Poles are at opposite ends of the earth, and in several other ways the poles are "opposites." The land under the North Polar area is shaped like a disc. It is covered by an ocean about 42,000 feet deep. The land in the South Polar region, however, bulges outward in high mountains. The North Polar area, or Arctic, is simply floating ice. The South Polar area, or Antarctic, is a continent covered with ice that is miles deep. The Antarctic is the highest continent in the world. The light over both poles is strange. Both poles have darkness at noon and light at midnight because of the earth's tilt. The North Pole is warmer than the South Pole because of the ocean under it. The South Pole, however, has eight times as much ice as the North Pole. Which of the two Poles would you like to visit?

1. What is the topic sentence? Write it.
2. Which four sentences do not give details that support the main idea? Write those sentences.

B. 3. Write a paragraph on any subject. Write a topic sentence and three detail sentences.

Friendly Letters

Sender's address
800 Alexander Ave.
Rochester, NY 14623
August 23, 19--

Dear Roxanne, ← Greeting

Body

We just returned from a two-day stay at Niagara Falls. I think one of the most thrilling moments of my life was standing on the rocks at the foot of the American Falls! See you soon.

Closing → *Your friend,*
Signature → *Deanna*

friendly letter
- The **friendly letter** has five parts. *(pages 386–388)*

heading
- The **heading** is in the upper right-hand corner. It contains the letter writer's address and the date. A comma is used between the name of the city and the state and between the day and the year in the date.

greeting
- The **greeting** starts at the left margin. It begins with a capital letter and is followed by a comma.

body
- The **body** of the letter is organized into paragraphs. Each paragraph is indented.

closing
- The **closing** is in a line with the heading at the end of the letter. The first word of the closing is capitalized. A comma follows the closing.

signature
- The **signature** is in a line with the closing.

Practice

Write a friendly letter to someone you really know or to an imaginary person.

Business Letters

Heading {
2513 Pacific Drive
Tacoma, Washington 98416
April 6, 19—

Ms. Linda Cartwright
Builtrite Electric Products } Inside Address
Edmond, Oklahoma 73034

Dear Ms. Cartwright: ⟵ Greeting

Two years ago I purchased a Builtrite electric mixer, model number 33402-4. Recently I broke one of the mixer blades. Would you please send me the name and address of the nearest outlet for this part? } Body

Closing ⟶ Yours truly,
Signature ⟶ *Rosemary Lewis*
Rosemary Lewis

- A **business letter** has six parts. *(pages 389–390)* — **business letter**
- The **heading** is in the upper right-hand corner. A comma is used between the city and the state and between the day and the year. — **heading**
- The **inside address** starts at the left margin. It shows the name and address of the business receiving the letter. — **inside address**
- The **greeting** begins at the left margin. It begins with a capital letter and is followed by a colon. — **greeting**
- The **body** tells why you are writing the letter. It should briefly and clearly give all the facts that the business needs in order to answer your letter or fill your order. — **body**
- The **closing** is in a line with the heading at the end of the letter. The first word of the closing is capitalized. A comma follows the closing. — **closing**
- The **signature** is in a line with the closing. The signature includes the writer's full name. — **signature**

Practice

Write a business letter. Make up any names and facts you need to have a complete letter, but sign your own name.

Envelopes

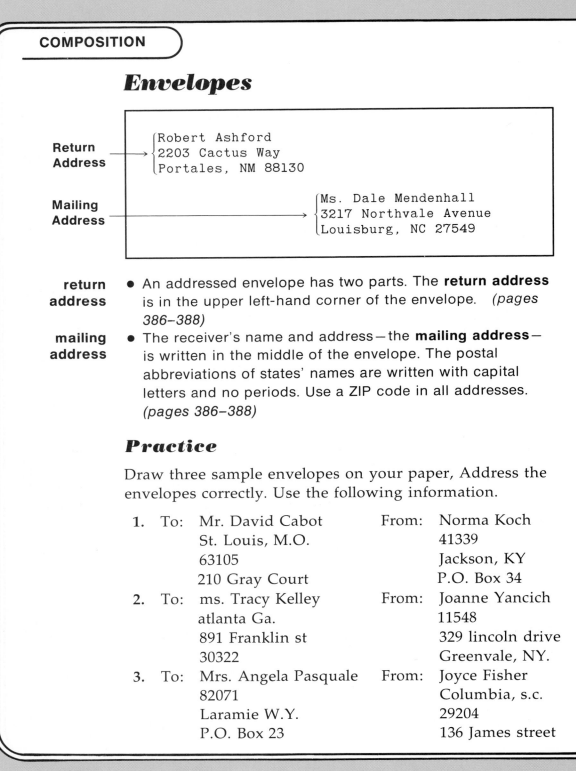

Return
Address → Robert Ashford
2203 Cactus Way
Portales, NM 88130

Mailing
Address → Ms. Dale Mendenhall
3217 Northvale Avenue
Louisburg, NC 27549

**return
address**
- An addressed envelope has two parts. The **return address** is in the upper left-hand corner of the envelope. *(pages 386–388)*

**mailing
address**
- The receiver's name and address—the **mailing address**—is written in the middle of the envelope. The postal abbreviations of states' names are written with capital letters and no periods. Use a ZIP code in all addresses. *(pages 386–388)*

Practice

Draw three sample envelopes on your paper. Address the envelopes correctly. Use the following information.

1. To: Mr. David Cabot
St. Louis, M.O.
63105
210 Gray Court

From: Norma Koch
41339
Jackson, KY
P.O. Box 34

2. To: ms. Tracy Kelley
atlanta Ga.
891 Franklin st
30322

From: Joanne Yancich
11548
329 lincoln drive
Greenvale, NY.

3. To: Mrs. Angela Pasquale
82071
Laramie W.Y.
P.O. Box 23

From: Joyce Fisher
Columbia, s.c.
29204
136 James street

Revising

- It is important to review your work after you write. Use **editing and proofreading marks** to show the changes you want to make to improve your writing. *(pages 24–26)*

Editing and Proofreading Checklist

Editing
1. **Did I express a complete thought in each sentence?**
2. **Did I write a good topic sentence for each paragraph?**
3. **Did I use detail sentences to support the main idea?**
4. **Did I write detail sentences that keep to the topic?**

Proofreading
5. **Did I begin each sentence with a capital letter?**
6. **Did I end each sentence with the correct punctuation mark?**
7. **Did I use other punctuation marks correctly?**
8. **Did I indent the first line of each paragraph?**
9. **Did I spell correctly?**
10. **Did I write neatly?**

Editing and Proofreading Marks

≡ capitalize
⊙ make a period
∧ add something
∧̓ add a comma
ⱽ̓ⱽ̓ add quotation marks
⤹ take something away
◯ spell correctly
ℍ indent the paragraph
/ make a lowercase letter
∿ tr transpose

Practice

Copy this paragraph. Make all the changes shown.

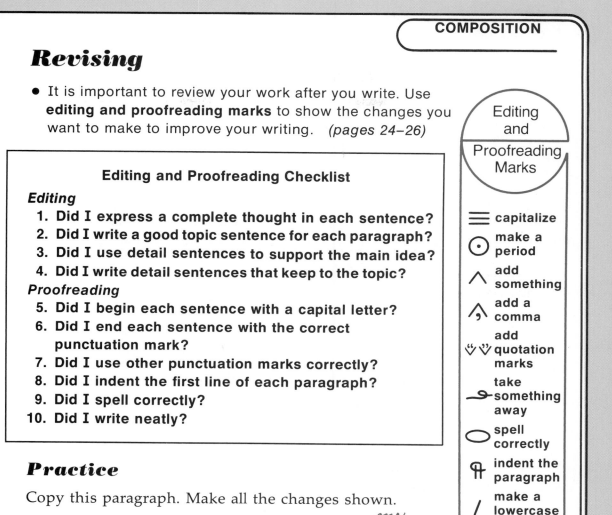

REVIEW HANDBOOK **433**

Names and Titles

person's name and titles
- Capitalize names and titles of people. *(pages 90–95)*

    Ms. Janet Dunne   President Franklin D. Roosevelt

pronoun I
- Capitalize the pronoun *I*. *(pages 27, 228–229)*

geographical names, holidays, and eras
- Capitalize geographical names and the names of holidays and historical periods. *(pages 90–91, 121)*

    Oak Lane   Labor Day   Middle Ages

abbreviations
- Capitalize abbreviations of parts of addresses. *(pages 94–95)*

    Blvd. (Boulevard)   St. (Street)   Ave. (Avenue)

proper adjectives
- Capitalize proper adjectives. *(pages 182–184)*

    Italian city   Greek mountain

first word of a sentence
- Capitalize the first word of a sentence. *(pages 2–3)*

    Did you hear the phone ring?   No, I didn't.

titles
- Capitalize the first word, the last word, and all other important words in the title of a written work. *(page 167)*

    Car and Driver (magazine)   Moby Dick (book)

days, months
- Capitalize days of the week and months of the year and their abbreviations. *(pages 94–95)*

    Tuesday   Thurs.   Nov.   May   Feb.

Practice

A. Write these names and titles correctly.

1. dr. marie rojas
2. charlotte's web
3. mr. peter ferro
4. newsweek
5. j. f. kennedy blvd.
6. french cooking
7. spanish music
8. houston, texas
9. rev. carl drasher
10. golden gate bridge

Periods

- Place a period at the end of a declarative or an imperative sentence. *(pages 2–3)*

  Oranges contain vitamin C.   Please eat your okra.

  to end sentences

- Place a period after an abbreviation. *(pages 94–95)*

  St. (Street)   Mr. (Mister)   Gen. (general)
  Nov. (November)   yd. (yard)   Mt. (mountain)

  in abbreviations

- Place a period after an initial. *(pages 94- 95)*

  Ulysses S. Grant   Rutherford B. Hayes

  after an initial

- Place a period after a number in the main topic and after a letter in the subtopic of an outline. *(pages 340–341)*

  I. Antique cars
     A. Cars through 1912
     B. Cars from 1913–1927

  in outlines

Practice

A. Write these groups of words correctly. Use periods where needed.

1. Dr Joan J Daimler
2. U S dollars
3. the year 453 BC
4. Agnes L White
5. A J Jones and Company
6. Capt J R Brown
7. Sen Everett M Dirksen
8. Mrs J J Johnson, Sr

B. Copy this outline correctly. Use periods where needed.

9. I Largest cities of the world   A Shanghai
   B Mexico City   C London

C. Follow the directions to write three sentences. Use periods wherever necessary.

10. Write a declarative sentence that gives a fact.
11. Write an imperative sentence that makes a request.
12. Write an imperative sentence that gives an order.

Commas

in dates
- Place a comma between the day and the year in a date. If the year is followed by more words in the sentence, place a comma after the year. *(pages 386–388)*

    The fiftieth star was added to the flag on July 4, 1960.
    On July 8, 1835, the Liberty Bell cracked.

in addresses
- Place a comma between the city and the state in an address. *(pages 386–388)*

    Wichita, Kansas   Tacoma, Washington

in letters
- Place a comma after the greeting in a friendly letter and after the closing of any letter. *(pages 386–388)*

    Dear Jennifer,   Sincerely yours,   Love,

in series
- Use commas to separate three or more items in a list, or series, in a sentence. *(pages 205–208)*

    Buy some milk, cheese, eggs, bread, and lettuce at the store.
    Turn right at the light, left at the next corner, and then right at the drugstore.

in compound sentences
- Place a comma before the conjunction *and*, *or*, or *but* in a compound sentence. *(pages 328–329)*

    Joan won first prize, and Carla won second prize.

in direct address
- Use commas to set off a noun in direct address. *(pages 332–333)*

    Please close the door, Frank, when you leave.

with introductory expressions
- Place a comma after the words *yes* and *no*, after mild interjections, and after two or more prepositional phrases when these items introduce a sentence. *(page 284)*

    Yes, the picnic will be held today.
    My, those puppies are cute!
    Under the table in the kitchen, you will probably find Rover, asleep.

- Place a comma between the closing marks of a direct quotation and the rest of the sentence unless a question mark or exclamation point is needed. *(pages 250–252)*

"I prefer the plaid sofa," she remarked.

- Place commas in parts of a bibliography. *(pages 338–339)*

Laird, Helene, and Laird, Charlton. "The
Anglo-Saxons." <u>The Tree of Language</u>, 1957, pp.
33–40.

- Use commas to set off most appositives. *(pages 282–283)*

Harriet Quimby, a magazine writer, was the first
licensed U.S. woman pilot.

Practice

Copy these sentences. Add commas where they are
needed.

1. "Yes this letter is for you Max" I said.
2. "Yes Brad I am going on a trip" Max my best friend told me.
3. "Oh I forgot about Ginger my pet rabbit" Max said.
4. "Well I will feed Ginger and I will pick up your mail too" I announced.
5. "You are a good friend" Max answered.
6. Max looked for his tennis racket in the attic out in the garage and in the cellar but he could not find it.
7. "No it is nowhere to be seen and I have looked everywhere" he told me.
8. "Say buddy you lent it to Henry your next-door neighbor" I reminded him.
9. "Ah so I did and I never got it back" said Max.
10. Max went to the phone dialed Henry's number and asked to speak to Henry.
11. "Hmm you are right about your racket" said Henry.
12. "Well I'll get it right now and I'll bring it over!"

Question Marks/Exclamation Points/Underlining

question mark
- Place a question mark at the end of an interrogative sentence. *(pages 2–3)*

   Did you get the job?   Who wrote this book?

exclamation point
- Place an exclamation point at the end of an exclamatory sentence. *(pages 2–3)*

   The train is leaving without us!

- Place an exclamation point after a strong interjection. *(pages 284- 285)*

   Help! I'm going to drop these dishes.

underlining
- Underline titles of books, plays, newspapers, magazines, movies, record albums, TV shows, and musical compositions. *(page 167)*

   <u>The New York Times</u> (newspaper)

Practice

Copy these sentences. Add question marks, exclamation points, and underlining where necessary.

1. Suzanne began to read her morning paper, The Newberg News.
2. "Wow I know that person on the front page" she exclaimed.
3. Why is Myra's picture under the headline "Newberg Woman Wins National Prize"
4. The article said that Ms. Myra Murdock won an award for her new novel, Wait Till the Sun Shines.
5. The novel was going to be made into a movie, which would be titled Stormy Weather.
6. "My goodness That certainly is exciting news," Suzanne exclaimed.

Quotation Marks and Dialog

- Place quotation marks around minor titles (titles of songs, articles, short stories, chapters in books, and minor poems). *(page 167)*

  with minor titles

  "The Mysterious Cat" (poem)

- Place quotation marks directly before and after each direct quotation. If the quotation is divided into two parts by other words, place quotation marks only around the quoted words. *(pages 250–252)*

  with direct quotations

  "What movie shall we see?" asked Jan.
  "I saw the movie at the Rialto," said Kim. "Let's go to the Strand," she added.

- If a direct quotation consists of several sentences, do not close the quotation until the speaker is finished. *(pages 250–252)*

  with end punctuation

  Mark announced, "Tryouts for the hockey team will be held tomorrow. Sign up now if you wish."

- Always place commas and periods *inside* the closing quotation marks. Place question marks and exclamation points inside the closing quotation marks if the quotation itself is a question or an exclamation. *(pages 250–252)*

  Jean said, "I forgot to bring my lunch."
  "That was a terrific catch!" the baseball fan exclaimed.
  "What time is it?" asked Jack.
  Who said, "A penny saved is a penny earned"?

- When you write conversation or dialog, begin a new paragraph every time the speaker changes. *(pages 250–252)*

  with dialog

  "Where are you going for your vacation?" asked Val.
  "I haven't decided whether to go to the mountains or to the seashore," said Sam.

Practice

Copy these sentences. Add commas, quotation marks, and end punctuation marks wherever they are needed.

1. Does this store sell both books and music asked Ann.
2. Yes, it does answered Dale. Let's go in.
3. Ann picked up a poetry book and began reading the poem To a Waterfowl
4. Dale looked at the sheet music for the songs Gentle on My Mind and How Am I to Know
5. Ann asked, Shall I buy this book
6. It is up to you answered Dale, while humming the melody to the song Eleanor Rigby
7. Look at this exclaimed Ann excitedly.
8. What is so exciting asked Dale.
9. The editor who collected these poems, said Ann, is Renée R. Greenley.
10. Who is that asked Dale.
11. Dr. Greenley was my English teacher last year Ann said.
12. Here is a poem by Dr Greenley Ann continued.
13. Why don't you buy the book suggested Dale, and ask Dr. Greenley to autograph it for you
14. That is a terrific idea exclaimed Ann.
15. Were the other people in the shop thinking Those girls are making too much noise
16. Which song are you going to buy Ann asked.
17. Dale answered by holding up the song Michelle
18. This is not a new song she said, but I really like it
19. I like it too agreed Ann.
20. Well, we found what we were looking for said Dale.
21. Then let's leave now remarked Ann.
22. Leaving the store Ann commented It's cold out.
23. I'm glad I'm wearing my warm coat she added.
24. Me too answered Dale so let's hurry home.
25. We'll be in time for dinner they thought.

Hyphens and Apostrophes

- Use a hyphen to syllabicate at the end of a line. Do not syllabicate before a single final letter. *(page 75)*

   gro-cery   cul-ti-vate

hyphen

- Use an apostrophe for possessive nouns but not for possessive pronouns. *(pages 96–97, 232–233)*

   Jane's   cities'   Bruce's
   hers   its   ours

apostrophe with possessive noun

- Use an apostrophe to form contractions of verbs and of the adverb *not*. *(pages 192–193, 234)*

   we're   she's   wouldn't   can't

apostrophe in contractions

Practice

A. Use hyphens to show where each word would be divided into syllables at the end of a line. You may use a dictionary if you need to. (In a dictionary the entry words—not the pronunciations—show where to divide the words.)

1. blueberry
2. former
3. plastic
4. propeller
5. promotion
6. unconscious
7. cyclone
8. boundless
9. cheerfulness
10. chariot
11. chemical
12. headache

B. Write the possessive nouns described below.

13. belonging to Ed
14. belonging to children
15. belonging to James
16. belonging to puppies
17. belonging to a story
18. belonging to schools
19. belonging to women
20. belonging to science

C. Write the contractions described below.

21. they + are
22. we + have
23. I + am
24. have + not

Semicolons and Colons

semicolon in compound sentences

- Use a semicolon to take the place of a comma and a conjunction in a compound sentence. *(pages 328–329)*

    The bedroom needs two coats of paint; the bathroom needs just one.

colon in greeting

- Place a colon after the greeting of a business letter. *(pages 389–390)*

    Dear Mr. Greenspan: Gentlemen:

colon in time of day

- Place a colon between the hour and the minute in the time of day. *(page 75)*

    9:45 A.M.   3:29 P.M.   7:37 A.M.

Practice

A. Copy these sentences. Take out each comma and conjunction, and replace them with a semicolon.

1. Bob spaded the garden, and Jean planted the seeds.
2. She planted two rows of beets, but she only planted one row of radishes.
3. Bob covered the seeds carefully, and then he walked on the seed rows to press the seeds down.
4. The seeds had to be covered, or birds would eat any seeds they spotted.

B. Write the greeting of a business letter for each of these.

5. Ms. Amanda Warsawa
6. Mr. J. B. Cornwallis
7. Pres. P. G. Arnaud
8. Mrs. Bernadette Cunningham

C. Write the following hours and minutes in numerals.

9. nine twenty-two P.M.
10. eleven fourteen A.M.
11. twelve fifty-nine A.M.
12. four forty-four P.M.
13. six twelve A.M.
14. one eight P.M.

Troublesome Words

- Use the word *a* before a word that begins with a consonant sound. Use *an* before a word that begins with a vowel sound. *(pages 182–183)*

  a, an

  <u>a</u> horse   <u>an</u> orange   <u>a</u> street   <u>an</u> honor

- Always use the pronoun *I* as a subject pronoun. Always use the pronoun *me* as an object pronoun. Use the pronoun *myself* only when the subject and the pronoun refer to the same person. *(pages 228–233)*

  I, me

  <u>I</u> looked at the notebooks. They were for <u>me</u>.
  <u>I</u> asked <u>myself</u> a question.

- Use *their* when you mean "belonging to them." Use *there* when you mean "in that place." Use *they're* as a contraction of *they are.* *(pages 232–235)*

  their, there, they're

  The children raised <u>their</u> hands.
  Put the groceries over <u>there</u>.
  <u>They're</u> going to arrive at noon.

- Use *its* when you mean "belonging to it." Use *it's* as a contraction for *it is.* *(pages 232–233, 234–235)*

  its, it's

  <u>Its</u> cover hints that <u>it's</u> an interesting book.

- Use *your* when you mean "belonging to you." Use *you're* as a contraction of *you are.* *(pages 232–233, 234–235)*

  your, you're

  Here is <u>your</u> umbrella.   <u>You're</u> late for work.

- Use the preposition *at* to show that someone or something is already in a certain place. Use the preposition *to* to show movement toward something. *(pages 278–279)*

  at, to

  Jake is <u>at</u> school.   The children are going <u>to</u> the zoo.

- Use the preposition *in* to mean "already inside." Use the preposition *into* to show movement from the outside to the inside. *(pages 278–279)*

  in, into

  <u>In</u> the house she puts ice <u>into</u> the glass.

among,
between
- Use the preposition *among* to refer to three or more. Use the preposition *between* to refer to two. *(pages 278–279)*

> Divide the party favors <u>among</u> all the children.
> There is a fence <u>between</u> the two houses.

beside,
besides
- Use the preposition *beside* to mean "at the side of." Use the preposition *besides* to mean "in addition to." *(pages 278–279)*

> The table is <u>beside</u> the chair.
> Who <u>besides</u> Tuwa is going to the fair?

Practice

A. Write the correct pronoun(s) from the choices below.

1. Yes, (I, me, myself) am studying geology.
2. Please give that rock sample to (I, me, myself).
3. I just bought (I, me, myself) this geology reference book.
4. (Your, You're) sure to find geology interesting too.
5. You will find (you're, your) first field trip fascinating.
6. Yet being outdoors has (its, it's) own rewards.
7. If (its, it's) warm enough next Tuesday, we will go to Red Rock Canyon and study (its, it's) formations.

B. Copy each sentence. Choose the correct word in parentheses ( ).

8. Joanne and Rosa are waiting (in, into) the forest with (there, their, they're) cameras.
9. (They're, There, Their) hoping to photograph some deer when they come (at, to) the pond.
10. Joanne saw a fawn pass (between, among) two pine trees over (they're, there, their), just (beside, besides) the large rock.
11. Now the fawn is (at, to) the pond and is stepping (in, into) the water (among, between) the water plants.
12. (Beside, Besides) the fawn, what else can you see?

Agreement

- A verb must agree with its subject in number. *(pages 330–331)*

  subject-verb agreement

  She <u>sings</u> very well.
  <u>Guppies</u> and <u>swordtails</u> <u>are</u> tropical fish.
  The twins or <u>I</u> <u>am</u> <u>going</u> to the store.
  <u>Ted</u> and his two <u>brothers</u> <u>are</u> at home now.

- A pronoun must agree with its antecedent in number and use. *(pages 226–227)*

  pronoun-antecedent agreement

  Richard was sleepy. <u>He</u> began to yawn.

Practice

A. Rewrite each sentence. Choose the correct words to make the subject and verb agree.

1. Our school (is, are) offering special classes after school.
2. Many people (have, has) signed up for aerobic dancing.
3. Cynthia and Joan (wants, want) to take ceramics.
4. A list of courses (is, are) posted on a bulletin board.
5. At least one (is, are) often canceled before September.
6. The course in gourmet cooking (attract, attracts) many.
7. Ms. Jonas and Dr. Perry (teach, teaches) shorthand.
8. Each year (bring, brings) new students and new courses.

B. Rewrite each sentence. Choose the correct word to make each pronoun agree with its antecedent.

9. Vincent stepped back to admire (he, his, him) painting.
10. Many have tried to be artists, and (he, they, them) failed.
11. Mrs. Ogelthorpe admired art, and (they, her, she) decided to collect (them, their, it).
12. Sharlene has just finished (she, her, hers) painting, and (it, they, them) is still wet.

MORE PRACTICE

UNIT 1

Understanding Kinds of Sentences   pages 2–3

Copy these sentences, adding correct punctuation. Then write what kind of sentence each one is.

1. Thomas Anthony Dooley was a famous doctor
2. Did you know that he worked in Southeast Asia
3. He set up hospitals in Laos and Vietnam
4. How helpful he was to the sick
5. Find out more about this dedicated doctor

Understanding Complete Subjects and Predicates
pages 4–5

Copy these sentences. Draw one line under each complete subject and two lines under each complete predicate.

1. Many kinds of animals have shells.
2. A tough shell covers the stag beetle.
3. Turtles and tortoises have shells on their backs.
4. Some animals, like birds, are formed within a shell.
5. The shells of many mollusks are very beautiful.

Understanding Simple Subjects and Predicates
pages 6–7

Copy these sentences. Draw one line under each simple subject and two lines under each simple predicate.

1. Only one person ever invented a complete system of writing.
2. He was Sequoya, a Cherokee Indian.

3. He spent many years developing the system.
4. The written language helped to unite the Cherokee.
5. Books were published in the Cherokee language.

Locating the Subjects of Sentences   pages 8–9

Copy these sentences. Draw one line under each subject.
Write *(you)* after each sentence in which the subject is
you (understood).

1. Where are the sheep?
2. That Hampshire ewe is friendly.
3. Catch that ram!
4. Is that lamb the newest one?
5. What is the sheep population of Australia?

Understanding Word Order in Sentences   pages 10–11

Copy these sentences. Draw one line under each subject.
Then write *natural* after each sentence in natural order
and *inverted* after each sentence in inverted order.

1. In that tree is the robins' nest.
2. The birds wait for the eggs to hatch.
3. Inside the shells baby birds are developing.
4. Soon they will peck their way out.
5. Out of their shells come the baby robins.
6. From their mouths come tiny peeps.
7. The baby birds are hungry.
8. The other robins must bring them food.
9. From the tree fly the adult robins.
10. Soon the babies will have plenty of food.

Using the Dictionary   pages 14–15

Decide which words would fall between the guide words
peppermint and *perfect*. Write the words.

1. Persia   2. perch   3. peppercorn
4. perceive   5. percent   6. performance
7. period   8. peppery   9. percussion

Using a Dictionary Entry   pages 16–17

Read these sentences. The underlined word in each sentence has more than one meaning. Find the underlined words in your dictionary, and copy the correct meaning for each sentence.

1. Maria sat on her <u>perch</u> in the apple tree.
2. While waiting in the office, José began to <u>leaf</u> through a magazine.
3. The house looks <u>even</u> worse than before.
4. What do you get when you <u>cross</u> a lemon with a canary?
5. Please <u>divide</u> 1,398,493,777,928 by 437,000.

Writing Effective Sentences   pages 21–23

Rewrite these sentences using specific words and devices of variety wherever possible. Make up any additional information you need.

1. My friend next door is a real pal.
2. We do lots of stuff together.
3. Sometimes our friends join us here.
4. When the weather is nice, we eat outside.
5. Sports keep us pretty busy.

Revising Sentences   pages 24–26

Copy these sentences. Then revise them for variety to make them more effective. Use editing and proofreading marks to help you. Finally, rewrite the sentences as you would want them to appear in your finished work.

1. Do you have a favorite holiday?
2. Some people enjoy Halloween.
3. Some people enjoy Thanksgiving.
4. Some people like to celebrate the Fourth of July.
5. Some people like New Year's Day because they are sports fans, and these people like to have a day full of football games.

Mechanics Practice   page 27

Copy these sentences. Use capital letters and punctuation marks wherever they are needed.

1. do you like sports
2. are you a spectator or a participant
3. baseball is considered our national pastime
4. surveys show that football has attracted many fans
5. soccer is especially popular with young players
6. what game do you like best
7. my favorite is football
8. football is so exciting
9. i try to guess which plays will be chosen
10. that last football game was terrific

Distinguishing Between Biography and Autobiography
pages 28–33

Write two paragraphs that tell about you or a friend of yours. Write the first paragraph as it would appear in your *biography*. Write the second paragraph as it would appear in your *autobiography*.

UNIT 2

Understanding Paragraphs and Main Ideas   pages 40–42

Read this paragraph. Then write in your own words the main idea of the paragraph.

The cheetah, which can run at 70 miles (112 km) per hour, is probably the fastest creature we know. The garden snail, which moves at 170 feet (5100 cm) per hour, is certainly among the slowest. Can you guess how a human runner compares with other creatures? Clocked at racing speeds of 27 miles (43.2 km) per hour, the human is faster than a squirrel. A person, however, is slower than a rabbit, a house cat, or a grizzly bear.

Understanding Topic Sentences and Detail Sentences
pages 43–44

Copy these sentences. Next to each write *topic sentence* if it expresses a main idea and *detail sentence* if it states a detail.

1. My dog Rolf is a good swimmer.
2. When a giant wave knocked me down, it was Rolf who pulled me to shore.
3. Rolf is also a good watchdog.
4. He warned us when burglars tried to break into our house.
5. Rolf is the best dog anyone could have.
6. He barked until my parents woke up.
7. Rolf trapped the burglars in a corner of the living room, and they could not escape.
8. When the police arrived at our house, they told us that we were lucky to have such a good dog.

Understanding Appropriate Details   pages 45–47

Here is a topic sentence followed by several detail sentences. Select the detail sentences that develop the topic. Then write all the appropriate sentences in correct paragraph form.

Many animal groups have interesting names.

1. You already know that ants live in colonies.
2. Fish swim in schools, and geese fly in flocks, or gaggles.
3. Locusts, of course, come in plagues, and wolves travel in packs.
4. The young of ducks are called *ducklings.*
5. The king of the beasts is found in a pride of lions.
6. I never learned the names for groups of ostriches, alligators, or emus.
7. By the way, what are young alligators called?
8. I do know, however, that horses, cattle, and sheep all belong to herds.

Using the Library   pages 50–51

Copy these sources of information. Next to each one write whether it would be found in the *reference, fiction, nonfiction,* or *periodicals* section of a library.

1. a biography of Babe Didrikson Zaharias
2. an atlas
3. a current *National Geographic*
4. a novel set during the Civil War
5. a book about a career in nursing
6. a dictionary of mythology
7. a collection of short stories

Using the Card Catalog   pages 52–53

Copy this book information. Next to each item write whether you would use the *title card,* the *author card,* or the *subject card* to find it.

1. a book about the gold rush
2. a book called *Ivanhoe*
3. a book by Robert Louis Stevenson
4. a book about art masterpieces in the Louvre
5. a book by James Fenimore Cooper
6. a book called *Daily Life in Ancient Rome*
7. a book by Madeline L'Engle

Using the Dewey Decimal System   pages 54–55

Copy these book titles. Next to each title write the number of the Dewey Decimal System under which each book would appear.

1. *Plato's Philosophy*
2. *Famous Civil War Battles*
3. *How to Learn Japanese*
4. *Works of Shakespeare*
5. *Introduction to Biology*
6. *Famous Artworks by Famous Women*
7. *How the U.S. Government Works*

Writing Time-Order Paragraphs   pages 59–60

The sentences in this time-order paragraph are mixed up. Rewrite the paragraph correctly.

1. Next I had her checked by a veterinarian.
2. I decided to buy a cat to keep me company.
3. Finally I brought her home.
4. Then I picked out a chocolate-point Siamese.
5. First I went to a cat show and examined Angoras, tabbies, calicos, and Persians.
6. The handlers at the cat show told me that tabbies and calicos had the best dispositions.
7. After that, I could not decide between the blue-point and the chocolate-point Siamese kittens.
8. I had nearly chosen a calico when I saw the Siamese.

Writing Space-Order Paragraphs   pages 61–66

This mixed-up paragraph begins at a distance and moves closer. Rewrite it correctly.

1. The borders just inside the wall were full of old-fashioned flowers: primroses, lilacs, and lavender.   2. At the center of the lawn where I sat, there stood a statue of a leaping deer darting away from an unseen hunter. 3. Closer in than the paths lay a lawn, well tended and luxurious.   4. The garden at the estate was enclosed by a stone wall that had been made many years before. 5. Within the borders were paths that formed a pleasant walk about the garden.

Paragraphs of Comparison and Contrast   pages 67–72

Choose a pair of subjects such as those below. Then choose three qualities and make a comparison or contrast outline like the one on page 67. Write a paragraph using your outline. Edit and proofread your work.

cats and mice   bicycles and cars

Revising Paragraphs   pages 73–74

Copy this contrast paragraph as it is, and add editing and proofreading marks to show how you would change it. Then write the paragraph in final form.

1. Whole milk and skim milk differ in appearance, in taste, and in health value.   2. Skim milk, on the other hand, is a watery, bluish-white color.   3. Whole milk is thick and white.   4. Whole milk tastes creamy. 5. However, doctors say that skim milk is better for adults. 6. Whole milk is necessary for the proper growth of infants and young children.   7. Skim milk, in contrast, tastes bland and watery and seems unpleasant to many people.

Mechanics Practice   page 75

Rewrite these sentences using capital letters and punctuation wherever necessary.

1. The alarm clock rang at 7:15 am.
2. When the second alarm clock rang at 7:59 am, Bob decided to get up.
3. The 8:22 am bus was late, so he didn't arrive at work until 9:15 am.
4. The workday sped by, and quitting time came at exactly 5:00 pm.
5. With luck he'd be home in time to catch the 7:20 pm show at the Bijou.

Reading a One-Act Play   pages 76–81

Select a one-act play, read it, and answer these questions.

1. When and where does the play take place?
2. Who are the major characters and who are the less important characters?
3. What is the plot of the play?
4. What is the conflict that is central to the plot?
5. What is the meaning of the title of the play?

UNIT 3

Understanding Common and Proper Nouns
pages 90–91

Copy these sentences. Draw one line under the common nouns and two lines under the proper nouns.

1. On Arbor Day we will plant a Douglas fir in the park.
2. Mayor Jacobi will use a silver shovel to dig the first hole.
3. Reporters from the Biloxi Weekly Journal and the Louisiana Times will be present.
4. Of course someone will recite the poem "Trees" by Joyce Kilmer.
5. The Edison School Ecology Club is sponsoring the event.

Understanding Singular and Plural Nouns   pages 92–93

Copy these sentences. Write *singular* or *plural* above each underlined noun.

1. The young of several animals are called cubs.
2. Bears, foxes, and tigers all have cubs.
3. A young deer is called a fawn.
4. Baby ducks, called ducklings, follow their mother everywhere.
5. A cygnet is a young swan.

Understanding Abbreviations   pages 94–95

Using a dictionary or other reference book, write the abbreviations for the following words.

1. March
2. Senator
3. Wyoming
4. Place
5. Friday
6. Saint Paul
7. Doctor
8. Road
9. General
10. Iowa
11. Boulevard
12. Editor

Understanding Possessive Nouns   pages 96–97

Copy these singular nouns. Then write the singular possessive, the plural, and the plural possessive forms of each. You should have four columns.

1. woman   2. fox   3. monkey
4. child   5. puppy   6. spy

Using the Encyclopedia   pages 100–101

Using the set of encyclopedias pictured here, write the *number* of the volume you would use for information on these subjects.

1. chariot   2. flintlock   3. J. S. Bach
4. Timbuktu   5. amaryllis   6. nightshade

Using Atlases and Almanacs   pages 102–103

Which of these questions can best be answered by using an *atlas* and which by an *almanac*? Copy these questions, and write the name of the reference you would use to answer each one.

1. What is the location of Poland?
2. Which countries surround Bolivia?
3. Who are the members of the Baseball Hall of Fame?
4. What is the state flower of Alaska?
5. What is the population of Indonesia?

Writing a How-to Paragraph   pages 104–111

Listed below is a topic sentence and a set of instructions in the wrong order. Rewrite the information in correct order. Be sure to add transitional expressions.

French toast is a good breakfast that is easy to make.

1. Beat eggs lightly, and add milk and cinnamon.
2. Serve with maple syrup.
3. You will need 2 eggs, 4 slices of bread, ¼ cup (60 ml) of milk, and ¼ teaspoon (1.25 ml) of cinnamon.
4. In a hot, greased frying pan fry the bread until it is brown and crispy.
5. Dip bread in the mixture to coat lightly.

Writing a Paragraph of Cause and Effect   pages 112–118

Choose one of these sentences. (The first two sentences are causes; the last two sentences are effects.) Copy the sentence and write four detail sentences to support it.

■ I have always loved chocolate.
■ I once borrowed my brother's paints without asking him.
■ I never watch television anymore.
■ Now I look forward to winter.

Revising a Paragraph   pages 119–120

Using the paragraph you wrote for the previous exercise, revise it for clarity as well as for correct spelling and punctuation.

Mechanics Practice   page 121

Copy these sentences. Add capital letters and punctuation marks wherever necessary.

1. My family traveled to grand rapids, michigan, on june 8, 1983.
2. We stayed there until independence day.

3. Then we traveled to minnesota, where many people speak the swedish or norwegian language.

4. These people are scandinavian in origin; their ancestors traveled across the atlantic ocean to come to the united states years ago.

5. My friend jans uncle, sen carl lorenson, came to America on july 4 1926.

Reading News Stories, Features, and Editorials
pages 122–127

Read this news story. Then list on your paper the six questions each news story must answer. Write the answers the story gives.

The sixth-grade class of Edison School will present "Tales of Pippi" on May 2 and 3 in the school auditorium. The presentation has been adapted by the sixth-graders themselves from the popular novel *Pippi Longstocking*. Proceeds from the play will be used to buy a new curtain for the stage.

UNIT 4

Understanding Action Verbs   pages 134–135

Copy these sentences. Draw one line under each action verb.

1. Veronica likes trees.
2. She wanted a birch tree on her bedroom wall.
3. She studied many drawings at the library.
4. Next, Veronica sketched a model for herself.
5. She will paint her wall tomorrow.
6. Veronica's sketch shows a single tree in a field.
7. Blue sky and white clouds provide the background.
8. Under the birch tree grow many wild flowers.
9. Veronica's painting will take about a week.
10. Then she will paint a seascape on my wall.

Understanding Linking Verbs pages 136–137

Copy these sentences. Draw one line under each linking verb.

1. The night sky is beautiful.
2. Stars appear as bright points of light.
3. These suns are invisible during the day.
4. At night they become guiding lights.
5. Stars seem numberless.
6. Stars are gaseous spheres.
7. These gases are extremely hot.
8. From earth the stars appear tiny.
9. Many, however, are larger than our planet.
10. Close up, the stars would seem huge.

Understanding Helping Verbs and Main Verbs
pages 138–139

Copy these sentences. Draw one line under each main verb and two lines under each helping verb.

1. Special training was required for knighthood.
2. A boy might spend several years as a page.
3. At 14 the youth was made a squire.
4. Squires were trained by knights and other teachers.
5. Knights have always represented loyalty, honor, bravery, and courtesy.
6. Most knights are remembered from famous stories.
7. King Arthur had assembled knights at Camelot.
8. Sir Kay and Sir Gawain had come from England.
9. Sir Lancelot had traveled all the way from France.
10. These men were called ''Knights of the Round Table.''

Understanding Principal Parts of Regular Verbs
pages 140–141

Write the three principal parts of these verbs.

1. dwell   2. summon   3. grant
4. remind   5. pass   6. answer

Understanding Principal Parts of Irregular Verbs I
pages 142–143

Copy these sentences. Draw one line under each irregular verb. After each sentence write which principal part was used to form it.

1. Everyone has come to the picnic.
2. We brought plenty of food.
3. We will drink the lemonade first.
4. Everyone has swum in the lake.
5. We should begin the barbecue.

Understanding Principal Parts of Irregular Verbs II
pages 144- 145

Copy these sentences. Draw one line under each irregular verb. After each sentence write which principal part was used to form it.

1. Everyone knows about the Wright brothers.
2. They have been written into history.
3. They flew the first plane at Kitty Hawk.
4. Everyone spoke about the flight.
5. Would you have flown in that plane?

Understanding Verb Tenses   pages 146–147

Copy these sentences. Draw one line under each verb. After each sentence write the tense of the verb.

1. Joel and Marcy will cook dinner tonight.
2. Last week they burned the spaghetti.
3. Tonight they will make an omelet.
4. They never tried that before.
5. We can always eat peanut butter and jelly.
6. Bob is the worst cook of all.
7. Once he boiled all the water out of a pot.
8. Of course the pot burned.
9. He was boiling water for cocoa.
10. Will he ever learn?

Understanding Verb Tenses: Present Perfect Tense
pages 148-149

Copy these sentences. Draw one line under each verb in the present perfect tense.

1. Have you ever visited this museum before?
2. Then you have never seen my favorite painting.
3. The tour guide has described the masterpiece.
4. Everyone has studied the collection.
5. No one has enjoyed this trip more than I.

Understanding Verb Complements   page 150–151

Copy these sentences. Draw one line under each verb, and after the sentence write *transitive* or *intransitive*. If the verb has a complement, circle the complement, and after the sentence write *direct object* or *predicate nominative*.

1. Spain is a beautiful land with more than 1,400 castles and palaces.
2. These buildings reflect the influence of other cultures in Spain.
3. The cathedral at Seville is a product of French Gothic architecture.
4. The Romans built many bridges and aqueducts in Spain.
5. The Moors built mosques and palaces during the Middle Ages.

Understanding the Parts of a Book   pages 154–155

Copy these items. Next to each write the name of the part of a book in which each item would be found.

1. © 1982
2. Life in Australia 135
3. **al ca zar** (al'-käz-ər) *n.:* a Spanish fortress or palace
4. Oxford University Press
5. education, 91, 98–111

Skimming and Scanning   pages 156–157

1. Skim the table of contents of one of your textbooks.
2. Write the names of the main sections listed on that page.
3. Scan the index to find one entry of interest to you.
4. Write the pages on which it can be found.

Prewriting and Composing—Book Report
pages 158–163

Write a book report on a book you have recently read. Make a form like the one on page 158 to summarize your ideas. Use your form to write your report.

Revising a Book Report   pages 164–166

Following the book report guidelines on page 165, revise the report you did for the previous exercise. Be sure that all the necessary parts have been included. Check your grammar and punctuation.

Mechanics Practice   page 167

Copy these sentences, punctuating each of the titles correctly.

1. My brother watches captain kangaroo.
2. We subscribe to national geographic.
3. My favorite book is the yearling.
4. I read a poem called the adventures of isabel.
5. We read the piedmont daily news every day.

Reading Myths   pages 168–173

Read a nature myth. Then answer these questions.

1. What situation or part of nature does this myth explain?
2. How is the message of the myth still true today?
3. Is a god or goddess connected in some way with this myth? If so, tell what role he or she has.
4. In a brief paragraph tell the story of the myth.

UNIT 5

Understanding Common, Proper, and Predicate Adjectives pages 182–184

Copy these sentences. Draw one line under each common adjective and two lines under each proper adjective. Circle any predicate adjectives.

1. The adventures of the heroic Cid are told in the Spanish poem *El Cid.*
2. African tales describe Anasi, the wise spider.
3. Mischievous Loki is popular in Scandinavian stories.
4. Paul Bunyan's famous ox in American stories was blue.
5. The angry Vishnu appears in Hindu tales.
6. *The Iliad* is a Greek tale.
7. It tells the famous story of the Trojan horse.
8. *The Odyssey* concerns the travels of a great hero.
9. Odysseus is more famous than many other heroes.
10. His exciting adventures end in beautiful Ithaca.

Comparing with Adjectives pages 185–187

Write the comparative and superlative forms of these adjectives.

1. brave
2. lonely
3. good
4. terrible
5. few
6. many

Understanding Adverbs pages 188–189

Copy each sentence. Draw one line under each adverb, and circle the word it modifies.

1. Amateur photographers usually enjoy their craft.
2. Today's cameras make picture taking fairly easy.
3. Focus and lighting are often automatic.
4. Composing the picture still challenges the photographer.
5. Children and animals are very popular subjects.

Comparing with Adverbs   pages 190–191

Copy these adverbs. Next to each write its degree of comparison.

1. impatiently   2. earlier   3. more often
4. most   5. less accurately   6. far

Using Adjectives and Adverbs   pages 192–193

Copy these sentences. Write whether the underlined words are adjectives or adverbs.

1. The school band ran a car wash <u>yesterday</u>.
2. They had posted <u>many</u> advertisements.
3. <u>Thirty</u> cars were washed during the afternoon.
4. All the volunteers worked <u>hard</u>.
5. They were <u>wet</u> and <u>tired</u> when they went home.

Understanding Prefixes   pages 196–197

Write these words on your paper. Draw one line under each prefix. Write the definition of each word.

1. unfit   2. illogical   3. impolite
4. remake   5. prepay   6. foresee

Understanding Suffixes   pages 198-199

Copy these words. Draw one line under each suffix. Draw two lines under any base word that changes before the suffix is added. Write the original base word.

1. justly   2. trustful   3. judgment
4. fearless   5. believable   6. sincerely

Understanding Roots   pages 200–201

Copy these words. Draw a line between the roots or base words used to form each one.

1. audiovisual   2. geothermal   3. biology
4. microsurgery   5. television   6. thermostat
7. automation   8. geography   9. perimeter

Prewriting and Composing—Descriptive Paragraph
pages 202-208

Make a diagram like the one on page 202 to describe an object or a scene. Write a descriptive paragraph that will make your readers experience what you describe by appealing to their five senses.

Revising a Descriptive Paragraph   pages 209–210

Revise and rewrite the paragraph you wrote for the previous exercise. Be sure you have used sensory words.

Mechanics Practice   page 211
Rewrite these sentences, using capital letters and commas wherever necessary to correct the adjectives used.

1. At our school students can study the french latin german and spanish languages.
2. There will be a trip to paris for french-speaking students.
3. Many jobs are open to people who speak both the spanish and the english languages.
4. We made replicas of japanese and portuguese flags.
5. In school we sampled african portuguese and indian food.

Understanding Imagery in Lyric Poetry   pages 212–219

Read several lyric poems from a collection of poetry. Find examples of these figures of speech. Write the title and author of the poem in which each figure of speech appears. Write the lines from the poem that illustrate each one.

1. simile
2. metaphor
3. alliteration
4. assonance
5. consonance

UNIT 6

Understanding Pronouns and Antecedents
pages 226- 227

Copy these sentences. Draw one line under each pronoun.
Draw an arrow from each pronoun to its antecedent.

1. Janice is working at a nursery where she learns all about plants.
2. Janice likes hydrangeas because they have large flower clusters.
3. Janice's boss teaches her about the plants.
4. The owner is very proud of her nursery.
5. Janice hopes that she will have a plant shop someday.

Understanding Subject Pronouns   pages 228–229

Copy these sentences. Draw one line under each subject pronoun.

1. Our coach said that we have a good team.
2. We had a game scheduled for today, but it was rained out.
3. Tod was supposed to pitch, so he was disappointed.
4. Jan pitches for our team when we face the Tigers.
5. Elliot and Judy wish they had tried out for the team.

Understanding Object Pronouns   pages 230–231

Copy these sentences. Draw one line under each direct object pronoun and two lines under each indirect object pronoun.

1. Tim's mother was happy because Tim gave her some flowers.
2. Lilacs grow in the garden, and we pick them.
3. This is our first rose. Would you like it?
4. Tim planted violets, and he will give you some.
5. Hand him the garden tools and the seed packets.

Understanding Possessive and Reflexive Pronouns
pages 232–233

Copy these sentences. Draw one line under each possessive pronoun and two lines under each reflexive pronoun.

1. Hazel did well on her quiz.
2. Now she wants to give herself a treat.
3. Becky and Chris studied hard for their courses.
4. They put themselves on a strict schedule.
5. Now their school work has improved.
6. They congratulated themselves on their hard work.

Using Pronouns Correctly   pages 234–235

Rewrite these sentences. Substitute the correct pronoun contraction for the underlined words and choose the correct object pronoun in parentheses ( ).

1. Chris said she will see (us, we) at the fair.
2. We will show (she, her) our prizes.
3. I am sure she will be proud of (we, us).
4. Meg and John said they will meet (we, us) later.
5. I will look for (he, them) at the horse show.
6. They would call us if (they, them) changed plans.

Understanding Homophones and Homographs
pages 238–239

Copy these pairs of words. Next to each group write whether the words are *homophones* or *homographs*.

1. wound/wound   2. steel/steal   3. bark/bark
4. break/brake   5. eye/aye   6. reel/real

Understanding Compound Words   pages 240–241

Join words from this list to make five compound words.

stop   ill   rail   road   tempered
school   watch   ball   house   base

Prewriting, Composing, and Revising — Short Story
pages 242–249, 257–260

Make a diagram like the one on page 243. Write the opening paragraph for a short story. Introduce the setting and characters. Tell something about the plot. Revise your work.

Writing Dialog in a Story   pages 250–252

Rewrite the following sentences, adding correct punctuation.

1. Little Pig, Little Pig, let me come in demanded the wolf.
2. The little pig answered Not by the hair of my chinny-chin-chin.
3. Then I'll huff and I'll puff said the wolf and I'll blow your house in.
4. This chair is too hard said Goldilocks and this chair is too soft.
5. Goldilocks smiled and said But this chair is just right.
6. However she grinned I didn't like the oatmeal much.
7. Hello said Red Riding Hood to the wolf.
8. The wolf answered Hello yourself, Red.
9. These goodies said Red are for my grandma.
10. Yes replied the wolf and they look mighty good.

Making Transitions Within and Between Paragraphs
pages 253–256

Copy this paragraph, completing it with the proper transitional words.

The Kims had eagerly planned their camping trip. They left the house at 5:00 A.M. on Monday. _____ that day they reached a lakeside campsite. _____ they cooked dinner and cleaned up. _____ they unpacked their sleeping bags and went to bed early. They did not, _____, have a comfortable night. _____ they were driven from their campsite by hundreds of frogs. _____ they gave up the idea of camping and headed for home.

Revising a Story   pages 257–260

Rewrite this short story by adding, changing, or taking away sentences to give the story unity. Add proper punctuation as well. Be sure to begin a new paragraph for each new speaker.

When he was walking to the fair, Simon met a pie distributor. Simon was wearing a big hat. Sir, said Simon, let me try one of your pies. Of course young fellow said the pie distributor. First I must ask if you can afford to buy one. The pie distributor had delicious cherry, apple, and lemon meringue pies. Well, I have no money, Simon began. In that case said the pie distributor come back someday when you do.

Mechanics Practice   page 261

Copy these sentences, adding capital letters and punctuation wherever needed in the conversation. Be sure to begin a new paragraph for each new speaker.

Why did you tell me youd see me later asked Johnny. You know Im going to the moon tomorrow. What I meant was that Ill see you when you get back answered Louis. I hope youll bring me a moon rock or two. Im not sure theyll let me take any rocks on the space shuttle commented Johnny. I will however try to get you a plant or two for your collection. Youre a real pal exclaimed Louis. When I go to Saturn next year, Ill bring something back for you too.

Understanding the Parts of a Story   pages 262–269

Read a short story. Then answer these questions about the story after writing the title and author.

1. What do you learn in the introduction?
2. What is the problem in the story?
3. How does the story reach a climax?
4. What is the resolution?
5. What is the setting?

UNIT 7

Understanding Prepositions and Prepositional Phrases
pages 278–279

Copy these sentences. Draw one line under each preposition and two lines under each object of the preposition.

1. Many people enjoy the excitement of skiing.
2. They like riding to the top of the slope.
3. Skiing down the slope, they feel wonderful.
4. Beginners turn with a <u>snowplow</u>.
5. The <u>christie</u> is used by advanced skiers.

Using Prepositional Phrases as Adjectives and Adverbs
pages 280–281

Copy these sentences. Draw one line under each prepositional phrase, and circle the word it modifies. Tell whether it is used as an adjective or as an adverb.

1. Myths are stories of gods and heroes.
2. Some myths explain the beginning of the world.
3. Other myths explain forces of nature.
4. These stories have endured in popularity.
5. People recognize many important truths in the myths.

Understanding Appositives   pages 282- 283

Copy these sentences. Draw one line under the appositive in each sentence and two lines under the noun or pronoun to which the appositive refers.

1. The sea horse, the only fish with a grasping tail, is found on the Atlantic coast.
2. Its real name, <u>hippocampus</u>, means "sea horse monster."
3. The sea nettle, a jellyfish, causes painful stings.
4. The sea slug, a mollusk, lacks a shell as an adult.
5. A beautiful creature, the sea slug is brightly colored.

Understanding Interjections   pages 284-285

Copy these sentences. Draw one line under the words that are interjections.

1. Oh! It's scary in here.
2. Ah, there's a light ahead.
3. Oops! The light went out.
4. Ugh! What was that?
5. Whoops! I'm not staying to find out.

Understanding Conjunctions   pages 286-287

Copy these sentences. Circle the conjunction in each sentence. Then draw one line under the words, phrases, or short sentences that are joined by each conjunction.

1. Shellfish are popular in restaurants, but some people find them distasteful.
2. Shellfish can be cooked, or they can be served raw.
3. Their texture and their taste are unusual.
4. Both lobster and baked clams are popular.
5. Scallops can be shelled and cooked, but shrimp must be deveined as well.

Combining Sentences   pages 288-289

Combine each pair of sentences with a conjunction. Use the one that shows the meaning given in parentheses ( ).

1. I just borrowed a new book.
   I am eager to read it. (addition)
2. We borrow books from the library.
   We buy paperbacks at the store. (choice)
3. I like mysteries.
   My brother prefers science fiction. (contrast)
4. Do you like fantasy?
   Do you prefer realism? (choice)
5. The Borrowers used to be my favorite series.
   Now I prefer the Narnia. (contrast)

Understanding Analogies   pages 292–293

Copy these analogies, adding the correct answer to each one.

1. NEIGH : HORSE :: meow :
2. JUNE : SUMMER :: December :
3. KNEE : LEG :: elbow :
4. WINDOW : GLASS :: candle :
5. TADPOLE : FROG :: caterpillar :

Understanding Fact and Opinion   pages 294–295

Copy these sentences. Write *opinion* for each sentence that gives an opinion and *fact* for each sentence that gives a fact.

1. Cooked meat tastes better than raw meat.
2. Cold soups are delicious.
3. Fad diets attract many people.
4. Many vegetables are eaten raw.
5. Eggs taste delicious.

Reasoning Logically   pages 296–297

Each of these statements is illogical. Write the type of error in reasoning used, and explain how you knew that it was illogical.

1. When you buy *Softies,* you are buying tissues of the highest quality.
2. A vote for Geraldine Spear is a vote for the best leader.
3. Why not lose weight now at Nat's Fitness Spa?

Prewriting and Composing — Composition of Opinion   pages 298–304

Write a composition explaining how you feel about one of the following. Use a diagram like the one on page 298 to summarize your ideas.

football   baby-sitting
grandparents   computers in the classroom

Revising a Composition   pages 305–308

Revise the composition of opinion that you wrote for the exercise you just completed. Be sure that your reasoning is logical. Check to see that you have written all three parts of the composition. Finally, recopy your work.

Mechanics Practice   page 309

Rewrite these sentences, adding commas and exclamation points where needed.

1. Oh do you think this house is haunted?
2. This house a scary place has been abandoned for years.
3. Wow Look at the wall around it.
4. The gate a heavy wrought-iron piece was forged by hand.
5. Ah I knew we could open it.

Enjoying Humorous Literature   pages 310–317

Read a humorous story or article. Then work on these activities.

1. Copy one example of informal vocabulary.
2. Copy one example of exaggeration.
3. Name the subject that is being treated humorously.

UNIT 8

Understanding Compound Subjects and Predicates
pages 324–325

Copy these sentences. Draw one line under the compound subject or compound predicate in each sentence.

1. The caterer and his assistants prepared for the party.
2. They basted and baked for a week in advance.
3. The freezers and refrigerators were filled.
4. They cooked new creations and prepared old favorites.
5. They chose the dishes and examined the linens.

Understanding Clauses   pages 326–327

Copy these sentences. Draw one line under each independent clause.

1. Marigold is interested in exploring caves, but her brother prefers mountain climbing.
2. Marigold likes to find underground caverns, but Sam prefers to breathe fresh air.
3. Marigold enjoys scary adventures, and her brother enjoys tests of skill.
4. For excitement their parents go scuba diving, or they go ballooning.
5. Their vacations are exciting, and their activities are adventurous.
6. My friends Rana, Tapa, and Aiku have recently become very interested in physical fitness.
7. They jog three times a week, and they have taken up tennis and swimming as well.
8. They have asked me to join them, but I have never been very good at sports.
9. After two weeks of discussion, Rana finally took me with her to the jogging track.
10. My jogging really wasn't bad at all, but with a little practice I can do even better.

Understanding Compound Sentences   pages 328–329

Copy only the compound sentences. If a sentence is not compound, write *not compound.*

1. You can build amazing machines with motorized craft kits.
2. Terrence made a crane with a power winch, and Justine built an elevator.
3. Gregory built an oil drilling rig with a cam shaft.
4. Alicia worked on a Dutch windmill, and Ted constructed a carnival loop.
5. Do you want to make a machine, or would you like to study one instead?

Understanding Subject-Verb Agreement
pages 330–331

Copy these sentences. Use the correct verb in parentheses ( ).

1. The members of our class (has, have) planned an international supper.
2. Each student (bring, brings) a different dish.
3. Students and their families (attends, attend) together.
4. They (chooses, choose) souvlaki, pierogies, or couscous.
5. Our group (is, are) the first to sponsor such a supper.
6. The supper (is, are) the highlight of international week at school.
7. Some students (prepare, prepares) a program of singing and dancing from several countries.
8. This year two students (is, are) playing the balalaika at the international show.
9. Eight boys and girls from Mr. Petersen's class (has, have) been practicing all week.
10. They (plan, plans) to present three folk dances from Czechoslovakia.

Understanding Varied Sentences   pages 332–333

Copy these sentences. After each tell how the original underlined sentence has been made more interesting.

1. Sodium, a silvery-white metallic element, has many uses.
2. Sodium nitrate is used in fertilizer, and sodium bicarbonate is used in soap.
3. Sodium salts are used in carbonated drinks and in fire extinguishers.
4. In laboratories and hospitals scientists use sodium for research.
5. A special process, electrolysis, is used to extract sodium from sodium compounds.

Taking Notes   pages 336–337

Use the information contained in Understanding Varied Sentences to make a set of notes about sodium.

Preparing a Bibliography   pages 338–339

Write the information about these sources in correct bibliographic form.

1. Cecil Forsyth's book Orchestration published in 1941 by the Macmillan Company of New York
2. Carolyn Jabs's article "Is buying a wood stove your heating solution?" in Workbench magazine in September 1981, pages 104–108
3. "Soddy, Frederick," an article published in World Book Encyclopedia, Volume 17, page 464, written by Henry M. Leicester, published by Field Enterprises Educational Corporation, Chicago.
4. A book called All about earth-sheltered homes written by H. A. Spirakis and published by Weather Vane Press of Ontario, Vermont in 1983.

Outlining   pages 340–341

Copy this part of an outline about orchestra instruments. Make any corrections needed in capitalization, punctuation, and indentation.

THE BRASS SECTION OF AN ORCHESTRA
I. trumpets
a. have valves
b. related to cornets
II. french horns
a. have valves
b. related to hunting horns
III. trombones
a. have slides
b. related to medieval sackbut

Writing a Research Report   pages 345–348

In the correct order copy these steps for writing a research report.

1. Write the report.
2. Locate sources of information.
3. Choose a topic.
4. Write an outline.
5. Take notes.

Revising a Research Report   pages 349–350

This paragraph was written from the outline on the brass section of an orchestra. Rewrite it so that it will be complete.

The brass section of the orchestra has several different kinds of instruments. Trumpets are instruments with valve action. They are related to cornets but are more difficult to play. French horns are another type of valve instrument. Trombones developed from the medieval sackbut.

Mechanics Practice   page 351

Write this mixed-up outline correctly.

The Library   B. Tennis Pros   III. Biography
I. fiction   B. Treasure Island   A. The Babe
II. nonfiction   A. The Yearling   Ruth Story
A. A book of Kites   B. Insects

Recognizing Stories in Verse   pages 352–359

Read a narrative poem in a collection of poetry. Then answer these questions.

1. What is the title and who is the author of the poem?
2. Who are the characters in the poem?
3. What is the plot, or story?
4. Give an example of alliteration or assonance.
5. Give an example of a simile or a metaphor.

UNIT 9

Listening in Class   pages 366–367

Copy the instruction words listed in column A. Next to each word write the correct explanation from the list in column B.

A	B
1. describe	give the meaning
2. compare	tell how or why
3. contrast	show how two or more things are alike
4. explain	show how two or more things are different
5. define	create a word picture

Conducting a Meeting   pages 368–369

Copy the terms listed in column A. Next to each term write the correct explanation from column B.

A	B
1. chairperson	order of a meeting
2. secretary	person who runs the meeting
3. motion	called on to speak
4. recognized	person who writes the minutes
5. parliamentary procedure	a suggestion for action

Making Introductions   pages 370–371

Copy these statements. Label each *true* or *false*.

1. If you are introducing a person to a group, mention the name of the group first.
2. If the person being introduced is standing, you should remain seated.
3. If you introduce two people, you should mention both persons' names.
4. It is courteous to shake hands.
5. The purpose of an introduction is to put people at ease.

Interviewing   pages 372–373

In the correct order write these steps for interviewing.

1. Ask questions.
2. Write about the interview.
3. Call for an appointment.
4. Take notes.
5. Prepare questions.

Presenting an Oral Report   pages 374–375

Make an outline for an oral report about a hobby or an interest you have. Explain how to do something, or try to interest the audience in your hobby.

Understanding Synonyms and Antonyms
pages 378–379

Copy these words. Then write one synonym and one antonym for each.

1. false   2. reckless   3. sadness
4. thrifty   5. modern   6. strong

Using the Thesaurus   pages 380–381

1.–5. Look up the word *say* in a thesaurus. Write five sentences. Use a synonym with a different shade of meaning in each sentence.

Writing a Friendly Letter   pages 382–388

Rewrite this letter in correct form. Label the parts of the letter.

92 Elm Street Evanston Illinois 60202 September 8, 19-- Dear Scooter, When you told me about the strange bugs you had seen outside your house, I went to the library and looked them up. The green cicadas you saw are called dog-day cicadas because they come out in July and August when the dog star is seen in the sky. I saw a picture of them, and I think they're neat too. While we're on the subject of

animals, I want to tell you I'm getting a dog. She's a fox terrier, and she's six weeks old. I'm going to name her Cricket. Our soccer team just started practicing. We'll be all ready when you come to our first game. Your friend, Jimmie

Writing a Business Letter   pages 389–390

Write a business letter requesting a free catalog from The Book Barn, 121 Broad Street, Palisades Park, New Jersey 07650. Use your own address as the address of the sender. Then address the envelope you would use to send it.

Revising a Business Letter   page 393

Revise your business letter. Be sure the language is suited to the purpose and the audience for which it was intended.

Mechanics Practice   page 393

Rewrite this letter in correct form and with proper punctuation.

901 forest boulevard milwaukee wisconsin 53207 March 21, 19-- never fail seed company box 221 greenwood south carolina 29646 dear sir or madam I read in your catalog that you publish a zone map showing the appropriate climate for each of your plants please send me a copy I am enclosing two seed packets to receive my free map thank you very much sincerely yours frances miller

Reading the Letters of Famous People   pages 394–397

Find a collection of letters in the library. Read one of the letters and answer these questions.

1. What does the letter reveal about the sender?
2. Does the letter give a picture of the times in which it was written? If so, give examples.
3. Is the language formal or informal?
4. To whom was the letter written? What relationship does the writer have with the receiver of the letter?
5. Describe in a few sentences the message in the letter.

INDEX

Biographies, 28-33, 37, 449
  Thor Heyerdahl, Viking Scientist
    (excerpt), 30-31
  Walt Disney: Master of Make-Believe, 33
Book(s), parts of, 154-155, 175-176, 460
Book reports, 158-166, 176, 461
British terms, 47
Business letters. *See* Letters

Call number, 53, 54-55
Capitalization
  of abbreviations and initials, 94-95, 434
  of *A.M.* and *P.M.,* 75, 85
  to begin sentences, 2-3, 13, 24-26, 27,
    37, 131, 211, 222, 362-363, 414, 434,
    449, 453, 456-457, 464
  of days and months, 94-95, 434, 454
  of direct quotations, 250-252
  editing marks for. *See* Editing and
    proofreading marks
  of *I,* 27, 228-229, 434
  in letters, 479
  in outlines, 340-341, 351, 362
  of proper adjectives, 211
  of proper nouns, 90-91, 121, 362-363,
    393, 434, 456-457, 464
  in quotations, 250-252, 261, 273, 362-
    363, 439-440, 467, 468
  of titles, 167, 176, 338-339, 434
Card catalog, 52-53, 83, 451. *See also*
  Author card; Call number; Dewey
  Decimal system; Subject card; Title card
Carroll, Lewis, 353-355
Cause and effect paragraphs, 112-120, 131,
  456
Chairperson, 368-369, 376, 477
Characters
  in narrative poetry, 352-359
  in plays, 76-81, 85
  in short stories, 245-249, 262-269
Choice
  conjunctions showing, 288-289, 291
  transitional words showing, 253-256
Clauses, 326-327, 332-333, 334, 360, 361,
  402, 415, 473
  defined, 326
  independent, 326-327, 332-333, 415, 473
  to vary sentences, 332-333, 335, 361,
    448, 474

Climax
  defined, 268
  in narrative poetry, 352-359
  in short stories, 262-269
Closed compound, 240-241
  defined, 240
Colon
  in business letters, 389-390, 393, 442, 479
  in times of day, 75, 85, 442
Combining sentences
  with adjectives and adverbs, 192-193, 221
  with conjunctions, 288-289, 319, 320,
    470
Commands. *See* Imperative sentences
Commas
  in addresses, 393, 401, 436, 479
  with appositives, 282-283, 309, 321, 332-
    333, 437, 472
  in bibliographies, 338-339, 437
  in compound sentences, 328-329, 351,
    436
  with compound subjects and
    predicates, 324-325
  with conjunctions, 288-289, 324-325,
    326-327, 328-329, 351
  in dates, 121, 386-388, 393, 401, 436
  in direct address, 332-333, 436
  editing marks for. *See* Editing and
    proofreading marks
  in greetings and closings of letters, 386-
    388, 393, 401, 436, 479
  with interjections, 284-285
  with introductory expressions, 309, 321,
    436
  with prepositional phrases, 309, 332-
    333, 362-363, 472
  in quotations, 250-252, 273, 332-333,
    351, 362-363, 436-437, 467, 468
  in series, 205-208, 211, 222, 436, 464
  with transitional expressions, 254-256,
    261, 309
Common adjectives, 182-184, 220, 424, 462
  defined, 424
Common nouns, 90-91, 98, 128, 179, 274,
  402, 417, 454
  defined, 90
Comparative degree
  of adjectives, 185-187
  of adverbs, 190-191, 425
  defined, 185, 190

for writing, 18-26, 56-66, 67-74, 104-111,
112-120, 158-166, 202-210, 242-260,
298-308, 340-350, 382-392
"To Memorize," 23, 42, 118, 137, 187,
241, 293, 348, 367
Cross-references, 100-101

Dates, 121, 386-388, 393, 401, 436
D'Aulaire, Ingri and Edgar, 168-171
Day, Clarence, 262-269
Days of the week, 94-95, 434
Declarative sentences, 2-3, 12, 21-23, 27, 34,
36, 86, 178, 402, 406, 414, 446
defined, 2, 414
diagraming, 406
punctuation, 2, 27, 414, 435
Definitions, 16-17, 36
Degrees of comparison
adjectives, 185-187, 194, 424
adverbs, 190-191, 195, 425
Deleting. *See* Editing and proofreading
marks
Descriptive paragraphs, 202-210, 222, 464
Details
in paragraphs, 45-47, 49, 82-83, 87
in sentences, 43-44, 450
Dewey Decimal system, 54-55, 83, 451
Diagraming sentences, 404-413
Dialog
of play, 76-81, 85, 439-440, 468
of story, 250-252, 257-260, 262-269, 272,
332-333, 439, 467
Dickinson, Emily, 187
Dictionary
abbreviations in, 94-95
alphabetical order in, 14-15, 36
boldface type, 14-15
definitions, 14-15, 36, 448
entry words, 16, 448
guide words, 14-15, 36, 447
multiple meanings, 17, 36
pronunciation key, 16
syllabication, 16-17
Direct address, 332-333, 436
Direct objects, 150-151, 153, 175, 179, 230-
231, 236, 270, 407
defined, 150
diagraming, 407
pronouns as, 230-231, 234-235, 426, 465
Direct quotations. *See also* Quotations
defined, 250
Directions, listening to, 366-367, 376, 477
Disney, Walt, 33
Drafting. *See* Composing
Driscoll, Louise, 42

Editing. *See* Revising
Editing and proofreading marks, 24-26, 64-
66, 73-74, 110-111, 119-120, 164-166,
209-210, 257-260, 305-308, 349-350, 391,
392, 433
Editorials, 122-127, 131, 457
Effect, and cause, paragraphs of, 112-120,
131, 456
Encyclopedia, 100-101, 130, 455
Enright, Elizabeth, 269
Entry words
in dictionary, 16, 448
in thesaurus, 380-381, 399, 478
Envelopes, addressing, 387-388, 389-390,
400, 432
Exclamation point, 2-3, 250-252, 284-285,
309, 321, 438, 446, 449, 472
with quotation marks, 250-252
Exclamatory sentences, 2-3, 12, 21-23, 27,
34, 36, 86, 178, 406, 414, 446
defined, 2, 414
diagraming, 406
punctuation of, 414

Fact, telling opinion from, 294-295, 320, 471
Famous people, letters of, 394-397, 401, 479
Feature articles, 122-127, 131, 457
Fiction, 50-51
Among the Dolls, 173
Mrs. Frisby and the Rats of NIMH, 127
My Side of the Mountain, 219
P.S. Write Soon, 397
The Saturdays, 269
Figures of speech
defined, 213
in poetry, 212-219
sports terms as, 285
Fonteyn, Margot, 359
Friendly letter. *See* Letters
Future tense verbs, 146-147, 153, 175, 365
defined, 146

Geographical names
abbreviations of, 94-95, 99, 129, 434,
454
capitalization of, 90-91, 121, 393, 417,
434
George, Jean, 219
Glossary, 154-155
Good and *well,* 192-193
Guide words, dictionary, 14-15, 36, 447

Hans, Marcie, 217
Helping verbs, 138-139, 152, 174, 179, 420,
458

Paragraphs (continued)
    of comparison, 67-74, 84-85, 452
    of contrast, 67-74, 84-85, 452
    defined, 40
    descriptive, 202-210, 222, 464
    detail sentences in, 43-44, 45-47, 49, 60,
        62, 82-83, 87, 178, 208, 275, 429, 450,
        456
    of dialog, 250-252, 257-260, 262-269,
        272, 332-333, 439
    how-to, 104-111, 130, 456
    indenting, 75
    introductory sentence, 208
    keeping to topic in, 45-46, 275, 450
    main idea of, 40-42, 48-49, 82, 87, 429,
        449
    organization of, 59-60, 61-63, 67-69, 82-
        83, 452
    space-order, 56-58, 61-66, 84, 208, 452
    time-order, 56-60, 64-66, 84, 208, 452
    topic sentences in, 43-44, 45-47, 48-49,
        60, 62, 64-66, 82-83, 87, 178, 275,
        402, 429, 450
    transitions within and between, 253-256,
        467
    unity in, 45-47, 49, 87, 178, 275
Parallel structure
    in outlines, 340-341
    in sentences, 286-287
Parliamentary procedure, 368-369
Past participles, 140-141, 142-143, 144-145,
    421-422
Past tense verbs, 140-141, 146-147, 148-149,
    153, 175, 179, 274, 403, 421-422, 423,
    458, 460
    defined, 146
People
    introductions of, 370-371, 376, 398-399,
        403, 477
    names and titles of, 94-95, 434, 435
Period
    in abbreviations and initials, 94-95, 121,
        435
    ending sentences with, 2-3, 326-327,
        414, 435, 446, 449, 453, 479
    in outlines, 340-341, 351, 435
    in quotations, 250-252
Periodical section, in the library, 50-51, 83
Phonetic respelling, 16-17
Place names. See Geographical names
Plays
    "The Land We Love," 76-81
Plays, reading, 76-81, 453
Plot
    in narrative poetry, 352, 356-359

    in plays, 76, 80-81
    in short stories, 242-249, 262, 268-269
Plural nouns, 92-93, 98, 99, 128, 129, 179,
    275, 417, 418, 454
    defined, 92
    forming possessive, 92-93, 99, 129, 179, 418
    pronouns, 226-227, 228-229, 230-231,
        232-233
P.M., 75, 85
Poems
    "Flashlight," 233
    "Fog," 214
    "Godfrey Gordon Gustavus Gore," 357-
        358
    "Hope Is a Thing with Feathers," 187
    "January," 212
    "Red," 223
    "Serve Me a Slice of Moon," 217
    "Spring Thunder," 216
    "Swift Things Are Beautiful," 293
    "The Toucan," 233
    "Velvet Shoes," 215
    "The Walrus and the Carpenter," 353-
        355
    "What Is Once Loved," 241
    "Within Your Heart," 42
Poetry
    alliteration, 213-219, 223
    assonance, 213-219, 223
    consonance, 213-219, 223
    imagery, 212-219, 223, 464
    lyric, 212-219, 223, 464
    metaphor, 213-219
    narrative, 352-359, 363, 476
    rhythm and rhyme in, 223, 352-359
    simile, 213-219, 223
    titles of, 167, 176, 439
Positive degree of comparison
    adjectives, 185-187, 424
    adverbs, 190-191, 425
    defined, 185, 190
Possessives
    defined, 232
    diagraming, 408
    nouns, 96-97, 99, 129, 179, 408, 441, 455
    pronouns, 232-233, 237, 271, 408, 426,
        441, 443
Postal abbreviations, 432
Predicate
    adjectives, 182-184, 220, 410, 419
    complete, 4-5, 6-7, 12, 34, 86, 416, 446
    compound, 324-325, 332-333, 334, 335,
        360, 402, 413, 416, 472
    nominative, 150-151, 153, 175, 179, 409,
        419, 460

order of, in sentences, 10-11, 13
simple, 6-7, 12, 34-35, 86, 134, 324-325, 402, 416, 446-447
Prefixes, 196-197, 221, 463
defined, 196
invention words, 11
Prepositional phrases, 278-279, 290, 318, 332-333, 361, 403, 412, 427, 469
as adjectives and adverbs, 280-281, 290, 318, 469
defined, 278
diagraming, 412
punctuation of, 309, 332-333
to vary sentences, 332-333, 335, 361
Prepositions, 278-279, 290, 318, 427, 443-444, 469
defined, 278
objects of, 278-279, 290, 427
troublesome, 443-444
Present perfect tense verbs, 148-149, 153, 175, 423
defined, 148
Present tense verbs, 146-147, 153, 175, 423
defined, 146
Prewriting
brainstorming, 18-20, 33, 202-204, 218-219
choosing and arranging details, 56-58, 81
diagraming, 56-58, 67-69, 112-114, 131, 202-204, 222, 242-244, 272, 298-300, 321, 464, 467, 471
framed paragraph, 104-106, 130
generating ideas, 298-300
listmaking, 56-58, 81, 316, 358-359, 382-385, 389, 397, 400
note taking, 127, 222, 336-337, 361, 362, 371-372
outlining, 67-69, 172, 340-344, 362
preparing a bibliography, 338-339
skimming and scanning, 156-157
summarizing plots, 158-160, 176, 242-244, 461
establishing tone, 382-385, 400
Principal parts, of verbs, 140-141, 142-143, 144-145, 152, 174-175, 403, 421-422
irregular verbs, 142-143, 144-145, 152, 174-175, 421-422, 459
regular verbs, 140-141, 152, 174-175, 421-422, 458
Pronouns, 226-227, 234-235, 236-237, 270, 274, 403, 426, 445, 465
antecedents, 226-227, 236, 426, 445, 465
contractions, 261, 271, 466
correct usage of, 234-235, 271, 466

defined, 226
I/me, 228-229, 232-233, 443
object, 230-231, 236-237, 270-271, 426, 465
possessive, 232-233, 237, 271, 408, 426, 441, 443, 466
reflexive, 232-233, 237, 271, 426, 466
Scandinavian influence on, 97
subject, 228-229, 236, 270, 426, 465
Pronunciation key, in dictionary, 16
Proofreading. *See* Revising
Proper adjective, 182-184, 220, 424, 462
defined, 183
Proper nouns, 90-91, 98, 128, 179, 402, 417, 454
defined, 90
Proverbs, 23
Punctuation marks. *See types of*

Question mark, 2-3, 250-252, 438, 446, 449
Questions, 2-3, 12, 21-23, 27, 34, 36, 86, 103, 178, 406, 414, 446
Quotation marks
British term for, 47
in dialog, 250-252, 439-440
in direct quotations, 250-252, 261, 273, 351, 362-363, 439-440, 467, 468
for titles, 167, 176, 351, 439-440, 461
Quotations, direct, 250-252

Rands, William Brighty, 357-358
Reading
autobiographies and biographies, 28-33, 37, 49
humorous literature, 310-317, 321, 472
letters, 394-397, 401, 479
myths, 168-173, 177, 461
newspapers, 122-127, 131, 457
plays, 76-81, 85, 453
poetry, 212-219, 223, 352-359, 363, 464, 476
short stories, 242-244, 262-269, 273
skimming and scanning, 156-157, 176, 461
Reasoning logically, 296-297, 320, 471
Receiver's address, 387-388, 389-390, 400, 432
Record albums, titles of, 139, 438
Reference books, 50-51. *See also* Almanac; Atlas; Dictionary; Encyclopedia; Thesaurus
Reflexive pronouns, 232-233, 237, 271, 426, 466
defined, 232

Reports
    book, 158-166, 176, 461
    interviews, 372-373, 377, 399
    making outline for, 340-341
    oral, 374-375, 377, 399
    research, 342-348, 476
Request, letter of. *See* Letters
Research reports
    bibliography of, 338-339, 361, 475
    note taking for, 336-337, 361, 475
    outlining, 340-341, 351, 362, 475, 478
    rough draft for, 342-344
Resolution
    defined, 268
    in narrative poetry, 356-358
    in short stories, 268
Result, transitional words showing, 253-256
Return address, 387-388, 389-390, 400, 432
Review Handbook, 414-445
Revising
    addressing envelopes, 391-392
    autobiographies, 33
    book reports, 164-166, 176, 461
    checklist for, 24-26, 317, 321, 433, 464
    compositions of opinion, 305-308, 321,
        472
    diagrams, 58
    humorous compositions, 317
    letters, 391-392
    lists, 58
    myths, 172-173
    paragraphs, 60, 63, 64-66, 73-74, 110-
        111, 119-120, 209-210, 222, 464
    plays, 81
    poetry, 218-219, 358-359
    reports, 349-351, 362, 476
    sentences, 24-26, 36
    stories, 251-252, 257-260, 272, 467, 468
Rhythm and rhyme, in poetry, 223, 352-359
Rodowsky, Colby, 397
Roots
    defined, 200
    invention words, 11
    of words, 200-201, 221, 463
Rough draft, 218-219, 342-344

Sandburg, Carl, 214
Scandinavian influence, on the English
    language, 97
Scanning, skimming and, 156-157, 176, 461
Semicolon, 328-329, 351, 403, 442
Sentences
    capital letters to begin, 2-3, 13, 24-26,
        27, 37, 131, 211, 222, 362-363, 414,
        434, 449, 453, 456-457, 464

combining with adjectives and adverbs,
    192-193, 221
combining with conjunctions, 288-289,
    319, 320, 470
compound, 328-329, 332-333, 334-335,
    360, 402, 413, 415, 442, 473
declarative, 2-3, 12, 21-23, 27, 34, 36, 86,
    178, 402, 406, 414, 446
defined, 2
detail, 43-44, 45-47, 49, 60, 62, 82-83, 87,
    178, 208, 275, 429, 450, 456
diagraming, 404-413
exclamatory, 2-3, 12, 21-23, 27, 34, 36,
    86, 178, 406, 414, 446
imperative, 2-3, 12, 27, 34, 36, 86, 178,
    406, 414, 446
interrogative, 2-3, 12, 21-23, 27, 34, 36,
    86, 178, 406, 414, 446
parallel structure in, 286-287
parts of, 4-5, 6-7, 8-9, 12, 13, 34-35, 178
punctuation at end of, 2-3, 9, 13, 24-26,
    27, 37, 85, 131, 414
simple, 328-329, 415
topic, 43-44, 45-47, 48-49, 60, 62, 64-66,
    82-83, 87, 178, 275, 402, 429, 450
varying, 332-333, 335, 361, 448, 474
word order in, 10-11
    inverted, 10-11, 13, 21-23, 24-26, 35,
        86-87, 178, 405, 447
    logical, 46
    natural, 10-11, 13, 24-26, 35, 86-87,
        178, 405, 447
Series, commas in, 205-208, 211, 222, 436, 464
Setting
    in narrative poetry, 352, 357-358
    in short stories, 245, 248-249, 262, 268-269
Short stories, 245-249, 257-260, 262-269,
    272, 273
    characters, 245-249, 262-269
    complication, 248, 268-269, 273
    "Father Wakes Up the Village," 262-269
    "Horse Crazy," 245-247
    introduction, 245, 262, 268, 273
    plot, 245-249, 262-269
    resolution, 248, 268-269, 273
    setting, 245, 248-249, 262, 268-269
Shulevitz, Uri, 118
Silverstein, Shel, 223
Similar ideas, transitional words, showing,
    253-256, 272
Simile, 213-219, 223
    defined, 213
Simple predicates, 6-7, 12, 34-35, 86, 134,
    324-325, 402, 416, 446-447
    defined, 6

Underlining, of book titles, 167, 438, 461
Understood subjects, 8-9, 13, 35, 416, 447
    defined, 8
    diagraming, 406
Unit Tests, 34-37, 82-87, 128-131, 174-177, 220-223, 270-275, 318-321, 360-363, 398-401
Updike, John, 212

Van Doren, Mark, 216
Verbs
    action, 134-135, 152, 153, 174, 179, 274, 420, 457
    complements of, 150-151, 153, 175, 179, 230-231, 236, 270, 274, 407, 409, 419, 460
    defined, 134
    future tense, 146-147, 153, 175, 365
    helping, 138-139, 152, 174, 179, 420, 458
    intransitive, 150-151, 175, 274, 420, 460
    irregular, 142-143, 144-145, 152, 174-175, 421-422, 459
    linking, 136-137, 152, 153, 174, 179, 274, 420, 458
    main, 138-139, 174, 179, 403, 404-413, 420, 458
    past participles, 140-141, 142-143, 144-145, 421-422
    past tense, 140-141, 146-147, 148-149, 153, 175, 179, 274, 403, 421-422, 423, 458, 460
    plural, 330-331
    present perfect tense, 148-149, 153, 175, 423
    present tense, 146-147, 153, 175, 423
    principal parts of, 140-141, 142-143, 144-145, 152, 174-175, 403, 421-422
    regular, 140-141, 152, 174-175, 421-422, 458
    singular, 330-331
    subject-verb agreement, 330-331, 361
    tense, 140-141, 146-147, 148-149, 153, 175, 179, 274, 403, 421-422, 423, 458, 459, 460
    transitive and intransitive, 150-151, 175, 274, 420, 460

Verse, stories in, 352, 359, 363
Vocabulary building
    compound words, 240-241, 261, 272, 286, 466
    prefixes, 196-197, 221, 463
    suffixes, 198-199, 221, 463
    using dictionary/glossary, 14-15, 16-17, 36, 154-155, 447, 448

Well and *good,* 192-193
White, E.B., 394-395
Words
    Anglo-Saxon, 87
    base, 196-197, 198-199, 221
    British, 47
    compound, 240-241, 261, 272, 286, 466
    division of, at the end of a line, 16-17, 75, 85
    Norman French, 87
    Old English, 97, 285
    order of, in sentences, 10-11, 13, 21-23, 24-26, 35, 86-87, 178, 405, 447
    origins of, 11, 87, 97, 135, 191, 229, 285, 373
    roots of, 200-201, 221, 463
    sound descriptions, in different languages, 331
    sports, 285
    troublesome, 192-193, 234-235, 443-444
Writing. *See* Composing
Wylie, Elinor, 215

You (understood), 8-9, 13, 35, 416, 447
    defined, 8
    diagraming, 406
Young adult section in the library, 50-51, 83
Your and *you're,* 385

ZIP code, 386-388, 432

PHOTO CREDITS

ART CREDITS